D0434302

7

ONE WEEK
LOAN

2 9 FEB 2000

- 1 MAY 1998   0 9 NOV 2000

3 0 APR 1997

1 9 MAY 1997   2 5 SEP 1998

- 5 SEP 1997   15 MAR 1999   1 2 JAN 2001
                     17 MAR 1999
- 3 DEC 1997
                                        21 SEP 2001
10 DEC 1997
                     0 5 MAY 1999
                     28 OCT 1999   30/7/01
11 FEB 1998

                     1 4 FEB 2000   31 JUL 2002
0 8 JAN 1999
                     21 FEB 2000

                     1 3 MAR 2000   3 1 MAR 2003

Z

An Introduction to
Formal Methods

Second Edition

Antoni Diller
School of Computer Science
University of Birmingham

JOHN WILEY & SONS
Chichester · New York · Brisbane · Toronto · Singapore

Other Wiley Editorial Offices

John Wiley & Sons, Inc., 605 Third Avenue,
New York, NY 10158-0012, USA

Jacaranda Wiley Ltd, 33 Park Road, Milton,
Queensland, 4064, Australia

John Wiley & Sons (Canada) Ltd, 22 Worcester Road,
Rexdale, Ontario M9W 1L1, Canada

John Wiley & Sons (SEA) Pte Ltd, 37 Jalan Pemimpin #05-04,
Block B, Union Industrial Building, Singapore 2057

Library of Congress Cataloging-in-Publication Data
Diller, Antoni.
Z : an introduction to formal methods / Antoni Diller. – 2nd ed.
p. cm.
Includes bibliographical references and index.
ISBN 0 471 93973 0
1. Z (Computer program language) I. Title,
QA76.73 Z2D55 1994
005.1'2–dc20   94-4943
                                                           CIP

British Library Cataloguing in Publication Data

A catalogue record for this book is available from the British Library

ISBN 0 471 93973 0

Produced from camera-ready copy supplied by the author using LaTeX.
Printed and bound in Great Britain by Redwood Books, Trowbridge, Wilts.

This book is dedicated to my niece,
Laura Diller.

Contents

Preface   xv

Acknowledgements   xix

I   Tutorial   1

1   Introduction   3
   1.1   What is Z? 3
   1.2   Specification Foretaste 5
   1.3   Numbers 7

2   First-order Logic   9
   2.1   Propositional Calculus 9
     2.1.1   Introduction 9
     2.1.2   Truth-functional Connectives and Constant Formulas 10
     2.1.3   Model-theory 15
     2.1.4   Useful Laws 19
   2.2   Predicate Calculus 23
     2.2.1   Introduction 23
     2.2.2   Types 24
     2.2.3   Declarations 24
     2.2.4   Quantifiers 25
     2.2.5   Term-forming Operators 27
   2.3   Exercises 28

3   Set Theory   31
   3.1   Ways of Making Sets 31
     3.1.1   Enumeration 31
     3.1.2   Set Comprehension 32
   3.2   Relations between Sets (and their Members) 33
     3.2.1   Membership and Equality 33
     3.2.2   Subset 33
   3.3   Some Special Sets 34
     3.3.1   Empty Sets 34

	3.3.2	Power Sets	35
3.4	Operations on Sets		35
	3.4.1	Union	35
	3.4.2	Intersection	35
	3.4.3	Difference	36
	3.4.4	Symmetric Difference	36
	3.4.5	Useful Laws	37
	3.4.6	Generalized Union and Intersection	38
3.5	Exercises		38

4 Internal Telephone Directory   **41**

4.1	Introduction		41
4.2	Cartesian Products and Relations		42
4.3	The State Space		43
	4.3.1	The Domain of a Relation	44
	4.3.2	The Range of a Relation	45
	4.3.3	The Union of Two Relations	46
	4.3.4	Schemas	46
4.4	Adding an Entry to the Database		48
	4.4.1	The First Account	48
	4.4.2	Schema Operations	49
	4.4.3	A Concise Specification	53
	4.4.4	Dealing with Errors	53
	4.4.5	The Total Specification	54
4.5	Interrogating the Database by Person		55
	4.5.1	The Image of a Relation	55
	4.5.2	Specifying the Operation	56
4.6	Interrogating the Database by Number		57
	4.6.1	Relational Inversion	58
	4.6.2	Specifying the Operation	58
4.7	Removing an Entry from the Database		59
4.8	Someone Joining the University		60
4.9	Someone Leaving the University		60
	4.9.1	Domain Restriction	60
	4.9.2	Domain Anti-restriction	61
	4.9.3	Specifying the Operation	62
4.10	Specifying a User-interface		62
4.11	Presenting a Formal Specification		64
	4.11.1	Definition Before Use	64
	4.11.2	The Format of a Sequential System	65
	4.11.3	Combining Z and Descriptive Text	68
	4.11.4	Conventions for Identifiers	68
4.12	Exercises		69

5 More about Relations and Schemas **71**
  5.1 Relations 71
      5.1.1 Composition 71
      5.1.2 Identity, Powers and Closures 72
      5.1.3 Range Restriction and Anti-restriction 74
      5.1.4 Overriding 76
  5.2 Schemas 77
      5.2.1 Horizontal Form 77
      5.2.2 Renaming 78
      5.2.3 Hiding 79
      5.2.4 Composition 79
      5.2.5 Piping 84
      5.2.6 As Types 86
      5.2.7 The θ Operator 87
  5.3 Exercises 88

6 Functions **91**
  6.1 Introduction 91
  6.2 Specifying a Weather Map 91
      6.2.1 Introduction 91
      6.2.2 Updating the Weather Map 92
      6.2.3 Looking up the Temperature of a Region 93
  6.3 Constrained Functions 93
      6.3.1 Introduction 93
      6.3.2 Potentially Non-finite Functions 94
      6.3.3 Finite Functions 94
  6.4 Function Definition 95
      6.4.1 Enumeration 95
      6.4.2 Set Comprehension 95
      6.4.3 The λ-notation 95
  6.5 Modelling Arrays 96

7 Sequences **97**
  7.1 Fundamental Ideas 97
  7.2 Defining Sequences 97
  7.3 Sequence Manipulating Functions 98
  7.4 Exercises 101

8 Bags **103**
  8.1 Introduction 103
  8.2 Bag Manipulating Functions 103
  8.3 A Specification of Sorting 105
  8.4 The Specification of a Vending Machine 106
      8.4.1 Introduction 106
      8.4.2 Pricing Goods 108

  8.4.3 Acceptable Coins 109
  8.4.4 Restocking 109
  8.4.5 Buying 111
  8.4.6 Profit Taking 114

9 Free Types   **115**
  9.1 Introduction 115
  9.2 Lists as a Free Type 115
  9.3 Specifying Sequence Proofs 116
      9.3.1 Introduction 116
      9.3.2 The Specifications 119
  9.4 The Formal Treatment of Free Types 120

II Methods of Reasoning   **123**

10 Formal Proof   **125**
  10.1 Propositional Calculus 125
      10.1.1 Introduction 125
      10.1.2 Notational Conventions 128
      10.1.3 Themata 128
      10.1.4 Start Sequents and Proofs 130
      10.1.5 Derived Thematic Rules 133
      10.1.6 Further Examples of Proofs 137
      10.1.7 Soundness and Completeness 140
  10.2 Predicate Calculus 140
      10.2.1 Introduction 140
      10.2.2 Quantifier Rules 140
      10.2.3 Examples of Proofs 142
      10.2.4 Useful Laws 146
  10.3 Theorems, Sequents and Themata 148
  10.4 Exercises 150

11 Rigorous Proof   **151**
  11.1 Introduction 151
  11.2 Reasoning about Sets 151
  11.3 Reasoning about Tuples 156
  11.4 Mathematical Induction 157
  11.5 Induction for Sequences 158
  11.6 Exercises 159

12 Immanent Reasoning   **161**
  12.1 Introduction 161
  12.2 Specifying a Classroom 161
  12.3 Schemas and Formulas 162

12.4 The Initialization Proof Obligation 163
12.5 Constructing Theories about Specifications 164
12.6 Investigating Preconditions 165
12.7 Totality 168
12.8 Operation Refinement 169

13 Reification and Decomposition **171**
13.1 Introduction 171
13.2 Modelling Sets by Sequences 172
    13.2.1 Correctness of Operation Modelling 173
    13.2.2 Modelling Set Intersection 176
    13.2.3 Modelling Set Difference 178
13.3 Reification and Decomposition using Schemas 180
    13.3.1 Introduction 180
    13.3.2 Example Specification and Design 180
    13.3.3 Relating Specification and Design 181
    13.3.4 Correctness of Design 181
    13.3.5 General Correctness of Design 186

14 Floyd–Hoare Logic **189**
14.1 Introduction 189
14.2 Hoare Triples 190
14.3 Start Sequents and Themata 191
    14.3.1 Introduction 191
    14.3.2 Structural Rules 191
    14.3.3 The *skip* Command 192
    14.3.4 Substitution 192
    14.3.5 Assignment 192
    14.3.6 Sequencing 193
    14.3.7 The **while**-loop 194
    14.3.8 The Conditional 195
    14.3.9 The **for**-loop 195
14.4 Total Correctness 196
14.5 Using Mathematical Variables 196
14.6 Verification Conditions 197
    14.6.1 Introduction 197
    14.6.2 The *skip* Command 198
    14.6.3 Assignment 198
    14.6.4 The Conditional 198
    14.6.5 Sequencing 199
    14.6.6 The **while**-loop 199
    14.6.7 The **for**-loop 199
    14.6.8 An Example 200
14.7 Conclusion 200

15 Getting to Program Code   **203**
  15.1 The Transformation Recipe 203
  15.2 Modelling a Simple Bank Account 204
      15.2.1 Adding Messages 206
  15.3 A Sales Database 208
      15.3.1 Informal Account 208
      15.3.2 The State Space 209
      15.3.3 The Operations 210
      15.3.4 The User-interface 213
      15.3.5 Calculating Preconditions 215
      15.3.6 The Implementation 215
  15.4 Conclusion 219

III Case Studies   **221**

16 Two Small Case Studies   **223**
  16.1 The Bill of Materials Problem 223
      16.1.1 Introduction 223
      16.1.2 Representing the Database 223
      16.1.3 Specifying Parts Explosion 224
      16.1.4 Another Specification 225
  16.2 A Route Planner 228
      16.2.1 Introduction 228
      16.2.2 The State Space 230
      16.2.3 The Operations 230

17 Wing's Library Problem   **233**
  17.1 Introduction 233
  17.2 Basic Types and User-defined Sets 234
  17.3 The State of the System 235
  17.4 The Operations 238
      17.4.1 Checking Out and Returning Copies of Books 238
      17.4.2 Adding and Removing Copies of Books 243
      17.4.3 Interrogating the Library Database 249

18 Partial Specification of a Text-editor   **255**
  18.1 Introduction 255
  18.2 Basic Types 255
  18.3 The State Space 256
  18.4 The Operations 256
      18.4.1 Operations to the Left of the Cursor 256
      18.4.2 Operations to the Right of the Cursor 259
  18.5 The *Doc2* State 262
      18.5.1 Promoting *Doc1* Operations to *Doc2* Ones 265

18.6 The *Doc3* Model 266
    18.6.1 Putting a Window on the Unbounded Display 266
18.7 Conclusion 268

IV   Specification Animation   269

19 Animation using Miranda   271

19.1 Introduction 271
19.2 The Animation 271
    19.2.1 Overall Structure 271
    19.2.2 Basic Types 271
    19.2.3 The State Space 272
    19.2.4 The Initial State 273
    19.2.5 The Operations 273
    19.2.6 The Miranda Script 275

V   Reference Manual   279

20 Methods of Definition   281

20.1 Axiomatic Description 281
20.2 Generic Definition 282
20.3 Schema Definition 283

21 Formal Definitions   285

21.1 Sets 285
    21.1.1 Relations between Sets 285
    21.1.2 Operators on Sets 285
    21.1.3 Generalized Union and Intersection 286
    21.1.4 Finite Sets 286
    21.1.5 Smallest and Largest Elements 287
21.2 Relations 287
    21.2.1 Introduction 287
    21.2.2 Domains and Ranges 287
    21.2.3 Inversion 288
    21.2.4 Domain Restriction and Anti-restriction 288
    21.2.5 Range Restriction and Anti-restriction 288
    21.2.6 Composition 289
    21.2.7 Image 289
    21.2.8 Iteration and Closures 289
    21.2.9 Overriding 290
21.3 Functions 290
    21.3.1 Possibly Non-finite Functions 290
    21.3.2 Finite Functions 292

21.3.3 Lambda Abstraction 292
21.4 Sequences 292
    21.4.1 Basic Definitions 292
    21.4.2 Sequence Constructors 292
    21.4.3 Sequence Destructors 293
    21.4.4 Reversing a Sequence 294
    21.4.5 Disjointness and Partitioning 294
21.5 Bags 295
    21.5.1 Basic Definitions 295
    21.5.2 Bag Manipulating Operators 295

22 Rules and Obligations   **299**
22.1 First-order Logic 299
    22.1.1 Start Sequents 299
    22.1.2 Themata 299
22.2 Reasoning about Sets 303
22.3 Reasoning about Tuples 304
22.4 Floyd–Hoare Logic 304
22.5 Induction 305
    22.5.1 Mathematical Induction 305
    22.5.2 Induction for Sequences 306
22.6 Proof Obligations for Refinement 306
    22.6.1 Operation Refinement 306
    22.6.2 Data Refinement 307

VI Appendices   **309**

A Variable Conventions   **311**

B Answers to Exercises   **313**

C Glossary of Terms   **333**

D Glossary of Symbols   **351**

Bibliography   **357**

Index   **363**

Preface

Origins and Intended Audience

This book is about the formal specification language Z. It is based on various lecture courses that I have given in the School of Computer Science at the University of Birmingham since October 1987. (Some of these were given jointly with my colleague Tom Axford, but this book does not make use of any of his material.) Needless to say, what is presented here has undergone much revision and elaboration during the process of turning it into book form.

Given its origins this book can be used as a textbook for introductory courses on Z and formal methods, but it is also suitable for people who want to learn Z on their own. I assume that the reader has some knowledge of the basic ideas of set theory, but I do not assume any great familiarity with formal methods. This book is an *introductory* book on Z, so it does not cover some of the more esoteric features of that language.

Organization of the Material

This book is divided into six parts. Part I is a tutorial introduction to Z which covers the basic mathematical toolkit and the fundamental ideas of the schema calculus. Many exercises are provided and—to help people using this book on their own in order to learn Z—answers are provided in appendix B to *every* exercise set. Personally, I find it annoying when textbooks which contain exercises contain either no answers or only answers to selected exercises; therefore, I have included answers to all the exercises.

Part II looks at methods of reasoning. As well as looking at both formal and rigorous proof, I also cover the important issues of data refinement and operation decomposition. This part also contains two chapters which deal with the topic of how a Z specification can be related to program code. Chapter 14 presents the basic ideas of Floyd–Hoare logic and chapter 15 shows how Z schemas describing operations can be transformed into the formulas of such a logic. The method presented is illustrated by means of two case studies.

Part III contains four specification case studies: two small ones and two fairly large ones. The two small ones are of the bill of materials problem and of a route planner. (The route planner specification was suggested to me by my colleague Tom Axford.) The first large case study is of Wing's library problem and the second is a partial specification of a display-oriented text-editor, based on Sufrin's specification. One of the distinctive features of this book is the large number of case studies provided. In addition to the four contained in this part of the book, no less than eleven others are included in other parts. These range in size from the 21-page specification of a library database down to the specification of an operation that raises three to the power of an arbitrary non-negative number, which consists of a single schema. Most of the specifications contained in this book are original, but I have also included some well-known favourites like the classroom specification, the bill of materials specification and an updated and revamped version of Sufrin's editor specification. In part I of the book when a new Z data type is introduced, it is usually illustrated by means of a case study. Thus, a telephone directory is used to illustrate relations, a weather map to illustrate functions, sorting to illustrate both sequences and bags, a vending machine to illustrate bags and a theorem-checker and theorem-prover to illustrate sequences and free types (in this case, trees).

In part IV I look at how a Z specification can be animated using a high-level modern functional programming language.

Part V is a reference manual. It consists of three chapters. In chapter 20 the various methods of definition available in Z are explained and in chapter 21 formal definitions are given of the most frequently used symbols in Z. These are needed in order to reason about the operations those symbols stand for as explained in chapter 11. The final chapter in this part of the book lists all the rules that are needed to reason about Z that have been mentioned in other parts of the book, together with a summary of the proof obligations that have to be discharged to show that one specification is a refinement of another one.

Part VI consists of four appendices as well as the bibliography and index. Appendix A contains a list of the uses to which I put all the single-letter identifiers used in this book. Appendix B contains answers to all the exercises set in this book. Appendix C is a glossary of terms. This is included for two reasons. The first is that, as readers of this book will have different backgrounds, it is impossible for me to assume that they all have familiarity with a particular specialized vocabulary. (The terminology used about Z is drawn from several sources.) Rather than define all these terms in the body of the book, most of these definitions are collected together in the glossary. The second is that some of the terms used about Z have several meanings and the account given in the glossary makes clear how I am using them. Appendix D is a glossary of symbols. As well as giving a very brief account of the meaning of each symbol, page references are given—where appropriate—to where the symbol in question has its meaning explained and where it is formally defined.

Changes from the First Edition

The major additions in this edition are the two entirely new chapters explaining how a Z specification can be related to program code, namely chapters 14 and 15, and the new appendix containing a glossary of terms used in Z, which is appendix C. The only major deletion has been the removal of the chapter which showed how a specification could be animated in Prolog.

As well as these major changes, many further revisions and additions have been made. Some of the more important ones are listed here:

- Chapter 1 has been entirely rewritten and a section on numbers and the basic numerical operators available in Z included.

- In chapter 4—in which the specification of a telephone directory is presented— new material has been added at the beginning and the end of the chapter. At the beginning the section on Cartesian products has been expanded and a new section added which contains an informal account of the functionality of the system being specified. At the end, the section on the structure and organization of a Z specification document has been considerably expanded.

- Schema piping and the use of schemas as types is included for the first time in chapter 5.

- Chapters 10 and 11, on formal and informal reasoning, respectively, have been considerably revamped and a uniform proof-theory is presented. Thus, first-order logic, set theory—and later, in chapter 14, Floyd–Hoare logic—are all presented in the form of a single-conclusion sequent calculus.

- Several new exercises—and their answers—have been included.

Some of the revisions in and additions to this edition have been made as a result of changes in the Z language itself. The notation used in this book conforms to that of standard Z as it is defined in the second edition of the reference manual written by Spivey (1992). A number of changes were made in standard Z between the first and second editions of that manual. Some of the more important changes in this category are listed here:

- In the second edition of Spivey's manual the overriding operator $\oplus$ is defined in such a way that it makes a relation out of two other relations, whereas in the first edition it made a function out of two other functions. This has necessitated the moving of the section on overriding from the chapter on functions to chapter 5, where various operations on relations are discussed.

- In the first edition of Spivey's manual the operator $\_^{-1}$ was used to form the inverse of both homogeneous and heterogeneous relations, but in the second edition this operator became $\_^{\sim}$. The operator $\_^{-1}$ can only be applied to homogeneous relations. This has necessitated many—admittedly minor—changes throughout the book.

- In the second edition of Spivey's manual the symbol $\in$ is used for bag membership, instead of the word 'in' that was used in the first edition, $\sharp$ is introduced as a synonym for *count* and several new operators on bags are added, such as $\otimes$, $\sqsubseteq$ and $\uplus$. I have included an account of all these new symbols.

These are only a selection of the changes and emendations that I have made to the text. I do not think that a single page has been left unaltered. Furthermore, the material contained here has been considerably reorganized, though only minor changes have been made to the case studies used. This is because I know that many people used the first edition of this book as a set book for courses on Z and I hope that they will use this second edition as well and keeping the case studies and many of the examples the same means that they will not have to spend much time updating any course material that makes use of those case studies and examples. I am keen to hear from those people who have read this book and also from those who have used it to teach Z from. I can be contacted by email at `A.R.Diller@cs.bham.ac.uk` or by normal mail at the School of Computer Science, University of Birmingham, Birmingham, B15 2TT, England. Some of the improvements to this edition were made at the suggestion of correspondents and my gratitude to them is expressed in the acknowledgements section which follows this preface.

Antoni Diller
Birmingham
January 1994

Acknowledgements

The following trademarks are used in this book. 'Miranda' is a trademark of Research Software Ltd. 'TEX' is a trademark of the American Mathematical Society. 'Kit Kat' and 'Aero' are registered trademarks of Société des Produits Nestlé S.A., Vevey, Switzerland.

This book was typeset using LaTeX and I am grateful to Mike Spivey for providing me with a copy of the TEX macros he wrote for producing the various boxes and notations used in Z. Some of the Z symbols used in this edition were produced with help from his *f*uzz package, though that was not used to typeset the entire book. I would also like to thank Makoto Tatsuta for giving me a copy of his style file `proof.sty` containing the TEX macros that he wrote for producing tree proofs. I am also grateful to Tom Axford for the `\enclose` macro used in chapter 9. Although I think that LaTeX is—on the whole—a very good package of TEX macros, there are certain design decisions made by Lamport that I disagree with. In particular, throughout this book I use the TEX commands `\eqalign` and `\eqalignno` in preference to LaTeX's `\eqnarray`. More about this can now be found in my book on LaTeX, namely (Diller 1993).

I am indebted to a large number of people for my knowledge of Z and for many of the ideas contained in this book. I initially learnt Z from Bernard Sufrin and Ib Sørensen of Oxford University's Programming Research Group and I am grateful to them—and Mike Spivey—for answering many questions about Z. In the first edition of this book I thanked Rachid Anane, Tom Axford, Richard Billington and Mark Tarver for their helpful comments on parts of the manuscript as I was writing it and I repeat that thanks here. In addition I would like to express my gratitude to the following people who either noticed errors in the first edition or made helpful comments about how it could be improved: Ananda Amatya, Paul Ammann, Roberto Barros, Stephen J. Bevan, Rosemary Docherty, Stephen Gilmore, Peter Greenfield, Lindsay Groves, Howard Goodman, Darrel Ince, Steve King, Soren Larsen, Dave Love, George Row, Garurank P. Saxena, A.A. Sayficar, Phil Windley and Leszek Zarzycki.

I apologize for any omissions of acknowledgement and will correct them when the opportunity arises if they are drawn to my attention. Needless to say, any mistakes contained in this book are my own responsibility.

Part I

Tutorial

1

Introduction

1.1 What is Z?

Z is a language, but knowing this does not tell you very much about it because there are many different kinds of language, such as natural language and programming language. Z, however, does not belong to either of these kinds of language. Programming languages are used in order to express algorithms in a form that can be executed by a computer and natural languages are used by human beings in order to communicate with each other about an extremely wide range of topics. Although Z is neither a natural language nor a programming language, it shares some characteristics with languages belonging to both of these kinds. On the one hand, Z is a *formal* language and this is one thing that it shares with every programming language. They all have a precisely defined syntax. On the other hand, Z is used for communication by some people, but about a very narrow range of topics, namely the specification and design of software systems. It is, in fact, a *formal specification language* and it is based on conventional mathematical notations—though it occasionally departs from what is normal in mathematics.

Not only is the grammar of Z based on that of the language used in mathematics, but its semantics is also based on that of *classical* mathematics and the word 'classical' is important here. The reason for this is that other specification languages are based on non-classical mathematics. Classical mathematics is founded on two-valued logic and set theory and so is Z, but some approaches to specification are built on deviant logics.[1] For example, VDM is based on one of the three-valued logics and some specification notations are derived from intuitionistic logic and mathematics.

Although built on some of the central theories of classical mathematics, the Z language is not identical to that used there. The main difference is that Z has a precise syntax, whereas the language of mathematics has never been subjected to a formal process of standardization. A definitive version of the grammar of Z has yet to appear, but I have decided to treat the language defined in the second edition of

---

[1]The word 'deviant' is used here in a technical sense. See, for example, (Haack 1974), p. 4, where a *deviant* logic is defined to be one which shares the the same syntax as that used in classical logic, but which has a different class of theorems—though, of course, there may be some overlap.

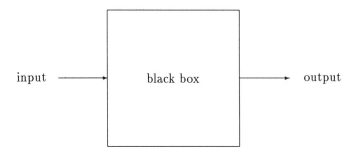

Figure 1.1: Black box specification.

Spivey's book *The Z Notation: A Reference Manual* (1992) as constituting standard
Z and wherever the phrase 'standard Z' occurs in this book it is the language that is
described in Spivey's manual that is being referred to.[2]

As already mentioned, the main use to which Z is put is that of specifying software
systems. Although Z is not a programming language, the reason why someone uses it
is because at the end of the day he or she wants to write or help to produce a computer
program written in a real programming language that runs on an actual machine. The
ultimate goal of using Z in a software project is that of producing demonstrably correct
software. In other words, what people who use Z are trying to do is to write bug-free
computer programs.[3] Using Z in this process has several advantages. It allows us, for
example, to make use of representational and procedural (or operational) abstraction.

Representational abstraction involves using high-level mathematical data types—
like sets, relations, functions, sequences, bags, trees and so on—in the specification
of software systems without worrying about how these are going to be eventually
implemented. This has the beneficial consequence that in solving a specific problem we
are allowed to think using types most suited to the problem in hand, rather than being
forced at a premature stage to think in terms of the baroque data types available in
most programming languages.[4] Later on, when the specification has been finished, we
can start thinking about how those high-level data types can be *reified* or *decomposed*
into data types that are more like those found in conventional, high-level programming
languages.

Using *procedural abstraction* we ignore issues relating to *how* a task is to be carried
out and focus instead on accurately stating *what* has to be done. One of the things

---

[2]There are slight differences between Spivey's dialect of Z and those defined in (Brien and Nicholls
1992) and in appendices A and B of (Hayes 1993).

[3]In a recent article Fetzer (1988) has argued forcefully that there is an unbridgeable gap between
the abstract world in which formal specifications, correctness proofs and ideal programming languages
live and the concrete world of actual programs written in real programming languages running on
physical machines. This led to a lively exchange in subsequent issues of the *Communications of the
ACM* (in which journal Fetzer's article was published). It would be out of place to discuss Fetzer's
ideas here, but the report (Diller 1991) is my first attempt to evaluate his arguments.

[4]This is an example of the divide-and-conquer problem-solving strategy.

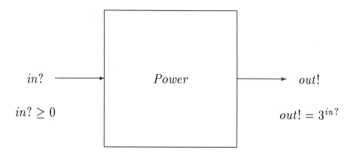

Figure 1.2: Calculating powers specification.

that people find difficult to do when they start writing formal specifications is to stop thinking procedurally. In writing a specification it is best to think declaratively. Issues relating to efficiency and even implementability should be shelved for the time being. There is a time and a place to think about how a specification is going to be implemented efficiently, but this is best done when the specification has been finished. Using procedural abstraction operations are specified by means of their input-output behaviour, that is to say, by stating their preconditions and postconditions. The use of this abstraction technique is illustrated in the next section.

1.2   Specification Foretaste

In Z operations are specified by their input-output behaviour. The means by which the output is produced from the input is regarded as a black box as shown in Fig. 1.1. The specifier as specifier is not interested in the contents of the black box. All that he or she is interested in is the relationship that exists between the output and the input. In order to make the discussion more concrete I will consider the problem of specifying the operation which calculates the result of raising three to the power of some non-negative integer which is the input to the operation. The input-output behaviour of this operation, which I call *Power*, is shown in Fig. 1.2. The input is represented by the integer-valued variable *in?* and the fact that it is non-negative is captured by the formula $in? \geq 0$. Note that the identifier *in?* ends in a question mark. It is conventional in Z to distinguish input variables from other sorts of variable by making the last character of the name of an input variable a question mark.

The output of the *Power* operation is represented by the integer-valued variable *out!* in Fig. 1.2 and its relation to the input *in?* is given by the formula $out! = 3^{in?}$. Note that the identifier *out!* ends in an exclamation mark. It is conventional in Z to distinguish output variables from other sorts of variable by making the last character of the name of an output variable an exclamation mark.

In Z the specification shown diagrammatically in Fig. 1.2 is packaged up into what is known as a *schema* and the *Power* schema looks like this:

```
function POWERA(X: INTEGER);
begin
  if X = 0 then
    POWERA := 1
  else
    POWERA := 3 * POWERA(X − 1)
end;
```

```
function POWERB(X: INTEGER);
begin
  if X = 0 then
    POWERB := 1
  else if EVEN(X) then
    POWERB := SQUARE(POWERB(X div 2))
  else
    POWERB := 3 * POWERB(X − 1)
end;
```

Figure 1.3: Two implementations of *Power*.

$$\begin{array}{|l} \hline \_Power_____ \\ in?, out!: \mathbf{Z} \\ \hline in? \geq 0 \\ out! = 3^{in?} \\ \hline \end{array}$$

Every schema has a name and this occurs at the top of the schema box and it makes a gap in the top horizontal line of the box. (The name 'box' is now fairly standard even though the right-hand edge is missing.) The contents of the box are separated by a short horizontal line. In the top region of the box, which is known as the *declaration-part* of the schema, there occur one or more declarations and in the bottom region of the box, which is known as the *predicate-part* of the schema, there occur one or more formulas. (There is an unfortunate tendency in the Z community to call formulas *predicates* and even I succumbed to this in the first edition of this book (Diller 1990). In this second edition formulas are called *formulas*. Calling the bottom region of the schema box the predicate-part is now so firmly established, however, that to call it something else would only cause confusion and so I have decided to stick to the established terminology.)

In the declaration-part of *Power* there occurs the declaration $in?, out!: \mathbf{Z}$ which tells us that both $in?$ and $out!$ are integer-valued variables. The type of all integers is represented by the letter $\mathbf{Z}$, which in this book is set in boldface type, though sometimes in books on Z it appears in blackboard bold as Z. $\mathbf{Z}$ is in fact the only predefined type in standard Z.

In the predicate-part of the schema *Power* there occur the two formulas $in? \geq 0$

and $out! = 3^{in?}$. The first of these tells us that $in?$ must be a non-negative number and the second of them tells us that the output is three raised to the power of the input.

Even though the operation specified by the schema *Power* is very simple there are many different programs which implement it. Two of these are shown as Pascal functions in Fig. 1.3. Currently, there is no standard way of linking a Z specification to program code, though several approaches are the topic of active research. For example, King (1990) uses the refinement calculus developed by Morgan (1990) to get to program code from a Z specification, Wordsworth (1992), chapter 7, uses some of Dijkstra's work for this and later on in this book—in chapter 15—I show how a Z specification can be linked to program code through the formulas of a Floyd–Hoare logic.

1.3   Numbers

As already mentioned, the type of all integers is represented in Z by the letter **Z** and, not surprisingly, there are several relations available for comparing integers and also a number of binary functions defined on them. Z contains the following relations: = (equality), $\neq$ (difference), $<$ (strictly less than), $\leq$ (less than or equal to), $\geq$ (greater than or equal to) and $>$ (strictly greater than). It also contains the following binary functions: $+$ (addition), $-$ (subtraction), $*$ (multiplication), **div** (integer division) and **mod** (modulo). The last two are defined so that truncation takes place towards minus infinity (Spivey 1992, p. 108). This means that if $j \neq 0$, then the following equation relates **div** and **mod**:

$$i = (i \text{ div } j) * j + i \text{ mod } j,$$

where i and j are integers. We also have that when j is positive and i is any integer then $0 \leq i \text{ mod } j < j$. This last formula is defined in Z to mean exactly the same as $0 \leq i \text{ mod } j \wedge i \text{ mod } j < j$, where the symbol $\wedge$ is the conjunction sign. In fact, in Z it is always true that a formula like

$$t_1 \ F_1 \ t_2 \ F_2 \ t_3 \ldots t_{n-1} \ F_{n-1} \ t_n,$$

where t_i, for $1 \leq i \leq n$, is a term and F_i, for $1 \leq i < n$, is a binary, infix relation symbol, is equivalent in every way to the conjunctive formula

$$(t_1 \ F_1 \ t_2) \wedge (t_2 \ F_2 \ t_3) \wedge \ldots \wedge (t_{n-1} \ F_{n-1} \ t_n),$$

which is made up out of $n - 1$ conjuncts, where $n > 1$.

Z also contains the unary functions $-$ (unary minus) and *succ* (the successor function) which returns $i + 1$ when given the argument i, for $i \geq 0$.

2

First-order Logic

2.1 Propositional Calculus

2.1.1 Introduction

There are two main ways of studying any logical system, namely the proof-theoretic and the model-theoretic. *Model-theory* or (*formal*) *semantics* deals with concepts like truth, interpretation and satisfiability, whereas *proof-theory* deals with proofs. In this section I describe the model-theory of the propositional calculus and in chapter 10 I discuss its proof-theory.

Z uses the classical, two-valued propositional calculus in which every formula is postulated to be either true or false, but not both. No third truth-value is permitted, nor is it allowed for a formula to lack a truth-value.[1] The only two truth-values permitted are truth and falsity. In this chapter these will be represented by t and f, respectively. The following are examples of formulas:

$$2 + 7 = 9, \tag{2.1}$$
$$3 > 9, \tag{2.2}$$
$$10 \in \varnothing. \tag{2.3}$$

Formula (2.1) is true, (2.2) is false and (2.3) is also false.

Although the truth-functional connectives $\neg$, $\wedge$, $\vee$, $\Rightarrow$ and $\Longleftrightarrow$ are all part of the Z language, in this section on the propositional calculus they are discussed in isolation, that is to say, apart from the other constructs of Z. To be precise, I deal with the language *prop*, of the propositional calculus, whose abstract syntax is given as follows:[2]

$$A ::= ident$$
$$| \neg A$$

---

[1] It is possible to devise n-valued logics which have n truth-values. The specification language of VDM, for example, uses a 3-valued logic. In using Z, however, you should always be aware that it is based on classical logic. For more information about many-valued logics see (Ackermann 1967).

[2] Note that the symbols ::= and | used here are *not* the symbols belonging to Z which look the same and are used to define a free type.

$$| \ A_1 \wedge A_2$$
$$| \ A_1 \vee A_2$$
$$| \ A_1 \Rightarrow A_2$$
$$| \ A_1 \Longleftrightarrow A_2,$$

where *ident* represents any alphanumeric identifier, whose first character is not a numeral, and A, A_1 and A_2 are formulas. If A is a formula generated by this abstract syntax, then it is known as a *formula of the propositional calculus* or simply as a *formula* if calling it this does not lead to confusion. For illustrative purposes, however, I sometimes use formulas like (2.1), (2.2) and (2.3) in examples.

If A is a formula in whose construction no truth-functional connective was used, then A is known as a *primitive* or *atomic* formula. If one or more truth-functional connectives were used in the construction of A, then A is known as a *non-atomic* formula. Imagine a tree representing the construction of a non-atomic formula. Then the connective at the root is the *main connective* of the formula. For example, let P, Q and R be primitive formulas. Then the main connective of the formula $(P \wedge Q) \vee (R \Rightarrow P)$ is $\vee$. This can be seen from the following construction tree:

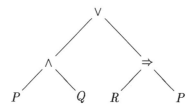

Let A be a non-atomic formula whose main connective is $\neg$. Then the formula B, which is such that $\neg B$ is the same formula as A, is known as the *immediate constituent* of A. Similarly, let A be a non-atomic formula whose main connective is $\heartsuit$, where $\heartsuit$ is one of $\wedge$, $\vee$, $\Rightarrow$ or $\Longleftrightarrow$. Then the formulas B and C, which are such that $B \heartsuit C$ is the same formula as A, are known as the *immediate constituents* of A. A formula B is a *constituent* of a non-atomic formula A if either B is an immediate constituent of A or B is a constituent of one of the immediate constituents of A.

2.1.2 Truth-functional Connectives and Constant Formulas

The letters A, B, C, P, Q, R and these letters decorated with numerical subscripts are used consistently in this book to stand for arbitrary formulas. A *one-place truth-functional connective* is an operator which makes a formula out of one other formula. The reason for the name is that the truth-value of the resulting formula depends only on the truth-value of the formula which is its immediate constituent. Similarly, a *two-place truth-functional connective* is an operator which makes a formula out of two other formulas.

Negation

The negation sign ¬ is a one-place truth-functional connective. Thus, it makes a formula out of another formula. For example, applying it to the formulas (2.1), (2.2) and (2.3), respectively, yields the three formulas:

$$\neg(2 + 7 = 9), \tag{2.4}$$
$$\neg(3 > 9), \tag{2.5}$$
$$\neg(10 \in \varnothing). \tag{2.6}$$

Of these, (2.4) is false, (2.5) is true and (2.6) is also true. The meaning of the negation sign is fully determined by the following basic truth-table:

P	$\neg P$
t	f
f	t

A formula $\neg P$ is false iff P is true and $\neg P$ is true iff P is false. (The phrase 'if and only if' occurs so frequently in discussions of logic that it is usually abbreviated to 'iff'.)

Conjunction

The conjunction sign $\wedge$ is a two-place truth-functional connective. Thus, it makes a formula out of two other formulas. For example, combining the two formulas (2.1) and (2.2), in that order, by means of it results in the formula $(2 + 7 = 9) \wedge (3 > 9)$. This can be read as '$2 + 7 = 9$ and $3 > 9$'. A formula whose main connective is $\wedge$ is known as a *conjunction* or as a *conjunctive formula* and the two immediate constituents are known as *conjuncts*. The meaning of the conjunction sign is completely given by this basic truth-table:

P	Q	$P \wedge Q$
t	t	t
t	f	f
f	t	f
f	f	f

This says that a conjunction is true iff both of its conjuncts are true.

Disjunction

The sign for disjunction $\vee$ is a two-place truth-functional connective. Thus, it makes a formula out of two other formulas. For example, combining the two formulas (2.1) and (2.2), in that order, by means of it results in the formula $(2 + 7 = 9) \vee (3 > 9)$. This can be read as '$2 + 7 = 9$ or $3 > 9$'. A formula whose main connective is $\vee$ is known as a *disjunction* or as a *disjunctive formula* and the two immediate constituents are known as *disjuncts*. The meaning of the disjunction sign is given by the following basic truth-table:

P	Q	$P \vee Q$
t	t	t
t	f	t
f	t	t
f	f	f

Thus, a disjunction is false iff both its disjuncts are false. Such a disjunction is known as *non-exclusive* or *inclusive* disjunction. The reason why it is called this is because $P \vee Q$ is true when both P and Q are true, that is to say, inclusive disjunction *includes* this, whereas exclusive disjunction *excludes* this. There is no symbol for exclusive disjunction in standard Z, but using $\|$ for this allows its basic truth-table to be displayed:[3]

P	Q	$P \| Q$
t	t	f
t	f	t
f	t	t
f	f	f

Thus, a formula $P \| Q$ is true iff its immediate constituents have different truth-values.

Implication

The implication sign $\Rightarrow$ is a two-place truth-functional connective. Thus, it makes a formula out of two other formulas. For example, combining the two formulas (2.1) and (2.2), in that order, by means of it results in the formula $(2 + 7 = 9) \Rightarrow (3 > 9)$, which can be read as 'if $2 + 7 = 9$, then $3 > 9$'. A formula whose main connective is $\Rightarrow$ is known variously as an *implication*, an *implicative formula*, a *conditional (formula)* or a *hypothetical (formula)*. Let $P \Rightarrow Q$ be an implicative formula. Then the constituent P is known as the *antecedent* or the *protasis* and the component Q is known as the *consequent* or the *apodosis*. The meaning of the implication sign is fully determined by the following basic truth-table:

P	Q	$P \Rightarrow Q$
t	t	t
t	f	f
f	t	t
f	f	t

A conditional formula is false iff its antecedent is true and its consequent is false.

---

[3]Some authors use the symbol $\equiv$ for the bi-implication sign and $\not\equiv$ as the sign for exclusive disjunction.

Bi-implication

The bi-implication sign $\Longleftrightarrow$ is a two-place truth-functional connective. Thus, it makes a formula out of two other formulas. For example, combining the two formulas (2.1) and (2.2), in that order, by means of it results in the formula $(2 + 7 = 9) \Longleftrightarrow (3 > 9)$, which can be read as '$2 + 7 = 9$ if and only if $3 > 9$'. A formula whose main connective is $\Longleftrightarrow$ is known as a *bi-implication* or as a *biconditional (formula)*. The constituents of a biconditional are not given any special names. The meaning of the bi-implication sign is fully determined by the following basic truth-table:

P	Q	$P \Longleftrightarrow Q$
t	t	t
t	f	f
f	t	f
f	f	t

A biconditional is true iff both of its immediate constituents have the same truth-value.

Constant Formulas

Z also contains two constant formulas, namely the always true and the always false formulas. The former of these is symbolized by *true* and the latter by *false*. The constant formulas *true* and *false* should be carefully distinguished from the truth-values t and f. The latter are used to give the meanings of formulas. The relation between a formula and its truth-value is similar to that which holds between a name and its bearer. I am different from the name 'Antoni Diller', but my name stands for or denotes or refers to me—similarly with formulas and their truth-values. The formula '$2 + 3 = 5$' refers to the truth-value t. Another difference is that the constant formulas can be combined with other formulas by means of the truth-functional connectives. For example, both *true* $\Rightarrow 2 + 3 = 5$ and $7 > 3 \wedge$ *false* are legitimate examples of formulas of Z. The truth-values t and f, however, cannot be used in this way. They belong to the meta-language we use to talk about the propositional calculus and are not part of that language themselves. It is also worth pointing out that this means that Z does not have a Boolean data type.

Precedence and Associativity of the Connectives

The negation sign binds most strongly, so $\neg P \vee Q$ means $(\neg P) \vee Q$ and not $\neg(P \vee Q)$. The conjunction sign binds more strongly than any truth-functional connective except the negation sign, and then come the signs for disjunction, implication and bi-implication, in that order. So, $P \vee Q \wedge R \Rightarrow P$ means $(P \vee (Q \wedge R)) \Rightarrow P$. The connective $\Rightarrow$ associates to the right, whereas $\wedge$, $\vee$ and $\Longleftrightarrow$ all associate to the left. So, $P \wedge Q \wedge R \Rightarrow P \Rightarrow R$ means $((P \wedge Q) \wedge R) \Rightarrow (P \Rightarrow R)$. Sometimes when writing complicated formulas parentheses are used even when they are not needed in order to make the structure of the formula clearer. Thus, many people would choose to write

$$P \vee (Q \wedge R) \Longleftrightarrow (P \vee Q) \wedge (P \vee R)$$

rather than

$$P \vee Q \wedge R \Longleftrightarrow (P \vee Q) \wedge (P \vee R),$$

even though the two displayed formulas have exactly the same meaning.

Ways of Defining the Connectives

So far I have introduced the five truth-functional connectives available in standard Z and given the meaning of each one of them independently of the others, but is is possible to define all of these connectives using only a subset of them. For example, we can take negation and disjunction as primitive and define all the other connectives like this:

$$P \wedge Q == \neg(\neg P \vee \neg Q),$$
$$P \Rightarrow Q == \neg P \vee Q,$$
$$P \Longleftrightarrow Q == \neg(\neg(\neg P \vee Q) \vee \neg(\neg Q \vee P)).$$

The sign $==$ used here is the Z notation for an abbreviation definition. The left-hand side is being defined to mean the same as the right-hand side.[4]

In fact, there exist connectives in terms of which all the others can be defined. One example of such a connective is Sheffer's stroke, which has the following basic truth-table:

P	Q	$P \mid Q$
t	t	f
t	f	t
f	t	t
f	f	t

Sheffer's stroke is also known as the sign for *alternative denial*. A formula $P \mid Q$ is false iff both P and Q are true. It is possible to define $\neg$, $\wedge$, $\vee$, $\Rightarrow$ and $\Longleftrightarrow$ in terms of $\mid$. First, we define $\neg$ and $\vee$ like this:

$$\neg P == P \mid P,$$
$$P \vee Q == (P \mid P) \mid (Q \mid Q).$$

Then, we use the previous definitions.

---

[4]See section 20.1 below and (Spivey 1992), pp. 50 and 80, for more information about abbreviation definitions.

2.1.3 Model-theory

Semantic Validity

In order to explain the important notion of semantic validity I need to define quite a few terms.[5]

The formulas of the propositional calculus can be divided into the atomic and the non-atomic ones. An *atomic formula* is one that does not contain any of the truth-functional connectives, whereas a *non-atomic formula* contains at least one truth-functional connective.

An *interpretation* $\mathcal{I}$ *of the atomic formulas of the propositional calculus* is a function which associates each atomic formula with one and only one truth-value. Each such interpretation can be extended in a unique way to an *interpretation* $\mathcal{V}$ (*of the propositional calculus*) which is a function that associates *every* formula with one and only one truth-value. This is done as follows:[6]

$$\mathcal{V}(P) = \mathcal{I}(P), \quad \text{for all atomic formulas } P;$$

$$\mathcal{V}(\neg P) = \begin{cases} t, & \text{if } \mathcal{V}(P) = f, \\ f, & \text{if } \mathcal{V}(P) = t; \end{cases}$$

$$\mathcal{V}(P \wedge Q) = \begin{cases} t, & \text{if } \mathcal{V}(P) = \mathcal{V}(Q) = t, \\ f, & \text{otherwise}; \end{cases}$$

$$\mathcal{V}(P \vee Q) = \begin{cases} f, & \text{if } \mathcal{V}(P) = \mathcal{V}(Q) = f, \\ t, & \text{otherwise}; \end{cases}$$

$$\mathcal{V}(P \Rightarrow Q) = \begin{cases} f, & \text{if } \mathcal{V}(P) = t \text{ and } \mathcal{V}(Q) = f, \\ t, & \text{otherwise}; \end{cases}$$

$$\mathcal{V}(P \Longleftrightarrow Q) = \begin{cases} t, & \text{if } \mathcal{V}(P) = \mathcal{V}(Q), \\ f, & \text{otherwise}. \end{cases}$$

A formula P is *true in an interpretation* $\mathcal{V}$ if $\mathcal{V}(P) = t$ and it is *false in an interpretation* $\mathcal{V}$ if $\mathcal{V}(P) = f$.

A *sequent* is an ordered pair consisting of a set of formulas Γ and a single formula P. In this book such a sequent is written $\Gamma \mapsto P$.[7] A member of the set Γ is known as a *premise* and the formula P is called the *conclusion* of the sequent.

---

[5]The following account of the basic ideas of the model-theory of the propositional calculus is the way in which these notions are defined if the propositional calculus is being studied in isolation. In the case of Z, the truth-functional connectives form only a small part of a much richer language the formal semantics of which is fairly complicated—see, for example, (Spivey 1988). Thus, the account given in the text is best thought of as a "first approximation" to the proper semantics of the truth-functional connectives as they appear in Z. Readers who are new to formal semantics may profit from studying a more detailed account of the model-theory of the propositional calculus in, for example, (Hunter 1971), part 2, and (Gallier 1986), section 3.3.

[6]The following definition does not contain clauses for exclusive disjunction or alternative denial because the signs for these are not part of standard Z.

[7]See the entry under the heading *sequent* in the glossary of terms contained in appendix C for the reasons why this notation was chosen.

The capital Greek letters Γ, Δ and Σ are used to stand for sets of formulas, which may well be empty. The set consisting of, say, the three formulas P, Q and R is written

$$P, Q, R$$

Furthermore, Γ, Δ represents the union of Γ and Δ and Γ, P represents the union of Γ and the set that just consists of P.

A sequent $\Gamma \mapsto P$ is (*semantically*) *valid* (*in the propositional calculus*) iff there does not exist an interpretation in which every member of Γ is true and in which P is false. When a sequent $\Gamma \mapsto P$ is semantically valid we also say that P is a (*semantic*) *consequence* of Γ and that Γ (*semantically*) *entails* P. When P is a semantic consequence of the set of formulas Γ, we write $\Gamma \models P$. When Γ is the empty set, the notation $\models P$ is used as an alternative to $\varnothing \models P$. The symbol $\models$ is known as the (*semantic*) *turnstile* and it represents a *relation* in the meta-language used to talk about the propositional calculus. Thus, $\Gamma \models P$ is a *statement* that can be either true or false, whereas $\Gamma \mapsto P$ stands for a (structured) object. The relation $\models$ consists of all those sequents $\Gamma \mapsto P$ where P is a semantic consequence of Γ.

For example, the sequent $P, P \Rightarrow Q \mapsto Q$ is semantically valid. That this is indeed valid can be shown as follows. First, we draw up a truth-table:

P	Q	P	$P \Rightarrow Q$	$\mapsto$	Q
t	t	t	t		t
t	f	t	f		f
f	t	f	t		t
f	f	f	t		f

Note that we do not write anything in the column headed by the symbol $\mapsto$. This is because $\mapsto$ is not a truth-functional connective. It is a symbol used in the meta-language of the propositional calculus to form sequents.[8] Each row of such a truth-table corresponds to a single interpretation of the propositional calculus. If a column in the truth-table is headed by a non-atomic formula, then its truth-value in any row is worked out by looking at the basic truth-tables of the connectives that occur in it. Alternatively, the relevant clauses of the definition of $\mathcal{V}$ can be consulted.

The way we use this truth-table is to look at those rows in which the conclusion of the sequent, namely Q, is false. If all the premises in such a row are true, then the sequent is not valid. If there does not exist a row in which the conclusion is false and all the premises true, then the sequent is valid. Note that the rows in which the conclusion is true are irrelevant to the issue of whether or not the sequent is valid. In the case of the sequent $P, P \Rightarrow Q \mapsto Q$ there are only two rows in which the conclusion is false. In neither of these are all the premises true; hence, the sequent is valid.

---

[8] Note that Z also contains a symbol that looks like $\mapsto$. The meta-linguistic and the object language symbols have a similar meaning, but they are, nonetheless, different symbols.

Tautologies and Contradictions

A formula is *satisfiable* if there exists an interpretation in which it is true. A *tautology* is a formula that is true in every interpretation and a *contradiction* is a formula that is false in every interpretation. Thus, the formula Q is a tautology iff the sequent $\emptyset \mapsto Q$ is valid. Sometimes, $\mapsto Q$ is written instead of $\emptyset \mapsto Q$. (Tautologies are also known as *logical truths* and contradictions are also known as *logical falsehoods*. When several logical systems are being discussed, these terms are sometimes qualified to indicate which logical system they apply to. For example, not every logical truth of classical logic is a logical truth of intuitionistic logic.)

One of the simplest tautologies is $P \lor \neg P$. This is true—in classical logic—no matter what the truth-value of P is.[9] This can be straightforwardly shown by constructing a truth-table, thus:

P	$P \lor \neg P$
t	t
f	t

If we look at the main column headed by the main connective of the formula $P \lor \neg P$, that is to say, the disjunction sign, we see that only t occurs in that column. As a row of the truth-table corresponds to an interpretation, this means that $P \lor \neg P$ is true in every interpretation. Therefore, it is a tautology.

Another simple tautology is $P \Rightarrow P$. This can be shown like this:

P	$P \Rightarrow P$
t	t
f	t

Another example of a tautology is the formula $(P \Rightarrow Q) \lor (Q \Rightarrow P)$. That this is a tautology is rather surprising, but the following truth-table shows that it is:

P	Q	$(P \Rightarrow Q)$	$\lor$	$(Q \Rightarrow P)$
t	t	t	t	t
t	f	f	t	t
f	t	t	t	f
f	f	t	t	t

---

[9]This tautology is known as *the law of the excluded middle*. Mathematicians and logicians of the intuitionistic school do not accept that it is logically valid. Intuitionistic ideas will not be pursued here—though they have their uses in computing. See (Dummett 1977) and (Martin-Löf 1984) for more information about intuitionistic logic.

Truth-tables can also be used to show that a formula is not a tautology. Consider, for example, the truth-table of the formula $(P \Rightarrow Q) \Rightarrow (Q \Rightarrow P)$:

P	Q	$(P \Rightarrow Q)$	$\Rightarrow$	$(Q \Rightarrow P)$
t	t	t	t	t
t	f	f	t	t
f	t	t	f	f
f	f	t	t	t

When P is false and Q is true, then $(P \Rightarrow Q) \Rightarrow (Q \Rightarrow P)$ is false. Thus, it is not a tautology. It is not necessary to draw the entire truth-table in order to show that a formula is not a tautology; it is sufficient to give the truth-values of P and Q that serve as a counter-example, that is to say, make the formula false.

The final example of a truth-table that I give is one that involves three constituent formulas. The following truth-table shows that the formula $(P \Rightarrow Q) \vee (Q \Rightarrow R)$ is a tautology:

P	Q	R	$(P \Rightarrow Q)$	$\vee$	$(Q \Rightarrow R)$
t	t	t	t	t	t
t	t	f	t	t	f
t	f	t	f	t	t
t	f	f	f	t	t
f	t	t	t	t	t
f	t	f	t	t	f
f	f	t	t	t	t
f	f	f	t	t	t

There is a close connection between the notions of validity and being a tautology. As already mentioned, $\varnothing \models Q$ iff the formula Q is a tautology. Furthermore, $P \models Q$ iff $P \Rightarrow Q$ is a tautology. More generally, we have that $P_1, P_2, \ldots, P_n \models Q$ iff $P_1, P_2, \ldots, P_{n-1} \models P_n \Rightarrow Q$ and that $P_1, P_2, \ldots, P_n \models Q$ iff $P_1 \Rightarrow P_2 \Rightarrow \ldots \Rightarrow P_{n-1} \Rightarrow P_n \Rightarrow Q$ is a tautology.

Semantic Equivalence

Two formulas P and Q are (*semantically*) *equivalent* iff both of the sequents $P \mapsto Q$ and $Q \mapsto P$ are valid. The notation $P \models\!\models Q$ is used to represent the fact that P and Q are semantically equivalent. Thus, $\models\!\models$ is a symbol for a meta-linguistic relation. Only single formulas can be written either side of $\models\!\models$. Note that P and Q are semantically equivalent iff $P \Longleftrightarrow Q$ is a tautology. The formula $P \Longleftrightarrow Q$, however, is part of the Z language, whereas the notation $P \models\!\models Q$ only occurs in the meta-language that is used in this book to talk about the Z language.

For example, to show that $P \Rightarrow Q$ and $\neg P \vee Q$ are semantically equivalent we have to show that the two sequents $P \Rightarrow Q \;\longmapsto\; \neg P \vee Q$ and $\neg P \vee Q \;\longmapsto\; P \Rightarrow Q$ are both valid. To establish this we split it into two cases. First, we show that $P \Rightarrow Q \;\longmapsto\; \neg P \vee Q$ is valid. This is established by considering the following truth-table:

P	Q	$P \Rightarrow Q$	$\longmapsto$	$\neg P \vee Q$
t	t	t		t
t	f	f		f
f	t	t		t
f	f	t		t

The row to consider is that in which the conclusion $\neg P \vee Q$ is false. In this case the premise $P \Rightarrow Q$ is not true; therefore the sequent is valid.

Next, we show that $\neg P \vee Q \;\longmapsto\; P \Rightarrow Q$ is valid. This is established by considering the following truth-table:

P	Q	$\neg P \vee Q$	$\longmapsto$	$P \Rightarrow Q$
t	t	t		t
t	f	f		f
f	t	t		t
f	f	t		t

The row to consider is that in which the conclusion $P \Rightarrow Q$ is false. In this case the premise $\neg P \vee Q$ is not true; therefore the sequent is valid. Combining these two results shows that $P \Rightarrow Q$ and $\neg P \vee Q$ are semantically equivalent.

2.1.4 Useful Laws

Negation

The following laws are sometimes useful in manipulating negated formulas:

$$\neg \neg P \;=\!\!\models\; P,$$
$$\neg true \;=\!\!\models\; false,$$
$$\neg false \;=\!\!\models\; true.$$

Conjunction

Conjunction is idempotent, commutative and associative and every tautology is a two-sided unit for it:[10]

$$P \wedge P =\!\models P,$$
$$P \wedge Q =\!\models Q \wedge P,$$
$$(P \wedge Q) \wedge R =\!\models P \wedge (Q \wedge R),$$
$$P \wedge taut =\!\models P,$$
$$taut \wedge P =\!\models P,$$

where *taut* is any logical truth.

Disjunction

Disjunction is idempotent, commutative and associative and every contradiction is a two-sided unit for it:

$$P \vee P =\!\models P,$$
$$P \vee Q =\!\models Q \vee P,$$
$$(P \vee Q) \vee R =\!\models P \vee (Q \vee R),$$
$$P \vee contra =\!\models P,$$
$$contra \vee P =\!\models P,$$

where *contra* is any contradiction.

Implication

Implication is neither idempotent, nor commutative nor associative. Every tautology is a left unit for it, but it does not have a right unit:

$$taut \Rightarrow P =\!\!\!|\models P,$$

where *taut* is any tautology.

Bi-implication

Bi-implication is not idempotent. It is, however, commutative and associative and every tautology is a two-sided unit for it:

$$P \Longleftrightarrow Q =\!\models Q \Longleftrightarrow P,$$
$$(P \Longleftrightarrow Q) \Longleftrightarrow R =\!\models P \Longleftrightarrow (Q \Longleftrightarrow R),$$
$$P \Longleftrightarrow taut =\!\models P,$$
$$taut \Longleftrightarrow P =\!\models P,$$

where *taut* is any tautology.

---

[10] The meaning of terms like *idempotent*, *commutative*, *associative* and *unit* are all explained in the glossary contained in appendix C.

Distributive Laws

Conjunction distributes forwards through itself and disjunction. Although it does not distribute forwards through implication and bi-implication, there is in both of those cases a one-way semantic entailment:

$$P \wedge (Q \wedge R) \; =\!\!\models \; (P \wedge Q) \wedge (P \wedge R),$$
$$P \wedge (Q \vee R) \; =\!\!\models \; (P \wedge Q) \vee (P \wedge R),$$
$$P \wedge (Q \Rightarrow R) \; \models \; (P \wedge Q) \Rightarrow (P \wedge R),$$
$$P \wedge (Q \Longleftrightarrow R) \; \models \; (P \wedge Q) \Longleftrightarrow (P \wedge R).$$

Conjunction distributes backwards through itself and disjunction. Although it does not distribute backwards through implication and bi-implication, there is in both of those cases a one-way semantic entailment:

$$(P \wedge Q) \wedge R \; =\!\!\models \; (P \wedge R) \wedge (Q \wedge R),$$
$$(P \vee Q) \wedge R \; =\!\!\models \; (P \wedge R) \vee (Q \wedge R),$$
$$(P \Rightarrow Q) \wedge R \; \models \; (P \wedge R) \Rightarrow (Q \wedge R),$$
$$(P \Longleftrightarrow Q) \wedge R \; \models \; (P \wedge R) \Longleftrightarrow (Q \wedge R).$$

Disjunction distributes forwards through conjunction, disjunction, implication and bi-implication:

$$P \vee (Q \wedge R) \; =\!\!\models \; (P \vee Q) \wedge (P \vee R),$$
$$P \vee (Q \vee R) \; =\!\!\models \; (P \vee Q) \vee (P \vee R),$$
$$P \vee (Q \Rightarrow R) \; =\!\!\models \; (P \vee Q) \Rightarrow (P \vee R),$$
$$P \vee (Q \Longleftrightarrow R) \; =\!\!\models \; (P \vee Q) \Longleftrightarrow (P \vee R).$$

Disjunction distributes backwards through conjunction, disjunction, implication and bi-implication:

$$(P \wedge Q) \vee R \; =\!\!\models \; (P \vee R) \wedge (Q \vee R),$$
$$(P \vee Q) \vee R \; =\!\!\models \; (P \vee R) \vee (Q \vee R),$$
$$(P \Rightarrow Q) \vee R \; =\!\!\models \; (P \vee R) \Rightarrow (Q \vee R),$$
$$(P \Longleftrightarrow Q) \vee R \; =\!\!\models \; (P \vee R) \Longleftrightarrow (Q \vee R).$$

Implication distributes forwards through conjunction, disjunction, implication and bi-implication:

$$P \Rightarrow (Q \wedge R) \; =\!\!\models \; (P \Rightarrow Q) \wedge (P \Rightarrow R),$$
$$P \Rightarrow (Q \vee R) \; =\!\!\models \; (P \Rightarrow Q) \vee (P \Rightarrow R),$$
$$P \Rightarrow (Q \Rightarrow R) \; =\!\!\models \; (P \Rightarrow Q) \Rightarrow (P \Rightarrow R),$$
$$P \Rightarrow (Q \Longleftrightarrow R) \; =\!\!\models \; (P \Rightarrow Q) \Longleftrightarrow (P \Rightarrow R).$$

Implication does not distribute backwards through either conjunction, disjunction, implication or bi-implication. However, in the case of disjunction and implication, the following one-way semantic entailments hold:

$$(P \vee Q) \Rightarrow R \models (P \vee R) \Rightarrow (Q \vee R),$$
$$(P \Rightarrow Q) \Rightarrow R \models (P \Rightarrow R) \Rightarrow (Q \Rightarrow R).$$

Bi-implication does not distribute forwards through conjunction, nor through disjunction, nor through implication nor through itself. However, the following three one-way semantic entailments hold:

$$(P \Longleftrightarrow Q) \wedge (P \Longleftrightarrow R) \models P \Longleftrightarrow (Q \wedge R),$$
$$P \Longleftrightarrow (Q \vee R) \models (P \Longleftrightarrow Q) \vee (P \Longleftrightarrow R),$$
$$P \Longleftrightarrow (Q \Rightarrow R) \models (P \Longleftrightarrow Q) \Rightarrow (P \Longleftrightarrow R).$$

Bi-implication does not distribute backwards through any of the other four connectives. However, the following three one-way semantic entailments hold:

$$(P \Longleftrightarrow R) \wedge (Q \Longleftrightarrow R) \models (P \wedge Q) \Longleftrightarrow R,$$
$$(P \vee Q) \Longleftrightarrow R \models (P \Longleftrightarrow R) \vee (Q \Longleftrightarrow R),$$
$$(P \Rightarrow Q) \Longleftrightarrow R \models (P \Longleftrightarrow R) \Rightarrow (Q \Longleftrightarrow R).$$

De Morgan's Laws

The following four semantic equivalences are known collectively as de Morgan's laws:

$$\neg(P \wedge Q) \models\!\mid \neg P \vee \neg Q,$$
$$\neg(P \vee Q) \models\!\mid \neg P \wedge \neg Q,$$
$$P \wedge Q \models\!\mid \neg(\neg P \vee \neg Q),$$
$$P \vee Q \models\!\mid \neg(\neg P \wedge \neg Q).$$

Miscellaneous Useful Laws

The next group of laws that I list all involve one or other of the constant formulas *true* and *false*.

$$\models \quad true,$$
$$P \models \quad true,$$
$$false \models \quad P,$$
$$P \vee true \models\!\mid true,$$
$$P \wedge false \models\!\mid false,$$
$$P \Rightarrow false \models\!\mid \neg P.$$

The following group of laws does not make use of either of the constant formulas *true* or *false*.

$$\models \neg(P \wedge \neg P),$$
$$\models P \vee \neg P,$$
$$P \models\!\models P,$$
$$P \wedge Q \models P,$$
$$P \wedge Q \models Q,$$
$$P \models P \vee Q,$$
$$Q \models P \vee Q,$$
$$P \wedge Q \models\!\models (P \vee \neg Q) \wedge Q,$$
$$P \vee Q \models\!\models (P \wedge \neg Q) \vee Q.$$

The tautology $\neg(P \wedge \neg P)$ is known as the law of non-contradiction and $P \vee \neg P$ is the law of the excluded middle, which is also known as *tertium non datur*. The tautology $((P \Rightarrow Q) \Rightarrow P) \Rightarrow P$ that appears first in the next list of laws is known as Peirce's law.

$$\models ((P \Rightarrow Q) \Rightarrow P) \Rightarrow P,$$
$$\models (P \Rightarrow Q) \vee (Q \Rightarrow R),$$
$$Q \models P \Rightarrow Q,$$
$$\neg P \models P \Rightarrow Q,$$
$$\neg P \Rightarrow P \models P,$$
$$P \Rightarrow \neg P \models \neg P,$$
$$P \Rightarrow Q \models\!\models \neg(P \wedge \neg Q),$$
$$P \Rightarrow Q \models\!\models \neg P \vee Q,$$
$$P \Rightarrow Q \models\!\models \neg Q \Rightarrow \neg P,$$
$$(P \wedge Q) \Rightarrow R \models\!\models (P \Rightarrow R) \vee (Q \Rightarrow R),$$
$$(P \vee Q) \Rightarrow R \models\!\models (P \Rightarrow R) \wedge (Q \Rightarrow R),$$
$$(P \wedge Q) \vee (\neg P \wedge R) \models\!\models (P \Rightarrow Q) \wedge (\neg P \Rightarrow R).$$

2.2 Predicate Calculus

2.2.1 Introduction

My treatment of the predicate calculus is different from my treatment of the propositional calculus. In this section I describe the use of the predicate calculus informally. It would have been possible for me to explain the model-theory of the predicate calculus, but this is more complicated than that of the propositional calculus, so I decided not to include it. The interested reader is referred to (Hunter 1971), part 3, and (Gallier 1986), section 5.3, for an account of this.

2.2.2 Types

One of the distinctive features of Z is that it is a typed language. Whenever a variable is introduced for the first time in a specification document its type must be given. A *type* is just a collection of objects. To be precise, a type—according to Spivey (1992), p. 24—is a special sort of expression, that is to say, something linguistic. It is common, however, also to call the set that a type stands for a *type*—even though a more accurate name for this set is the *carrier* of that type. This slightly inaccurate way of talking is followed in this book.

Because the basic type of all integers—represented as $\mathbf{Z}$—is used so frequently in specifications, it does not have to be introduced in any special way. (In order to ensure no confusion, the type $\mathbf{Z}$ consists of all the negative whole numbers, zero and all the positive whole numbers.) Every other basic type, however, that is used in a specification document has to be introduced by means of a *basic type definition*. In this chapter I use—for illustrative purposes—the type *Europe*, which is the collection of all European states. The basic type definition which introduces this into a specification document looks like this:

$$[\mathit{Europe}]$$

That is to say, the *basic type* (or *given set* as it is sometimes known) that is being introduced is enclosed in square brackets and placed on a line by itself. If more than one given set is being introduced, then the names of the basic types involved are separated by commas.

2.2.3 Declarations

To indicate an object's type, say that x is an integer, we write $x \colon \mathbf{Z}$. This can be read as either 'x is an integer' or 'The type of x is $\mathbf{Z}$'. To say that France is a European state we write *france*$\colon$ *Europe*. Such type assigning phrases are known as *basic declarations*. It is also possible to introduce several variables simultaneously in a basic declaration. For example, in the basic declaration

$$i, j, k \colon \mathbf{Z}$$

three variables are introduced, namely i, j and k, and each of them is declared to be an integer. Several basic declarations can be combined together to form a *declaration*. The distinct basic declarations need to be separated by means of semicolons. For example, in the declaration

$$\mathit{germany}, \mathit{italy}, \mathit{poland} \colon \mathit{Europe}; p, q, r, s \colon \mathbf{Z}$$

seven variables are declared: three variables of type *Europe*, namely *germany*, *italy* and *poland*, and four variables of type $\mathbf{Z}$, namely p, q, r and s.

2.2.4 Quantifiers

Restricted Quantifiers

Using the truth-functional connectives introduced earlier in this chapter we can write things like:

$$(1 < 11) \wedge (2 < 11) \wedge (4 < 11) \wedge (7 < 11) \wedge (8 < 11). \tag{2.7}$$

But this is very cumbersome. The predicate $\_ < 11$ appears five times. (Note the use of the underscore to indicate the 'gap' in the predicate.) This violates our desire for abstraction. We should avoid 'requiring something to be stated more than once'. We should 'factor out the recurring pattern'.[11] Luckily in Z there is a more concise way of expressing (2.7). We can use the *restricted universal quantifier* as follows:

$$\forall x \colon \mathbf{Z} \mid x \in \{1, 2, 4, 7, 8\} \bullet x < 11.$$

This can be read as 'Every integer which is in the set $\{1, 2, 4, 7, 8\}$ is (such that it is) less than 11'. The letter x here is a variable. Because Z is a typed language, whenever we introduce a variable we have to give its type. So, following the symbol $\forall$—known as the *universal quantifier*—there occurs a declaration. The occurrence of x in the declaration is called its *binding* occurrence. The remaining occurrences of x in this formula are *bound* occurrences. They are *bound by* the binding occurrence. If a variable other than x occurred in either of the formulas $x \in \{1, 2, 4, 7, 8\}$ or $x < 11$, then they would be said to be *free*.[12]

The sentence 'Every European state which has a common border with Albania also has a common border with Bulgaria' can be translated into the following Z formula:

$$\forall x \colon Europe \mid x \ borders \ albania \bullet x \ borders \ bulgaria,$$

where $\_ borders \_$ means $\_$ has a common border with $\_$. (My knowledge of geography is so poor that I do not know if this is true or false.)

The restricted universal quantifier applies to *all* things belonging to some set which have a particular property. There is another quantifier which only applies to *some* things. This is the *restricted existential quantifier*, which applies to *some* things which have a particular property. If we wanted to say in Z that some integer between 0 and 5, inclusive, is equal to its own square, then—without the restricted existential quantifier—we would have to write:

$$(0 = 0 * 0) \vee (1 = 1 * 1) \vee (2 = 2 * 2) \vee (3 = 3 * 3) \vee (4 = 4 * 4) \vee (5 = 5 * 5).$$

This is cumbersome and the same pattern of expression is used six times. A better way of writing it is:

$$\exists x \colon \mathbf{Z} \mid 0 \leq x \leq 5 \bullet x = x * x,$$

---

[11] The quotations here are part of what—in the area of programming language design—MacLennan (1987), p. 53 and elsewhere, calls *the abstraction principle* and which he formulates as, 'Avoid requiring something to be stated more than once; factor out the recurring pattern.'

[12] This terminology is defined more rigorously in section 10.2.2 below. Some authors do not distinguish between the *binding* and the *bound* occurrence of a variable. They call both sorts of occurrence *bound* ones.

and this is read as 'There exists some integer (which is) greater than or equal to 0 and less than or equal to 5 such that it is equal to its own square'.

The sentence 'Some European state which has a common border with Albania is a member of the EC' can be translated into Z as:

$$\exists x\colon Europe \mid x \ borders \ albania \bullet ec \ x,$$

where $ec \_$ means $\_$ is a member of the European Community.

Unrestricted Quantifiers

In Z we often want to say things about *all* integers without restriction or about *all* things belonging to some other set. For this purpose we use unrestricted quantifiers. For example, the sentence 'Every integer is equal to itself' gets translated into:

$$\forall x\colon \mathbf{Z} \bullet x = x.$$

This formula makes use of the *unrestricted universal quantifier* and to translate the sentence 'Some integer is equal to its own square' into Z you need to make use of the *unrestricted existential quantifier* as follows:

$$\exists x\colon \mathbf{Z} \bullet x = x * x.$$

The Z translation of 'Every European state is a member of NATO' is:

$$\forall x\colon Europe \bullet nato \ x,$$

where $nato \_$ means $\_$ is a member of NATO. The translation of 'Some European state has a common border with Iceland' into Z is:

$$\exists x\colon Europe \bullet x \ borders \ iceland.$$

Note that in Z we can write things like $\forall x\colon U \bullet P$ and $\exists x\colon U \bullet P$ even when U is not a type. Let U and V be members of the same type such that $U \subset V$. Then $\forall x\colon U \bullet P$ is equivalent to $\forall x\colon V \bullet x \in U \Rightarrow P$ and $\exists x\colon U \bullet P$ is equivalent to $\exists x\colon V \bullet x \in U \land P$.

Connection between Restricted and Unrestricted Quantifiers

Let D be a declaration and P and Q formulas. Then we have the following two laws:

$$(\forall D \mid P \bullet Q) \Longleftrightarrow (\forall D \bullet P \Rightarrow Q),$$
$$(\exists D \mid P \bullet Q) \Longleftrightarrow (\exists D \bullet P \land Q).$$

Unique Quantifiers

The symbol $\exists_1$ represents the *unique quantifier* and the notation

$$\exists_1 x \colon X \mid P \bullet Q$$

is used to mean that there exists exactly one thing x belonging to the set X which satisfies the formula P such that it also satisfies Q. Let D be a declaration and P and Q formulas. Then we have the following law:

$$(\exists_1 D \mid P \bullet Q) \Longleftrightarrow (\exists_1 D \bullet P \wedge Q).$$

This relates the restricted and the unrestricted forms of a unique quantification. The unrestricted unique quantifier satisfies the following law:

$$(\exists_1 x \colon X \bullet P(x)) \Longleftrightarrow (\exists x \colon X \bullet (P(x) \wedge (\forall y \colon X \bullet P(y) \Rightarrow x = y))).$$

The notation $P(x)$ means that the variable x can occur free in the predicate P. If $P(x)$ and $P(y)$ both occur in the same context, then $P(y)$ is the same as $P(x)$, except that y has been substituted for all free occurrences of x in $P(x)$.

2.2.5 Term-forming Operators

Definite Descriptions

Definite descriptions in Z are constructed by means of the μ-operator. For example, the term

$$\mu x \colon \mathbf{Z} \mid x > 0 \wedge x^3 = 1 \bullet 2 * x$$

refers to the unique integer of the form $2 * x$, where x has the property that it is greater than zero and its cube is equal to one. In other words, the μ-term displayed above refers to the number two, as the only integer greater than zero whose cube is one is one.

    The general form of a μ-term in Z is $\mu D \mid P \bullet t$, where D is a declaration, P a formula and t a term. If P is absent, then its default is the constant formula *true*. That is to say, $\mu D \bullet t$ is the same as $\mu D \mid true \bullet t$. If only a single variable is declared in D and t is absent, then t is assumed to be the variable declared in D. Thus, $\mu x \colon X \mid P$ is the same as $\mu x \colon X \mid P \bullet x$. If more than one variable is declared in D and t is absent, then t is assumed to be the ordered n-tuple made up out of the n variables declared in D in the order in which they occur in D. Thus, $\mu x_1 \colon X_1; x_2 \colon X_2; \ldots; x_n \colon X_n \mid P$ is the same as $\mu x_1 \colon X_1; x_2 \colon X_2; \ldots; x_n \colon X_n \mid P \bullet (x_1, x_2, \ldots, x_n)$.

Conditional Terms

The construction

$$\textbf{if } P \textbf{ then } t \textbf{ else } u$$

is used in Z to form *conditional terms*. In any situation in which P is satisfied the value of the displayed term is t and its value is u in any situation in which P is not satisfied. For example, let x, y and z all be integer-valued variables. Then the value of the variable z in the formula

$$z = \text{if } x > y \text{ then } x - y \text{ else } y - x$$

is the same as that of $x - y$ if $x > y$ and it is the same as that of $y - x$ if $x \leq y$. Note that Z does not contain a construct for forming conditional *formulas*.

Local Definitions

The term

$$(\text{let } x == i + j + k \bullet x(x - i)(x - j)(x - k))^3$$

is syntactically equivalent to the following one:

$$(x(x - i)(x - j)(x - k) \; [i + j + k/x])^3,$$

where $t[u/x]$ represents the term that results when the term u is substituted for all free occurrences of x in the term t. This, in turn, is equivalent to

$$((i + j + k)(j + k)(i + k)(i + j))^3$$

after performing the substitution and carrying out some simple algebraic manipulation. More generally, the term

$$(\text{let } x_1 == t_1; x_2 == t_2; \ldots; x_n == t_n \bullet u)$$

is equivalent to $u[t_1/x_1, t_2/x_2, \ldots, t_n/x_n]$, which represents the simultaneous substitution of t_i for x_i in u (for $1 \leq i \leq n$). Note that the parentheses are part of the syntax of the **let**-construction in Z and that none of the x_i can occur in any of the t_j, where i and j lie between 1 and n.

Z also contains another version of the **let**-construction. In this the *formula*

$$(\text{let } x_1 == t_1; x_2 == t_2; \ldots; x_n == t_n \bullet P),$$

where P is a formula, is equivalent to $P[t_1/x_1, t_2/x_2, \ldots, t_n/x_n]$, which represents the simultaneous substitution of t_i for x_i in P (for $1 \leq i \leq n$). Note that the parentheses are part of the syntax of the **let**-construction in Z and that none of the x_i can occur in any of the t_j, where i and j lie between 1 and n.

2.3   Exercises

2.1) Which of the following formulas are tautologies and which are not?

  a) $P \wedge P$.

  b) $P \wedge \neg Q$.

  c) $(P \Rightarrow Q) \Rightarrow P$.

d) $P \Rightarrow (Q \Rightarrow P)$.

e) $P \Rightarrow (Q \Rightarrow (P \Rightarrow P))$.

f) $(P \wedge Q) \Rightarrow P$.

g) $P \Rightarrow (P \wedge Q)$.

h) $((P \wedge Q) \Rightarrow R) \Longleftrightarrow ((P \Rightarrow R) \vee (Q \Rightarrow R))$.

2.2) Which of the following sequents are valid and which are not?

a) $\neg P \Rightarrow P \vdash P$.

b) $P \vdash Q \Rightarrow (P \wedge Q)$.

c) $P \Rightarrow Q, P \Rightarrow \neg Q \vdash \neg P$.

d) $(P \wedge Q) \Longleftrightarrow P \vdash P \Rightarrow Q$.

e) $Q \Rightarrow R \vdash (P \vee Q) \Rightarrow (P \vee R)$.

f) $P_1 \Rightarrow P_2, P_3 \Rightarrow P_4 \vdash (P_1 \vee P_3) \Rightarrow (P_2 \vee P_4)$.

2.3) Define the truth-functional connectives $\vee$, $\Rightarrow$ and $\Longleftrightarrow$ in terms of $\neg$ and $\wedge$.

2.4) The connective $\downarrow$ has the following basic truth-table:

P	Q	$P \downarrow Q$
t	t	f
t	f	f
f	t	f
f	f	t

A formula $P \downarrow Q$ is true iff both P and Q are false. The connective $\downarrow$ is sometimes known as the sign for *joint denial* and a formula $P \downarrow Q$ can be read as 'neither P nor Q'. Define the connectives $\neg$, $\vee$, $\wedge$, $\Rightarrow$ and $\Longleftrightarrow$ in terms of $\downarrow$.

2.5) Express the following formulas using restricted quantifiers:

a) $(2 + 3 = 4) \wedge (2 + 3 = 5) \wedge (2 + 3 = 7) \wedge (2 + 3 = 19)$.

b) $(2 + 3 = 4) \vee (2 + 3 = 5) \vee (2 + 3 = 7) \vee (2 + 3 = 19)$.

2.6) Translate the following English sentences into Z:

a) Every integer strictly less than 3 is not equal to 7.

b) Some integer strictly less than 3 is not equal to 7.

c) Every even integer less than 9 is not odd.

d) Some European state which is a member of the EC has a common border with Belgium.

e) Every European state which is a member of the EC is not a member of NATO.

3

Set Theory

3.1 Ways of Making Sets

A set or class is a collection of objects which satisfy some property. There are two main ways of making sets in Z and they are by *enumeration* and by *comprehension*.

3.1.1 Enumeration

Some sets can be specified by writing down all their elements. This is specifying a set *extensionally* or by *enumeration*. This method of making sets is only feasible for small finite sets. The elements of the set are simply listed or enumerated. Thus, the set of the first seven prime numbers can be enumerated as follows:

$$\{2, 3, 5, 7, 11, 13, 17\}.$$

Another notation is also sometimes used for the introduction of sets by enumeration, especially sets of messages in a specification, and that is the following:

$$Report ::= \text{'Okay'}$$
$$| \text{ 'At top of document'}$$
$$| \text{ 'At bottom of document'}.$$

This is just a restricted use of Z's notation for introducing *free types*. The definition of *Report* just given is equivalent to[1]

$$Report == \{\text{'Okay', 'At top of document', 'At bottom of document'}\}.$$

The sign $==$ used here is the Z notation for an abbreviations definition. When this sign is used what appears on its left-hand side is being defined to mean the same as what appears on its right-hand side.

The notation $\_ .. \_$ is used for number ranges. Thus,

$$89 .. 94 = \{89, 90, 91, 92, 93, 94\}.$$

---

[1]This equivalence follows from the way in which free types are treated in Z. It is fully justified in section 9.4 below. The whole of chapter 9 is devoted to the topic of free types and their use in specifications.

3.1.2 Set Comprehension

Set comprehension allows us to make a set from other sets. For example, the set comprehension term $\{\, n\colon \mathbf{Z} \mid n \geq 0 \bullet n \,\}$ represents the set of all the non-negative whole numbers. This is used so often that it is given a standard one-letter name in Z by means of the abbreviation definition:

$$\mathbf{N} == \{\, n\colon \mathbf{Z} \mid n \geq 0 \bullet n \,\}.$$

As another example, the set comprehension

$$\{\, n\colon \mathbf{N} \mid n \neq 0 \wedge n \bmod 2 = 0 \bullet n \,\},$$

where mod is Z's remainder operator, defines the set of all positive even numbers.[2] Note that both these set comprehensions have three main parts to them and these are separated by a vertical line | and a bullet •. In both cases, the part to the left of the vertical line is a declaration, the part between the vertical line and the bullet is a formula and the part to the right of the bullet is a term. In the case of the second example this is shown in this way:

$$\{\ \overbrace{n\colon \mathbf{N}}^{\text{declaration}}\ \mid\ \overbrace{n \neq 0 \wedge n \bmod 2 = 0}^{\text{formula}}\ \bullet\ \overbrace{n}^{\text{term}}\ \}.$$

If the term in a set comprehension is identical to the only variable introduced in the declaration, then it can be omitted.[3] In other words, if the term of a set comprehension is absent, the default value is the symbol that occurs in the declaration (on the left-hand side of the colon) assuming that this contains only a single declaration. Thus, we could define the set of even numbers like this:

$$evens == \{\, n\colon \mathbf{N} \mid n \neq 0 \wedge n \bmod 2 = 0 \,\}.$$

In a set comprehension there is no need for the term to be a simple variable; it can be a complex expression. Thus, another way in which to specify the set of positive even numbers is:

$$\{\, n\colon \mathbf{N} \mid n \neq 0 \bullet 2 * n \,\}.$$

As another example, consider the following definition of the set of all the squares of the non-negative numbers:

$$squares == \{\, n\colon \mathbf{N} \mid true \bullet n * n \,\}.$$

---

[2] Note that 0 is not thought of as an even number. This is just a convention. If you place your money on *evens* in roulette in a British casino and 0 comes up, then you lose half your bet. (The casino still has a 1.35% edge.) Clearly, casino owners are in two minds about whether 0 is even or not!

[3] If the declaration D in a set comprehension $\{\, D \mid P \,\}$ introduces more than one variable, then the absent term is assumed to be the n-tuple made up out of the variables declared in D in the same order. Thus, $\{\, x_1\colon X_1; x_2\colon X_2; \ldots; x_n\colon X_n \mid P \,\}$ is equivalent by definition to the term $\{\, x_1\colon X_1; x_2\colon X_2; \ldots; x_n\colon X_n \mid P \bullet (x_1, x_2, \ldots, x_n) \,\}$.

Note that the formula in this set comprehension is the always true formula. When this happens it is possible to abbreviate the set comprehension by leaving *true* out, like this:

$$squares == \{\, n: \mathbf{N} \bullet n * n \,\}.$$

It is possible for both these abbreviatory conventions to be used in a single set comprehension. Thus, the set comprehension $\{\, n: \mathbf{N} \,\}$ is short for $\{\, n: \mathbf{N} \mid true \bullet n \,\}$ and that is just a roundabout way of writing the set of natural numbers $\mathbf{N}$.

In a set comprehension $\{\, x: U \mid P \bullet t \,\}$ the set U does not have to be a type. Let U and V be subsets of the same type X such that $U \subset V$. Then, $\{\, x: U \mid P \bullet t \,\}$ is equivalent to $\{\, x: V \mid x \in U \wedge P \bullet t \,\}$.

3.2 Relations between Sets (and their Members)

3.2.1 Membership and Equality

The relations of set membership and equality are represented in Z by means of the symbols $\in$ and $=$, respectively. To show that an object x is a member of a set X we write $x \in X$, thus:

$$3 \in \{1, 3, 5, 7, 9\},$$

$$4 \in evens,$$

$$4 \in \{\, n: \mathbf{N} \mid n < 10 \,\}.$$

The formula $x \in X$ is true if x is a member of the set X and the formula $x = y$ is true if x and y are the same object. If a set has been introduced by enumeration, then we can establish the truth of a set membership formula by simply going through all the enumerated objects and checking whether or not they are identical to the term which occurs on the left-hand side of the relation $\in$. For example,

$$3 \in \{1, 3, 5, 7, 9\} \Longleftrightarrow (3 = 1 \vee 3 = 3 \vee 3 = 5 \vee 3 = 7 \vee 3 = 9).$$

When a set has been introduced by comprehension, we need the following law in order to check the truth of formulas involving that set comprehension:

$$x \in \{\, D \mid P \bullet t \,\} \Longleftrightarrow \exists D \mid P \bullet t = x,$$

where D is a declaration, P a formula, t a term and x a variable that is not declared in D. For example,

$$i \in \{\, n: \mathbf{N} \mid n \neq 0 \bullet 2 * n \,\} \Longleftrightarrow \exists n: \mathbf{N} \mid n \neq 0 \bullet 2 * n = i.$$

3.2.2 Subset

Let U and V be sets of the same type $\mathbf{P}\, X$. Then U is a *subset* of V iff every member of U is also a member of V. This is written $U \subseteq V$ and the following law is often useful in manipulating the subset relation:

$$U \subseteq V \Longleftrightarrow (\forall x: X \bullet x \in U \Rightarrow x \in V).$$

The following are some examples of true formulas involving the subset relation:

$$\{1,2,3\} \subseteq \{1,2,3\},$$
$$\{1,2,3\} \subseteq \mathbf{N},$$
$$\{1,2,3\} \subseteq \{\, n \colon \mathbf{N} \mid n < 10 \,\}.$$

The subset relation $\subseteq$ is reflexive, antisymmetric and transitive:[4]

$$U \subseteq U,$$
$$U \subseteq V \wedge V \subseteq U \Rightarrow U = V,$$
$$U \subseteq V \wedge V \subseteq W \Rightarrow U \subseteq W,$$

for all sets U, V and W which are of the same type. In other words, the subset relation $\subseteq$ on sets is a partial order.

Let U and V be sets of the same type $\mathbf{P}\,X$. Then U is a *proper subset* of V iff U is not the same as V and U is a subset of V. This is written as $U \subset V$ and is represented symbolically as:

$$U \subset V \Longleftrightarrow (U \neq V \wedge U \subseteq V).$$

The proper subset relation $\subset$ is irreflexive, asymmetric and transitive:

$$\neg(U \subset U),$$
$$U \subset V \Rightarrow \neg(V \subset U),$$
$$U \subset V \wedge V \subset W \Rightarrow U \subset W,$$

for all sets U, V and W of the same type.

3.3   Some Special Sets

3.3.1   Empty Sets

Intuitively you might think that there is a unique empty set, since any set which contains no members is the same as any other set which contains no members. Unfortunately, this is false in a typed set theory like Z. Here there are an infinite number of empty sets, one for each type. The definition of the empty set in Z is, therefore, generic:[5]

$$\varnothing[X] == \{\, x \colon X \mid false \,\}.$$

The empty set $\varnothing[X]$ can also be written $\{\ \}[X]$. Usually the type of an empty set is omitted, since the context makes it clear which one is being used.

---

[4] The meanings of terms like *reflexive*, *antisymmetric* and *transitive* are all explained in the glossary contained in appendix C.

[5] More information about generic definitions is contained in section 20.2.

3.3.2   Power Sets

If X is a set, then so is $\mathbf{P}\,X$, which is known as the *power set* of X. A useful property of power sets is that

$$U \in \mathbf{P}\,X \Longleftrightarrow U \subseteq X.$$

That is to say, something is a member of $\mathbf{P}\,X$ iff it is a subset of X. In other words, $\mathbf{P}\,X$ is the collection of all the subsets of X. For example,

$$\mathbf{P}(\{1,2\}) = \{\varnothing, \{1\}, \{2\}, \{1,2\}\}.$$

The set of non-empty subsets of an arbitrary set X is represented as $\mathbf{P}_1\,X$ and is defined as:

$$\mathbf{P}_1\,X == \{\, U : \mathbf{P}\,X \mid U \neq \varnothing[X]\,\}.$$

For example,

$$\mathbf{P}_1(\{1,2\}) = \{\{1\}, \{2\}, \{1,2\}\}.$$

3.4   Operations on Sets

3.4.1   Union

The union of two sets U and V of the same type is just the set obtained by pooling all their members. This is written as $U \cup V$. For example, if *available* represents the set of all the copies of books in a library that are available for borrowing and *checkedout* represents the set of all copies of books currently borrowed, then *available* $\cup$ *checkedout* represents the set of all copies of books owned by the library that can be borrowed, that is to say, that are not reference copies which cannot legitimately be removed from the library. The following law is sometimes useful in manipulating expressions whose main operator is $\cup$:

$$x \in U \cup V \Longleftrightarrow (x \in U \lor x \in V).$$

Set union is idempotent, commutative and associative and the empty set is a two-sided unit for it:

$$U \cup U = U,$$
$$U \cup V = V \cup U,$$
$$(U \cup V) \cup W = U \cup (V \cup W),$$
$$U \cup \varnothing = U,$$
$$\varnothing \cup U = U.$$

3.4.2   Intersection

If U and V are sets of the same type, then the intersection of U and V is the set which consists of everything that is both in U and in V. This is represented as $U \cap V$. For example, to show that no copy of a book in a library is both available for check-out and checked out at the same time we write:

$$available \cap checkedout = \varnothing,$$

where $\varnothing$ represents the empty set which consists of no copies of books. The following law is sometimes useful in manipulating expressions whose main operator is $\cap$:

$$x \in U \cap V \Longleftrightarrow (x \in U \wedge x \in V).$$

Set intersection is idempotent, commutative and associative. If the intersection operator is used with sets all of which belong to the same type $\mathbf{P}\,X$, then the type X is a two-sided unit for this intersection operator. These properties are expressed in symbols in this way:

$$U \cap U = U,$$
$$U \cap V = V \cap U,$$
$$(U \cap V) \cap W = U \cap (V \cap W),$$
$$U \cap X = U,$$
$$X \cap U = U,$$

where U, V and W are all subsets of the type X.

3.4.3   Difference

The notation $U \setminus V$ denotes the set consisting of all those elements of U which are not in V. In other words, you take out of U everything that is in V. For example, in the abbreviation definition

$$\mathbf{N}_1 == \mathbf{N} \setminus \{0\},$$

the symbol $\mathbf{N}_1$ is being defined to be the set of non-negative numbers *excluding* 0. So, $\mathbf{N}_1$ consists of all the positive whole numbers. Note that the combination of symbols $\mathbf{N}_1$ is part of standard Z. Set difference is also used in the following abbreviation definition:

$$odds == \mathbf{N}_1 \setminus evens.$$

The set *evens* was defined earlier to be the set of all positive even numbers. In this abbreviation definition *odds* is being defined to be the set of all positive odd numbers.

The following law is sometimes useful in manipulating expressions whose main operator is $\setminus$:

$$x \in U \setminus V \Longleftrightarrow (x \in U \wedge x \notin V).$$

Set difference is neither idempotent, nor commutative nor associative. The empty set is a right unit for set difference, but it does not have a left unit:

$$U \setminus \varnothing = U.$$

3.4.4   Symmetric Difference

The notation $U \bigtriangleup V$ represents the symmetric difference of the sets U and V, which must belong to the same type:

$$U \bigtriangleup V == (U \setminus V) \cup (V \setminus U).$$

The following law is sometimes useful in manipulating expressions whose main operator is $\triangle$:

$$x \in U \triangle V \iff (x \in U \cup V \land x \notin U \cap V).$$

Symmetric difference is not idempotent, but it is commutative and associative and the empty set is a two-sided unit for it:

$$U \triangle V = V \triangle U,$$
$$(U \triangle V) \triangle W = U \triangle (V \triangle W),$$
$$U \triangle \varnothing = U,$$
$$\varnothing \triangle U = U,$$

where U, V and W are all sets of the same type.

It should be noted that the symmetric difference operator is not part of standard Z as defined by Spivey (1992), but it can be introduced by means of the abbreviation definition just given when it is required. The symbol $\triangle$ is the only symbol discussed in this chapter which is not part of standard Z.

3.4.5 Useful Laws

In this section a number of useful laws relating the various set-theoretic operators are collected together. In all the following laws it is assumed that U, V and W all belong to the same type $\mathbf{P}\,X$.

$$U \cup X = X,$$
$$U \cap \varnothing = \varnothing,$$
$$X \setminus X = \varnothing,$$
$$X \setminus \varnothing = X,$$
$$X \setminus (X \setminus U) = U.$$

Set union distributes both forwards and backwards through set intersection and set intersection distributes both forwards and backwards through set union:

$$U \cup (V \cap W) = (U \cup V) \cap (U \cup W),$$
$$(U \cap V) \cup W = (U \cup W) \cap (V \cup W),$$
$$U \cap (V \cup W) = (U \cap V) \cup (U \cap W),$$
$$(U \cup V) \cap W = (U \cap W) \cup (V \cap W).$$

The remaining laws relate set difference to union and intersection:

$$X \setminus (U \cap V) = (X \setminus U) \cup (X \setminus V),$$
$$X \setminus (U \cup V) = (X \setminus U) \cap (X \setminus V),$$
$$U \cup (V \setminus W) = (U \cup V) \setminus (W \setminus U),$$
$$U \cap (V \setminus W) = (U \cap V) \setminus W$$
$$(U \cup V) \setminus W = (U \setminus W) \cup (V \setminus W),$$
$$U \setminus (V \cap W) = (U \setminus V) \cup (U \setminus W).$$

3.4.6   Generalized Union and Intersection

Let xss be a set of objects which are themselves sets. Then, the generalized union of xss, which is represented in Z as $\bigcup xss$, is the set which consists of all those things which are members of at least one of the sets that is an element of xss. For example,

$$\bigcup\{\{0,1,2\},\{5,7,9\},\{1,2,3,5,7,9\},\{767,789\}\} =$$
$$\{0,1,2,3,5,7,9,767,789\}.$$

The following law is sometimes useful in manipulating generalized unions:

$$x \in \bigcup xss \iff (\exists xs\colon xss \bullet x \in xs),$$

where $x\colon X$, $xs\colon \mathbf{P}\,X$ and $xss\colon \mathbf{P}(\mathbf{P}\,X)$, for some type X.

Let xss be a set of objects which are themselves sets. Then, the generalized intersection of xss, which is represented as $\bigcap xss$, is the set which consists of all those things which belong to every set which is a member of xss. For example,

$$\bigcap\{\{0,1,2\},\{5,7,9\},\{1,2,3,5,7,9\},\{767,789\}\} = \varnothing,$$
$$\bigcap\{\{0,1,2\},\{1,2,9\},\{1,2,3,5,7,9\},\{1,2,7\}\} = \{1,2\}.$$

The following law is sometimes useful in manipulating generalized intersections:

$$x \in \bigcap xss \iff (\forall xs\colon xss \bullet x \in xs),$$

where $x\colon X$, $xs\colon \mathbf{P}\,X$ and $xss\colon \mathbf{P}(\mathbf{P}\,X)$, for some type X.

3.5   Exercises

3.1) Let the sets zer, low, eve, bla, red, odd and hig (all of which are subsets of $0\mathinner{\ldotp\ldotp}36$) be defined like this:

$$zer == \{0\},$$
$$low == 1\mathinner{\ldotp\ldotp}18,$$
$$eve == \{\,n\colon \mathbf{N} \mid 1 \le n \wedge n \le 18 \bullet 2*n\,\},$$
$$bla == \{2,4,6,8,10,11,13,15,17,20,22,24,26,28,29,31,33,35\},$$
$$red == (1\mathinner{\ldotp\ldotp}36)\setminus bla,$$
$$odd == \{\,n\colon \mathbf{N} \mid 0 \le n \wedge n \le 17 \bullet 2*n+1\,\},$$
$$hig == 19\mathinner{\ldotp\ldotp}36.$$

European roulette players will have no difficulty recognizing these sets! Let U be a set of roulette numbers. Then the probability of a number from U coming up is $\#U/37$, where $\#U$ is the size or cardinality of the set U.

a) List the elements of $red \cap odd$.

b) List the elements of $(low \cup eve) \cap bla$.

c) List the elements of $(1..36) \setminus (red \cup eve)$.

d) List the elements of $bla \triangle odd$.

e) List the elements of $low \cap eve \cap bla$.

f) What is the probability of a member of low winning?

g) What is the probability of a member of $low \cup eve$ winning?

h) What is the probability of a member of $bla \cup red$ winning?

i) What is the probability of a member of $low \cap eve \cap bla$ winning?

j) What is the probability of a member of $bla \triangle odd$ winning?

3.2)   a) Let $U = \{2, 3, 5, 7, 11, 13, 17\}$ and $V = \{0, 1, 2, 3, 4, 5\}$. Write down $U \cup V$, $U \cap V$ and $U \setminus V$.

b) Write down the sets $10..15 \cup 12..18$, $10..15 \cap 12..18$ and $10..15 \setminus 12..18$.

c) Let $U = \{ x \colon N \mid x < 27 \}$. Write down the sets $U \cap \{ x \colon N \mid x \bmod 3 = 1 \}$ and $U \cap \{ x \colon N \mid x \operatorname{div} 7 = 2 \}$.

d) The countries *england*, *france* and *spain* are all European states, that is to say, *england, france, spain: Europe*. Write down all the members of the following power set $\mathbf{P}(\{england, france, spain\})$.

3.3)   a) Write down a set comprehension which defines all the leap years between 1900 and 2100, inclusive.

b) Write down two set comprehensions which define, respectively, the set of all European states which are members of the European Community and those which are members of the Warsaw Pact.

4

Internal Telephone Directory

4.1 Introduction

In this chapter I introduce the idea of a relation as a set of ordered pairs as well as various operations that can be performed on relations. In order to make this material easier to absorb I develop the ideas and notations associated with relations in conjunction with the specification of a telephone directory of the sort that is used internally inside a large organization such as a university.[1] The functionality of the system to be specified is as follows:

> A university wants to computerize its internal telephone directory. The database must keep a record of all the people who are currently members of the university (as only they can have telephone extensions). The database must cope with the possibility that one person may be reached at several extensions and also with the possibility that several people might have to share an extension. Six operations are to be provided, namely
>
> (1) that of adding an entry to the database, where an *entry* is an association between a person and a telephone extension,
>
> (2) that of interrogating the database by person (in which case the output is the set of telephone extensions at which that person can be reached),
>
> (3) that of interrogating the database by extension number (in which case the output is the set of people who can be reached at that extension),
>
> (4) that of removing an entry from the database,
>
> (5) that of adding a person to the database's record of who is currently a member of the university and
>
> (6) that of removing a person from the database along with all those entries in which he or she figures.

---

[1]This specification derives ultimately from one used by Spivey in various talks and which also appears in (Spivey 1988), pp. 2–7. I have altered it, however, better to serve my purposes.

The order of these operations may seem a bit strange, but it was chosen for pedagogic reasons. It allows various operations on relations to be introduced gradually.

In the next section I explain how the set of all relations between two sets is defined in Z and after that I start on the task of specifying the internal telephone number database. At the end of the chapter I say something about the way in which a Z specification should be presented.

4.2 Cartesian Products and Relations

If X and Y are sets, then so is $X \times Y$, their *Cartesian product* or *cross product*. The Cartesian product $X \times Y$ of two sets X and Y is the set of *all* the ordered pairs whose first elements are drawn from X and whose second elements are drawn from Y. An example of a cross product is:

$$\{1,3\} \times \{2,4\} = \{(1,2),(1,4),(3,2),(3,4)\}.$$

The usual way to express the fact that the ordered pair made up out of 3 and 2 is a member of this Cartesian product is like this:

$$(3,2) \in \{1,3\} \times \{2,4\},$$

but often it is clearer to write $3 \mapsto 2$ for $(3,2)$, so the above fact would be written as:

$$3 \mapsto 2 \in \{1,3\} \times \{2,4\}.$$

What is important about an ordered pair is that it is a structured object made up out of two components one of which comes first and the other second.

We are all familiar with relations in arithmetic like $n \geq m$ or n is divisible by m. Relations are used extensively in Z and—as is customary in mathematics—a relation is just thought of as a set of ordered pairs. A relation F between X and Y is a subset of the Cartesian product $X \times Y$, that is to say, $F \subseteq X \times Y$. The set of *all* relations between elements drawn from X and Y is written as $X \leftrightarrow Y$. This is, in fact, just another way of writing $\mathbf{P}(X \times Y)$. The standard way of defining the set of all relations between X and Y is:

$$X \leftrightarrow Y == \mathbf{P}(X \times Y).$$

To indicate that F is a relation between X and Y it needs to be declared as $F: X \leftrightarrow Y$. As already mentioned, the formula $x \mapsto y \in F$ states that the ordered pair $x \mapsto y$ is a member of the relation F. It is sometimes clearer to write this as $x \underline{F} y$, where the symbol for the relation is written as an infix operator. Note that when an ordinary identifier is used as an infix relation symbol it has to be underlined. Thus, it would be wrong to write $x F y$ if F had been declared to be of type $X \leftrightarrow Y$.

Z uses many different sorts of symbol. For example, the symbol $\geq$ is used for the relation of one number being greater than or equal to another number. When such a relation is declared underscores are used to indicate where its arguments are to go. Thus, $\_ \geq \_: \mathbf{Z} \leftrightarrow \mathbf{Z}$. It is possible to write $7 \mapsto 4 \in (\_ \geq \_)$ to express the fact that 7 is greater than or equal to 4, but it is much more common to write this as $7 \geq 4$.

4.3   The State Space

In order to specify the telephone directory we need to be able to refer to all the people who might end up in the database and also to all the possible phone numbers that the telephone exchange can handle. So, let *Person* be the type of all people and let *Phone* be the type of all possible internal telephone numbers. Since we are engaged in writing a *specification* there is no need at this stage to consider how we are going to eventually represent people and numbers in a program. To make decisions about such issues at this time is premature. The way in which the *basic types* or *given sets* *Person* and *Phone* are introduced into a Z specification document is by means of a *basic type definition* like this:

$$[Person, Phone]$$

The relation that exists between people and their internal telephone numbers I am going to denote by means of the identifier *telephones*, thus:

$$telephones: Person \leftrightarrow Phone.$$

This means that *telephones* $\subseteq$ *Person* $\times$ *Phone*. So, for example, in the case of the University of Birmingham, we have

$$(diller, 4794) \in telephones.$$

This can be written equivalently as

$$diller \mapsto 4794 \in telephones.$$

It is possible for one person to have more than one internal telephone. This happens, for example, if he or she is a very important person:

$$jarratt \mapsto 4936 \in telephones,$$
$$jarratt \mapsto 5317 \in telephones.$$

Similarly, if you are not very important, then you might have to share your internal telephone:

$$smith \mapsto 3174 \in telephones,$$
$$jones \mapsto 3174 \in telephones.$$

For the time being, let that be the entire state of the database:

$$telephones = \{jarratt \mapsto 4936,$$
$$jarratt \mapsto 5317,$$
$$diller \mapsto 4794,$$
$$smith \mapsto 3174,$$
$$jones \mapsto 3174\}.$$

This can be represented by means of a diagram as in Fig. 4.1. The relation *telephones* belongs to the set *Person* $\leftrightarrow$ *Phone*. The type *Person*, however, contains *every* possible person, the type *Phone* includes *every* conceivable internal telephone number and the set *Person* $\leftrightarrow$ *Phone* contains *all* the relations between *Person* and *Phone*. The small relation *telephones* is just one of these.

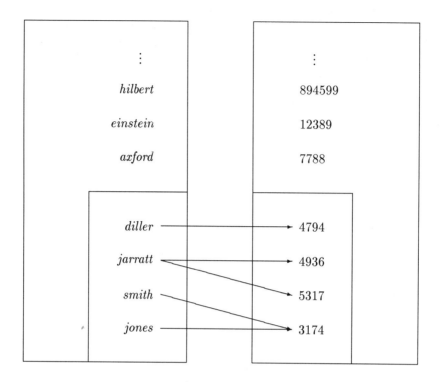

Figure 4.1: Graphical representation of *telephones*.

4.3.1   The Domain of a Relation

One thing that we might be interested in knowing is the set of people in the database who have telephone extensions. In our example, that would be the set consisting of *diller*, *jarratt*, *smith* and *jones*. The set consisting of just these four people is the *domain* of the relation *telephones* and it is written like this:

$$\text{dom } telephones = \{diller, jarratt, smith, jones\}.$$

In the diagram in Fig. 4.1 the domain of the relation *telephones* is represented by all the names that occur inside the inner rectangle on the left-hand side of the picture. A person x is a member of the set dom *telephones*, that is to say, the domain of the relation *telephones*, iff there exists a phone to which he or she stands in the relation *telephones*:

$$x \in \text{dom } telephones \iff \exists y\colon Phone \bullet x \mapsto y \in telephones.$$

The type of dom *telephones* is **P** *Person*. In our example, *einstein* is not in the set dom *telephones* because he does not have a phone associated with him in the database. Note that the way in which the term 'domain' is used in Z is different from the way in which it is conventionally used in mathematics. In ordinary mathematical discourse the relation $F: X \leftrightarrow Y$ would be said to have the domain X. This, however, is not Z speak. Some authors call X the *from-set* and Y the *to-set* and I will follow them in doing so.[2] In general, if $F: X \leftrightarrow Y$ is a relation and x is a member of X, then

$$x \in \operatorname{dom} F \iff \exists y: Y \bullet x \mapsto y \in F.$$

The following laws are sometimes useful in manipulating the domain operator:

$$\operatorname{dom} \varnothing = \varnothing,$$
$$\operatorname{dom}\{x \mapsto y\} = \{x\},$$
$$\operatorname{dom}\{x_1 \mapsto y_1, \ldots, x_n \mapsto y_n\} = \{x_1, \ldots, x_n\},$$
$$\operatorname{dom}(F \cup G) = (\operatorname{dom} F) \cup (\operatorname{dom} G),$$
$$\operatorname{dom}(F \cap G) \subseteq (\operatorname{dom} F) \cap (\operatorname{dom} G),$$

where $x, x_1, \ldots, x_n: X$, $y, y_1, \ldots, y_n: Y$ and $F, G: X \leftrightarrow Y$.

4.3.2 The Range of a Relation

The range of the relation *telephones* is the set of all the phones that are associated with a person. So,

$$4794 \in \operatorname{ran} \textit{telephones},$$
$$833335 \notin \operatorname{ran} \textit{telephones},$$
$$\operatorname{ran} \textit{telephones} = \{3174, 5317, 4936, 4794\}.$$

In the diagram in Fig. 4.1 the range of the relation *telephones* is represented by all the phone numbers that occur inside the inner rectangle on the right-hand side of the picture. A phone y is a member of the set ran *telephones*, that is to say, the range of the relation *telephones*, iff there exists a person to which it stands in the relation *telephones*:

$$y \in \operatorname{ran} \textit{telephones} \iff \exists x: \textit{Person} \bullet x \mapsto y \in \textit{telephones}.$$

The type of ran *telephones* is **P** *Phone*. In general, if $F: X \leftrightarrow Y$ is a relation and y is a member of Y, then

$$y \in \operatorname{ran} F \iff \exists x: X \bullet x \mapsto y \in F.$$

The following laws are sometimes useful in manipulating the range operator:

$$\operatorname{ran} \varnothing = \varnothing,$$
$$\operatorname{ran}\{x \mapsto y\} = \{y\},$$
$$\operatorname{ran}\{x_1 \mapsto y_1, \ldots, x_n \mapsto y_n\} = \{y_1, \ldots, y_n\},$$
$$\operatorname{ran}(F \cup G) = (\operatorname{ran} F) \cup (\operatorname{ran} G),$$
$$\operatorname{ran}(F \cap G) \subseteq (\operatorname{ran} F) \cap (\operatorname{ran} G),$$

where $x, x_1, \ldots, x_n: X$, $y, y_1, \ldots, y_n: Y$ and $F, G: X \leftrightarrow Y$.

---

[2]This terminology is used, for example, by McMorran and Powell (1993), p. 58, and Wordsworth (1992), p. 73. Woodcock and Loomes (1988), p. 99, call X the *source* and Y the *target* of the relation $F: X \leftrightarrow Y$.

4.3.3   The Union of Two Relations

A relation is just a particular kind of set. Every relation is a set, but not every set is a relation. So, we can use the usual set-theoretic operations on relations. Things like set union, for example. Say we want to add an association between a *Person* and a *Phone* to our database. The existing state of the database I have been calling *telephones* and the new state I will call *telephones'*. The prime indicates that it is the *after* state; the unprimed version is the *before* state. Suppose what we want to add is the fact that Axford can now be reached at extension 7788; that is to say, we want to add the ordered pair *axford* $\mapsto$ 7788 to our database. I am going to call such associations between people and phones *entries*. So, we have got:

$$telephones' = telephones \cup \{axford \mapsto 7788\}.$$

The new database now consists of the following entries:

$$\begin{aligned}
telephones' = \{&jarratt \mapsto 4936, \\
&jarratt \mapsto 5317, \\
&diller \mapsto 4794, \\
&smith \mapsto 3174, \\
&jones \mapsto 3174, \\
&axford \mapsto 7788\}.
\end{aligned}$$

This relation is pictured in the diagram Fig. 4.2.

4.3.4   Schemas

Z contains a two-dimensional graphical notation—called a *schema*—for grouping together all the relevant information that belongs to a state description. Schemas are used for several different purposes in Z, but one of their uses is to make precise what the *state space* of a given specification is. The state space is defined by means of a *state schema* and in the case of the telephone database the state schema is called *PhoneDB*. It is defined like this:

```
┌─ PhoneDB ──────────────────────────────────
│  members: P Person
│  telephones: Person ↔ Phone
├────────────────────────────────────────────
│  dom telephones ⊆ members
└────────────────────────────────────────────
```

In order to make the example a little bit more interesting I have included the set *members* in the state. This set consists of all the members of the university whose telephone directory we are modelling. The formula that appears in the predicate-part of the schema *PhoneDB* forms the *state invariant* of the specification. Only members of the university can have telephones.

In order to specify a state transformation we need to represent the before and after states. In Z the *after* state is represented by *decorating* all the variables with a prime.

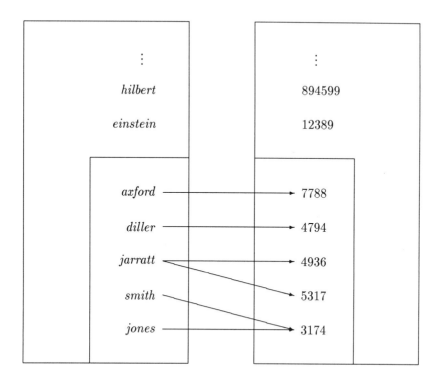

Figure 4.2: Graphical representation of *telephones'*.

PhoneDB is the name of a schema which represents a before state. Decorating a schema name with a prime, for example, *PhoneDB'*, represents the *after* state. *PhoneDB'* is the same as *PhoneDB*, except that every *variable* has been decorated with a prime. This is an example of *schema decoration*. The schema *PhoneDB'* is, therefore:

$$
\begin{array}{|l}
\hline
\quad PhoneDB' \\\hline
members' : \mathbf{P}\ Person \\
telephones' : Person \leftrightarrow Phone \\\hline
\operatorname{dom} telephones' \subseteq members' \\\hline
\end{array}
$$

Note that the type identifiers *Person* and *Phone* have not been decorated with a prime. It is only variables that are local to the schema that are decorated. The local variables are those that occur on the left-hand side of a colon in a declaration that appears in the declaration-part of the schema.

Note also that the definition of *PhoneDB'* just given is not a legal Z definition of a schema, because every defined schema name must be an undecorated identifier. It is only included here to show you what *PhoneDB'* looks like when written out in full. More is said about this restriction on schema names on p. 66 below.

4.4 Adding an Entry to the Database

4.4.1 The First Account

The operation of adding an entry to our database is represented by means of the following schema:

$$
\begin{array}{|l}
\hline
\_\,AddEntry \rule{6cm}{0.4pt} \\
\quad members, members': \mathbf{P}\, Person \\
\quad telephones, telephones': Person \leftrightarrow Phone \\
\quad name?: Person \\
\quad newnumber?: Phone \\
\hline
\quad \mathrm{dom}\ telephones \subseteq members \\
\quad \mathrm{dom}\ telephones' \subseteq members' \\
\quad name? \in members \\
\quad name? \mapsto newnumber? \notin telephones \\
\quad telephones' = telephones \cup \{name? \mapsto newnumber?\} \\
\quad members' = members \\
\hline
\end{array}
$$

Notice that question marks occur in some of the identifiers of this schema, namely *name?* and *newnumber?* This is how inputs are indicated in Z. The identifier *name?* represents the person who is getting a new telephone extension and *newnumber?* is the extension that he or she is getting. The formulas

$$name? \in members,$$

$$name? \mapsto newnumber? \notin telephones,$$

are the two *preconditions* of the operation *AddEntry*. You cannot add an entry involving somebody who is not a member of the university into the database and you cannot add an entry that is already in the database. The state invariant involving only before variables, namely the formula

$$\mathrm{dom}\ telephones \subseteq members,$$

is not normally thought of as a precondition for the operation specified by means of the schema *AddEntry*. In talking about the various formulas that occur in the predicate-part of a schema specifying an operation I use the terms '(before) state invariant' and 'precondition' as being mutually exclusive. That is to say, one and the same formula cannot be both a precondition and a state invariant in a single schema. One of the differences between the before state invariant and the preconditions of a schema is that the invariant is a 'precondition' of *every* operation defined on the state. It is best to think of the before state invariant as a 'precondition' to the entire specification, rather than as being specific to any one operation.

To return to the schema *AddEntry*, if the operation specified by this schema is carried out in any state in which the two preconditions are satisfied, then the formula

$$telephones' = telephones \cup \{name? \mapsto newnumber?\}$$

describes what happens. The relation *telephones'* is the same as *telephones* except that it also contains the entry *name?* $\mapsto$ *newnumber?* The formula *members'* = *members* is needed in order to capture the fact that the collection of people who are members of the university is not affected by this operation.

4.4.2 Schema Operations

I am going to take a short break from developing the telephone number database in order to deal with some schema operations and conventions which will greatly reduce the length of specifications. These will enable us to specify complex operations concisely and perspicuously. The schema operations and conventions that I am going to look at are:

(1) Linking schemas with propositional connectives.

(2) Schema inclusion.

(3) The Δ and Ξ conventions.

Linking Schemas with Propositional Connectives

Let S and T be two schemas. Then it is possible to combine S and T by means of the two-place truth-functional connectives to form $S \wedge T$, $S \vee T$, $S \Rightarrow T$ and $S \Longleftrightarrow T$. These all have very similar meanings, so I will consider $S \heartsuit T$, where $\heartsuit$ can be any of $\wedge$, $\vee$, $\Rightarrow$ or $\Longleftrightarrow$. The schema $S \heartsuit T$ is formed by merging the declarations of S and T and by combining the formulas in their predicate-parts by means of the connective $\heartsuit$. If either S or T has more than one formula in its predicate-part, then these have to be combined together into a single conjunctive formula. Let *Alpha* and *Beta* be the following two schemas:

```
┌─ Alpha ──────────────
│  x: Z
│  U, V: P Z
├──────────────────────
│  x ∈ V
│  U ⊆ V
└──────────────────────
```

```
┌─ Beta ──────────────
│  x, y: Z
│  U: P Z
├─────────────────────
│  x ≠ y
│  x + y ∈ U
└─────────────────────
```

Let *Gamma* $\hat{=}$ *Alpha* $\heartsuit$ *Beta*. The symbol $\hat{=}$ is used to define schemas. So, I am defining *Gamma* to be equivalent to the schema obtained by linking *Alpha* and *Beta* with the connective $\heartsuit$. When written out in full *Gamma* looks like this:

```
┌─ Gamma ──────────────────────────────────────────
│  x, y: Z
│  U, V: P Z
├───────────────────────────────────────────────────
│  (x ∈ V ∧ U ⊆ V) ♡ (x ≠ y ∧ x + y ∈ U)
└───────────────────────────────────────────────────
```

For example, if $\heartsuit$ is $\vee$, then the schema *Delta* $\overset{\wedge}{=}$ *Alpha* $\vee$ *Beta* has the following expansion:

```
┌─ Delta ─────────────────────────────────────────────
│ x, y: Z
│ U, V: P Z
├─────────────────────────────────────────────────────
│ (x ∈ V ∧ U ⊆ V) ∨ (x ≠ y ∧ x + y ∈ U)
```

In order for it to be possible to combine two schemas S and T by means of a two-place truth-functional connective any variable declared in both S and T must have the same type in both of them. It is possible, however, in Z to have a declaration $x : U$, where U is not a type. For example, in the declaration $y : 1 .. 57$ the type of y is **Z**, because **Z** is a type in Z but $1 .. 57$ is not. In every Z specification that makes use of more than one type all the types involved are postulated to be pairwise disjoint. The possibility of having a declaration $x : U$, where U is not a type, in a schema slightly complicates the way in which schemas are combined by means of the two-place truth-functional connectives. For example, let *Epsilon* and *Zeta* be the following two schemas:

```
┌─ Epsilon ─────────────────       ┌─ Zeta ─────────────────
│ y: 1 .. 57                       │ y: N
│ U: P Z                           │ U: P N
├───────────────────────           ├─────────────────────────
│ y ∈ U                            │ y > 23
```

Then, before we can combine *Epsilon* and *Zeta* by means of a truth-functional connective $\heartsuit$, we have to transform both of them so that the expression that follows the colon in the declaration involving y in *Epsilon* is the same as what follows the colon in the declaration involving y in *Zeta* and similarly for the variable U. Making changes to the declarations in *Epsilon* and *Zeta* also involves adding formulas to their predicate-parts. Seeing the transformed versions of these schemas will clarify this explanation.

```
┌─ TransEpsilon ─────────────       ┌─ TransZeta ─────────────
│ y: N                              │ y: N
│ U: P Z                            │ U: P Z
├───────────────────────           ├─────────────────────────
│ y ∈ 1 .. 57                       │ U ∈ P N
│ y ∈ U                             │ y > 23
```

It is now possible to combine *TransEpsilon* and *TransZeta* by means of a truth-functional connective, say $\Rightarrow$, to form a new schema, say, *Eta*:

```
┌─ Eta ─────────────────────────────────────────────
│ y: N
│ U: P Z
├───────────────────────────────────────────────────
│ (y ∈ 1 .. 57 ∧ y ∈ U) ⇒ (U ∈ P N ∧ y > 23)
```

More generally, let S and T be the schemas:

```
┌─ S ──────────────────────┐      ┌─ T ──────────────────────┐
│  x: U                    │      │  x: V                    │
│  D                       │      │  E                       │
│ ─────────────            │      │ ─────────────            │
│  P                       │      │  Q                       │
└──────────────────────────┘      └──────────────────────────┘
```

where U and V are both subsets of the same type X and $U \subset V$, D and E are declarations and P and Q are formulas. Then, before we can combine S and T by means of a truth-functional connective we have to transform S into *Theta*:

```
┌─ Theta ──────────────────────────────────────────────┐
│  x: V                                                 │
│  D                                                    │
│ ─────────────                                         │
│  x ∈ U                                                │
│  P                                                    │
└───────────────────────────────────────────────────────┘
```

If every variable y that is declared in both *Theta* and T has the property that X is the same as Y—when $y: X$ is a declaration in *Theta* and $y: Y$ is a declaration in T—then *Theta* and T can be combined by means of a truth-functional connective. If this is not the case, then further transformations need to be applied to either *Theta* or T before such combination becomes possible.

Note that in order to combine schemas by means of the truth-functional connectives it is not always necessary to *normalize* them. What normalizing a schema involves is replacing every set U, say, which occurs in a declaration $x: U$, with the type of which U is a subset and adding a formula to the predicate-part of the schema involved to constrain the variable appropriately.

Schema normalization, however, is mandatory when we want to form the negation of a schema. Thus, the negation of the schema *Epsilon* defined above is *not* the schema *Iota*; it is, rather, the schema *Kappa*:

```
┌─ Iota ──────────────────┐      ┌─ Kappa ──────────────────┐
│  y: 1..57               │      │  y: Z                     │
│  U: P Z                 │      │  U: P Z                   │
│ ─────────────           │      │ ─────────────             │
│  y ∉ U                  │      │  ¬(y ∈ 1..57 ∧ y ∈ U)    │
└──────────────────────────┘      └───────────────────────────┘
```

These are different. For example, if $U = \mathbf{N}$, then y can have the value of -17 in *Kappa* but not in *Iota*.

Schema Inclusion

A schema name S may be *included* in the declaration-part of another schema T. The effect of this is that the declarations of S are now considered part of T and the formulas in the predicate-parts of S and T are pooled together. The only restriction is that if a variable x is declared in both S and T, then it must have the same type in both of them. (Sometimes it may be necessary to transform the schemas involved—in a way analogous to that described when considering how schemas can be combined using truth-functional connectives—before including one schema in another one.) For example, consider the following two schemas:

```
┌─ Lambda ──────────────────        ┌─ Mu ──────────────────────
│  x, y: Z                          │  Lambda
│  U: P Z                           │  V: P Z
├──────────────                     ├──────────────
│  x < y                            │  x ∈ V
└──────────────────────────        └──────────────────────────
```

Here, the schema *Lambda* is included in the schema *Mu*. Expanding *Mu* we get:

```
┌─ Mu ──────────────────────────────────────────────────────
│  x, y: Z
│  U, V: P Z
├──────────────
│  x < y
│  x ∈ V
└──────────────────────────────────────────────────────────
```

The Δ and Ξ Conventions

Usually, $\Delta State$ is the schema obtained by combining the before and after versions of *State*. This can be defined using either schema inclusion as:

```
┌─ Δ State ──────────────────────────────────────────────────
│  State
│  State'
└──────────────────────────────────────────────────────────
```

or, alternatively, using schema conjunction, thus $\Delta State \mathrel{\widehat{=}} State \wedge State'$. In the case of the telephone number database $\Delta PhoneDB$ is:

```
┌─ Δ PhoneDB ────────────────────────────────────────────────
│  members, members': P Person
│  telephones, telephones': Person ↔ Phone
├──────────────
│  dom telephones ⊆ members
│  dom telephones' ⊆ members'
└──────────────────────────────────────────────────────────
```

This can be written more concisely as either:

$$\Delta PhoneDB \mathrel{\widehat{=}} PhoneDB \wedge PhoneDB'$$

or—using schema inclusion—in this way:

```
┌─ΔPhoneDB ──────────────────────────────────────
│ PhoneDB
│ PhoneDB'
│
└─────────────────────────────────────────────────
```

This is the usual way of understanding $\Delta State$, but it is not mandatory. In Z you are allowed to define $\Delta State$ to be whatever you want it to be, but if you do use it in a non-standard way make absolutely certain that any reader of your specification will be aware of what you are doing. Throughout this book I always use Δ schemas in the standard way explained here.

The schema $\Xi PhoneDB$ is used in the specification of operations that do not change the state of the database:

```
┌─ΞPhoneDB ──────────────────────────────────────
│ ΔPhoneDB
├─────────────────────────────────────────────────
│ members' = members
│ telephones' = telephones
└─────────────────────────────────────────────────
```

What I said above about the standard meaning of Δ schema also applies to Ξ schemas. They too can be redefined to suit your purposes.

4.4.3 A Concise Specification

Using the Δ convention it is now possible to concisely specify the operation of adding an entry to the database. It is as follows:

```
┌─AddEntry ──────────────────────────────────────
│ ΔPhoneDB
│ name?: Person
│ newnumber?: Phone
├─────────────────────────────────────────────────
│ name? ∈ members
│ name? ↦ newnumber? ∉ telephones
│ telephones' = telephones ∪ {name? ↦ newnumber?}
│ members' = members
└─────────────────────────────────────────────────
```

4.4.4 Dealing with Errors

I will now look at what happens when the preconditions of the schema *AddEntry* are not fulfilled. That is to say, the cases when either of the following is true:

$$name? \notin members, \tag{4.1}$$

$$name? \mapsto newnumber? \in telephones. \tag{4.2}$$

When either of these two formulas is true, we want to output a suitable error message. Dealing with errors again reveals the peculiar status enjoyed by the before state invariant, since we do not have to consider what happens when dom *telephones* $\not\subseteq$ *members*. This possibility can never arise.

When an error occurs we do not want the state of the database altered in any way, so the schema which deals with the situation in which (4.1) is true will include the schema $\Xi PhoneDB$. The schema in question is:

$$
\begin{array}{|l}
\hline
\_NotMember _____ \\
\Xi PhoneDB \\
name?: Person \\
rep!: Report \\
\hline
name? \notin members \\
rep! = \text{`Not a member'} \\
\hline
\end{array}
$$

The error situation in which (4.2) is true is dealt with by the following schema:

$$
\begin{array}{|l}
\hline
\_EntryAlreadyExists _____ \\
\Xi PhoneDB \\
name?: Person \\
newnumber?: Phone \\
rep!: Report \\
\hline
name? \mapsto newnumber? \in telephones \\
rep! = \text{`Entry already exists'} \\
\hline
\end{array}
$$

4.4.5   The Total Specification

The next schema I am going to introduce just outputs the message 'Okay' in order to inform the user that the transaction he or she requested to be carried out has in fact been successfully carried out.

$$
\begin{array}{|l}
\hline
\_Success _____ \\
rep!: Report \\
\hline
rep! = \text{`Okay'} \\
\hline
\end{array}
$$

It is now possible to define the total specification of the operation of adding an entry to the database.

$$
DoAddEntry \;\hat{=}\; AddEntry \wedge Success
$$
$$
\vee
$$
$$
NotMember
$$
$$
\vee
$$
$$
EntryAlreadyExists.
$$

In order to illustrate the utility of Z to concisely express quite complicated operations I will show what the schema *DoAddEntry* looks like when expanded.

```
┌─ DoAddEntry ─────────────────────────────────────────────────
│ members, members': P Person
│ telephones, telephones': Person ↔ Phone
│ name?: Person
│ newnumber?: Phone
│ rep!: Report
├──────────────────────────────────────────────────────────────
│ dom telephones ⊆ members
│ dom telephones' ⊆ members'
│ ((name? ∈ members ∧
│ name? ↦ newnumber? ∉ telephones ∧
│ telephones' = telephones ∪ {name? ↦ newnumber?} ∧
│ members' = members ∧
│ rep! = 'Okay')
│              ∨
│ (name? ∉ members ∧
│ members' = members ∧
│ telephones' = telephones ∧
│ rep! = 'Not a member')
│              ∨
│ (name? ↦ newnumber? ∈ telephones ∧
│ members' = members ∧
│ telephones' = telephones ∧
│ rep! = 'Entry already exists'))
└──────────────────────────────────────────────────────────────
```

I think that you will agree that the Δ and Ξ conventions and the linking of schemas using truth-functional connectives leads to concise and well-structured specifications.

4.5 Interrogating the Database by Person

4.5.1 The Image of a Relation

The next operation that I want to specify concerning the telephone database is that of finding out all the telephone numbers where a particular individual can be reached. In order to do this I need to introduce the idea of a *relational image*. Given, for example, the relation *telephones* as enumerated on p. 43 above and a set of elements of type *Person*, say {*jarratt*}, we want this operation to return all the telephones associated with *jarratt*, that is to say, all the extensions at which he can be reached. This is known as the *relational image* of a set through a relation and it is written:

$$telephones(\!|\{jarratt\}|\!) = \{4936, 5317\}.$$

The fundamental property of the relational image operator is that

$$y \in F(\!|U|\!) \iff (\exists x : X \bullet x \in U \wedge x \mapsto y \in F),$$

where $y\colon Y$, $F\colon X \leftrightarrow Y$ and $U\colon \mathbf{P}\,X$. Thus, $F(\!|U|\!)$ is the set of all those things in Y which can be reached from U. Using the convention that $\exists x\colon U \bullet P$ is short for $\exists x\colon X \bullet x \in U \wedge P$, if $U \subseteq X$, this can also be expressed in the following way:

$$y \in F(\!|U|\!) \iff (\exists x\colon U \bullet x \mapsto y \in F).$$

The following laws are sometimes useful in manipulating the relational image operator:

$$F(\!|U_1 \cup U_2|\!) = F(\!|U_1|\!) \cup F(\!|U_2|\!),$$
$$F(\!|U_1 \cap U_2|\!) \subseteq F(\!|U_1|\!) \cap F(\!|U_2|\!),$$

where $F\colon X \leftrightarrow Y$ and $U_1, U_2\colon \mathbf{P}\,X$.

I will now give some more examples of the use of the relational image of a set. The set of people known to our database is represented by dom *telephones*. Let us call this set *known*:

$$known == \mathrm{dom}\ telephones.$$

We might want to partition the set *known* into *staff* and *proles*:

$$staff \cup proles = known,$$
$$staff \cap proles = \varnothing.$$

Thus, in the small database that I am using for illustrative purposes we have:

$$staff = \{diller, jarratt\},$$
$$proles = \{smith, jones\}.$$

Given these definitions of *staff* and *proles* the set *telephones*$(\!|staff|\!)$ is the set of all staff telephone numbers, that is to say, the set of all extensions at which a staff member of the university can be reached and *telephones*$(\!|proles|\!)$ is the set of all prole telephone numbers, that is to say, the set of all extensions at which a non-staff member of the university can be reached. In our particular database we have:

$$telephones(\!|staff|\!) = \{4794, 4936, 5317\},$$
$$telephones(\!|proles|\!) = \{3174\}.$$

4.5.2 Specifying the Operation

The operation *FindPhones* has as its input a person—represented by the identifier *name*?—and as its output it has a set of telephone numbers—represented by the identifier *numbers*! Recall that outputs end conventionally with an exclamation mark. Interrogating the database does not alter it, so we have to include the formulas

$$members' = members,$$
$$telephones' = telephones,$$

in the required schema and this is best done by including the schema $\Xi PhoneDB$ in the declaration-part of *FindPhones*, which is defined as follows:

```
┌─ FindPhones ──────────────────────────────────────────────
│ ΞPhoneDB
│ name?: Person
│ numbers!: P Phone
├────────────────────────────────────────────────────────────
│ name? ∈ dom telephones
│ numbers! = telephones(|{name?}|)
└────────────────────────────────────────────────────────────
```

Now I deal with what happens when the formula *name?* ∈ dom *telephones* is not satisfied. In that case an error message is output.

```
┌─ UnknownName ─────────────────────────────────────────────
│ ΞPhoneDB
│ name?: Person
│ rep!: Report
├────────────────────────────────────────────────────────────
│ name? ∉ dom telephones
│ rep! = 'Unknown name'
└────────────────────────────────────────────────────────────
```

Thus the complete specification of the operation to interrogate the database by person is given by means of the schema *DoFindPhones*, which is defined like this:

$$DoFindPhones \;\hat{=}\; FindPhones \wedge Success$$
$$\vee$$
$$UnknownName.$$

It would be possible to give more detailed error messages by distinguishing between the case when we input a name of someone who is not a member of the university—that is to say, the case when the formula *name?* ∉ *members* is true—and the case when the input name is of a member of the university, but one who does not have an extension. This latter possibility would hold if the formula:

$$name? \in members \wedge name? \notin \text{dom } telephones$$

were true. This possibility, however, will not be pursued here.

4.6   Interrogating the Database by Number

I have just described an operation which outputs the set of telephone numbers at which a particular member of the university can be reached. Similarly, we can specify an operation which outputs all the names associated with a particular telephone number. In order to specify this operation I will have to make use of the inverse of the relation *telephones*.

4.6.1   Relational Inversion

Given any relation F you can form its inverse $F^\sim$. If F is a member of $X \leftrightarrow Y$, then $F^\sim$ is a member of $Y \leftrightarrow X$. $F^\sim$ is F with each element flipped over, so:

$$y \mapsto x \in F^\sim \iff x \mapsto y \in F.$$

An example will make this idea clearer. With *telephones* as shown in Fig. 4.1 on p. 44 above *telephones*$^\sim$ is the following:

$$\begin{aligned}
telephones^\sim = \{ &4936 \mapsto jarratt, \\
&5317 \mapsto jarratt, \\
&4794 \mapsto diller, \\
&3174 \mapsto smith, \\
&3174 \mapsto jones \}.
\end{aligned}$$

The following laws, where $F: X \leftrightarrow Y$, are sometimes useful in manipulating the relational inversion operator:

$$(F^\sim)^\sim = F,$$
$$\mathrm{dom}(F^\sim) = \mathrm{ran}\ F,$$
$$\mathrm{ran}(F^\sim) = \mathrm{dom}\ F.$$

4.6.2   Specifying the Operation

Using the inverse of the relation *telephones* it is now possible to specify what happens when we successfully interrogate the database in order to find out all the people who can be reached at a particular extension.

```
┌─ FindNames ─────────────────────────────────
│ ΞPhoneDB
│ names!: P Person
│ number?: Phone
├─────────────────────────────────────────────
│ number? ∈ ran telephones
│ names! = telephones~⦇{number?}⦈
└─────────────────────────────────────────────
```

In order to specify the total operation we have to state what happens when the precondition of the schema *FindNames* is not satisfied.

```
┌─ UnknownNumber ─────────────────────────────
│ ΞPhoneDB
│ number?: Phone
│ rep!: Report
├─────────────────────────────────────────────
│ number? ∉ ran telephones
│ rep! = 'Unknown number'
└─────────────────────────────────────────────
```

Now it is possible to specify the total operation of interrogating the database by number:

$$DoFindNames \;\hat{=}\; FindNames \wedge Success$$
$$\vee$$
$$UnknownNumber.$$

4.7   Removing an Entry from the Database

We need to be able to specify the operation of removing an entry from the database in order to capture what happens when somebody can no longer be reached at a particular extension. This operation is specified by the schema *RemoveEntry*:

```
┌─ RemoveEntry ──────────────────────────────
│ ΔPhoneDB
│ oldnumber?: Phone
│ name?: Person
├─────────────────────────────────────────────
│ name? ↦ oldnumber? ∈ telephones
│ telephones' = telephones \ {name? ↦ oldnumber?}
│ members' = members
└─────────────────────────────────────────────
```

RemoveEntry has only a single precondition, namely:

$$name? \mapsto oldnumber? \in telephones.$$

This states that you can only remove an entry from the database if that entry actually is present in the database. What happens in the case when this precondition is violated is captured by the following schema:

```
┌─ UnknownEntry ─────────────────────────────
│ ΞPhoneDB
│ oldnumber?: Phone
│ name?: Person
│ rep!: Report
├─────────────────────────────────────────────
│ name? ↦ oldnumber? ∉ telephones
│ rep! = 'Unknown entry'
└─────────────────────────────────────────────
```

The complete specification of the operation of removing an entry from the database is given by the schema *DoRemoveEntry*:

$$DoRemoveEntry \;\hat{=}\; RemoveEntry \wedge Success$$
$$\vee$$
$$UnknownEntry.$$

4.8   Someone Joining the University

The final things that I want to specify concerning the internal telephone number database are the operations of someone joining the university and someone leaving. First, someone joining. This is specified by means of the schema *AddMember*:

```
┌─ AddMember ──────────────────────────────────
│ ΔPhoneDB
│ name?: Person
├──────────────────────────────────────────────
│ name? ∉ members
│ members' = members ∪ {name?}
│ telephones' = telephones
└──────────────────────────────────────────────
```

The operation can only go wrong in one way, namely if *name?* ∈ *members*. What happens in this case is captured by means of the following schema:

```
┌─ AlreadyMember ─────────────────────────────
│ ΞPhoneDB
│ name?: Person
│ rep!: Report
├─────────────────────────────────────────────
│ name? ∈ members
│ rep! = 'Already a member'
└─────────────────────────────────────────────
```

Thus, the complete specification of the operation of adding a member is:

$$DoAddMember \;\hat{=}\; AddMember \land Success$$
$$\lor$$
$$AlreadyMember.$$

4.9   Someone Leaving the University

In order to specify the operation of someone leaving the university we first need to introduce another operation on relations, namely domain anti-restriction. This is closely connected to domain restriction, so I will discuss both of these operators next.

4.9.1   Domain Restriction

Consider the relation *ages*: *Person* $\leftrightarrow$ $\mathbb{N}$ which associates people with their ages. An example of *ages* is:

$$ages = \{arch \mapsto 23,$$
$$bell \mapsto 30,$$
$$cox \mapsto 27,$$
$$fry \mapsto 53,$$
$$hart \mapsto 21\}.$$

Say that we are only interested in the ages of males. We restrict the relation *ages* so that the first elements of all ordered pairs in the restricted relation have to be male. Let *male*: $\mathbf{P}$ *Person* and $\{arch, cox, fry\} \subseteq male$. Then we have:

$$male \triangleleft ages = \{arch \mapsto 23,$$
$$cox \mapsto 27,$$
$$fry \mapsto 53\}.$$

male $\triangleleft$ *ages* is a relation which is a subset of *ages*. The following law expresses the fundamental property of the domain restriction operator:

$$x \mapsto y \in U \triangleleft F \Longleftrightarrow (x \in U \land x \mapsto y \in F),$$

where $x: X$, $y: Y$, $U: \mathbf{P} X$ and $F: X \leftrightarrow Y$. The following laws are sometimes useful in manipulating the domain restriction operator:

$$U \triangleleft F \subseteq F,$$
$$\mathrm{dom}(U \triangleleft F) = U \cap (\mathrm{dom}\, F),$$
$$U_1 \triangleleft (U_2 \triangleleft F) = (U_1 \cap U_2) \triangleleft F,$$
$$(U_1 \cup U_2) \triangleleft F = (U_1 \triangleleft F) \cup (U_2 \triangleleft F),$$
$$U \triangleleft (F \cup G) = (U \triangleleft F) \cup (U \triangleleft G),$$

where $F, G: X \leftrightarrow Y$ and $U, U_1, U_2: \mathbf{P} X$.

4.9.2   Domain Anti-restriction

Domain anti-restriction is sometimes known as *domain subtraction* or *domain core-striction*. Say that we are interested in the ages of women. Let *female*: $\mathbf{P}$ *Person* and $\{bell, hart\} \subseteq female$. Then we have:

$$female \triangleleft ages = \{bell \mapsto 30,$$
$$hart \mapsto 21\}.$$

Assuming that nobody is both male and female, that is to say, that the sets *male* and *female* partition the set *Person*:

$$male \cup female = Person,$$
$$male \cap female = \varnothing,$$

we could also write:

$$male \triangleleft ages = \{bell \mapsto 30,$$
$$hart \mapsto 21\}.$$

male $\triangleleft$ *ages* is a relation which is a subset of *ages*. The fundamental property of the domain anti-restriction operator $\triangleleft$ is:

$$x \mapsto y \in U \triangleleft F \Longleftrightarrow (x \notin U \land x \mapsto y \in F),$$

where $x: X$, $y: Y$, $U: \mathbf{P}\,X$ and $F: X \leftrightarrow Y$. Domain anti-restriction distributes forwards through set union:

$$U \vartriangleleft (F \cup G) = (U \vartriangleleft F) \cup (U \vartriangleleft G),$$

and domain restriction and anti-restriction are related in the following way:

$$(U \vartriangleleft F) \cup (U \vartriangleleft F) = F,$$

where $U: \mathbf{P}\,X$ and $F, G: X \leftrightarrow Y$.

4.9.3   Specifying the Operation

The operation of removing someone, and all entries in which they figure, from the database is specified by the following schema:

```
┌─ RemoveMember ──────────────────────────────────────
│ ΔPhoneDB
│ name?: Person
├─────────────────────────────────────────────────────
│ name? ∈ members
│ members' = members \ {name?}
│ telephones' = {name?} ⊲ telephones
└─────────────────────────────────────────────────────
```

This goes wrong if *name?* $\notin$ *members*. This case is captured by means of the schema *NotMember*, which has already been discussed. The complete specification of this operation is given by the schema *DoRemoveMember*:

$$DoRemoveMember \mathrel{\widehat{=}} RemoveMember \wedge Success$$
$$\vee$$
$$NotMember.$$

4.10   Specifying a User-interface

The Z specification of the telephone number database cannot be directly implemented as an interactive program. In order to do this we need to augment it slightly. First, we add a type *Command* of all possible commands. The type *Command* contains, at least, the following commands: *ae* ('add entry'), *fp* ('find phones'), *fn* ('find names'), *re* ('remove entry'), *am* ('add member') and *rm* ('remove member'). Thus, we have that $\{ae, fp, fn, re, am, rm\} \subseteq Command$. The basic type *Command* has to be introduced by means of a basic type definition like this:

$$[Command]$$

Then we need to specify in some way that the issuing of the command *ae*, for example, is to be associated with the operation specified by *DoAddEntry*. The schema *DoAddEntryCommand* captures the fact that the command *ae* has been given:

$$DoAddEntryCommand \mathrel{\widehat{=}} [cmd?: Command \mid cmd? = ae].$$

The definition of the schema *DoAddEntryCommand* makes use of the *horizontal form* of a schema. The definition just given is equivalent in every way to the following vertical schema definition:[3]

```
┌─ DoAddEntryCommand ─────────────────────────────────────
│ cmd?: Command
├─────────────────────────────────────────────────────────
│ cmd? = ae
└─────────────────────────────────────────────────────────
```

The schemas *DoFindNamesCommand*, *DoFindPhonesCommand* and so on are defined analogously to the way in which *DoAddEntryCommand* is defined:

$$DoFindPhonesCommand \triangleq [cmd?: Command \mid cmd? = fp],$$

$$DoFindNamesCommand \triangleq [cmd?: Command \mid cmd? = fn],$$

$$DoRemoveEntryCommand \triangleq [cmd?: Command \mid cmd? = re],$$

$$DoAddMemberCommand \triangleq [cmd?: Command \mid cmd? = am],$$

$$DoRemoveMemberCommand \triangleq [cmd?: Command \mid cmd? = rm].$$

We can now specify an operation *CODoAddEntry* which captures the requirement that the operation *DoAddEntry* is only to be carried out when the command *ae* has been issued:

$$CODoAddEntry \triangleq DoAddEntryCommand \wedge DoAddEntry.$$

Analogously to the way in which *CODoAddEntry* was defined we can define the following schemas:

$$CODoFindPhones \triangleq DoFindPhonesCommand \wedge DoFindPhones,$$

$$CODoFindNames \triangleq DoFindNamesCommand \wedge DoFindNames,$$

$$CODoRemoveEntry \triangleq DoRemoveEntryCommand \wedge DoRemoveEntry,$$

$$CODoAddMember \triangleq DoAddMemberCommand \wedge DoAddMember,$$

$$CODoRemoveMember \triangleq DoRemoveMemberCommand \wedge DoRemoveMember.$$

The letters *CO*, by the way, come from the initial letters of the phrase 'carry out'.

The schema *UnknownCommand* records the fact that a command has been issued which is not known to the system:

```
┌─ UnknownCommand ────────────────────────────────────────
│ ΞPhoneDB
│ cmd?: Command
│ rep!: Report
├─────────────────────────────────────────────────────────
│ cmd? ∉ {ae, fp, fn, re, am, rm}
│ rep! = 'Unknown command'
└─────────────────────────────────────────────────────────
```

---

[3]The horizontal form of a schema definition is explained more fully in section 5.2.1 in the next chapter.

It is now possible to specify the entire internal telephone number database by means of a single schema:

$$PhoneDatabase \stackrel{\wedge}{=} CODoAddMember$$
$$\vee$$
$$CODoRemoveMember$$
$$\vee$$
$$CODoAddEntry$$
$$\vee$$
$$CODoRemoveEntry$$
$$\vee$$
$$CODoFindPhones$$
$$\vee$$
$$CODoFindNames$$
$$\vee$$
$$UnknownCommand.$$

How this specification can be animated using Miranda is the topic of chapter 19.

4.11 Presenting a Formal Specification

So far in this chapter I have presented the specification of an internal telephone number database in a way that has been guided by pedagogic concerns. This is not, however, necessarily the same as the order in which the material would be presented in a Z specification document. In this section I want to say a few things about the format of such a document.

4.11.1 Definition Before Use

The global organization of any document written in Z is governed by the principle that before a name can be used it has to be defined. This is known as the *definition before use* principle (Spivey 1992, p. 47). In the case of the telephone directory specification this principle was violated a small number of times for didactic reasons. The main way in which it was contravened was that the set of messages *Report* was used before it had been properly introduced. Before the first use of this set it should have been defined in the following—or some other—way:

$$Report ::= \text{'Okay'}$$
$$| \text{ 'Not a member'}$$
$$| \text{ 'Entry already exists'}$$
$$| \text{ 'Unknown name'}$$
$$| \text{ 'Unknown number'}$$
$$| \text{ 'Unknown entry'}$$
$$| \text{ 'Already a member'}$$
$$| \text{ 'Unknown command'}.$$

The definition of the set *Report* makes use of what, in Z, is known as a *free type definition*. Chapter 9 contains more information about this kind of definition.

4.11.2 The Format of a Sequential System

The principle of definition before use has to be obeyed by *every* document written in Z. The remaining considerations apply only to specifications of sequential systems—such as the telephone directory specification contained in this chapter—which are written in Z. In this book the following structure is usually followed in presenting specifications and many published Z specifications exhibit the same pattern. Note that not all of these components are present in every specification.

(1) *Basic types*: Near the beginning of the document there occurs a basic type definition in which all the given sets used in the specification are declared.

(2) *Global constants*: If the specification makes use of any global constants, then they should be properly introduced near the beginning of the document by means of an axiomatic description.[4]

(3) *User-defined sets*: Many specifications make use of a set of messages or reports that are output by the system being described. The set of messages needed by a specification is usually introduced by means of a free type definition. If the specification employs any other user-defined sets, they should be introduced here as well.

(4) *The state space*: Every sequential system needs a state schema which spells out what the state space of the system being specified is. Such a state schema is defined here. Sometimes the main state schema is made up out of several other schemas. If this is the case, then those other schemas have to be defined here and how they need to be joined together to form the main state schema needs to be made explicit.

(5) *The Δ and Ξ schemas*: Although the schemas $\Delta State$ and $\Xi State$ have a default definition in Z, namely

$$\Delta State \triangleq State \wedge State',$$

$$\Xi State \triangleq [\Delta State \mid \theta State' = \theta State],$$

where *State* is the state schema, many specifications repeat those definitions after the state schema has been given.[5] If the Δ and Ξ schemas are defined in a non-standard way, then those unusual definitions should be placed here.

---

[4] Axiomatic description is one of the methods of definition available in Z. It is explained in section 5.1.2 below and also in chapter 20.

[5] The horizontal form of schema definition used to define $\Xi State$ is explained in section 5.2.1 below and the θ operator is explained in section 5.2.7.

(6) *The initial state*: In specifying the internal telephone directory I did not mention the initial state, but the definition of this state occurs in a specification document before the various operations are defined. In the case of the telephone database the initial state is described by means of the schema *InitPhoneDB'*, where the schema *InitPhoneDB* is defined as follows:

```
┌─ InitPhoneDB ──────────────────────────────
│ PhoneDB
├────────────────────────────────────────────
│ members = ∅
│ telephones = ∅
└────────────────────────────────────────────
```

Conventionally in Z the variables in the schema describing the initial state are primed. Concerning this, Woodcock and Loomes (1988), p. 113, write:

> We can regard the initialization of a system as a peculiar kind of operation that creates a state out of nothing; there is no before state, simply an after state, with its variables decorated.

Note that the name of every defined schema must be an identifier that is not decorated in any way. In particular, it cannot be decorated by means of a prime or a subscript. Thus, it is *not* possible to define the initial state schema as follows:

```
┌─ InitPhoneDB' ─────────────────────────────
│ PhoneDB'
├────────────────────────────────────────────
│ members' = ∅
│ telephones' = ∅
└────────────────────────────────────────────
```

The reason for this is that in Z there is a convention about the effect of decorating a schema name and this convention would break down if it were allowed to define decorated identifiers as arbitrary schemas. (The convention is that if you decorate the name of a schema, that means that every identifier local to that schema is decorated in the same way.)

As well as defining the initial state it is a good idea to prove that an initial state exists. That such a state does in fact exist is a proof obligation known, not surprisingly, as the *initialization proof obligation*.[6] To satisfy this requirement in this case we have to prove that the following formula is a theorem:

$$\exists members': \mathbf{P}\ Person;\ telephones': Person \leftrightarrow Phone\ |$$
$$\operatorname{dom} telephones' \subseteq members' \bullet$$
$$\operatorname{dom} telephones' \subseteq members' \wedge members' = \emptyset \wedge telephones' = \emptyset.$$

This formula is indeed a theorem of first-order logic. In general, the initialization proof obligation requires us to prove that the formula $\exists State' \bullet InitState'$ is a

---

[6] For more information about this proof obligation see section 12.4 below.

theorem, where *State* is the state schema and *InitState'* is the initial state schema. If this formula is not a theorem, then we have made a mistake somewhere in our specification and this needs to be remedied. (Note that, in general, several states may satisfy the initial state schema. The above has been written as if the initial state is unique—with suitable modifications it also applies to the case when there are several initial states.)

(7) *The operations*: Following the initial state there come the schemas which define the various operations that can be performed on the system being specified. The specification of each operation follows the same pattern:

   (a) In the first place there occurs the definition of the schema which represents the successful completion of some operation.

   (b) After the schema which defines the successful completion of an operation has been given the various error schemas that say what happens when the preconditions of this schema are not satisfied are defined.

   (c) Following the schemas mentioned in (a) and (b) above comes the specification of the total operation. A *total* operation in Z is one which is defined for all states which satisfy the state invariant (which is the conjunction of all the formulas that occur in the predicate-part of the state schema).

(8) *The user-interface*: This is usually absent from published Z specifications, but the specification of a user-interface was included in the specification of an internal telephone directory given earlier in this chapter.

Some authors—for example, Wordsworth (1992), pp. 148–151—suggest a slightly different arrangement of the components of a specification document. In part (7) I say that the specification of each operation should follow the same pattern. Wordsworth, however, favours a layout in which *all* the schemas representing successful operations are defined before *any* error schemas are defined and the specifications of the total operations are only given after *all* the error schemas have been defined. Which format you prefer is largely a matter of taste.

Sometimes it is useful to define an 'okay' schema which combines the specification of a successful operation with the schema that outputs a message saying that the operation has been successfully performed. For example, it would have been possible in the telephone directory specification to define a schema *AddEntryOkay* like this:

$$AddEntryOkay \triangleq AddEntry \land Success.$$

The total operation *DoAddEntry* could then have been defined as follows:

$$DoAddEntry \triangleq AddEntryOkay$$
$$\lor$$
$$NotMember$$
$$\lor$$
$$EntryAlreadyExists.$$

The convention that a schema name *OpOkay* is defined to be *Op* ∧ *Success*, where *Op* is a schema corresponding to a successful operation, is used in chapter 15 as there are advantages to be gained from doing so when the implementation method described there is being used.

4.11.3   Combining Z and Descriptive Text

One of the most important things to remember in writing a Z document is that it should *not* consist solely of mathematical symbols. There should be a substantial amount of English prose. In general, there will be more English prose than Z notation. It is a good idea to begin the specification document with a brief introduction which informally gives an overview of the system of which you are going to present a formal specification.

Accompanying each paragraph of a Z specification there should be some descriptive text which explains the significance of the Z. (A *paragraph* in Z is, for example, a basic type definition or an axiomatic description or the definition of a schema or a free type definition. See (Spivey 1992), p. 143, for a fuller and more precise account of what a paragraph in Z is.) People differ on whether the prose description should precede or follow the Z paragraph, but wherever you decide to put it you should be consistent. (For textbooks, however, this requirement is relaxed! On the whole, in this book, the explanation of what a schema does follows the Z specification of that schema, but in giving formal definitions of Z operators in chapter 21 the informal description of an operator's behaviour precedes the formal account.) The informal account of a Z paragraph should not just consist of a translation into natural language of the formal notation, rather it should elaborate on the formal account and make explicit how it relates to the real world.[7]

4.11.4   Conventions for Identifiers

It is a good idea when writing a Z specification to use meaningful identifiers for global names. In particular, the names chosen for basic types, global constants, free types and schemas should be meaningful. This is useful as a mnemonic device for the specifier—who can easily remember what a schema named *JW14Gii* does?—and, in addition, it helps a reader of the specification to understand what the named entities are and how they relate to the other components of the specification.

Furthermore, when writing a specification it is a good idea to have a consistent policy on the *form* that identifiers take. In this book, for example, all schema names begin with an initial capital letter and all embedded words in a schema name also begin with a capital letter. Examples of this convention can be seen in the identifiers *EntryAlreadyExists*, *PhoneDatabase* and *AlreadyMember*.

In this book, when specifying a total operation the name of the schema involved always begins with the word *Do*. Examples of this convention can be seen in the identifiers *DoAddEntry* and *DoFindNames*. The name of a schema which contains a formula

---

[7]In writing this section I have been helped by the very useful report by Macdonald (1991), called *Z Usage and Abusage*, and I recommend this to everyone who is about to use Z in the real world.

that tests whether or not a particular command has been given ends with the component *Command*. Examples of this convention are the identifiers *DoAddEntryCommand* and *DoAddMemberCommand*. The name of a schema which combines the total specification of some operation with a test whether or not a particular command has been given begins with the letters *CO* ('carry out'). Examples of this convention are the identifiers *CODoAddEntry* and *CODoRemoveMember*. Furthermore, the initial state schema is always called *InitState'*, where *State* is the name of the state schema.

The convention described above which governs the form that the name of an 'atomic' schema takes is also used for the name of a basic type and also for the name of a user-defined global constant or variable. (The name of an 'atomic' schema is one which contains neither the component *Okay*, nor *Do*, nor *Command*, nor *CO* nor *Init*.) *Phone* and *Person* are examples of the names of basic types and *Report*, *Europe* and *Month* are examples of names of user-defined sets. (Some people use a different convention. They use identifiers composed entirely of capital letters for the names of basic types. For example, Spivey (1992), p. 3, uses *NAME* and *DATE* and McMorran and Powell (1993), p. 84, use *CHAR* and *SUBJECT* as the names of basic types. In this book identifiers made up entirely of capital letters are used as program variables in, for example, chapters 14 and 15.)

The name of an element belonging to a basic type or a user-defined type begins with a lowercase letter and embedded words in that name also begin with lowercase letters.

4.12 Exercises

4.1) Let *Room* be the type of all rooms and let *occupies*: *Person* $\leftrightarrow$ *Room* be a relation such that $x \mapsto y \in occupies$ iff the person x has been allocated to the room y. (The type *Person* is the same type as was used in the specification of the telephone directory. The types *Person* and *Room* are distinct basic types.) Such a relation might be used in the specification of a database that keeps track of who occupies which room in an organization. As *occupies* is a relation it is possible for one person to occupy more than one room and it is possible for one room to be occupied by several people. The members of the relation *occupies* are defined by enumeration to be the following:

$$occupies == \{arch \mapsto m7,$$
$$bell \mapsto m5,$$
$$cox \mapsto g3,$$
$$cox \mapsto m3,$$
$$dove \mapsto g8,$$
$$earl \mapsto g4,$$
$$fry \mapsto g4\}.$$

a) Write out all the members of the set dom *occupies*.

b) Write out all the members of the set ran *occupies*.

c) Write down a formula which captures the fact that the set dom *occupies* and the set ran *occupies* have no elements in common.

d) The set *aigroup*: **P** *Person* is the set of members of the AI group. It is defined like this: *aigroup* == {*cox*, *dove*, *earl*, *fry*}. State in English what the term *occupies*(|*aigroup*|) represents. Write down all the members of this set.

e) The set *ground*: **P** *Room*, which is the collection of rooms on the ground floor, is defined like this:

$$ground == \{g1, g2, g3, g4, g5, g6, g7, g8\}.$$

Write down a formula that expresses the fact that every member of the AI group has a room on the ground floor.

f) Write down the elements of the set *aigroup* ◁ *occupies*.

g) The set *fmgroup*: **P** *Person* is the set of members of the Formal Methods group. It is defined like this: *fmgroup* == {*arch*, *bell*, *cox*}. Write down the members of the set (*aigroup* ◁ *occupies*)(|*fmgroup*|).

h) Write down the members of the set (*aigroup* ◁ *occupies*)~.

i) Write down all the members of the set

$$(aigroup ◁ occupies)~(|(aigroup ◁ occupies)(|fmgroup|)|).$$

j) Write down the members of the set (*aigroup* ◁ *occupies*)~.

4.2) Specify by means of a schema *Films* a database for recording information about films. The database must be capable of holding information about who directed a particular film and about the writer of the film's screenplay. Every film in the database must have a director and writer associated with it. Provision must also be made for films that are directed by several people and written by more than one person.

State what the schemas Δ*Films*, Ξ*Films* and *InitFilms'* are.

Specify the operation of adding information to the database concerning a film with only one director and only one writer.

Specify two operations which interrogate the database in order to find out all the films directed by a particular individual and all the films written by a specific person.

5

More about Relations and Schemas

5.1 Relations

5.1.1 Composition

In this section I discuss the idea of forward relational composition. This is a way of making a relation out of two other relations. I begin by introducing it informally by means of a concrete example and then I discuss it more generally.

Let *Person* be the type of all people, let *Dog* be the type of all dogs and let *Breed* be the type of all the different breeds of dog that there are. The relation $has: Person \leftrightarrow Dog$ tells us who owns which dog. It is possible for a person to own more than one dog and a dog can be jointly owned by two or more people. One example of the relation *has* is given here:

$$has = \{cox \mapsto rover,$$
$$cox \mapsto rex,$$
$$hart \mapsto lassie,$$
$$fry \mapsto lassie,$$
$$gray \mapsto plato\}.$$

The relation $isa: Dog \leftrightarrow Breed$ tells us the breed of any particular dog. One example of the *isa* relation follows:

$$isa = \{rover \mapsto alsatian,$$
$$rex \mapsto labrador,$$
$$lassie \mapsto labrador,$$
$$plato \mapsto bulldog,$$
$$socrates \mapsto terrier,$$
$$aristotle \mapsto terrier\}.$$

Given all this information one of the things that we might be interested in is that of knowing which breeds of dog are favoured by which people. For example, does *dove* own a *bulldog* or a *terrier* or some other breed of dog, if he owns a dog at all? Clearly a person x owns a dog of breed z iff there exists a dog y such that x owns y and y belongs to the breed z, that is to say, if $x \mapsto y \in has$ and $y \mapsto z \in isa$. The relation that we are interested in is given extensionally as follows:

$$\{cox \mapsto alsatian,$$
$$cox \mapsto labrador,$$
$$hart \mapsto labrador,$$
$$fry \mapsto labrador,$$
$$gray \mapsto bulldog\}.$$

The relation $has \, \mathbin{\raise1pt\hbox{$\circ$}} \, isa$ is one which holds between people and breeds iff the person in the relation owns a dog of that breed. The relation $has \, \mathbin{\raise1pt\hbox{$\circ$}} \, isa$ is known as the *forward relational composition*—or simply the *relational composition* or even the *composition*—of has and isa. Symbolically, we have that

$$x \mapsto z \in has \, \mathbin{\raise1pt\hbox{$\circ$}} \, isa \iff (\exists y\colon Dog \bullet x \mapsto y \in has \wedge y \mapsto z \in isa).$$

In general, where $x\colon X$, $z\colon Z$, $F\colon X \leftrightarrow Y$ and $G\colon Y \leftrightarrow Z$, we have that

$$x \mapsto z \in F \, \mathbin{;} \, G \iff (\exists y\colon Y \bullet x \mapsto y \in F \wedge y \mapsto z \in G).$$

The following laws hold for forward relational composition:

$$(F \, \mathbin{;} \, G) \, \mathbin{;} \, H = F \, \mathbin{;} \, (G \, \mathbin{;} \, H),$$
$$F \, \mathbin{;} \, (G_1 \cup G_2) = (F \, \mathbin{;} \, G_1) \cup (F \, \mathbin{;} \, G_2),$$
$$(F_1 \cup F_2) \, \mathbin{;} \, G = (F_1 \, \mathbin{;} \, G) \cup (F_2 \, \mathbin{;} \, G),$$
$$(F \, \mathbin{;} \, G)^{\sim} = G^{\sim} \, \mathbin{;} \, F^{\sim},$$

where $F, F_1, F_2\colon X_1 \leftrightarrow X_2$, $G, G_1, G_2\colon X_2 \leftrightarrow X_3$ and $H\colon X_3 \leftrightarrow X_4$. The first of these states that relational composition is transitive, the second that composition distributes forwards through set union and the third that it also distributes backwards through set union. The fourth of these laws states that the inverse of the composition of two relations is the same as the composition of the inverse of the second one with the inverse of the first one.

Z also contains a backward relational composition operator which is symbolized by the sign $\circ$ and this is defined so that $z \mapsto x \in G \circ F$ iff $x \mapsto z \in F \, \mathbin{;} \, G$.

5.1.2   Identity, Powers and Closures

Let $F\colon X \leftrightarrow Y$ be a relation. Then if X is different from Y, the relation F is known as a *heterogeneous* relation and if X is the same set as Y, then F is known as a *homogeneous* relation. The simplest homogeneous relation between elements of the set X is the *identity relation* id X, which is defined straightforwardly as $\{x\colon X \bullet x \mapsto x\}$.

Let $parent\colon Person \leftrightarrow Person$ be a relation such that $x \mapsto y \in parent$ iff y is a (natural) parent of x. Then the relation $parent$ is a homogeneous relation. One of the things that it is possible to do with such relations is to compose them with themselves. Thus, we can form the relation $parent \, \mathbin{;} \, parent$. This is such that $x \mapsto y \in$

parent ; parent iff x is a grandchild of y. The relation *parent ; parent* can be written as $parent^2$. Similarly, we can form the relation *parent ; parent ; parent*. This is such that $x \mapsto y \in parent \; ; \; parent \; ; \; parent$ iff x is a greatgrandchild of y. The relation *parent ; parent ; parent* can also be written as $parent^3$. This process could, obviously, be repeated as many times as desired.

More generally, let $F \colon X \leftrightarrow X$ be a homogeneous relation. Then we have:

$$F^0 = \mathrm{id}\, X,$$
$$F^1 = F,$$
$$F^2 = F \; ; F,$$
$$F^3 = F \; ; F \; ; F,$$
$$F^4 = F \; ; F \; ; F \; ; F,$$

and clearly the process could be carried on indefinitely. When n is a positive number greater than or equal to two, then F^n is F composed with itself $n-1$ times.

The *transitive closure* of a homogeneous relation F is the relation obtained by forming the union of all F's iterations except F^0. It is symbolized as F^+. If *parent* is as explained above, then $x \mapsto y \in parent^+$ iff y is an ancestor of x. The *reflexive-transitive closure* of a relation F is the relation obtained by forming the union of all F's iterations *including* F^0. It is symbolized as F^*.

It is also possible to have negative powers of homogeneous relations. F^{-n} is defined in Z to be equivalent to $(F^\sim)^n$, where $n \geq 1$. Note that the operator $\_^{-1}$ can only be applied to homogeneous relations, whereas the relational inverse operator $\_^\sim$ can be applied to both homogeneous and heterogeneous relations. Of course, if F is a homogeneous relation, then $F^{-1} = F^\sim$. Let $n \colon \mathbf{Z}$ be an integer. Then the notation *iter n F* is also available in Z. It means the same as F^n.

Given the relation *parent* as explained above it is possible to define other relations in terms of it. For example, let *sibling: Person ↔ Person* be a relation such that $x \mapsto y \in sibling$ when x and y are siblings, that is to say, they are different people who have both of their natural parents in common. When x is a person, the term $parent(\!(\{x\}\!)\!)$ is the set which consists of all of x's natural parents. The relation *sibling* can be defined as follows:

$$\begin{array}{|l}
\hline
sibling \colon Person \leftrightarrow Person \\
\hline
\forall x, y \colon Person \bullet \\
\quad x \mapsto y \in sibling \Longleftrightarrow \\
\qquad (x \neq y \wedge parent(\!(\{x\}\!)\!) = parent(\!(\{y\}\!)\!))
\end{array}$$

The method of definition employed here is known as an *axiomatic description* in Z and one form this kind of definition can take is

$$\begin{array}{|l}
\hline
D \\
\hline
P \\
\end{array}$$

where D is a declaration which introduces one or more global variables and P is an optional formula that constrains the values that can be taken by the variables introduced in D. If P is absent, the default is the formula *true*. (The variables declared in D cannot have been previously declared globally and their scope extends to the end of the specification.)

5.1.3 Range Restriction and Anti-restriction

Range restriction and anti-restriction are similar operators to domain restriction and anti-restriction, except that they work on the range of a relation rather than on its domain. (Range anti-restriction is also known as range *corestriction* or range *subtraction*.) I will introduce both of these operators by means of examples.

Let *Month* be the set consisting of all twelve of the months of the year. It can be defined by enumeration like this:

$$Month == \{jan, feb, mar, apr, may, jun, jul, aug, sep, oct, nov, dec\}.$$

Let the relation *normal*: *Month* $\leftrightarrow$ $\mathbf{N}$ be such that $x \mapsto y \in normal$ iff the month x has y days in it. I am assuming that the year in question is not a leap year. The relation *normal* can be specified extensionally as follows:

$$\begin{aligned}
normal == \{&jan \mapsto 31, \\
&feb \mapsto 28, \\
&mar \mapsto 31, \\
&apr \mapsto 30, \\
&may \mapsto 31, \\
&jun \mapsto 30, \\
&jul \mapsto 31, \\
&aug \mapsto 31, \\
&sep \mapsto 30, \\
&oct \mapsto 31, \\
&nov \mapsto 30, \\
&dec \mapsto 31\}.
\end{aligned}$$

Range restriction is represented by the symbol $\rhd$ and the term $normal \rhd \{30\}$ represents that relation which results when the relation *normal* has had its range restricted to the set which just consists of the number 30.

$$normal \rhd \{30\} = \{apr \mapsto 30, jun \mapsto 30, sep \mapsto 30, nov \mapsto 30\}.$$

A pair $x \mapsto y$ is a member of $normal \rhd \{30\}$ iff its second component y is in $\{30\}$. So, the set of all the months that have exactly 30 days in them is denoted by means of the expression $\mathrm{dom}(normal \rhd \{30\})$.

Let $x: X$, $y: Y$, $F: X \leftrightarrow Y$ and $V: \mathbf{P} Y$. Then, in general, we have the following fundamental property of range restriction:

$$x \mapsto y \in F \rhd V \Longleftrightarrow (x \mapsto y \in F \wedge y \in V).$$

The following laws are sometimes useful in dealing with range restriction:

$$F \triangleright V \subseteq F,$$
$$F \triangleright V = F \, \mathbin{;} \operatorname{id} V,$$
$$\operatorname{ran}(F \triangleright V) = (\operatorname{ran} F) \cap V,$$
$$(F \triangleright V_1) \triangleright V_2 = F \triangleright (V_1 \cap V_2),$$
$$F \triangleright (V_1 \cup V_2) = (F \triangleright V_1) \cup (F \triangleright V_2),$$
$$(F \cup G) \triangleright V = (F \triangleright V) \cup (G \triangleright V),$$

where $F, G: X \leftrightarrow Y$ and $V, V_1, V_2 : \mathbf{P} Y$.

Range anti-restriction is represented by the symbol $\triangleright\!\!\!-$ and the term *normal* $\triangleright\!\!\!-$ $\{30\}$ represents that relation which results when the relation *normal* has had its range anti-restricted to the set which just consists of the number 30.

$$\begin{aligned}
normal \triangleright\!\!\!- \{30\} = \{jan &\mapsto 31, \\
feb &\mapsto 28, \\
mar &\mapsto 31, \\
may &\mapsto 31, \\
jul &\mapsto 31, \\
aug &\mapsto 31, \\
oct &\mapsto 31, \\
dec &\mapsto 31\}.
\end{aligned}$$

An ordered pair $x \mapsto y$ is a member of *normal* $\triangleright\!\!\!-$ $\{30\}$ iff its second component y is *not* in $\{30\}$. So, the set of all the months that do not have 30 days in them is denoted by means of the expression $\operatorname{dom}(normal \triangleright\!\!\!- \{30\})$.

Let $x: X$, $y: Y$, $F: X \leftrightarrow Y$ and $V: \mathbf{P} Y$. Then, in general, we have the following fundamental property of range anti-restriction:

$$x \mapsto y \in F \triangleright\!\!\!- V \iff (x \mapsto y \in F \wedge y \notin V).$$

Range anti-restriction distributes backwards through set union:

$$(F \cup G) \triangleright\!\!\!- V = (F \triangleright\!\!\!- V) \cup (G \triangleright\!\!\!- V),$$

and the following law relates range restriction and anti-restriction:

$$(F \triangleright V) \cup (F \triangleright\!\!\!- V) = F,$$

where $F, G: X \leftrightarrow Y$ and $V: \mathbf{P} Y$.

If a relation has both its domain and its range restricted, then it does not matter which operator is applied first. Similarly, if a relation has both its domain and range anti-restricted, then it does not matter which operator is applied first. In fact, if either the domain restriction or the domain anti-restriction operators are applied to a relation as well as either of the range restriction or anti-restriction operators, then the order in which the operators are applied is irrelevant. The following laws summarize this:

$$(U \lhd F) \rhd V = U \lhd (F \rhd V),$$
$$(U \blacktriangleleft F) \rhd V = U \blacktriangleleft (F \rhd V),$$
$$(U \lhd F) \blacktriangleright V = U \lhd (F \blacktriangleright V),$$
$$(U \blacktriangleleft F) \rhd V = U \blacktriangleleft (F \rhd V),$$

where $U: \mathbf{P}\, X$, $F: X \leftrightarrow Y$ and $V: \mathbf{P}\, Y$.

5.1.4   Overriding

The way in which overriding works is easy to grasp with the aid of an example. Let *Month*, again, be the set consisting of all the months and let *leap: Month* $\leftrightarrow$ $\mathbf{N}$ be a relation such that $x \mapsto y \in$ *leap* iff the month x has y days in it in a leap year. The relation *leap* is clearly the same as *normal* except for the number it associates with February. This connection between the relations *leap* and *normal* is captured using overriding as follows:

$$leap = normal \oplus \{feb \mapsto 29\}.$$

Just to make sure that you have grasped the significance of this I will spell out what *leap* is:

$$leap = \{jan \mapsto 31,$$
$$feb \mapsto 29,$$
$$mar \mapsto 31,$$
$$apr \mapsto 30,$$
$$may \mapsto 31,$$
$$jun \mapsto 30,$$
$$jul \mapsto 31,$$
$$aug \mapsto 31,$$
$$sep \mapsto 30,$$
$$oct \mapsto 31,$$
$$nov \mapsto 30,$$
$$dec \mapsto 31\}.$$

Let $x: X$, $y: Y$, $F, G: X \leftrightarrow Y$. Then the following formula holds for $F \oplus G$:

$$x \mapsto y \in F \oplus G \iff (x \mapsto y \in G \lor (x \mapsto y \in F \land x \notin \text{dom}\, G)).$$

We also have that $F \oplus G = G \cup ((\text{dom}\, G) \lhd F)$. Overriding is idempotent, associative and the empty set is a two-sided unit for it:

$$F \oplus F = F,$$
$$(F \oplus G) \oplus H = F \oplus (G \oplus H),$$
$$F \oplus \varnothing = F,$$
$$\varnothing \oplus F = F,$$

where $F, G, H: X \leftrightarrow Y$. Overriding, however, is not commutative. Where *leap* and *normal* are as above the following is a counter-example:

$$normal \oplus \{feb \mapsto 29\} \neq \{feb \mapsto 29\} \oplus normal.$$

In fact, $\{feb \mapsto 29\} \oplus normal$ is just the relation *normal*.

Let $U: \mathbf{P}\, X$, $F, G: X \leftrightarrow Y$ and $V: \mathbf{P}\, Y$. Then some further properties of $\oplus$ are:

$$U \lhd (F \oplus G) = (U \lhd F) \oplus (U \lhd G),$$
$$(F \oplus G) \rhd V \subseteq (F \rhd V) \oplus (G \rhd V).$$

5.2 Schemas

5.2.1 Horizontal Form

In the previous chapter many examples of schemas were given. Almost all of these were presented in what is known as the *vertical form*. For example, the state schema *PhoneDB* was defined like this:

PhoneDB

members: $\mathbf{P}$ *Person*
telephones: *Person* $\leftrightarrow$ *Phone*

dom *telephones* $\subseteq$ *members*

There is also, however, a *horizontal form* of schema definition and using this the state schema *PhoneDB* could be defined like this:

$$PhoneDB \;\hat{=}\; [members: \mathbf{P}\ Person; telephones: Person \leftrightarrow Phone \\ \mid \text{dom } telephones \subseteq members].$$

The general form of the right-hand side of such a schema definition is

$$[D_1; D_2; \ldots; D_n \mid P_1; P_2; \ldots; P_m],$$

where D_i, for $1 \leq i \leq n$, is a basic declaration and P_i, for $1 \leq i \leq m$, is a formula. Note that semicolons are used as separators both between the basic declarations and also between the formulas. Semicolons are also used in the vertical form of schema definition if we want to have either several definitions on a single line or several formulas on a single line. For example, the schema *InitPhoneDB* could have been defined like this:

InitPhoneDB

members: $\mathbf{P}$ *Person*; *telephones*: *Person* $\leftrightarrow$ *Phone*

dom *telephones* $\subseteq$ *members*; *members* $= \varnothing$; *telephones* $= \varnothing$

The horizontal form of schema definition is often used in order to define Ξ schemas and schemas representing the initial state. In the case of the internal telephone directory specification the schema $\Xi PhoneDB$ could have been defined like this:

$$\Xi PhoneDB \triangleq [\Delta PhoneDB \mid members' = members;\ telephones' = telephones].$$

Note that the Greek letters Δ and Ξ are the initial characters in the identifiers $\Delta PhoneDB$ and $\Xi PhoneDB$, respectively. These letters, however, can only occur as the initial characters of identifiers which are used as the names of schemas.

The horizontal form of schema definition is useful in 'extending' schemas either by adding a small number of declarations or by adding a small number of formulas. The word *extension* is—strictly speaking—inaccurate as what is happening is that a new schema is being defined. For example, the schema *TrendyPhoneDB* is obtained from *PhoneDB* by adding another declaration and *LimitedPhoneDB* is obtained by adding a formula:

$$TrendyPhoneDB \triangleq [PhoneDB;\ mobile\colon \mathbf{P}\ Phone],$$

$$LimitedPhoneDB \triangleq [PhoneDB \mid \#members \leq MaxSize],$$

where $\#$ is Z's cardinality operator that returns the size of a set and *MaxSize* is a constant representing the maximum number of people who can be members of the university.

5.2.2 Renaming

In this section I explain with the help of examples how schema renaming is done.[1] Consider the following simple schema:

```
┌─ S ──────────────────────────
│ x, y: N
│ V: P N
├──────────────────────────────
│ x ∈ V ⇒ y ∈ V
└──────────────────────────────
```

Schema renaming actually means renaming the local variables in the schema. The notation $S[m/x]$ means that every *free* occurrence of x in S is replaced by m. Let $T \triangleq S[m/x]$. Then the result of expanding T is the following schema:

```
┌─ T ──────────────────────────
│ m, y: N
│ V: P N
├──────────────────────────────
│ m ∈ V ⇒ y ∈ V
└──────────────────────────────
```

---

[1]Schema renaming is a part of standard Z according to (Spivey 1992), p. 31, though it was absent from the first edition of that book.

It might be easier to remember this if you think of it as $S[new/old]$. It is possible to perform several substitutions simultaneously. For example, if we now define T to be $S[n/x, W/V]$, then T is the following schema:

```
┌─ T ─────────────────────────────────────
│  n, y: N
│  W: P N
│  ─────────────────────
│  n ∈ W ⇒ y ∈ W
└──────────────────────────────────────────
```

5.2.3 Hiding

Let S be as above. Then the notation $S \setminus (x)$ is used to indicate the schema S with x hidden, that is to say, $S \setminus (x)$ is that schema in which x is removed from the declaration-part and existentially quantified over in the predicate-part. Let $T \triangleq S \setminus (x)$. Then the result of expanding T is the following schema:

```
┌─ T ─────────────────────────────────────
│  y: N
│  V: P N
│  ─────────────────────────────
│  ∃x: N • (x ∈ V ⇒ y ∈ V)
└──────────────────────────────────────────
```

It is possible to hide several variables at the same time. For example, if we now define T to be $S \setminus (x, V)$, then T is the following schema:

```
┌─ T ─────────────────────────────────────
│  y: N
│  ────────────────────────────────────────
│  ∃x: N; V: P N • (x ∈ V ⇒ y ∈ V)
└──────────────────────────────────────────
```

5.2.4 Composition

Schema composition is a way of relating the after state variables of one schema with the before state variables of another schema. The related variables must have the same base name. (The *base name* of a variable is what we are left with after we remove all the decorations from that variable. In this context a decoration is any subscript or any of the symbols !, ? and '.) Input and output variables are unaffected. For example, consider the schemas:

```
┌─ S ──────────────────        ┌─ T ──────────────────
│  x?, s, s', y!: N            │  x?, s, s': N
│  ─────────────────           │  ─────────────────
│  s' = s − x?                 │  s < x?
│  y! = s                      │  s' = s
└───────────────────────        └───────────────────────
```

In order to form $S \,\fatsemi\, T$ we go through the following four stages:

(1) We rename all the after state variables in S to something entirely new, for example, s^+. That is to say, we form $S[s^+/s']$.

(2) We rename all the before state variables in T to the same new thing, which—in this case—is s^+. That is to say, we form $T[s^+/s]$.

(3) We form the conjunction of the two renamed schemas obtained in (1) and (2) above, that is to say, we form $S[s^+/s'] \wedge T[s^+/s]$.

(4) We hide the variable—introduced in steps (1) and (2)—in the schema formed in step (3), that is to say, we form the schema $(S[s^+/s'] \wedge T[s^+/s]) \setminus (s^+)$. This is $S \,\fatsemi\, T$.

Let $Alpha \,\hat{=}\, S[s^+/s']$ and $Beta \,\hat{=}\, T[s^+/s]$, that is to say, $Alpha$ and $Beta$ are the schemas obtained by carrying out the transformations described in steps (1) and (2). The expanded versions of $Alpha$ and $Beta$ are the following schemas:

$$
\begin{array}{|l}
\underline{\;Alpha\;} \\
x?, s, s^+, y! : \mathbb{N} \\
\hline
s^+ = s - x? \\
y! = s \\
\hline
\end{array}
\qquad
\begin{array}{|l}
\underline{\;Beta\;} \\
x?, s^+, s' : \mathbb{N} \\
\hline
s^+ < x? \\
s' = s^+ \\
\hline
\end{array}
$$

The result of carrying out step (3) is the schema $Gamma \,\hat{=}\, S[s^+/s'] \wedge T[s^+/s]$, whose expansion is:

$$
\begin{array}{|l}
\underline{\;Gamma\;} \\
x?, s, s^+, s', y! : \mathbb{N} \\
\hline
s^+ = s - x? \\
y! = s \\
s^+ < x? \\
s' = s^+ \\
\hline
\end{array}
$$

The composition of two schemas S and T is written $S \,\fatsemi\, T$ and—in this case—it can be defined like this:

$$S \,\fatsemi\, T \,\hat{=}\, (S[s^+/s'] \wedge T[s^+/s]) \setminus (s^+).$$

Carrying out the operation described in step (4) above results in the schema $Delta \,\hat{=}\, S \,\fatsemi\, T$, whose expansion follows:

```
┌─ Delta ──────────────────────────────────
│ x?, s, s', y!: N
├──────────────────────────────────────────
│ ∃s⁺: N •
│         (s⁺ = s − x? ∧
│         y! = s ∧
│         s⁺ < x? ∧
│         s' = s⁺)
└──────────────────────────────────────────
```

The formula that results when we form the composition of two schemas can usually be considerably simplified. A law that is often useful in such simplification is the following one-point law:

$$P[t/y] \dashv\vdash \exists y: Y \bullet P \wedge y = t,$$

where t is a term of the same type as the variable y and y can occur free in the formula P. In the case of $S \,\mathbin{\raise1pt\hbox{\tiny 9}} T$ the predicate-part of that schema consists of the formula

$$\exists s⁺: N \bullet \underbrace{s⁺ = s − x? \wedge y! = s \wedge s⁺ < x?}_{P} \wedge s' = s⁺.$$

Taking $x⁺$ as y, s' as t and P as shown and using the above one-point law results in the formula

$$s' = s − x? \wedge y! = s \wedge s' < x?$$

Thus, the schema *Delta*, which is the composition of S with T, can be simplified to the following:

```
┌─ Delta ──────────────────────────────────
│ x?, s, s', y!: N
├──────────────────────────────────────────
│ s' = s − x?
│ y! = s
│ s' < x?
└──────────────────────────────────────────
```

Schema composition is a useful operation because it allows us to make new specifications out of old ones. In order to illustrate this I am going to consider the internal telephone number database presented in the previous chapter and I am going to show how the operation of someone changing one of their extensions can be composed out of the operations of removing an entry from the database and adding an entry to the database. What I am going to construct is the schema *RemoveEntry* $\mathbin{\raise1pt\hbox{\tiny 9}}$ *AddEntry*. In order to do this we have to go through the four stages mentioned above. Carrying out step (1) results in the schema *Alpha* which is a short name for the schema *RemoveEntry*[*members⁺*/*members'*][*telephones⁺*/*telephones'*]:

```
┌─ Alpha ─────────────────────────────────────────────────────────────
│ members, members⁺: P Person
│ telephones, telephones⁺: Person ↔ Phone
│ oldnumber?: Phone
│ name?: Person
├─────────────────────────────────────────
│ dom telephones ⊆ members
│ dom telephones⁺ ⊆ members⁺
│ name? ↦ oldnumber? ∈ telephones
│ telephones⁺ = telephones \ {name? ↦ oldnumber?}
│ members⁺ = members
└─────────────────────────────────────────────────────────────────────
```

Next we have to perform the operation mentioned in step (2) above. This results in the schema $Beta \hat{=} AddEntry[members^+/members][telephones^+/telephones]$:

```
┌─ Beta ──────────────────────────────────────────────────────────────
│ members⁺, members′: P Person
│ telephones⁺, telephones′: Person ↔ Phone
│ newnumber?: Phone
│ name?: Person
├─────────────────────────────────────────
│ dom telephones⁺ ⊆ members⁺
│ dom telephones′ ⊆ members′
│ name? ∈ members⁺
│ name? ↦ newnumber? ∉ telephones⁺
│ telephones′ = telephones⁺ ∪ {name? ↦ newnumber?}
│ members′ = members⁺
└─────────────────────────────────────────────────────────────────────
```

The next thing we have to find is:

$$RemoveEntry[members^+/members'][telephones^+/telephones']$$
$$\land AddEntry[members^+/members][telephones^+/telephones].$$

I shall call this schema *Gamma*:

```
┌─ Gamma ──────────────────────────────────────────────────────────────
│ members, members⁺, members': P Person
│ telephones, telephones⁺, telephones': Person ↔ Phone
│ oldnumber?, newnumber?: Phone
│ name?: Person
├──────────────────────────────────────────────────────────────────────
│ dom telephones ⊆ members
│ dom telephones⁺ ⊆ members⁺
│ dom telephones' ⊆ members'
│ name? ∈ members⁺
│ name? ↦ newnumber? ∉ telephones⁺
│ name? ↦ oldnumber? ∈ telephones
│ telephones' = telephones⁺ ∪ {name? ↦ newnumber?}
│ telephones⁺ = telephones \ {name? ↦ oldnumber?}
│ members' = members⁺
│ members⁺ = members
└──────────────────────────────────────────────────────────────────────
```

To obtain the composition of *RemoveEntry* and *AddEntry* we just existentially quantify over the variables introduced in steps (1) and (2) above. Let $Delta \stackrel{\wedge}{=} RemoveEntry \, \overset{\circ}{,} \, AddEntry$. Then *Delta* is the following schema:

```
┌─ Delta ──────────────────────────────────────────────────────────────
│ members, members': P Person
│ telephones, telephones': Person ↔ Phone
│ oldnumber?, newnumber?: Phone
│ name?: Person
├──────────────────────────────────────────────────────────────────────
│ ∃members⁺: P Person; telephones⁺: Person ↔ Phone •
│     dom telephones ⊆ members ∧
│     dom telephones⁺ ⊆ members⁺ ∧
│     dom telephones' ⊆ members' ∧
│     name? ∈ members⁺ ∧
│     name? ↦ newnumber? ∉ telephones⁺ ∧
│     name? ↦ oldnumber? ∈ telephones ∧
│     telephones' = telephones⁺ ∪ {name? ↦ newnumber?} ∧
│     telephones⁺ = telephones \ {name? ↦ oldnumber?} ∧
│     members' = members⁺ ∧
│     members⁺ = members
└──────────────────────────────────────────────────────────────────────
```

After simplification this turns out to be:

```
┌─ Delta ──────────────────────────────────────────────────────
│ ΔPhoneDB
│ oldnumber?, newnumber?: Phone
│ name?: Person
├──────────────────────────────────────────────────────────────
│ name? ∈ members
│ name? ↦ newnumber? ∉ telephones \ {name? ↦ oldnumber?}
│ name? ↦ oldnumber? ∈ telephones
│ telephones'
│       = telephones
│           \ {name? ↦ oldnumber?}
│           ∪ {name? ↦ newnumber?}
│ members' = members
└──────────────────────────────────────────────────────────────
```

One of the consequences of this is that it is possible for *newnumber?* and *oldnumber?* to be the same. There is little point in allowing this possibility, so in defining *ChangeEntry* it is excluded:

$$ChangeEntry \mathrel{\hat=} [RemoveEntry \mathbin{\text{\tiny\S}} AddEntry \mid newnumber? \neq oldnumber?].$$

5.2.5 Piping

Schema piping, represented by the symbol $\gg$, is a way of constructing a new schema out of two old ones by relating the output variables of one of those old schemas to the input variables of the other one. The variables that are identified are those that are the same after any exclamation or question marks have been removed. As as example, consider the two schemas S and T defined as follows:

```
┌─ S ─────────────────        ┌─ T ─────────────────
│ x?, s, s', y!: N            │ y?, t, t': N
├─────────────────────        ├─────────────────────
│ s' = s + x?                 │ y? > t
│ y! = 2 * s'                 │ t' = t + y?
└─────────────────────        └─────────────────────
```

In order to form $S \gg T$ we go through the following four stages:

(1) Every output variable in S whose base name is the same as that of an input variable in T is renamed to something entirely new. In the example, the only such variable is $y!$ in S, which corresponds to $y?$ in T. Let the entirely new variable be p. Then we form $S[p/y!]$.

(2) If $y!$ in S was renamed as p in step (1), then $y?$ in T is renamed to the same thing. That is to say, we form $T[p/y?]$.

(3) We form the conjunction of the two renamed schemas obtained in (1) and (2) above, that is to say, we form $S[p/y!] \wedge T[p/y?]$.

(4) We hide the variable that was introduced in steps (1) and (2) in the schema obtained in step (3). That is to say, we form $(S[p/y!] \wedge T[p/y?]) \setminus (p)$ and this is $S \gg T$.

Let $Alpha \triangleq S[p/y!]$ and let $Beta \triangleq T[p/y?]$. When expanded these look like this:

```
┌─ Alpha ──────────────────
│ x?, s, s', p: N
├──────────────────────────
│ s' = s + x?
│ p = 2 * s'
└──────────────────────────
```

```
┌─ Beta ──────────────
│ p, t, t': N
├─────────────────────
│ p > t
│ t' = t + p
└─────────────────────
```

The result of carrying out step (3) is the schema $Gamma \triangleq Alpha \wedge Beta$, whose expanded form is:

```
┌─ Gamma ──────────────────
│ x?, s, s', p, t, t': N
├──────────────────────────
│ s' = s + x?
│ p = 2 * s'
│ p > t
│ t' = t + p
└──────────────────────────
```

To obtain $S \gg T$ we hide p in $Gamma$. Let $Delta \triangleq (Alpha \wedge Beta) \setminus (p)$. Then $Delta$ looks like this:

```
┌─ Delta ──────────────────
│ x?, s, s', t, t': N
├──────────────────────────
│ ∃p: N •
│     (s' = s + x? ∧
│     p = 2 * s' ∧
│     p > t ∧
│     t' = t + p)
└──────────────────────────
```

Using the one-point law involving the existential quantifier in order to simplify the formula in the predicate-part of the schema *Delta* results in the following version of *Delta*:

```
┌─ Delta ──────────────────
│ x?, s, s', t, t': N
├──────────────────────────
│ s' = s + x?
│ 2 * s' > t
│ t' = t + 2 * s'
└──────────────────────────
```

5.2.6   As Types

In this section I discuss the use of schemas as types. I begin by considering a simple example. Let *Republic* and *Monarchy* be the following two schemas:

```
┌─ Republic ─────────────        ┌─ Monarchy ──────────────
│  leader: Person                │  leader: Person
│  people: P Person              │  people: P Person
│ ───────────────                │ ────────────────
│  leader ∈ people               │  leader ∉ people
└─────────────────────────       └──────────────────────────
```

In a republic the leader is one of the people. He is often called a *president* and the people of the republic are its *citizens*. In a monarchy the leader is usually called a *king* or a *queen* and the people are the monarch's *subjects*. The leader in this case is not one of the people. The schemas *Republic* and *Monarchy* define the same schema type, which is written ⟨ *leader*: *Person*; *people*: **P** *Person* ⟩. The order of the declarations in a schema type is not significant. The above schema type could, therefore, also be written as ⟨ *people*: **P** *Person*; *leader*: *Person* ⟩. Being a type a schema type can be written after the colon in a declaration like this:

$$usa: \langle\, leader: Person; people: \mathbf{P}\, Person \,\rangle.$$

The variable *usa* declared here is a structured object. The way in which its constituents are accessed is by means of the identifiers that precede the colons in the declarations inside the schema type. For example, *usa.leader* is a variable of type *Person* and *usa.people* is a variable of type **P** *Person*. Note that the full stops are part of these two identifiers. The variable *usa* represents a *binding* and the identifiers *usa.leader* and *usa.people* are the *components* of the binding. As an example of a binding we could have

$$\langle\, leader \Rrightarrow \text{Bill Clinton}, people \Rrightarrow \{\, p \mid p \text{ is a citizen of the USA} \,\}\rangle,$$

where I have deliberately not used Z syntax after the arrows ⇛ to emphasize the point that a binding is not something which is part of the Z language. It is part of the meta-language used to talk about Z and to give the language a meaning. Bindings—as Spivey (1992), p. 28, says—are more commonly called *assignments*, *interpretations* or *structures* in model-theory.

The schemas *Republic* and *Monarchy* can themselves occur after the colon in a declaration as they do in the following examples:

$$italy: Republic; uk: Monarchy.$$

Here, the variables *italy* and *uk* have exactly the same type and that type is the schema type ⟨ *leader*: *Person*; *people*: **P** *Person* ⟩. The fact that different formulas occur in the predicate-parts of the schemas *Republic* and *Monarchy* is irrelevant to the issue of determining to which *type* the variables *italy* and *uk* belong. This situation is analogous to the following. Let the schemas S and T be defined like this:

$$S \triangleq [x : \mathbf{Z} \mid x < 100],$$
$$T \triangleq [x : \mathbf{N} \mid x > 50].$$

Then the variable x declared in S has exactly the same type as that declared in T. They are both of type $\mathbf{Z}$. However, although these two variables have the same type, the two formulas

$$\forall S \bullet x \neq 0,$$
$$\forall T \bullet x \neq 0,$$

are not the same. When expanded they become, respectively,

$$\forall x : \mathbf{Z} \mid x < 100 \bullet x \neq 0,$$
$$\forall x : \mathbf{N} \mid x > 50 \bullet x \neq 0.$$

Something similar happens when the names of schemas are used as types. Consider the following two schemas:

```
__ Alpha _____        __ Beta _____
  japan: Republic                  japan: Monarchy
 _____                 _____
  #japan.people > 10,000,000       #japan.people > 10,000,000
```

The schemas *Alpha* and *Beta* are different. Although they contain exactly the same variables, the formulas in their expanded versions are different. These expanded versions are:

```
__ Alpha _____        __ Beta _____
  japan.leader: Person             japan.leader: Person
  japan.people: P Person           japan.people: P Person
 _____                 _____
  japan.leader ∈ japan.people      japan.leader ∉ japan.people
  #japan.people > 10,000,000       #japan.people > 10,000,000
```

5.2.7   The θ Operator

The schema *ElectNewLeader* represents the operation of a new leader of a republic being elected:

```
┌─ ElectNewLeader ──────────────────────────────────────────────
│ ΔRepublic
│ newleader?: Person
├───────────────────────────────────────────────────────────────
│ newleader? ∈ people
│ newleader? ≠ leader
│ leader' = newleader?
│ people' = people
└───────────────────────────────────────────────────────────────
```

If we declare *italy* to be of the schema type *Republic*, then we can specify the Italian election in this way:

```
┌─ ItalianElection ─────────────────────────────────────────────
│ ElectNewLeader
│ italy: Republic
├───────────────────────────────────────────────────────────────
│ italy.leader = leader
│ italy.people = people
└───────────────────────────────────────────────────────────────
```

The schema *Republic* only contains two variables, but in real-life applications a schema may contain a large number of variables and in such a case it would be tedious to include an identity statement corresponding to each one of those variables in the predicate-part of a schema built up analogously to the schema *ItalianElection*. Thus, in Z you are allowed to write:

```
┌─ ItalianElection ─────────────────────────────────────────────
│ ElectNewLeader
│ italy: Republic
├───────────────────────────────────────────────────────────────
│ italy = θRepublic
└───────────────────────────────────────────────────────────────
```

The expression $\theta Republic$ has a binding as its value. It contains the named components *leader* and *people*.

θ is often used to equate the before and after state variables in an operation. Thus, $\theta Republic' = \theta Republic$ is equivalent to the conjunction of the two formulas $leader' = leader$ and $people' = people$. Thus, instead of defining $\Xi Republic$ like this

$$\Xi Republic \mathrel{\hat{=}} [\Delta Republic \mid leader' = leader;\, people' = people]$$

many people writing a Z specification would use the following definition:

$$\Xi Republic \mathrel{\hat{=}} [\Delta Republic \mid \theta Republic' = \theta Republic].$$

5.3   Exercises

5.1) Let *father*, *mother*, *brother*, *firstcousin*, *grandfather* and *greatgrandmother* all be relations of type *Person* ↔ *Person*. Furthermore, $x \mapsto y \in father$ iff y is the father of x, $x \mapsto y \in mother$ iff y is the mother of x, $x \mapsto y \in brother$ iff x and y are brothers (not half-brothers), $x \mapsto y \in firstcousin$ iff x and y are first cousins, $x \mapsto y \in grandfather$ iff y is a grandfather of x and $x \mapsto y \in greatgrandmother$ iff y is a greatgrandmother of x.

a) Define the relation *brother* in terms of *father* and *mother*.

b) Define the relation *firstcousin* in terms of *father* and *mother*.

c) Give two definitions of the relation *grandfather* in terms of *father* and *mother*, one using variables and quantifiers and the other not.

d) What are the sets $grandfather(\!(\{x\}\!)\!)$ and $grandfather^\sim(\!(\{x\}\!)\!)$?

e) Give two definitions of the relation *greatgrandmother* in terms of *father* and *mother*, one using variables and quantifiers and the other not.

f) Write down an expression which represents the set of all a person x's ancestors.

5.2) This question relates to the specification of the internal telephone directory contained in the previous chapter. Often when someone joins the university they are given a telephone extension straight away. The operation *Join* can be defined using schema composition as *AddMember* ⨾ *AddEntry*. Work out what *Join* is by calculating it as explained in this chapter.

6

Functions

6.1 Introduction

In Z a *function* or *mapping* f from X to Y is a special kind of relation in which f maps an object x in X to at most one object y in Y. There are several different kinds of function in Z and the least constrained of these is the *partial function*. The set of all partial functions from X to Y is symbolized as $X \nrightarrow Y$ and is defined in this way:

$$X \nrightarrow Y == \{ f: X \leftrightarrow Y \mid (\forall x: X; y, z: Y \bullet x \mapsto y \in f \wedge x \mapsto z \in f \Rightarrow y = z) \}.$$

That is to say, there exists at most one object in Y corresponding to a single object in X. Note that if $f: X \nrightarrow Y$ is a partial function, then there may exist elements of the set X which are not the first components of any ordered pair which is a member of f.

Let $f: X \nrightarrow Y$ be a partial function, let $x \in \operatorname{dom} f$ and let y be the element of Y associated with x by f. Then, rather than writing $x \mapsto y \in f$, we often write $fx = y$. Parentheses can be placed around x if preferred, thus $f(x) = y$. Here, x is known as the *argument* of the function and y is its *value*.

6.2 Specifying a Weather Map

6.2.1 Introduction

In order to illustrate the use of functions in specifications, I am going to describe a simple weather map which just records the temperature (in degrees Celsius) of various regions of some country. Let *Region* be the type of all the regions that we might need to use. *Region* is a basic type, so it has to be introduced by means of a basic type definition like this:

$$[Region]$$

The state of the system is given by the schema *WeatherMap*:

```
┌─ WeatherMap ─────────────────────────────────────────
│ known: P Region
│ temp: Region ⇸ Z
├──────────────────────────────────────────────────────
│ dom temp = known
└──────────────────────────────────────────────────────
```

Here, *known* is the set of all the regions whose temperature is shown on the weather map and *temp* is the temperature function which returns the temperature associated with a region, given that region as its argument. The state invariant of the schema *WeatherMap* tells us that every region in the set *known* has a temperature associated with it. For example, the set *known* might be {*west, east, south, north*}. An example of the state of this system—with *known* as just enumerated—is

$$temp = \{west \mapsto 17, east \mapsto -3, south \mapsto 8, north \mapsto 0\}.$$

Because a function is just a special kind of relation, we can form its domain and range:

$$\text{dom } temp = \{west, east, south, north\},$$
$$\text{ran } temp = \{17, -3, 8, 0\}.$$

The schemas $\Delta WeatherMap$ and $\Xi WeatherMap$ are defined in the usual way:

$$\Delta WeatherMap \triangleq WeatherMap \wedge WeatherMap',$$
$$\Xi WeatherMap \triangleq [\Delta WeatherMap \mid known' = known; temp' = temp].$$

The initial state schema is $InitWeatherMap'$, where $InitWeatherMap$ is defined as follows:
$$InitWeatherMap \triangleq [WeatherMap \mid known = \varnothing; temp = \varnothing].$$

6.2.2   Updating the Weather Map

The specification of the operation of updating the weather map makes use of the overriding operator, which is symbolized as $\oplus$.

```
┌─ Update ─────────────────────────────────────────────
│ Δ WeatherMap
│ reg?: Region
│ deg?: Z
├──────────────────────────────────────────────────────
│ reg? ∈ known
│ temp' = temp ⊕ {reg? ↦ deg?}
│ known' = known
└──────────────────────────────────────────────────────
```

To illustrate the operation of *Update*, let *temp* be as above and let *reg?* = *west* and *deg?* = 13. Then, *temp'* is given by the equation

$$temp' = temp \oplus \{west \mapsto 13\}.$$

This has the consequence that *temp'* is the following function:

$$\{west \mapsto 13, east \mapsto -3, south \mapsto 8, north \mapsto 0\}.$$

Note that in the second edition of Spivey's reference manual (Spivey 1992, p. 102) overriding is defined so that it applies to relations and not just to functions. However, if f and g are both partial functions from X to Y, then so is $f \oplus g$. The following law, which occurs on p. 107 of Spivey's reference manual, captures this fact:

$$f \in X \nrightarrow Y \wedge g \in X \nrightarrow Y \Rightarrow f \oplus g \in X \nrightarrow Y.$$

6.2.3 Looking up the Temperature of a Region

Another operation that we might want to specify is that of looking up the temperature of a particular region. This is done by the schema *LookUp*:

```
┌─ LookUp ─────────────────────────────────────────
│ Ξ WeatherMap
│ reg?: Region
│ deg!: Z
├───────────────────────────────────────────────────
│ reg? ∈ known
│ reg? ↦ deg! ∈ temp
└───────────────────────────────────────────────────
```

Note that I have written $reg? \mapsto deg! \in temp$ here. This is done in order to emphasize the fact that in Z functions are just sets of ordered pairs which satisfy the property mentioned in section 6.1. It could have been written as $temp(reg?) = deg!$ using the more familiar notation for function application.

6.3 Constrained Functions

6.3.1 Introduction

There are quite a few different kinds of function in Z and they can be classified in several ways. For example, every function in Z can be thought of as either having or lacking each of the following four properties, namely those of

being definitely finite,

being definitely total,

being definitely injective or one-to-one and

being definitely surjective or onto.

6.3.2 Potentially Non-finite Functions

The collection of all partial functions from X to Y that has already been discussed is the least constrained of all the various collections of functions from X to Y that exist in Z in the sense that all the other collections are subsets of $X \nrightarrow Y$.

A function f from X to Y is *total* if dom $f = X$. The collection of all total functions from X to Y is symbolized as $X \longrightarrow Y$ and is defined like this:

$$X \longrightarrow Y == \{ f: X \nrightarrow Y \mid \text{dom } f = X \}.$$

A function f from X to Y is *one-to-one* or *injective* if $f(x_1) = f(x_2)$ implies that $x_1 = x_2$. The collection of all partial injections from X to Y is symbolized as $X \rightarrowtail Y$ and is defined like this:

$$X \rightarrowtail Y == \{ f: X \nrightarrow Y \mid (\forall x_1, x_2: \text{dom } f \bullet f(x_1) = f(x_2) \Rightarrow x_1 = x_2) \}.$$

A function f from X to Y is *onto* or *surjective* if ran $f = Y$. The collection of all partial surjections from X to Y is symbolized as $X \twoheadrightarrow Y$ and is defined in this way:

$$X \twoheadrightarrow Y == \{ f: X \nrightarrow Y \mid \text{ran } f = Y \}.$$

There are also arrows in Z which allow us to represent all the total injections, all the total surjections and all the bijections from X to Y. These are defined, respectively, in these ways:

$$X \rightarrowtail Y == (X \rightarrowtail Y) \cap (X \longrightarrow Y),$$
$$X \longrightarrow\!\!\!\!\rightarrow Y == (X \twoheadrightarrow Y) \cap (X \longrightarrow Y),$$
$$X \rightarrowtail\!\!\!\rightarrow Y == (X \longrightarrow\!\!\!\!\rightarrow Y) \cap (X \rightarrowtail Y).$$

For some reason Z does not contain a way of concisely referring to all the partial surjective injections (or partial injective surjections) from X to Y, but this set can be symbolized as $X \rightarrowtail\!\!\!\rightarrow Y$ and it can be defined in this way:

$$X \rightarrowtail\!\!\!\rightarrow Y == (X \rightarrowtail Y) \cap (X \twoheadrightarrow Y).$$

The different kinds of function that have been discussed in this section are shown in Table 6.1, where their various defining properties are also given.

6.3.3 Finite Functions

A *finite partial function* from X to Y is a partial function from X to Y whose domain is a finite subset of X. The set of all finite partial functions from X to Y is symbolized as $X \nrightarrow\!\!\!\!\rightarrow Y$ and is defined like this:

$$X \nrightarrow\!\!\!\!\rightarrow Y == \{ f: X \nrightarrow Y \mid \text{dom } f \in \mathbf{F}\, X \},$$

where $\mathbf{F}\, X$ means the set of all the finite subsets of X. A *finite injective function* is a finite function whose inverse is also a function. The set of all finite partial injections from X to Y can be defined like this:

$$X \rightarrowtail\!\!\!\!\rightarrow Y == \{ f: X \nrightarrow\!\!\!\!\rightarrow Y \mid f^{\sim} \in Y \nrightarrow\!\!\!\!\rightarrow X \}.$$

name	symbol	definitely total	definitely onto	definitely one-to-one
partial functions	$X \nrightarrow Y$	no	no	no
partial injections	$X \rightarrowtail\mkern-14mu\rightarrow Y$	no	no	yes
partial surjections	$X \nrightarrow\mkern-8mu\rightarrow Y$	no	yes	no
partial surjective injections	$X \rightarrowtail\mkern-14mu\rightarrow Y$	no	yes	yes
total functions	$X \rightarrow Y$	yes	no	no
total injections	$X \rightarrowtail Y$	yes	no	yes
total surjections	$X \twoheadrightarrow Y$	yes	yes	no
bijections	$X \rightarrowtail\mkern-18mu\twoheadrightarrow Y$	yes	yes	yes

Table 6.1: Kinds of function available in Z.

6.4 Function Definition

6.4.1 Enumeration

Small finite functions can be introduced by enumerating all their elements. I did this above in discussing the specification of the weather map when I illustrated a possible value of the partial function *temp*: *Region* $\nrightarrow$ **Z** as follows:

$$temp = \{west \mapsto 17, east \mapsto -3, south \mapsto 8, north \mapsto 0\}.$$

6.4.2 Set Comprehension

A function in Z is just a set of ordered pairs, so it can be specified by means of set comprehension. For example, the function *square*, which takes an integer as its argument and returns the square of that integer as its value, can be defined thus:

$$square == \{\, x \colon \mathbf{Z} \bullet x \mapsto x * x \,\}.$$

6.4.3 The λ-notation

The λ-notation is a very useful way of defining functions in Z. In using it, however, it is important not to forget that a function in Z is just a relation which has the property that every element in its domain is mapped to a single element in its range. Do not confuse the λ-notation of Z with the λ-calculus. Many of the characteristic features of the λ-calculus, such as the self-application of functions, are not possible with Z's λ-notation because they would violate the type discipline.[1]

As an example of the use of the λ-notation consider the problem of defining a function *cube* which cubes its argument. This can be done in this way:

$$cube == \lambda x \colon \mathbf{Z} \bullet x * x * x.$$

---

[1]There are several good books available on the λ-calculus. (Hindley and Seldin 1986) is a clear introduction to the subject and (Barendregt 1984) is a thorough treatment of the type-free λ-calculus.

The λ-term here is equivalent to the set comprehension $\{\, x\colon \mathbf{Z} \bullet x \mapsto x * x * x \,\}$. A λ-term $\lambda x\colon X \mid P \bullet t$, where P is a formula and t is a term, is defined in Z to mean exactly the same as $\{\, x\colon X \mid P \bullet x \mapsto t \,\}$. In fact, in general we have:

$$\lambda x_1\colon X_1; \ldots; x_n\colon X_n \mid P \bullet t == \{\, x_1\colon X_1; \ldots; x_n\colon X_n \mid P \bullet (x_1, \ldots, x_n) \mapsto t \,\}.$$

Related to the λ-notation is the topic of currying.[2] This is best explained by means of an example. The standard integer addition function $\_ + \_$ has type $\mathbf{Z} \times \mathbf{Z} \longrightarrow \mathbf{Z}$. This means that it takes a single (structured) argument, namely an ordered pair consisting of two integers, and returns an integer as its value. Sometimes it is useful to have a *curried* version of $\_ + \_$. I call this *add*. This is a function of type $\mathbf{Z} \longrightarrow (\mathbf{Z} \longrightarrow \mathbf{Z})$ defined like this:

$$add == \lambda i\colon \mathbf{Z} \bullet (\lambda j\colon \mathbf{Z} \bullet i + j).$$

The reason why curried functions are sometimes useful is that they can be partially parameterized. For example, $add\, 3$ is a function of type $\mathbf{Z} \longrightarrow \mathbf{Z}$ which adds 3 to its single integer argument and $add\, 77$ is a function of the same type which adds 77 to its argument.

6.5 Modelling Arrays

Arrays can be modelled in Z as functions from a range of numbers to some arbitrary set from which the elements of the array are drawn. For example, let *ArrMin* and *ArrMax* be integers that represent the two end points of an array of people. If *table* is the name of the array, then

$$table\colon ArrMin \mathinner{\ldotp\ldotp} ArrMax \longrightarrow Person.$$

To access an element in this array we simply apply it to the index of the element we are after. For example, if $i \in ArrMin \mathinner{\ldotp\ldotp} ArrMax$, then $table(i)$ is the person situated at the index i in the array *table*.

Updating an array is done using the overriding operator. If we wanted to replace the person in the array who is at location i by *gray*, then we would write

$$table' = table \oplus \{i \mapsto gray\},$$

where $table'\colon ArrMin \mathinner{\ldotp\ldotp} ArrMax \longrightarrow Person$ is another array of people. It is the same as *table* except that *gray* is located at point i.

A finite array can also be modelled as a partial function or even a finite partial function. If either of these options is chosen, then it becomes possible for there to be locations in the array which are not associated with any member of the set from which the elements of the array are drawn.

---

[2]This has nothing to do with Indian cuisine. The word 'currying' is derived from the surname of the logician Haskell Curry.

7

Sequences

7.1 Fundamental Ideas

The set of *all* finite sequences of elements drawn from a set X is denoted as seq X and to show that σ is a sequence of type seq X we write σ: seq X. Small finite sequences can be written enclosed in angle brackets with their elements separated by commas like this: $\langle x_1, x_2, \ldots, x_n \rangle$. The empty sequence in Z is written as $\langle\,\rangle$. The following are examples of sequences:

$$\langle feb, apr, dec, jan \rangle \in \text{seq } Month,$$
$$\langle 77, 5, 6 \rangle \in \text{seq } \mathbf{N},$$
$$\langle \langle\,\rangle, \langle feb, mar \rangle, \langle apr \rangle \rangle \in \text{seq(seq } Month),$$
$$\langle \{1, 2, 83\}, \varnothing, evens \rangle \in \text{seq}(\mathbf{P}\,\mathbf{N}).$$

7.2 Defining Sequences

The set of all finite sequences that have their elements drawn from X is defined like this:

$$\text{seq } X == \{\, f: \mathbf{N} \nrightarrow X \mid \text{dom } f = 1 \mathinner{.\,.} \#f \,\}.$$

So, a sequence of things drawn from the set X is a finite function from the non-negative whole numbers to X whose domain consists of all the numbers between 1 and $\#f$, that is to say, whose domain is an initial segment of the positive whole numbers. Recall that $\#$ is Z's cardinality operator. Applied to a finite set it returns the number of elements in that set. As already mentioned $\langle feb, apr, dec, jan \rangle$ is a sequence of months. Because of the way in which sequences are defined in Z, this is just another way of expressing the set

$$\{1 \mapsto feb, 2 \mapsto apr, 3 \mapsto dec, 4 \mapsto jan\}.$$

Because sequences are functions you can apply them to numbers. Let σ: seq X. Then $\sigma(1)$ is the first element of σ, $\sigma(2)$ is the second element of σ, $\sigma(3)$ is the third element of σ, and so on, assuming, of course, that they all exist. So, we have:

$$\langle feb, apr, dec, jan \rangle\ (3) = dec,$$
$$\langle feb, apr, dec, jan \rangle\ (1) = feb.$$

Because sequences are functions the empty sequence $\langle\ \rangle$ is just an alternative notation for the empty set $\emptyset$.

If X is a set, then $\mathrm{seq}_1 X$ is the set of all the non-empty, finite sequences which have their elements drawn from the set X and $\mathrm{iseq}\, X$ is the set of all injective sequences drawn from the set X. An injective sequence is one which does not contain any repetitions or duplicates, so $\langle jan, feb, mar \rangle$ is an injective sequence but $\langle jan, feb, jan \rangle$ is not. The sets $\mathrm{seq}_1 X$ and $\mathrm{iseq}\, X$ are defined like this:

$$\mathrm{seq}_1 X == \{\, f \colon \mathrm{seq}\, X \mid f \neq \langle\,\rangle \,\},$$
$$\mathrm{iseq}\, X == \mathrm{seq}\, X \cap (\mathbf{N} \rightarrowtail X).$$

7.3   Sequence Manipulating Functions

Concatenation for Sequences

Given two arbitrary sequences σ and τ, of the same type, $\sigma \frown \tau$ is the sequence which results from sticking them together, for example,

$$\langle jan, feb \rangle \frown \langle mar, apr, may \rangle = \langle jan, feb, mar, apr, may \rangle.$$

The formal definition of the concatenation operator is:

$$
\begin{array}{|l}
\hline
= [X] =\! \\
\ \_ \frown \_ \colon (\mathrm{seq}\, X) \times (\mathrm{seq}\, X) \longrightarrow (\mathrm{seq}\, X) \\
\hline
\forall \sigma, \tau \colon \mathrm{seq}\, X\ \bullet \\
\quad \sigma \frown \tau = \sigma \cup \{\, n \colon \mathrm{dom}\, \tau \ \bullet\ n + \#\sigma \mapsto \tau(n) \,\} \\
\hline
\end{array}
$$

The 'box' used in this definition, namely

$$
\begin{array}{|l}
\hline
= [X] =\! \\
x \colon X \\
\hline
P \\
\hline
\end{array}
$$

introduces a *generic definition*. It defines a whole family of variables x of generic type X which satisfy some formula P. When we actually come to use x we have to supply an actual type instead of the parameter X. For example, if we were dealing with numbers we would write $x[\mathbf{N}]$ and if we were dealing with European states we would write $x[Europe]$ and so on. Often the actual type is omitted when it can be deduced from the context.

The Functions *head, last, front* **and** *tail*

Given a non-empty sequence $\sigma: \mathrm{seq}_1 X$, *head* σ is the first element of σ, *last* σ is the last element of σ, *front* σ is the initial segment of σ which consists of all the elements of σ except the last and *tail* σ is the sequence which consists of all the members of σ except the first. For example,

$$head\langle jan, feb, mar, apr\rangle = jan,$$
$$last\langle jan, feb, mar, apr\rangle = apr,$$
$$front\langle jan, feb, mar, apr\rangle = \langle jan, feb, mar\rangle,$$
$$tail\langle jan, feb, mar, apr\rangle = \langle feb, mar, apr\rangle.$$

Let $\sigma: \mathrm{seq}_1 X$ be a non-empty sequence of elements drawn from X. Then the following two laws hold for σ:

$$\langle head\, \sigma\rangle \frown (tail\, \sigma) = \sigma,$$
$$(front\, \sigma) \frown \langle last\, \sigma\rangle = \sigma.$$

Filtering and Extraction

Let *winter* be the set of all the winter months. In Britain we have

$$winter = \{sep, oct, nov, dec, jan, feb, mar, apr\}.$$

The filtering operator $\upharpoonright$ has the following effect:

$$\langle jun, nov, feb, jul\rangle \upharpoonright winter = \langle nov, feb\rangle.$$

In general, if $\sigma: \mathrm{seq}\, X$ and $V \subseteq X$, then $\sigma \upharpoonright V$ is that sequence whose elements occur in the set V and the order in which those elements occur in $\sigma \upharpoonright V$ is the same as that in which they occur in σ.

Let *evens* be the set of positive even numbers. Then the extraction operator $\upharpoonleft$ has the following effect:

$$evens \upharpoonleft \langle jun, nov, feb, jul\rangle = \langle nov, jul\rangle.$$

In general, if $U \subseteq \mathbf{N}_1$ and $\sigma: \mathrm{seq}\, X$, then $U \upharpoonleft \sigma$ is that sequence of elements in σ that occur at a position in σ whose index occurs in the set U.

The Functions *after* **and** *drop*

Given a sequence σ and a natural number n, then σ *after* n is the sequence obtained by dropping the first n elements of σ, for example,

$$\langle jan, feb, mar, apr, may\rangle \text{ after } 3 = \langle apr, may\rangle.$$

It is sometimes useful to have a curried version of *after*; this is known as *drop*:

$$drop == \lambda n: \mathbf{N} \bullet (\lambda \sigma: \mathrm{seq}\, X \bullet \sigma \text{ after } n).$$

Note that the functions *after* and *drop* are not part of standard Z.

The Functions *for* and *take*

Given a sequence σ and a natural number n, σ *for* n is the sequence made up out of the first n elements of σ, for example,

$$\langle may, jun, jul, aug \rangle \; for \; 2 = \langle may, jun \rangle.$$

It is sometimes useful to have a curried version of *for*; this is known as *take*:

$$take == \lambda n \colon \mathbf{N} \bullet (\lambda \sigma \colon seq X \bullet \sigma \; for \; n).$$

Note that the functions *for* and *take* are not part of standard Z.

Reversing a Sequence

Given an arbitrary sequence σ, *rev* σ is the sequence which contains just the same elements as σ, but in reverse order, for example,

$$rev\langle aug, sep, oct, dec \rangle = \langle dec, oct, sep, aug \rangle.$$

Distributed Concatenation

In the first section of this chapter I had the following example of a sequence:

$$\langle\langle \; \rangle, \langle feb, mar \rangle, \langle apr \rangle\rangle \in seq(seq \; Month).$$

Applying the distributed concatenation operator $^\frown/$ to this yields a sequence of months:

$$^\frown/\langle\langle \; \rangle, \langle feb, mar \rangle, \langle apr \rangle\rangle = \langle feb, mar, apr \rangle.$$

More generally, if xss is a sequence of sequences whose elements belong to X, then $^\frown/\, xss$ is that sequence of elements drawn from X which results when all the sequences in xss have been concatenated together. Thus, if $xss \colon seq(seq X)$ is a sequence, then $^\frown/\, xss$ is $xss(1) ^\frown xss(2) ^\frown \ldots ^\frown xss(\#xss)$ and this belongs to the set $seq X$.

Disjointness and Partitioning

In discussing the specification of the internal telephone directory I said—on p. 56 above—that the sets *staff* and *proles* partition the set *known*. This was captured by means of the two formulas:

$$staff \cup proles = known,$$
$$staff \cap proles = \varnothing.$$

The two sets *staff* and *proles* are said to be *disjoint* and together they *partition* the set *known*. Because the ideas of disjointness and partitioning crop up quite frequently in specifications, there is a concise way of expressing them in Z. We can write:

$$disjoint \; \langle staff, proles \rangle,$$
$$\langle staff, proles \rangle \; partition \; known.$$

These relations also work for sequences of any length. In fact, the definition of these operators in (Spivey 1992), p. 122, is even more general, since it does not just apply to sequences of sets but to any indexed family of sets.

7.4   Exercises

7.1) Let $\sigma, \tau, \upsilon: \operatorname{seq} \mathit{Char}$ be sequences of characters defined like this:

$$\sigma == \langle \mathtt{A}, \mathtt{C}, \mathtt{K} \rangle,$$
$$\tau == \langle \mathtt{B}, \mathtt{L} \rangle,$$
$$\upsilon == \langle \mathtt{J} \rangle.$$

What are the following sequences?

a) $(\tau \frown \sigma) \frown (\upsilon \frown \sigma)$.

b) $\mathit{head}(\mathit{front}(\tau \frown \sigma))$.

c) $\mathit{last}(\mathit{front}(\tau \frown \sigma))$.

d) $\mathit{tail}(\mathit{front}(\tau \frown \sigma))$.

e) $\sigma \frown \tau$.

f) $\mathit{rev}(\sigma \frown \tau)$.

g) $\operatorname{dom}(\sigma \frown \tau)$.

h) $\operatorname{ran}(\sigma \frown \tau)$.

i) $(\sigma \frown \tau)^\sim$.

j) $(\sigma \frown \tau)^\sim \, \mathbin{;} \mathit{succ}^\sim \mathbin{;} (\sigma \frown \tau)$.

k) $(\{\mathtt{E} \mapsto 4, \mathtt{R} \mapsto 5\} \cup \sigma^\sim)^\sim$.

l) $(\sigma \frown \tau) \rhd \{\mathtt{A}, \mathtt{E}, \mathtt{I}, \mathtt{O}, \mathtt{U}\}$.

m) $(\tau \frown \sigma) \oplus \{3 \mapsto \mathtt{O}\}$.

n) $\{1 \mapsto 2, 2 \mapsto 1, 3 \mapsto 4, 4 \mapsto 5, 5 \mapsto 3\} \mathbin{;} ((\sigma \frown \tau) \oplus \{3 \mapsto \mathtt{E}\})$.

8

Bags

8.1 Introduction

This chapter is about bags, which sometimes are known as *families* or *multi-sets*. A bag of things is similar to a set in that the order of the elements is not important, but—unlike a set—the number of occurrences of each object in the bag is significant. Small finite bags can be written with 'fat' square brackets ⟦...⟧ enclosing the members of the bag, for example,

$$\llbracket bell, bell, cox, dove, dove, dove \rrbracket.$$

In this bag *bell* occurs twice, *cox* once and *dove* three times. Bags are like sets in that the elements of a bag are not ordered in any way. Thus, the bag just mentioned could be written:

$$\llbracket dove, bell, dove, bell, dove, cox \rrbracket.$$

This is a bag of people. Let *Person* denote the type of all people. Then bag *Person* is the type of all bags of people. In Z a bag is a partial function whose from-set is the set from which the elements of the bag are drawn and whose to-set is the set of positive whole numbers, so:

$$\text{bag } Person == Person \nrightarrow \mathbb{N}_1.$$

The bag considered above is thus the function $\{bell \mapsto 2, cox \mapsto 1, dove \mapsto 3\}$. In general, we have that bag $X == X \nrightarrow \mathbb{N}_1$. The empty bag is written as ⟦ ⟧ and this is identical to the empty set $\emptyset$.

8.2 Bag Manipulating Functions

The function *count* tells you how many times an object occurs in a bag. Let

$$L == \llbracket bell, bell, cox, dove, dove, dove \rrbracket.$$

Then we have:

$$count\ L\ bell = 2,$$
$$count\ L\ dove = 3,$$
$$count\ L\ earl = 0,$$
$$count\ L\ fry = 0.$$

Note that if a person x is not a member of the bag L, then $count\ L\ x$ is zero. Spivey (1992), p. 124, introduces the symbol $\sharp$ so that $L\ \sharp\ x$ is equivalent in every way to $count\ L\ x$.

The relation $\sqsubseteq$ holds between an object and a bag just in case that object is a member of the bag. It is analogous to the set membership relation $\in$. Using the previous example once again, we have that both $bell \sqsubseteq L$ and $\neg(earl \sqsubseteq L)$.[1]

If the bags L and M are both of the same type, then L is a sub-bag of M if each element of L also occurs in M and the number of times that it occurs in M is at least the same as the number of times that it occurs in L. To indicate that L is a sub-bag of M we write $L \sqsubseteq M$ and we have the following useful property:

$$L \sqsubseteq M \iff (\forall x\!:\! X \bullet count\ L\ x \leq count\ M\ x),$$

where $L, M\!:\! \text{bag}\ X$. The sub-bag relation is reflexive, antisymmetric and transitive:

$$L \sqsubseteq L,$$
$$L \sqsubseteq M \wedge M \sqsubseteq L \Rightarrow L = M,$$
$$L \sqsubseteq M \wedge M \sqsubseteq N \Rightarrow L \sqsubseteq N,$$

where $L, M, N\!:\! \text{bag}\ X$, for some set X. Thus, the sub-bag relation is a partial order in the world of bags.

The analogue in bag theory of set union is bag union, symbolized as $\uplus$. Here is an example of its use:

$$\{bell \mapsto 2,\ cox \mapsto 1, dove \mapsto 3\} \uplus \{bell \mapsto 3, earl \mapsto 1\}$$
$$= \{bell \mapsto 5, cox \mapsto 1, dove \mapsto 3, earl \mapsto 1\}.$$

In general, the number of times an object occurs in $L \uplus M$, where L and M are bags of the same type, is the sum of the number of times it occurs in L and in M. Bag union is not idempotent, but it is commutative and associative and the empty bag is a two-sided unit for it:

$$L \uplus M = M \uplus L,$$
$$(L \uplus M) \uplus N = L \uplus (M \uplus N),$$
$$L \uplus [\![\ ]\!] = L,$$
$$[\![\ ]\!] \uplus L = L,$$

where $L, M, N\!:\! \text{bag}\ X$, for some set X.

---

[1] Note that the symbol $\sqsubseteq$ was introduced in (Spivey 1992), p. 125. Previously, the symbol 'in' was used for bag membership.

The symbol ⊓ is used to represent what Hayes (1993), p. 258, calls the 'pairwise minimum of two bags'. Let L and M be bags belonging to the same type. Then the number of times that an object occurs in $L \sqcap M$ is the lesser of the two numbers which are the number of times that it occurs in L and the number of times that it occurs in M. For example,

$$\{fry \mapsto 7,\ earl \mapsto 2,\ gray \mapsto 89\} \sqcap \{hart \mapsto 11, fry \mapsto 2\}$$
$$= \{fry \mapsto 2\}.$$

The operator ⊓ is idempotent, commutative and associative, but it does not have a unit element:

$$L \sqcap L = L,$$
$$L \sqcap M = M \sqcap L,$$
$$(L \sqcap M) \sqcap N = L \sqcap (M \sqcap N),$$

where L, M and N are all bags belonging to the same type. Note that the pairwise minimum of two bags is not part of standard Z.

The symbol ⊔ is used to represent what Hayes (1993), p. 258, calls the 'pairwise maximum of two bags'. Let L and M be bags belonging to the same type. Then the number of times that an object occurs in $L \sqcup M$ is the greater of the two numbers which are the number of times that it occurs in L and the number of times that it occurs in M. For example,

$$\{fry \mapsto 7,\ earl \mapsto 2,\ gray \mapsto 89\} \sqcup \{hart \mapsto 11, fry \mapsto 2\}$$
$$= \{fry \mapsto 7,\ earl \mapsto 2,\ gray \mapsto 89,\ hart \mapsto 11\}.$$

The operator ⊔ is idempotent, commutative and associative and the empty bag is a two-sided unit for it:

$$L \sqcup L = L,$$
$$L \sqcup M = M \sqcup L,$$
$$(L \sqcup M) \sqcup N = L \sqcup (M \sqcup N),$$
$$L \sqcup [\![\,]\!] = L,$$
$$[\![\,]\!] \sqcup L = L,$$

where L, M and N are all bags belonging to the same type. Note that the pairwise maximum of two bags is not part of standard Z.

Given a sequence, the function *items* returns the bag of elements of the sequence, for example,

$$items\langle bell,\ earl,\ bell,\ bell \rangle = \{bell \mapsto 3,\ earl \mapsto 1\}.$$

8.3   A Specification of Sorting

The first example of a specification that I am going to give in this chapter is that of sorting a sequence of things into non-decreasing order. This will make use of both sequences and bags. The problem that I am going to specify requires that we are given a sequence *in?* of objects drawn from some set X and that the output of the operation must be a sequence *out!* in which all the elements occur in non-decreasing order. (I say 'non-decreasing' rather than 'increasing' in order to allow for the possibility of duplicates.) We can only sort things belonging to the set X if there is available a total order defined on the elements of X. A total order $F: X \leftrightarrow X$ is a relation which is reflexive, antisymmetric and transitive and which has the property that every object in X is related to every other object in X. An example of a total order is $\leq$ on the integers. The set of all total orders defined on the set X is represented as *totord X*.

In order to specify the operation of sorting using Z we need to define a generic function *nondecreasing*: $(X \leftrightarrow X) \longrightarrow \mathbf{P}(\operatorname{seq} X)$, which, given a total order as its argument, yields the set of all sequences that are in non-decreasing order according to that total order.

$$
\begin{array}{l}
= [X] = \\
\hline
\quad nondecreasing: (X \leftrightarrow X) \longrightarrow \mathbf{P}(\operatorname{seq} X) \\
\hline
\quad \forall F: X \leftrightarrow X; \sigma: \operatorname{seq} X \bullet \\
\qquad \sigma \in nondecreasing\, F \iff \\
\qquad\qquad (\forall i, j: \operatorname{dom} \sigma \mid i < j \bullet \sigma(i) \mapsto \sigma(j) \in F)
\end{array}
$$

Clearly, *nondecreasing F* is a set of sequences in non-decreasing order iff F is a total order. The specification of sorting can now be given as:

$$
\begin{array}{l}
\_\, Sort[X] \_ \\
\hline
\quad in?, out!: \operatorname{seq} X \\
\quad rel?: X \leftrightarrow X \\
\hline
\quad rel? \in totord\, X \\
\quad out! \in nondecreasing[X]\, rel? \\
\quad items(out!) = items(in?)
\end{array}
$$

We have to input the relation *rel?* because many different total orders can be defined on the same set. The output of the sort is non-decreasing. The output sequence must contain the same items as the input with the same frequency and this is captured by means of the formula $items(out!) = items(in?)$.

8.4   The Specification of a Vending Machine

8.4.1   Introduction

In order to specify a vending machine we need a set *Good* of all the items that can be bought from the machine. At any given time only a subset of *Good* will actually be available from the machine. The basic type *Good*, therefore, must be introduced by means of a basic type definition:

$$[Good]$$

The constant *Capacity* represents the maximum number of items of any sort that can be stored in the machine. The way such constants are introduced into a Z specification document is by means of an axiomatic description as follows:

$$| \ Capacity: \mathbf{N}$$

The state of the machine is specified by means of the schema *VendingMachine*:

```
┌─ VendingMachine ──────────────────────────────
│  coin: P N
│  cost: Good ⇸ N
│  stock: bag Good
│  float: bag N
├───────────────────────────────────────────────
│  dom stock ⊆ dom cost
│  dom float ⊆ coin
│  quantity(stock) ≤ Capacity
└───────────────────────────────────────────────
```

The set *coin* is the set of all acceptable coins. A coin is identified with its value in pence. The function *cost* returns the value of a good in pence. For example,

$$cost(aero) = 17,$$
$$cost(crisps) = 19,$$
$$cost(kitkat) = 19.$$

The bag *stock* records how many items of each type of good are currently stored in the machine. For example, if *stock* was equal to the bag

$$\{aero \mapsto 3, crisps \mapsto 11, kitkat \mapsto 1\}$$

this would tell us that currently the stock of the machine consists of 3 Aero bars, 11 bags of crisps and a single Kit Kat. The bag *float* records how many coins of each type are currently in the machine. For example, if *float* was equal to the bag

$$\{100 \mapsto 2, 20 \mapsto 3, 10 \mapsto 1, 2 \mapsto 57, 1 \mapsto 13\}$$

this would tell us that the float consists of two pound coins, three 20 pence coins, one 10 pence coin, 57 two-penny coins and 13 one-penny coins.

The formula dom *stock* ⊆ dom *cost* says that everything in the machine must have a price associated with it. The formula dom *float* ⊆ *coin* says that the money contained in this machine must be made up out of acceptable coins. The formula

$$quantity(stock) \leq Capacity$$

states that the total capacity of the machine must not be exceeded. The function *quantity* is not part of standard Z, but it can be defined as follows:

```
╔═[X]═══════════════════════════════════════════
║  quantity: bag X → N
╟───────────────────────────────────────────────
║  ∀x: X; j: N; L: bag X •
║     quantity⟦ ⟧ = 0 ∧
║     quantity({x ↦ j} ⊎ L) = j + quantity L
╚═══════════════════════════════════════════════
```

What the function *quantity* does is to take a bag of things and return the number of occurrences of any of them. For example,

$$quantity\{aero \mapsto 3, crisps \mapsto 11, kitkat \mapsto 1\} = 3 + 11 + 1 = 15.$$

The schemas Δ *VendingMachine* and Ξ *VendingMachine* are defined in the standard way:

$$\Delta VendingMachine \triangleq VendingMachine \wedge VendingMachine',$$

$$\Xi VendingMachine \triangleq [\Delta VendingMachine \mid \theta VendingMachine' = \theta VendingMachine].$$

Initially, the vending machine is empty. The initial state is given by means of the schema *InitVendingMachine'*, where *InitVendingMachine* is defined as follows:

```
┌─ InitVendingMachine ──────────────────────────────
│ VendingMachine
├───────────────────────────────────────────────────
│ coin = ∅
│ cost = ∅
│ stock = [ ]
│ float = [ ]
└───────────────────────────────────────────────────
```

Note that initially the function *cost'* is empty. This means that the machine—to begin with—contains no record of how much any item costs. Similarly, *coin'* is empty. To get the machine working both of these sets have to be updated.

8.4.2 Pricing Goods

The first operation that I am going to specify is that of giving a good a particular price. It can also be used to reprice an item that already has a price associated with it. This is straightforward:

```
┌─ Price ────────────────────────────────────────────
│ Δ VendingMachine
│ article?: Good
│ price?: N
├───────────────────────────────────────────────────
│ cost' = cost ⊕ {article? ↦ price?}
│ coin' = coin
│ stock' = stock
│ float' = float
└───────────────────────────────────────────────────
```

The item *article?* is the good that is having its price fixed and *price?* is how much it costs. The operation *Price* always succeeds. We can give a price to an item which the machine does not currently stock. Therefore, the total specification is given by:

$$DoPrice \triangleq Price \wedge Success,$$

where the schema *Success* is defined as follows:

```
┌─ Success ────────────────────────────────
│ rep!: Report
├──────────────────────────────────────────
│ rep! = 'Okay'
└──────────────────────────────────────────
```

8.4.3 Acceptable Coins

The next operation involves telling the machine that a particular coin is now acceptable.

```
┌─ Accept ─────────────────────────────────
│ ΔVendingMachine
│ den?: N
├──────────────────────────────────────────
│ den? ∉ coin
│ coin' = coin ∪ {den?}
│ cost' = cost
│ stock' = stock
│ float' = float
└──────────────────────────────────────────
```

The input *den?* ('denomination') represents the value of the coin that is now acceptable. The schema *Accept* has only a single precondition, namely the formula $den? \notin coin$; hence we need to cope with the situation in which this is not satisfied. This is accomplished by means of the following schema:

```
┌─ AlreadyAcceptable ──────────────────────
│ ΞVendingMachine
│ den?: N
│ rep!: Report
├──────────────────────────────────────────
│ den? ∈ coin
│ rep! = 'Coin already acceptable'
└──────────────────────────────────────────
```

The total operation of getting the machine to accept coins of a new denomination is *DoAccept*, which is defined in what, by now, must be a very familiar way to the reader:

$$DoAccept \triangleq Accept \land Success$$
$$\lor$$
$$AlreadyAcceptable.$$

8.4.4 Restocking

The next operation that I am going to specify is that of restocking the machine with more goods.

___ *ReStock* _____
Δ *VendingMachine*
new?: bag *Good*
_____
dom *new?* $\subseteq$ dom *cost*
stock $\sqcap$ *new?* = [[ ]]
quantity(*stock* $\uplus$ *new?*) $\leq$ *Capacity*
stock' = *stock* $\uplus$ *new?*
coin' = *coin*
cost' = *cost*
float' = *float*
_____

The input variable *new?* represents the bag of goods that are being used to restock the machine. The operation specified by means of the schema *ReStock* can go wrong in three different ways. It goes wrong if either of the following three preconditions are violated:

$$\text{dom } new? \subseteq \text{dom } cost, \tag{8.1}$$
$$stock \sqcap new? = [[\ ]], \tag{8.2}$$
$$quantity(stock \uplus new?) \leq Capacity. \tag{8.3}$$

The precondition (8.1) is not satisfied in any situation in which it is attempted to add some goods to the machine which do not have prices associated with them. What happens in that situation is specified by means of the schema *GoodsNotPriced*.

___ *GoodsNotPriced* _____
Ξ *VendingMachine*
new?: bag *Good*
rep!: *Report*
_____
$\neg$(dom *new?* $\subseteq$ dom *cost*)
rep! = 'Some goods are unpriced'
_____

The precondition (8.2) is not satisfied in any situation in which it is attempted to restock the machine with items that are already present in it. When (8.2) is not satisfied the schema *AlreadyStocked* specifies what happens:

___ *AlreadyStocked* _____
Ξ *VendingMachine*
new?: bag *Good*
rep!: *Report*
_____
stock $\sqcap$ *new?* $\neq$ [[ ]]
rep! = 'Cannot restock with previously stocked items'
_____

The precondition (8.3) is not satisfied in any situation in which it is attempted to restock the vending machine with too many things. When (8.3) is not satisfied the schema *CapacityExceeded* specifies what happens:

```
┌─ CapacityExceeded ──────────────────────────────
│ Ξ VendingMachine
│ new?: bag Good
│ rep!: Report
├─────────────────────────────────────────────────
│ quantity(stock ⊎ new?) > Capacity
│ rep! = 'Capacity exceeded'
└─────────────────────────────────────────────────
```

The total operation of restocking the machine with items to be sold is called *DoReStock* and it is defined in this way:

$$DoReStock \triangleq ReStock \wedge Success$$
$$\vee$$
$$GoodsNotPriced$$
$$\vee$$
$$AlreadyStocked$$
$$\vee$$
$$CapacityExceeded.$$

8.4.5 Buying

The next thing that I am going to specify is the operation of somebody buying an item from the vending machine. In the schema *Buy* the variable *in?* represents the coins that the buyer inserts into the machine and the variable *out!* represents the coins that the machine outputs as change. The buyer also needs to tell the machine what item he wants to buy from it. This is done by means of the input variable *article?* Note that *article?* is an input variable. It represents the information conveyed to the machine concerning which item is being bought.

```
┌─ Buy ───────────────────────────────────────────
│ Δ VendingMachine
│ in?, out!: bag N
│ article?: Good
├─────────────────────────────────────────────────
│ article? ∈ dom stock
│ sumbag(in?) ≥ cost(article?)
│ out! ⊑ float
│ dom in? ⊆ coin
│ sumbag(in?) = sumbag(out!) + cost(article?)
│ stock' ⊎ {article? ↦ 1} = stock
│ float' ⊎ out! = float ⊎ in?
│ coin' = coin
│ cost' = cost
└─────────────────────────────────────────────────
```

The function *sumbag* that is used in the schema *Buy* is not part of standard Z. It calculates the total value of a bag of numbers. For example,

$$sumbag\{2 \mapsto 7, 5 \mapsto 3\} = 14 + 15 = 29.$$

It is defined like this:

$$
\begin{array}{|l}
sumbag \colon \mathrm{bag}\,\mathbf{N} \longrightarrow \mathbf{N} \\
\hline
\forall i, j \colon \mathbf{N};\ L \colon \mathrm{bag}\,\mathbf{N}\ \bullet \\
\quad sumbag[\![\,]\!] = 0\ \wedge \\
\quad sumbag(\{i \mapsto j\} \uplus L) = i * j + sumbag\ L
\end{array}
$$

Note that I have used bag union in the definition of $sumbag$.

The formula $article? \in \mathrm{dom}\ stock$ is one of the preconditions of the operation Buy. You can only buy something from the vending machine if it is in the machine. The formula $out! \sqsubseteq float$ is another precondition of Buy. You cannot buy something from this machine if the machine does not have the correct amount of change to give you. The precondition $\mathrm{dom}\ in? \subseteq coin$ says that only acceptable coins can be used to buy goods. The formula

$$
sumbag(in?) = sumbag(out!) + cost(article?)
$$

says that the amount of money you put into the machine must have exactly the same value as the price of the thing you are buying added to your change. The formula

$$
stock' \uplus \{article? \mapsto 1\} = stock
$$

says that the item you buy from the machine is taken out of the machine and the formula

$$
float' \uplus out! = float \uplus in?
$$

says that the total value of the money in the machine is increased by the cost of the item you buy. This is because

$$
cost(article?) = sumbag(in?) - sumbag(out!).
$$

The operation specified by Buy can go wrong in four ways, namely if the item requested is not currently in stock, if the customer inserts too little money into the machine, if the machine does not have the exact change needed and if the customer tries to insert a coin which is not acceptable. What happens when the formula $article? \in \mathrm{dom}\ stock$ is not satisfied is specified by means of the schema $NotInStock$:

$$
\begin{array}{|l}
\underline{\quad NotInStock \quad\rule{6cm}{0pt}} \\
\Xi\,VendingMachine \\
article? \colon Good \\
rep! \colon Report \\
\hline
article? \notin \mathrm{dom}\ stock \\
rep! = \text{`Item not in stock'}
\end{array}
$$

What happens when the formula $sumbag(in?) \geq cost(article?)$ is not satisfied is specified by means of the schema $TooLittleMoney$:

```
┌─ TooLittleMoney ──────────────────────────────────────
│ Ξ VendingMachine
│ in?: bag N
│ article?: Good
│ rep!: Report
├───────────────────────────────────────────────────────
│ sumbag(in?) < cost(article?)
│ rep! = 'Insert more money'
└───────────────────────────────────────────────────────
```

What happens when the machine does not have the correct change to give is specified by means of the schema *ExactChangeUnavailable*. In this case the customer gets his money back. This is represented by means of the formula $out! = in?$

```
┌─ ExactChangeUnavailable ──────────────────────────────
│ Ξ VendingMachine
│ in?, out!: bag N
│ article?: Good
│ rep!: Report
├───────────────────────────────────────────────────────
│ ¬∃L: bag N • (L ⊑ float ∧ sumbag(in?) = sumbag(L) + cost(article?))
│ out! = in?
│ rep! = 'Correct change unavailable'
└───────────────────────────────────────────────────────
```

When the formula ran $in? \subseteq coin$ is not satisfied the schema *ForeignCoin* specifies what happens.

```
┌─ ForeignCoin ─────────────────────────────────────────
│ Ξ VendingMachine
│ in?: bag N
│ rep!: Report
├───────────────────────────────────────────────────────
│ ¬(ran in? ⊆ coin)
│ rep! = 'Unacceptable coin'
└───────────────────────────────────────────────────────
```

The total operation of someone buying an article from the vending machine is specified by means of the schema *DoBuy*, which is defined as follows:

$$DoBuy \triangleq Buy \wedge Success$$
$$\vee$$
$$NotInStock$$
$$\vee$$
$$TooLittleMoney$$
$$\vee$$
$$ExactChangeUnavailable$$
$$\vee$$
$$ForeignCoin.$$

8.4.6   Profit Taking

The final operation that I am going to specify here is that of money being removed
from the machine:

```
┌─ RemoveMoney ─────────────────────────────────────────────
│ Δ VendingMachine
│ profit!: bag N
├───────────────────────────────────────────────────────────
│ float' ⊎ profit! = float
│ coin' = coin
│ cost' = cost
│ stock' = stock
│
└───────────────────────────────────────────────────────────
```

The operation *RemoveMoney* goes wrong if you try removing money which is not
present in the machine.

```
┌─ Profiteering ────────────────────────────────────────────
│ Ξ VendingMachine
│ profit!: bag N
│ rep!: Report
├───────────────────────────────────────────────────────────
│ ¬∃L: bag N • (float' ⊎ L = float ∧ profit! = L)
│ rep! = 'Such profit non-existent'
└───────────────────────────────────────────────────────────
```

The total operation of money being removed legitimately from the machine is specified
by means of the schema *DoRemoveMoney*.

$$DoRemoveMoney \triangleq RemoveMoney \wedge Success$$
$$\vee$$
$$Profiteering.$$

9

Free Types

9.1 Introduction

Recursive structures, like lists and trees, are used very frequently in software engineering and in this chapter I show how lists of integers can be defined as *free types* in Z. Then I develop a specification of a proof-checker and theorem-prover for a Hilbert-style formalization of the propositional calculus. The set of well-formed formulas of the propositional calculus is defined to be a free type. To conclude the chapter I show how free types are formally defined in Z. This is done to emphasize the point that Z's free type notation is merely syntactic sugar. It adds nothing to the power of the language. A specification involving free types can be mechanically transformed into one in which they do not appear.

9.2 Lists as a Free Type

Although standard Z contains sequences and various operators defined on sequences, in order to illustrate how a free type is defined in Z I show how the type of all lists of integers can be defined.[1] It is done as follows:

$$List ::= nil \mid cons\langle\!\langle \mathbf{Z} \times List \rangle\!\rangle.$$

This says that a list is either the empty list *nil* or it is constructed from an integer and a list by applying the function *cons* to them in that order. The type of the constant *nil* is *List* and the function *cons* belongs to the set $\mathbf{Z} \times List \rightarrowtail List$. The list consisting of the integers 7, 13, 2 and 8, in that order, is represented by the term:

$$cons(7, cons(13, cons(2, cons(8, nil)))).$$

If we define $List_1$ to be $List \setminus \{nil\}$, then the familiar functions *car* and *cdr* can be defined like this:

---

[1] Note that it is impossible in Z to define, say, *List X*, that is to say, a set which consists of lists of elements drawn from some arbitrary set X, as a free type in Z.

$$car\colon List_1 \longrightarrow \mathbf{Z}$$
$$cdr\colon List_1 \longrightarrow List$$

$$car(cons(i, x)) = i$$
$$cdr(cons(i, x)) = x$$

Whenever you define a free type in Z you get an induction principle for free. In the case of lists, if you want to prove something about every list—that is to say, if you want to prove that $\forall x\colon List \bullet P(x)$ holds, for some formula P—then all you have to prove are that

(1) $P(nil)$ holds; and that

(2) $P(cons(i, x))$ holds on the assumption that $P(x)$ holds, which can be expressed in symbols like this:

$$\forall i\colon \mathbf{Z};\, x\colon List \bullet P(x) \Rightarrow P(cons(i, x)).$$

(1) is known as the *base case* and (2) is the *inductive step*.[2]

9.3   Specifying Sequence Proofs

9.3.1   Introduction

In chapter 10 I develop the proof-theory of first-order logic using a single-conclusion sequent calculus which is built on the idea that a proof is a particular kind of tree of sequents. There are many notions of a formal proof in mathematical logic and here I am going to look at the concept of a *sequence proof*. A logical system built on this notion of what constitutes a proof is known as a *Hilbert-style system* and in such a system the propositional calculus can be axiomatized as shown in Fig. 9.1. The logical system PS actually has an infinite number of axioms. For example, every substitution instance of the axiom PS1 is an axiom. Thus, all the following are axioms:

$$P \Rightarrow (P \Rightarrow P),$$
$$Q \Rightarrow (Q \Rightarrow Q),$$
$$(P \Rightarrow Q) \Rightarrow (R \Rightarrow (P \Rightarrow Q)).$$

A proof starts from axioms and succeeding formulas follow from earlier ones by means of *modus ponendo ponens*. The notion of a sequence proof can be defined as follows:

> A *sequence proof* of the formula A in the logical system PS is a finite sequence of formulas σ, such that each element of σ either is an axiom or follows from earlier elements of σ by means of *modus ponendo ponens* and the last element of σ is the formula A.

A sample proof is shown in Fig. 9.2.[3]

---

[2] Induction principles for numbers and sequences are discussed in sections 11.4 and 11.5, respectively, below.

[3] This example is taken from (Hunter 1971), pp. 73–74, and the system PS is also from there, p. 72.

Axioms

PS1	$A \Rightarrow (B \Rightarrow A)$
PS2	$(A \Rightarrow (B \Rightarrow C)) \Rightarrow ((A \Rightarrow B) \Rightarrow (A \Rightarrow C))$
PS3	$(\neg A \Rightarrow \neg B) \Rightarrow (B \Rightarrow A)$

Rule of inference

Modus ponendo ponens: from A and $A \Rightarrow B$ infer B

Figure 9.1: The Hilbert-style system PS.

$$\langle \ (\neg Q \Rightarrow \neg P) \Rightarrow (P \Rightarrow Q),$$
$$((\neg Q \Rightarrow \neg P) \Rightarrow (P \Rightarrow Q)) \Rightarrow$$
$$(\neg P \Rightarrow ((\neg Q \Rightarrow \neg P) \Rightarrow (P \Rightarrow Q))),$$
$$\neg P \Rightarrow ((\neg Q \Rightarrow \neg P) \Rightarrow (P \Rightarrow Q)),$$
$$(\neg P \Rightarrow ((\neg Q \Rightarrow \neg P) \Rightarrow (P \Rightarrow Q))) \Rightarrow$$
$$((\neg P \Rightarrow (\neg Q \Rightarrow \neg P)) \Rightarrow (\neg P \Rightarrow (P \Rightarrow Q))),$$
$$(\neg P \Rightarrow (\neg Q \Rightarrow \neg P)) \Rightarrow (\neg P \Rightarrow (P \Rightarrow Q)),$$
$$\neg P \Rightarrow (\neg Q \Rightarrow \neg P),$$
$$\neg P \Rightarrow (P \Rightarrow Q)$$
$$\rangle.$$

Figure 9.2: An example proof in PS.

Representing Formulas

In translating a Hilbert-style logical system into Z the first thing we have to do is to somehow represent the well-formed formulas that the system uses. This is done using Z's free type notation. Let *Ident* be the set of all the identifiers used in the object language of our logical system. Then the complete object language can be specified as the Z free type *Wff* in the following way:

$$Wff ::= at\langle\!\langle Ident \rangle\!\rangle$$
$$| \ \ neg\langle\!\langle Wff \rangle\!\rangle$$
$$| \ \ conj\langle\!\langle Wff \times Wff \rangle\!\rangle$$

$$| \quad disj \langle\!\langle \mathit{Wff} \times \mathit{Wff} \rangle\!\rangle$$
$$| \quad imp \langle\!\langle \mathit{Wff} \times \mathit{Wff} \rangle\!\rangle$$
$$| \quad equiv \langle\!\langle \mathit{Wff} \times \mathit{Wff} \rangle\!\rangle.$$

This says that a well-formed formula is either an atomic formula consisting of an identifier or the negation of a formula or the conjunction of two formulas or the disjunction
of two formulas or the implication formed from two formulas or the bi-implication
formed from two formulas. (The phrase 'well-formed formula' is often abbreviated to
'wff'.) The functions *at*, *neg*, *conj*, *disj*, *imp* and *equiv* are known as *constructors*. To
illustrate the use of this free type definition the formula $P \wedge \neg Q \Rightarrow R$ is depicted by
the term:

$$imp(\mathit{conj}(at\ P, neg(at\ Q)), at\ R),$$

and the formula $(P \Rightarrow Q) \vee (Q \Rightarrow P)$ is represented by:

$$disj(imp(at\ P, at\ Q), imp(at\ Q, at\ P)).$$

The resulting notation is, I hope you will agree, only marginally more difficult to read
than Lisp.

Representing Axioms

Because the logical system PS does not have a rule of substitution, the axioms PS1,
PS2 and PS3 are really axiom *schemas*.[4] In other words, they are *sets* of formulas.
Thus, they are represented in Z as follows:

> $ax1$, $ax2$, $ax3$: **P** *Wff*
>
> ---
>
> $ax1 = \{\ A, B\colon \mathit{Wff} \bullet imp(A, imp(B, A))\ \}$
> $ax2 = \{\ A, B, C\colon \mathit{Wff} \bullet$
> $\qquad imp(imp(A, imp(B, C)), imp(imp(A, B), imp(A, C)))\ \}$
> $ax3 = \{\ A, B\colon \mathit{Wff} \bullet imp(imp(neg\ A,\ neg\ B), imp(B, A))\ \}$

Here, $ax1$, $ax2$ and $ax3$ are the axiom schemas. The following are examples of axioms
corresponding to the schema $ax1$:

$$imp(at\ P, imp(at\ P, at\ P)),$$
$$imp(neg(at\ Q), imp(disj(at\ P, at\ R), neg(at\ Q))).$$

Representing Rules of Inference

A rule of inference is just a relation between a finite set of formulas and a formula.
The single rule of inference of PS, namely *modus ponendo ponens*, is thus defined like
this:

> mpp: **F** *Wff* $\leftrightarrow$ *Wff*
>
> ---
>
> $mpp = \{\ A, B\colon \mathit{Wff} \bullet \{A, imp(A, B)\} \mapsto B\ \}$

---

[4]This use of the word 'schema' has nothing to do with Z's two-dimensional schema notation.

Representing Proofs

The formula $isprf(\sigma, A)$ is true iff σ is a sequence proof of A in the logical system PS. It is defined like this in Z:

$$
\begin{array}{|l}
isprf: \operatorname{seq} \mathit{Wff} \leftrightarrow \mathit{Wff} \\
\hline
\forall \sigma: \operatorname{seq} \mathit{Wff}; \, A: \mathit{Wff} \bullet \sigma \mapsto A \in isprf \Longleftrightarrow \\
\quad ((\forall i: \operatorname{dom} \sigma \bullet (\sigma(i) \in ax1 \cup ax2 \cup ax3 \, \vee \\
\qquad (\exists j, k: \operatorname{dom} \sigma \mid j < i \wedge k < i \wedge j \neq k \bullet \\
\qquad \{\sigma(j), \sigma(k)\} \mapsto \sigma(i) \in mpp))) \wedge \sigma(\#\sigma) = A)
\end{array}
$$

Note that $isprf$ is not a function. The formula $isthm(A)$ is true iff A is a theorem of the logical system PS. It is defined in the following way:

$$
isthm(A) == \exists \sigma: \operatorname{seq} \mathit{Wff} \bullet isprf(\sigma, A).
$$

9.3.2 The Specifications

A Proof-checker

A proof-checker is a program that accepts as input a sequence of formulas $list?$ and a formula $form?$ and tests to see whether or not $list?$ is indeed a proof of $form?$ A proof-checker for the system PS can be specified as follows:

$$
\begin{array}{|l}
\underline{\quad ProofChecker \quad\qquad\qquad\qquad\qquad\qquad\qquad\qquad} \\
list?: \operatorname{seq} \mathit{Wff} \\
form?: \mathit{Wff} \\
rep!: \{\text{'yes'}, \text{'no'}\} \\
\hline
(list? \mapsto form? \in isprf \wedge rep! = \text{'yes'}) \\
\qquad \vee \\
(list? \mapsto form? \notin isprf \wedge rep! = \text{'no'})
\end{array}
$$

A Theorem-prover

A theorem-prover for PS is a program which accepts a formula $form?$ as input and tells you whether or not $form?$ is a theorem of PS. It can be specified as follows:

$$
\begin{array}{|l}
\underline{\quad TheoremProver \quad\qquad\qquad\qquad\qquad\qquad\qquad\qquad} \\
form?: \mathit{Wff} \\
rep!: \{\text{'yes'}, \text{'no'}\} \\
\hline
(isthm(form?) \wedge rep! = \text{'yes'}) \\
\qquad \vee \\
(\neg\, isthm(form?) \wedge rep! = \text{'no'})
\end{array}
$$

A Proof-generator

A proof-generator for PS is a program which accepts a formula *form?* as input and outputs a proof of *form?* if it is a theorem, otherwise it outputs the empty sequence. It can be specified as follows:

┌─ *ProofGenerator* ──────────────────────────────────
│ *form?*: *Wff*
│ *list!*: seq *Wff*
│ *rep!*: {'yes', 'no'}
├───
│ (*list!* ↦ *form?* ∈ *isprf* ∧ *rep!* = 'yes')
│   ∨
│ (¬ *isthm*(*form?*) ∧ *list!* = ⟨ ⟩ ∧ *rep!* = 'no')
└───

Discussion

The specifications of a theorem-prover and a proof-generator for PS contained in the schemas *TheoremProver* and *ProofGenerator* once again illustrate the technique of procedural abstraction, since they do not contain any information about how a theorem-prover or a proof-generator for PS could actually be implemented in a suitable programming language. They precisely state, however, a criterion for deciding whether or not any implementation is a theorem-prover or a proof-generator for PS.

9.4 The Formal Treatment of Free Types

As explained in (Spivey 1992), pp. 82–85, the notation for free types is purely syntactic. Although it adds nothing to the power of Z, the use of the free type notation for recursive data types makes their treatment more perspicuous. In this section I just want to show how we could have avoided the definition of the free type *Wff* given above. That definition is identical with the following one, which does not make use of free types at all:

┌───
│ *at*: *Ident* ↣ *Wff*
│ *neg*: *Wff* ↣ *Wff*
│ *conj*, *disj*, *imp*, *equiv*: (*Wff* × *Wff*) ↣ *Wff*
├───
│ disjoint ⟨ran *at*, ran *neg*, ran *conj*, ran *disj*, ran *imp*, ran *equiv*⟩
│ ∀*U*: **P** *Wff* •
│   (*at*⦇*Indent*⦈ ∪
│   *neg*⦇*Wff*⦈ ∪
│   *conj*⦇*Wff* × *Wff*⦈ ∪
│   *disj*⦇*Wff* × *Wff*⦈ ∪
│   *imp*⦇*Wff* × *Wff*⦈ ∪
│   *equiv*⦇*Wff* × *Wff*⦈ ⊆ *U*) ⇒ *Wff* ⊆ *U*
└───

The notation $\rightarrowtail$ is Z's way of denoting the type of all *total injective* functions between X and Y. To say that a function is *one-to-one* or an *injection* means that each element in the range of the function is the value of only one argument. The set of all total injective functions between X and Y can be defined as follows:

$$X \rightarrowtail Y \ == \ \{f: X \longrightarrow Y \mid f^{\sim} \in Y \nrightarrow X\}.$$

The reader is referred to section 3.10 of (Spivey 1992, pp. 82–85) for a more thorough treatment of free types. The only further thing that I want to do here is to substantiate the claim I made in chapter 3, namely that a free type definition of the form

$$W ::= a \mid b \mid c$$

is equivalent to the set enumeration

$$W \ == \ \{a, b, c\}.$$

This follows from the fact that the free type definition just amounts to this:

$$
\begin{array}{|l}
a, b, c : W \\
\hline
\text{disjoint } \langle \{a\}, \{b\}, \{c\} \rangle \\
\forall U : \mathbf{P}\, W \bullet \{a, b, c\} \subseteq U \Rightarrow W \subseteq U
\end{array}
$$

In this case, the three constants a, b and c are the only three members that the set W has.

Part II

Methods of Reasoning

10

Formal Proof

10.1 Propositional Calculus

10.1.1 Introduction

Logic is the study of inference and there are two main ways of studying the nature of inference mathematically, namely the model-theoretic and the proof-theoretic. *Model theory*, or *(formal) semantics* as it is sometimes known, deals with concepts like those of truth, interpretation and satisfiability. *Proof theory*, or *(formal) syntax* as it is sometimes known, deals with proofs. It is the topic of this chapter.

There are several different notions of proof in logic and the one I have chosen to present is that in which a proof is a tree of single-conclusion sequents, where such a sequent is an ordered pair consisting of a set of premises and a single conclusion. The resulting system of logic is known, not surprisingly, as a *single-conclusion sequent calculus*. A sequent is the formal analogue of an argument and before going into the nuts and bolts of proof construction I present the informal intuitions underlying this sort of logical system.

An *argument*—in a natural language like English—is a structured, linguistic entity made up out of a number of premises and a single conclusion. All the premises and the conclusion are propositions that can be either true or false. Thus, the following is an example of an argument:

> If Hart is breathing, then he is alive;
> Hart is not alive; $\qquad$ (10.1)
> therefore, Hart is not breathing.

As another example of an argument, we have the following:

> If Gray is snoring, then she is asleep;
> Gray is not asleep; $\qquad$ (10.2)
> therefore, Gray is not snoring.

Logic is not primarily the study of specific examples of arguments. It is, rather, the study of common *patterns* of reasoning. The two arguments (10.1) and (10.2) have the same structure and this can be exhibited by means of the following *argument schema*:

$$P \Rightarrow Q; \neg Q; \text{therefore, } \neg P. \tag{10.3}$$

In an argument schema variables or schematic letters, like P and Q, take the place of propositions. When these letters are replaced by propositions an argument results. An argument obtained in this way is said to be an *instance* of the corresponding schema. Thus, arguments (10.1) and (10.2) are both instances of the schema (10.3). When there is little danger of confusion argument schemas in this book will be referred to simply as *arguments*.

A *thema* is a structured, linguistic entity made up out of a collection of arguments and a single argument.[1] There is no standard terminology for the components of a thema, but I refer to the collection of arguments as the *input arguments* to the thema and the single argument as its *output argument*. Whereas an argument is made up out of a number of premises and a conclusion—all of which are propositions—a thema is made up out of a number of input arguments and an output argument—all of which are arguments. As an example of a thema we can take that one whose input is the single argument (10.2) and whose output argument is the following one:

> If Gray is snoring, then she is asleep;
> therefore, if Gray is not asleep, then she is not snoring.   (10.4)

The resulting thema can be written as a tree diagram with the output argument forming the root of the tree. Thus, the thema whose input argument is (10.2) and whose output argument is (10.4) is represented in this way:

> If Gray is snoring, then she is asleep;
> Gray is not asleep;
> therefore, Gray is not snoring.
> _____
> If Gray is snoring, then she is asleep;
> therefore, if Gray is not asleep, then she is not snoring.   (10.5)

Thema *schemas* are to be understood analogously to argument *schemas*. In a thema schema propositions are replaced with variables or schematic letters. The thema displayed as (10.5) is an instance of the thema schema (10.6).

$$\frac{P \Rightarrow Q; \neg Q; \text{therefore, } \neg P.}{P \Rightarrow Q; \text{therefore, } \neg Q \Rightarrow \neg P.} \tag{10.6}$$

Another instance of the same thema schema appears as (10.7).

> If Hart is breathing, then he is alive;
> Hart is not alive;
> therefore, Hart is not breathing.
> _____
> If Hart is breathing, then he is alive;
> therefore, if Hart is not alive, then he is not breathing.   (10.7)

---

[1]Note that the plural of *thema* is *themata*. Themata were introduced into logic by the Stoic logicians, but in recent times it is Geach more than anybody else who has stressed the difference between arguments and themata. See, for example, chapter 14 of (Geach 1976). Also useful is the discussion by Sanford (1989), pp. 22–26.

When there is no danger of confusion, thema schemas in this book will be referred to simply as *themata*.

In mathematical logic arguments and argument schemas are represented by sequents, where a *sequent* is an ordered pair consisting of a set of premises and a conclusion. Thus, the argument schema (10.3) is represented by means of the following sequent:[2]

$$\{P \Rightarrow Q, \neg Q\} \mapsto \neg P. \qquad (10.8)$$

Similarly, the thema schema (10.6) is represented by means of the following tree of sequents:

$$\frac{\{P \Rightarrow Q, \neg Q\} \mapsto \neg P}{\{P \Rightarrow Q\} \mapsto \neg Q \Rightarrow \neg P.} \qquad (10.9)$$

Although the first component of a sequent is a set, usually when a sequent is written the braces that are used when introducing a set by enumeration are left out. Thus, the sequent (10.8) is, more commonly, written as

$$P \Rightarrow Q, \neg Q \mapsto \neg P \qquad (10.10)$$

and the tree of sequents (10.9) is usually written as

$$\frac{P \Rightarrow Q, \neg Q \mapsto \neg P}{P \Rightarrow Q \mapsto \neg Q \Rightarrow \neg P.} \qquad (10.11)$$

When there is no danger of confusion, a tree of sequents like (10.11) is referred to as a *thema* and, for variety, such a thema is also known as a *(thematic) rule*.

The following tree of sequents is an example of a proof in a single-conclusion sequent calculus:

$$\frac{P \wedge Q \Rightarrow R \mapsto P \wedge Q \Rightarrow R \quad \dfrac{\dfrac{P \mapsto P \quad Q \mapsto Q}{P, Q \mapsto P \wedge Q} \wedge\text{-}int}{P \wedge Q \Rightarrow R, P, Q \mapsto R} \Rightarrow\text{-}elim}{\dfrac{P \wedge Q \Rightarrow R, P \mapsto Q \Rightarrow R}{P \wedge Q \Rightarrow R \mapsto P \Rightarrow (Q \Rightarrow R).} \Rightarrow\text{-}int} \Rightarrow\text{-}int$$

Later on in this chapter it is explained in more detail what the various components of this tree mean, but for the time being all that I want to emphasize is that in order to construct such a tree of sequents we need to know which sequents can legitimately be used as leaf nodes and we also need to know the specific thematic rules that can be used in order to make the tree. Sequents that can be used legitimately to form leaf nodes are known as *start sequents* and the stock of such sequents that we begin with are known as the *primitive* start sequents of the calculus that we are dealing with. Similarly, the stock of original themata of a particular calculus are known as the *primitive* themata of that calculus.

A third thing that we need to know in framing a single-conclusion calculus is what formulas can be used in order to form the sequents that make up proofs in that calculus. In the first part of this chapter the formulas that are used are those of the propositional calculus whose abstract syntax is given on pp. 9–10 of chapter 2.

---

[2]See the entry under the heading *sequent* in the glossary of terms contained in appendix C for an explanation of why the symbol $\mapsto$ is used to form sequents in this book.

10.1.2   Notational Conventions

A *sequent* is an ordered pair, written as $\Gamma \mapsto A$, where Γ is a set of formulas and A is a single formula. The set Γ is known as the set of *premises* of the sequent and the formula A is called its *conclusion*. The capital Greek letters Γ, Δ and Σ, sometimes with subscripts, are used for arbitrary—possibly empty—sets of formulas and the letters A, B, C, P, Q and R, sometimes with subscripts, are used for arbitrary formulas.[3] The set consisting of the formulas A, B and C is written:

$$A, B, C$$

Furthermore, Γ, Δ represents the union of Γ and Δ and Γ, A represents the set formed by adding A to the set Γ.

10.1.3   Themata

Introduction   A *thema* in the sequent calculus is a structured entity made up out of one or more *input sequents* and an *output sequent*. Themata are written in the following way:

$$\overbrace{\Gamma_1 \mapsto A_1}^{\text{first input sequent}} \quad \cdots \quad \overbrace{\Gamma_n \mapsto A_n}^{n\text{th input sequent}}$$
$$\underbrace{\Delta \mapsto B}_{\text{output sequent}} \quad name$$

Think of this as a mini-tree with n leaves and a root. Each leaf is an input sequent and the root is the output sequent. In this book the name of the thematic rule is written to the right of the horizontal line which separates the input sequents from the output sequent.

Let $\heartsuit$ be an arbitrary two-place truth-functional connective. Then an *elimination* rule for $\heartsuit$ is one in which $\heartsuit$ appears in the conclusion of at least one of the input sequents to the rule and $\heartsuit$ does not occur in the conclusion of the output sequent of the rule. An *introduction* rule for $\heartsuit$ is one in which $\heartsuit$ does not appear in the conclusion of any of the input sequents to the rule, but $\heartsuit$ does occur in the conclusion of the output sequent of the rule.

Conjunction   There are two elimination rules associated with conjunction. The first is $\wedge$-*elim*$_1$:

$$\frac{\Gamma \mapsto A \wedge B}{\Gamma \mapsto A.} \wedge\text{-}elim_1$$

Intuitively, this rule can be understood as follows. Assume that we have established in some way that the formula $A \wedge B$ follows from the set of formulas Γ, then the formula A by itself follows from the set of formulas Γ.

The second elimination rule for conjunction is $\wedge$-*elim*$_2$:

$$\frac{\Gamma \mapsto A \wedge B}{\Gamma \mapsto B.} \wedge\text{-}elim_2$$

---

[3]The letters A, B and C are mainly used in stating the thematic rules of the propositional and predicate calculuses.

Conjunction has a single introduction rule:

$$\frac{\Gamma \mapsto A \quad \Delta \mapsto B}{\Gamma, \Delta \mapsto A \wedge B.} \wedge\text{-}int$$

If A follows from the set of premises Γ and B follows from Δ, then $A \wedge B$ follows from the union of Γ and Δ.

Disjunction   There is one elimination rule associated with disjunction. It is called $\vee$-*elim*:

$$\frac{\Gamma \mapsto A \vee B \quad \Delta, A \mapsto C \quad \Sigma, B \mapsto C}{\Gamma, \Delta, \Sigma \mapsto C.} \vee\text{-}elim$$

This is the most complicated rule in the sequent calculus for propositional logic and for that reason I give several examples of its use later on in this chapter.

There are two introduction rules associated with disjunction, namely $\vee$-*int$_1$* and $\vee$-*int$_2$*:

$$\frac{\Gamma \mapsto A}{\Gamma \mapsto A \vee B,} \vee\text{-}int_1 \qquad \frac{\Gamma \mapsto B}{\Gamma \mapsto A \vee B.} \vee\text{-}int_2$$

Implication   There is one elimination rule associated with implication. It is called $\Rightarrow$-*elim*. It works like this:

$$\frac{\Gamma \mapsto A \quad \Delta \mapsto A \Rightarrow B}{\Gamma, \Delta \mapsto B.} \Rightarrow\text{-}elim$$

There is one introduction rule associated with implication. It is $\Rightarrow$-*int*:

$$\frac{\Gamma \mapsto B}{\Gamma \setminus \{A\} \mapsto A \Rightarrow B.} \Rightarrow\text{-}int$$

The formula A can occur in the set of premises Γ, but it does not have to.

Bi-implication   The elimination rules for bi-implication allow us to change them into implications:

$$\frac{\Gamma \mapsto A \Longleftrightarrow B}{\Gamma \mapsto A \Rightarrow B,} \Longleftrightarrow\text{-}elim_1 \qquad \frac{\Gamma \mapsto A \Longleftrightarrow B}{\Gamma \mapsto B \Rightarrow A.} \Longleftrightarrow\text{-}elim_2$$

There is a single introduction rule for bi-implication:

$$\frac{\Gamma \mapsto A \Rightarrow B \quad \Delta \mapsto B \Rightarrow A}{\Gamma, \Delta \mapsto A \Longleftrightarrow B.} \Longleftrightarrow\text{-}int$$

Negation, *false* **and** *true*   Negation has a single elimination rule:

$$\frac{\Gamma \mapsto A \quad \Delta \mapsto \neg A}{\Gamma, \Delta \mapsto false.} \neg\text{-}elim$$

Negation has a single introduction rule:

$$\frac{\Gamma, A \mapsto false}{\Gamma \mapsto \neg A.} \; \neg\text{-}int$$

The elimination and introduction rules for negation are easy to remember if you make use of the fact that $\neg A$ can be defined as $A \Rightarrow false$. Thus, they can be seen as special cases of the elimination and introduction rules for implication.

Associated with negation there is also a double negation elimination rule:[4]

$$\frac{\Gamma \mapsto \neg\neg A}{\Gamma \mapsto A.} \; \neg\neg\text{-}elim$$

The next rule only involves the constant formula *false*. It is known as *false* elimination:

$$\frac{\Gamma \mapsto false}{\Gamma \mapsto A.} \; false\text{-}elim$$

The final two primitive rules of the propositional calculus allow us to eliminate and introduce the constant formula *true*:

$$\frac{\Gamma \mapsto true}{\Gamma \mapsto \neg false,} \; true\text{-}elim \qquad \frac{\Gamma \mapsto \neg false}{\Gamma \mapsto true.} \; true\text{-}int$$

10.1.4 Start Sequents and Proofs

A (*correctly constructed*) *tree proof* (or simply a *proof* for short) in a single-conclusion sequent calculus—relative to a collection of primitive start sequents and a class of primitive themata—is a tree with a sequent located at each node which satisfies the following constraints:

(1) Every sequent located at a leaf node is a start sequent.

(2) Each mini-tree is a (substitution) instance of one of the themata, where a *mini-tree* is any tree obtained from the original tree which consists of a node and all of that node's children and nothing else.

In the case of the propositional calculus the collection of primitive start sequents consists of every sequent of the form $A \mapsto A$ and the class of primitive themata contains all the elimination and introduction rules given above.[5] An example of a correctly constructed tree proof is

$$\frac{\dfrac{P \wedge Q \mapsto P \wedge Q}{P \wedge Q \mapsto Q} \wedge\text{-}elim_2 \quad \dfrac{P \wedge Q \mapsto P \wedge Q}{P \wedge Q \mapsto P} \wedge\text{-}elim_1}{P \wedge Q \mapsto Q \wedge P.} \wedge\text{-}int$$

---

[4] For those of you with some knowledge of other logical systems, if the rule for double negation elimination is left out of the formal system being introduced, then the resulting system is *intuitionistic* logic.

[5] In the case of both the predicate calculus and Floyd–Hoare logic both the collection of primitive start sequents and the class of primitive themata contain members in addition to those given here.

The primitive start sequents are all assumed to be valid and all the members of the class of primitive themata are assumed to transmit validity from their input sequents to their respective output sequents, therefore a correctly constructed tree proof must have a valid sequent situated at its root. (A thema that transmits validity is said to be *correct*.) In fact, a sequent is defined to be (*syntactically*) *valid*—relative to a collection of primitive start sequents and a class of primitive themata—if there exists a correctly constructed tree proof which has it as its root.

When the sequent $\Gamma \mapsto A$ is valid, we write $\Gamma \vdash A$. The symbol $\vdash$ is known as the (*syntactic*) *turnstile* and it stands for a meta-linguistic relation between sets of formulas and formulas. When $\Gamma \vdash A$, we also say that A is a (*syntactic*) *consequence* of the set of formulas Γ and that the set of formulas Γ (*syntactically*) *entail* A. Note that whereas $\Gamma \mapsto A$ is an *object*, namely an ordered pair, $\Gamma \vdash A$ is a *statement* that can be either true or false.

Another metalinguistic relation is symbolized by $\dashv\vdash$. This is a homogeneous relation between formulas. An ordered pair (A, B) is a member of $\dashv\vdash$ iff A is a syntactic consequence of B and B is a syntactic consequence of A. When $A \dashv\vdash B$, we say that A and B are *syntactically equivalent*.

Sometimes in this kind of sequent calculus the start sequents are known as *axioms*. This terminology is not used in this book. In the context of a sequent calculus I think that it is more appropriate to call a *formula* A an *axiom* if it is postulated that the start sequent $\varnothing \mapsto A$ is valid. (Moreover, a sequent is an *object* and an axiom is a *formula*, therefore it is a mistake to call a sequent an axiom.) Let $\Gamma \mapsto A$ be a valid sequent. Then A is a *theorem* if $\Gamma = \varnothing$. Thus, the set of axioms is a subset of the set of theorems.

Some Examples of Proofs Some examples of tree proofs should make the above ideas clearer.

(1) First, I show that the sequent $\neg P \wedge Q \mapsto P \Rightarrow Q$ is valid:

$$\frac{\dfrac{\neg P \wedge Q \mapsto \neg P \wedge Q}{\neg P \wedge Q \mapsto Q} \wedge\text{-}elim_2}{\neg P \wedge Q \mapsto P \Rightarrow Q.} \Rightarrow\text{-}int$$

(2) The next example is a proof that the sequent $P \wedge Q \mapsto P \Longleftrightarrow Q$ is valid:

$$\frac{\dfrac{\dfrac{P \wedge Q \mapsto P \wedge Q}{P \wedge Q \mapsto Q} \wedge\text{-}elim_2}{P \wedge Q \mapsto P \Rightarrow Q} \Rightarrow\text{-}int \qquad \dfrac{\dfrac{P \wedge Q \mapsto P \wedge Q}{P \wedge Q \mapsto P} \wedge\text{-}elim_1}{P \wedge Q \mapsto Q \Rightarrow P} \Rightarrow\text{-}int}{P \wedge Q \mapsto P \Longleftrightarrow Q.} \Longleftrightarrow\text{-}int$$

(3) The next example is a proof that the sequent $P \wedge \neg Q \mapsto \neg(P \wedge Q)$ is valid:

$$\frac{\dfrac{\dfrac{P \wedge \neg Q \mapsto P \wedge \neg Q}{P \wedge \neg Q \mapsto \neg Q} \wedge\text{-}elim_2 \qquad \dfrac{\dfrac{P \wedge Q \mapsto P \wedge Q}{P \wedge Q \mapsto Q} \wedge\text{-}elim_1}{} \neg\text{-}elim}{P \wedge \neg Q, P \wedge Q \mapsto false}}{P \wedge \neg Q \mapsto \neg(P \wedge Q).} \neg\text{-}int$$

(4) The next example is a proof that the sequent $Q \mapsto P \wedge Q \Longleftrightarrow P$ is valid:

$$
\cfrac{
\cfrac{
\cfrac{
\cfrac{
\cfrac{P \wedge Q \mapsto P \wedge Q}{P \wedge Q \mapsto P} \wedge\text{-}elim_1
}{P \wedge Q \mapsto Q \Rightarrow P} \Rightarrow\text{-}int \quad \cfrac{Q \mapsto Q}{}
}{Q, P \wedge Q \mapsto P} \Rightarrow\text{-}elim
}{Q \mapsto P \wedge Q \Rightarrow P} \Rightarrow\text{-}int
\qquad
\cfrac{
\cfrac{
\cfrac{Q \mapsto Q \quad P \mapsto P}{Q, P \mapsto P \wedge Q} \wedge\text{-}int
}{Q \mapsto P \Rightarrow P \wedge Q} \Rightarrow\text{-}int
}{}
}{Q \mapsto P \wedge Q \Longleftrightarrow P.} \Longleftrightarrow\text{-}int
$$

(5) The tree proof

$$
\cfrac{P \mapsto P \quad P \Rightarrow Q \mapsto P \Rightarrow Q}{P, P \Rightarrow Q \mapsto Q} \Rightarrow\text{-}elim
$$

tells us that the sequent $P, P \Rightarrow Q \mapsto Q$ is valid. This is *modus ponendo ponens* (as a sequent).

(6) The tree proof

$$
\cfrac{
\cfrac{
\neg(P \wedge Q) \mapsto \neg(P \wedge Q) \quad \cfrac{P \mapsto P \quad Q \mapsto Q}{P, Q \mapsto P \wedge Q} \wedge\text{-}int
}{\neg(P \wedge Q), P, Q \mapsto false} \neg\text{-}elim
}{\neg(P \wedge Q), P \mapsto \neg Q} \neg\text{-}int
$$

tells us that the sequent $\neg(P \wedge Q), P \mapsto \neg Q$ is valid. This is *modus ponendo tollens* (as a sequent).

(7) The tree proof

$$
\cfrac{
P \vee Q \mapsto P \vee Q \qquad
\cfrac{
\cfrac{
\cfrac{\neg P \mapsto \neg P \quad P \mapsto P}{\neg P, P \mapsto false} \neg\text{-}elim
}{\neg P, P \mapsto Q} falseelim
\quad Q \mapsto Q
}{}
}{P \vee Q, \neg P \mapsto Q} \vee\text{-}elim
$$

tells us that the sequent $P \vee Q, \neg P \mapsto Q$ is valid. This is *modus tollendo ponens* (as a sequent).

(8) The tree proof

$$
\cfrac{
\cfrac{
\neg Q \mapsto \neg Q \qquad
\cfrac{P \mapsto P \quad P \Rightarrow Q \mapsto P \Rightarrow Q}{P, P \Rightarrow Q \mapsto Q} \Rightarrow\text{-}elim
}{\neg Q, P, P \Rightarrow Q \mapsto false} \neg\text{-}elim
}{\neg Q, P \Rightarrow Q \mapsto \neg P} \neg\text{-}int
$$

tells us that the sequent $\neg Q, P \Rightarrow Q \mapsto \neg P$ is valid. This is *modus tollendo tollens* (as a sequent).

Once a sequent has been shown to be valid it can be used as a start sequent in subsequent tree proofs. Such a sequent is known as a *derived* start sequent. Every sequent of the form $\Gamma \mapsto B$, where Γ is a finite set that contains the formula B, is a derived sequent. To establish this consider the following tree proof:

$$\dfrac{\dfrac{\dfrac{\dfrac{B \mapsto B}{B \mapsto A_1 \Rightarrow B}\Rightarrow\text{-}int \quad A_1 \mapsto A_1}{A_1, B \mapsto B}\Rightarrow\text{-}elim}{A_1, B \mapsto A_2 \Rightarrow B}\Rightarrow\text{-}int \quad A_2 \mapsto A_2}{A_1, A_2, B \mapsto B.}\Rightarrow\text{-}elim$$

This shows that every sequent of the form $\Gamma \mapsto B$ is valid when Γ contains two or three formulas one of which is B. Similarly, it could be established that every sequent of the form $\Gamma \mapsto B$, where Γ is a finite set containing B, is valid.

10.1.5 Derived Thematic Rules

The first example of a derived thematic rule discussed here is *modus ponendo tollens* (as a thema):

$$\dfrac{\Gamma \mapsto \neg(A \wedge B) \quad \Delta \mapsto A}{\Gamma, \Delta \mapsto \neg B.}\ mpt$$

This can be established by means of the following incomplete tree proof:

$$\dfrac{\dfrac{\Gamma \mapsto \neg(A \wedge B) \quad \dfrac{\Delta \mapsto A \quad B \mapsto B}{\Delta, B \mapsto A \wedge B}\wedge\text{-}int}{\Gamma, \Delta, B \mapsto false}\neg\text{-}elim}{\Gamma, \Delta \mapsto \neg B.}\neg\text{-}int$$

This tree proof is incomplete because not all of its leaf nodes are start sequents, but every rule used in its construction is a correct thematic rule. Thus, *if* both the sequents $\Gamma \mapsto \neg(A \wedge B)$ and $\Delta \mapsto A$ are valid, then so is $\Gamma, \Delta \mapsto \neg B$. So, the rule *mpt* is correct.[6]

The next example of a derived thematic rule is *modus tollendo ponens*:

$$\dfrac{\Gamma \mapsto A \vee B \quad \Delta \mapsto \neg A}{\Gamma, \Delta \mapsto B.}\ mtp$$

This can be established by means of the following incomplete tree proof:

$$\dfrac{\Gamma \mapsto A \vee B \quad \dfrac{\dfrac{\dfrac{\Delta \mapsto \neg A \quad A \mapsto A}{\Delta, A \mapsto false}\neg\text{-}elim}{\Delta, A \mapsto B}false\text{-}elim \quad B \mapsto B}{}}{\Gamma, \Delta \mapsto B.}\vee\text{-}elim$$

Another example of a derived thematic rule is *modus tollendo tollens*:

$$\dfrac{\Gamma \mapsto A \Rightarrow B \quad \Delta \mapsto \neg B}{\Gamma, \Delta \mapsto \neg A.}\ mtt$$

---

[6] A derived thema like *mpt* can be thought of as a *macro* which could be replaced by its defining incomplete tree proof in whatever tree proof it occurs.

Intuitively, this rule states that if we have established that the formula $\neg B$ follows from the set of formulas Δ and also that the formula $A \Rightarrow B$ follows from the set of formulas Γ, then the formula $\neg A$ follows from the union of Δ and Γ. The derived rule *mtt* can be established as follows:

$$\cfrac{\cfrac{A \mapsto A \quad \Gamma \mapsto A \Rightarrow B}{\Gamma, A \mapsto B}\;\Rightarrow\text{-}elim \quad \Delta \mapsto \neg B}{\cfrac{\Gamma, \Delta, A \mapsto false}{\Gamma, \Delta \mapsto \neg A.}\;\neg\text{-}int}\;\neg\text{-}elim$$

So, whenever we have managed to prove that the sequents $\Delta \mapsto \neg B$ and $\Gamma \mapsto A \Rightarrow B$ are both valid, then we can use the derived rule *mtt* to establish that the sequent $\Delta, \Gamma \mapsto \neg A$ is valid.

Some authors when setting up a single-conclusion sequent calculus for propositional logic include a number of so-called structural rules among the primitive themata. Usually, rules known as *cut* and *weakening* (or *thinning*) are included. The *cut* rule looks like this:

$$\cfrac{\Gamma \mapsto A \quad A, \Delta \mapsto B}{\Gamma, \Delta \mapsto B.}\;cut$$

There is no need, however, to include this as a primitive rule as it can be established to be a derived rule. There are several ways in which this can be done. The following is one of the most straightforward:

$$\cfrac{\Gamma \mapsto A \quad \cfrac{A, \Delta \mapsto B}{\Delta \mapsto A \Rightarrow B}\;\Rightarrow\text{-}int}{\Gamma, \Delta \mapsto B.}\;\Rightarrow\text{-}elim$$

Paulson (1987), p. 41, gives another derivation that makes use of the rules for disjunction:

$$\cfrac{\cfrac{\Gamma \mapsto A}{\Gamma \mapsto A \vee A}\;\vee\text{-}int_1 \quad A, \Delta \mapsto B \quad A, \Delta \mapsto B}{\Gamma, \Delta \mapsto B.}\;\vee\text{-}elim$$

Yet another derivation makes use of the rules governing negation:

$$\cfrac{\cfrac{\cfrac{A, \Delta \mapsto B \quad \neg B \mapsto \neg B}{A, \Delta, \neg B \mapsto false}\;\neg\text{-}elim}{\Delta, \neg B \mapsto \neg A}\;\neg\text{-}int \quad \Gamma \mapsto A}{\cfrac{\Gamma, \Delta, \neg B \mapsto false}{\cfrac{\Gamma, \Delta \mapsto \neg\neg B}{\Gamma, \Delta \mapsto B.}\;\neg\neg\text{-}elim}\;\neg\text{-}int}\;\neg\text{-}elim}$$

The weakening or thinning rule looks like this:

$$\cfrac{\Gamma \mapsto B}{\Gamma, A \mapsto B.}\;weak$$

It allows us to introduce additional formulas into the set of premises of a sequent while preserving validity. That the rule *weak* is a derived rule can be shown by means of the following tree proof:

$$\frac{\dfrac{\Gamma \;\mapsto\; B}{\Gamma \;\mapsto\; A \Rightarrow B}\;\Rightarrow\text{-}int \quad A \;\mapsto\; A}{\Gamma, A \;\mapsto\; B.}\;\Rightarrow\text{-}elim$$

Translating into a Linear Form Because tree proofs tend to become large many people who advocate this kind of sequent calculus actually use a linear style of presentation. For example, Suppes (1957), Lemmon (1965), Mates (1972), Schumm (1979), Newton-Smith (1985), Allen and Hand (1992) and Cass and Le Poidevin (1993) do this. In this section I show how to translate a tree proof into an equivalent linear one.

Using the proof of the sequent $P \Rightarrow Q, Q \Rightarrow R \;\mapsto\; P \Rightarrow R$ as an example, the first thing we have to do is to label each sequent. This results in the following proof:

$$\frac{\dfrac{1\colon P \;\mapsto\; P \quad 2\colon P \Rightarrow Q \;\mapsto\; P \Rightarrow Q}{3\colon P, P \Rightarrow Q \;\mapsto\; Q}\;\Rightarrow\text{-}elim \quad 4\colon Q \Rightarrow R \;\mapsto\; Q \Rightarrow R}{\dfrac{5\colon P \Rightarrow Q, Q \Rightarrow R, P \;\mapsto\; R}{6\colon P \Rightarrow Q, Q \Rightarrow R \;\mapsto\; P \Rightarrow R.}\;\Rightarrow\text{-}int}\;\Rightarrow\text{-}elim$$

When labelling a tree proof we only label an internal or root node when we have labelled every node—except that node—in the subtree which has that node as its root. Leaf nodes can be labelled at any time. We then linearize the proof to a sequence of 4-tuples:

1	(1)	P	*ass*
2	(2)	$P \Rightarrow Q$	*ass*
1,2	(3)	Q	1,2 $\Rightarrow$-*elim*
4	(4)	$Q \Rightarrow R$	*ass*
1,2,4	(5)	R	3,4 $\Rightarrow$-*elim*
2,4	(6)	$P \Rightarrow R$	5 $\Rightarrow$-*int*

Each line of such a sequence contains four elements. The leftmost is a set of numbers which represents the set of premises of a sequent. A number i in this set stands for the formula—the third element of the 4-tuple—in line i. Moving right, the number in parentheses (j) is the line number and to the right of this we have a formula. The rightmost item on every line is an annotation. The annotation *ass* stands for *assumption* and it is used to annotate sequents which are legitimate starting nodes of a tree proof, that is to say, they are instances of the start sequents of the calculus we are dealing with.

It should be noted that this linearization technique has certain limitations and these ensure that it cannot be successfully applied to every correctly constructed tree proof. (It can, however, be used to linearize every tree proof constructed out of the primitive start sequents and the primitive themata of the propositional calculus as given above.) The following are its main restrictions:

(1) It can only be applied successfully to tree proofs all of whose leaf nodes are of the form $A \;\mapsto\; A$ or $\varnothing \;\mapsto\; B$, where B is an axiom. It cannot cope with leaf nodes of the form $\Gamma \;\mapsto\; A$, where $A \in \Gamma$ and $\#\Gamma > 1$.

(2) It cannot be applied successfully to a tree proof which makes use either of the *cut* rule or the rule of thinning or any rule which involves either the construction or the taking apart of a formula that occurs in the set of premises of any sequent belonging to the rule.

The rule $\Rightarrow$-*int-l* illustrates the final restruction in clause (2). The derived rule $\Rightarrow$-*int-l* allows us to introduce the implication sign in a formula belonging to the set of premises of the output sequent of the rule:

$$\frac{\Gamma \mapsto A \quad \Delta, B \mapsto C}{\Gamma, \Delta, A \Rightarrow B \mapsto C.} \quad \Rightarrow\text{-}int\text{-}l$$

Another difficulty with this linearization method is best illustrated by means of an example. Consider the following tree proof:

$$\cfrac{A \mapsto A \quad \cfrac{\cfrac{\cfrac{P \mapsto P \quad P \Rightarrow Q \mapsto P \Rightarrow Q}{P, P \Rightarrow Q \mapsto Q} \Rightarrow\text{-}elim}{P, P \Rightarrow Q \mapsto Q \vee R} \text{ } \vee\text{-}int_1}{P \Rightarrow Q \mapsto P \Rightarrow (Q \vee R)} \Rightarrow\text{-}int \quad \cfrac{\cfrac{\cfrac{P \mapsto P \quad P \Rightarrow R \mapsto P \Rightarrow R}{P, P \Rightarrow R \mapsto R} \Rightarrow\text{-}elim}{P, P \Rightarrow R \mapsto Q \vee R} \text{ } \vee\text{-}int_2}{P \Rightarrow R \mapsto P \Rightarrow (Q \vee R)} \Rightarrow\text{-}int}{A \mapsto P \Rightarrow (Q \vee R),} \quad \vee\text{-}elim$$

where A is the formula $(P \Rightarrow Q) \vee (P \Rightarrow R)$. One of the many linearizations of this is the following proof:

1	(1)	P	*ass*
2	(2)	$P \Rightarrow Q$	*ass*
1, 2	(3)	Q	$1, 2 \Rightarrow\text{-}elim$
1, 2	(4)	$Q \vee R$	3 $\vee\text{-}int_1$
2	(5)	$P \Rightarrow (Q \vee R)$	$4 \Rightarrow\text{-}int$
6	(6)	P	*ass*
7	(7)	$P \Rightarrow R$	*ass*
6, 7	(8)	R	$6, 7 \Rightarrow\text{-}elim$
6, 7	(9)	$Q \vee R$	8 $\vee\text{-}int_2$
7	(10)	$P \Rightarrow (Q \vee R)$	$9 \Rightarrow\text{-}int$
11	(11)	$(P \Rightarrow Q) \vee (P \Rightarrow R)$	*ass*
11	(12)	$P \Rightarrow (Q \vee R)$	$5, 10, 11$ $\vee\text{-}elim$

The problem with this is that the formula P is assumed twice and as formulas are referred to by numbers in the leftmost column this means that both the numbers 1 and 6 relate to one and the same formula. In order to avoid such repetition and in order to allow proofs to be constructed in which assumptions are given a unique label people who favour this way of presenting proofs usually allow the re-use of sequents.

Making use of this feature the above linear proof can be rewritten as follows:

$$
\begin{array}{llll}
1 & (1) & P & ass \\
2 & (2) & P \Rightarrow Q & ass \\
1,2 & (3) & Q & 1,2 \Rightarrow\text{-}elim \\
1,2 & (4) & Q \vee R & 3 \vee\text{-}int_1 \\
2 & (5) & P \Rightarrow (Q \vee R) & 4 \Rightarrow\text{-}int \\
6 & (6) & P \Rightarrow R & ass \\
1,6 & (7) & R & 1,6 \Rightarrow\text{-}elim \\
1,6 & (8) & Q \vee R & 7 \vee\text{-}int_2 \\
6 & (9) & P \Rightarrow (Q \vee R) & 8 \Rightarrow\text{-}int \\
10 & (10) & (P \Rightarrow Q) \vee (P \Rightarrow R) & ass \\
10 & (11) & P \Rightarrow (Q \vee R) & 5,9,10 \vee\text{-}elim
\end{array}
$$

When linear proofs are presented in the remainder of this book they make use of this feature if it is appropriate to do so. This results in some proofs being shorter than they would be if this feature were not used.

10.1.6 Further Examples of Proofs

That conjunction distributes backwards through disjunction is proved first in this section. What is to be proved can be expressed in symbols as:

$$(P \vee Q) \wedge R \dashv\vdash (P \wedge R) \vee (Q \wedge R).$$

First, I prove that the sequent $(P \vee Q) \wedge R \mapsto (P \wedge R) \vee (Q \wedge R)$ is valid. This is done by means of the following proof:

$$
\begin{array}{llll}
1 & (1) & (P \vee Q) \wedge R & ass \\
1 & (2) & R & 1 \wedge\text{-}elim_2 \\
1 & (3) & P \vee Q & 1 \wedge\text{-}elim_1 \\
4 & (4) & P & ass \\
1,4 & (5) & P \wedge R & 4,2 \wedge\text{-}int \\
1,4 & (6) & (P \wedge R) \vee (Q \wedge R) & 5 \vee\text{-}int_1 \\
7 & (7) & Q & ass \\
1,7 & (8) & Q \wedge R & 7,2 \wedge\text{-}int \\
1,7 & (9) & (P \wedge R) \vee (Q \wedge R) & 8 \vee\text{-}int_2 \\
1 & (10) & (P \wedge R) \vee (Q \wedge R) & 3,6,9 \vee\text{-}elim
\end{array}
$$

The operation of the rule $\vee\text{-}elim$ is a bit tricky to get used to, so I explain its operation here in more detail. Recall the tree representation of the rule $\vee\text{-}elim$:

$$\frac{\Gamma \mapsto A \vee B \quad \Delta, A \mapsto C \quad \Sigma, B \mapsto C}{\Gamma, \Delta, \Sigma \mapsto C.} \vee\text{-}elim$$

Line (3) of the above proof is:

$$\overbrace{(P \vee Q) \wedge R}^{\Gamma} \mapsto \overbrace{P \vee Q}^{A \vee B}.$$

Line (6) is:

$$\frac{\overbrace{}^{\Delta}}{(P \vee Q) \wedge R,} \; \overbrace{P}^{A} \;\; \mapsto \;\; \frac{\overbrace{}^{C}}{(P \wedge R) \vee (Q \wedge R).}$$

And line (9) is:

$$\frac{\overbrace{}^{\Sigma}}{(P \vee Q) \wedge R,} \; \overbrace{Q}^{B} \;\; \mapsto \;\; \frac{\overbrace{}^{C}}{(P \wedge R) \vee (Q \wedge R).}$$

In this case Γ, Δ and Σ all happen to be the same. So, applying the graphical version of the rule $\vee$-*elim* we get

$$(P \vee Q) \wedge R \; \mapsto \; (P \wedge R) \vee (Q \wedge R),$$

which is represented in the above proof as line (10).

Second, we have to prove that the sequent $(P \wedge R) \vee (Q \wedge R) \; \mapsto \; (P \vee Q) \wedge R$ is valid. The following proof achieves this:

1	(1)	$(P \wedge R) \vee (Q \wedge R)$	*ass*
2	(2)	$P \wedge R$	*ass*
2	(3)	P	2 $\wedge$-*elim*$_1$
2	(4)	$P \vee Q$	3 $\vee$-*int*$_1$
2	(5)	R	2 $\wedge$-*elim*$_2$
2	(6)	$(P \vee Q) \wedge R$	4, 5 $\wedge$-*int*
7	(7)	$Q \wedge R$	*ass*
7	(8)	Q	7 $\wedge$-*elim*$_1$
7	(9)	$P \vee Q$	8 $\vee$-*int*$_2$
7	(10)	R	7 $\wedge$-*elim*$_2$
7	(11)	$(P \vee Q) \wedge R$	9, 10 $\wedge$-*int*
1	(12)	$(P \vee Q) \wedge R$	1, 6, 11 $\vee$-*elim*

I will again explain the last line of this proof in a bit more detail. Line (1) is:

$$\frac{\overbrace{}^{\Gamma}}{(P \wedge R) \vee (Q \wedge R)} \; \mapsto \; \frac{\overbrace{}^{A}}{(P \wedge R)} \vee \frac{\overbrace{}^{B}}{(Q \wedge R).}$$

Line (6) is:

$$\frac{\overbrace{P \wedge R}^{A}}{} \; \mapsto \; \frac{\overbrace{(P \vee Q) \wedge R.}^{C}}{}$$

Here Δ is the empty set. Line (11) is:

$$\frac{\overbrace{Q \wedge R}^{B}}{} \; \mapsto \; \frac{\overbrace{(P \vee Q) \wedge R.}^{C}}{}$$

Here, Σ is empty as well. So, the output sequent is:

$$(P \wedge R) \vee (Q \wedge R) \; \mapsto \; (P \vee Q) \wedge R.$$

This explains the meaning of line (12) in the above proof.

The next thing that I am going to prove is the following law of de Morgan:

$$\neg(P \vee Q) \dashv\vdash \neg P \wedge \neg Q.$$

First, I prove that the sequent $\neg P \wedge \neg Q \mapsto \neg(P \vee Q)$ is valid. The proof is as follows:

1	(1)	$\neg P \wedge \neg Q$	*ass*
2	(2)	$P \vee Q$	*ass*
1	(3)	$\neg P$	1 $\wedge$-*elim*$_1$
1, 2	(4)	Q	2, 3 *mtp*
1	(5)	$\neg Q$	1 $\wedge$-*elim*$_2$
1, 2	(6)	*false*	4, 5 $\neg$-*elim*
1	(7)	$\neg(P \vee Q)$	6 $\neg$-*int*

This illustrates the use of the derived rule *mtp*. The same result can be proved without the use of this rule, thus:

1	(1)	$\neg P \wedge \neg Q$	*ass*
2	(2)	$P \vee Q$	*ass*
1	(3)	$\neg P$	1 $\wedge$-*elim*$_1$
4	(4)	P	*ass*
1, 4	(5)	*false*	3, 4 $\neg$-*elim*
1, 4	(6)	Q	5 *false-elim*
7	(7)	Q	*ass*
1, 2	(8)	Q	2, 6, 7 $\vee$-*elim*
1	(9)	$\neg Q$	1 $\wedge$-*elim*$_2$
1, 2	(10)	*false*	8, 9 $\neg$-*elim*
1	(11)	$\neg(P \vee Q)$	10 $\neg$-*int*

This shows why derived themata, like *mtp*, can be thought of as macros, since their use can always be eliminated and replaced by applications of the primitive thematic rules.

Second, I prove that the sequent $\neg(P \vee Q) \mapsto \neg P \wedge \neg Q$ is valid as follows:

1	(1)	$\neg(P \vee Q)$	*ass*
2	(2)	P	*ass*
2	(3)	$P \vee Q$	2 $\vee$-*int*$_1$
1, 2	(4)	*false*	1, 3 $\neg$-*elim*
1	(5)	$\neg P$	4 $\neg$-*int*
6	(6)	Q	*ass*
6	(7)	$P \vee Q$	6 $\vee$-*int*$_2$
1, 6	(8)	*false*	1, 7 $\neg$-*elim*
1	(9)	$\neg Q$	8 $\neg$-*int*
1	(10)	$\neg P \wedge \neg Q$	5, 9 $\wedge$-*int*

10.1.7 Soundness and Completeness

So far in this chapter I have presented the proof-theory of the propositional calculus and in chapter 2 I presented its model-theory. This calculus is both complete and sound. To say that a logical system is *sound* means that if $\Gamma \vdash P$, then $\Gamma \models P$ and to say that a logical system is *complete* or *adequate* means that if $\Gamma \models P$, then $\Gamma \vdash P$. In the case of the propositional calculus—and also of the predicate calculus—the two notions of syntactic and semantic consequence are extensionally equivalent, but this is not true of all logical systems.

10.2 Predicate Calculus

10.2.1 Introduction

In the propositional calculus formulas are treated as units. The internal structure of a formula—in whose construction no truth-functional connective occurs—is irrelevant to the validity or invalidity of any sequent in which that formula appears. In the predicate calculus that internal structure becomes important. The predicate calculus is also known as *first-order logic*. Some authors distinguish between first-order logic with identity and first-order logic without identity. In this book, first-order logic is always assumed to include identity.

10.2.2 Quantifier Rules

Free, Binding and Bound Variable Occurrences

A *primitive* formula of the predicate calculus is one which does not contain either any truth-functional connectives or any quantifiers. For example, *x borders albania* is a primitive formula. Every occurrence of a variable x is free in a primitive formula. So, the only occurrence of x in *x borders albania* is free, both occurrences of x in *x borders x* are free and both the occurrence of x and that of y in *x borders y* are free.

In order to work out if a particular occurrence of x is free in an arbitrary formula A we use a recursive definition. An occurrence of the variable x is *free* in the formula A iff its being so follows from one or more of the following seven clauses:[7]

(1) An occurrence of x is free in $\neg A$ iff the corresponding occurrence of x is free in A.

(2) An occurrence of x is free in $A \wedge B$ iff the corresponding occurrence of x is free in A or B (depending on which conjunct it occurs in).

(3) An occurrence of x is free in $A \vee B$ iff the corresponding occurrence of x is free in A or B.

---

[7] Z also contains variable-binding operators in addition to the universal and existential quantifiers, but in this chapter those quantifiers are the only variable-binding operators that I discuss.

(4) An occurrence of x is free in $A \Rightarrow B$ iff the corresponding occurrence of x is free in A or B.

(5) An occurrence of x is free in $A \Longleftrightarrow B$ iff the corresponding occurrence of x is free in A or B.

(6) An occurrence of x is free in $\forall y : Y \bullet A$ iff x is different from y and that occurrence of x is free in A.

(7) An occurrence of x is free in $\exists y : Y \bullet A$ iff x is different from y and that occurrence of x is free in A.

The occurrence of a variable x in a quantified formula $\forall x : X \bullet A$ or $\exists x : X \bullet A$ following either the universal or the existential quantifier is called the *binding* occurrence of that variable and the formula A is called the *scope* of that binding occurrence. An occurrence of a variable x is *bound* in a formula $\forall x : X \bullet A$ or $\exists x : X \bullet A$ iff x is not a binding occurrence and the corresponding occurrence of x is free in A.

Note that it is *occurrences* of variables that are either free, binding or bound and not variables. This is because the same variable can occur both free and bound in the same formula. For example, consider the formula:

$$x \text{ } borders \text{ } y \wedge \forall x : Europe \bullet (y \text{ } borders \text{ } x \vee \exists x : Europe : x \text{ } borders \text{ } y).$$

All occurrences of y are free in this formula as is the first occurrence of x. The second and fourth occurrences of x are binding occurrences and the third and fifth occurrences of x are bound occurrences. The third occurrence of x is bound by the second occurrence and lies in its scope. The fifth occurrence of x is bound by the fourth occurrence and it lies within the scope of that occurrence.

The Universal Quantifier

There is one elimination rule associated with the universal quantifier, namely $\forall$-*elim*:

$$\frac{\Gamma \mapsto \forall x : X \bullet A}{\Gamma \mapsto A[t/x].} \text{ } \forall\text{-}elim$$

Here, t is any term of the same type as x. The notation $A[t/x]$ stands for that formula which is obtained by substituting t for all free occurrences of x in A.

There is a single introduction rule for the universal quantifier, namely $\forall$-*int*:

$$\frac{\Gamma \mapsto A}{\Gamma \mapsto \forall x : X \bullet A[x/a].} \text{ } \forall\text{-}int$$

Here, x is a variable and a a constant of the same type which does not occur in Γ.

The Existential Quantifier

There is one elimination rule associated with the existential quantifier, namely ∃-*elim*:

$$\frac{\Gamma \mapsto \exists x \colon X \bullet A \quad \Delta, A[a/x] \mapsto C}{\Gamma, \Delta \mapsto C.} \; \exists\text{-}elim$$

Here, a is a constant of the same type as x and a cannot occur in Γ, Δ, $\exists x \colon X \bullet A$ or C. The reason for using the letter C in the statement of this rule—rather than B—is to bring out the connection between this rule and the rule ∨-*elim*.

There is one introduction rule associated with the existential quantifier, namely ∃-*int*:

$$\frac{\Gamma \mapsto A[t/x]}{\Gamma \mapsto \exists x \colon X \bullet A.} \; \exists\text{-}int$$

Here, x is a variable and t is a term of the same type.

Identity

The elimination rule for identity is:

$$\frac{\Gamma \mapsto A \quad \Delta \mapsto t = u}{\Gamma, \Delta \mapsto B.} \; =\text{-}elim$$

Here, t and u are any terms of the same type and B is like A except that u has been substituted for t one or more times. There is no need to substitute u for *all* occurrences of t.

The way in which the identity sign is introduced into a tree proof is by allowing leaf nodes in a correctly constructed tree proof to have the form $\mapsto t = t$, where t is any term. This start sequent is known as $=$-*int*. In other words, any formula of the form $t = t$ is treated as an axiom.

10.2.3 Examples of Proofs

In order to illustrate the rules just introduced this section contains a number of sample proofs. The first sequent that is shown to be valid is

$$\forall x \colon X \bullet (P(x) \Rightarrow Q(x)), \forall x \colon X \bullet (Q(x) \Rightarrow R(x)) \; \mapsto \; \forall x \colon X \bullet (P(x) \Rightarrow R(x)),$$

where I write $P(x)$, $Q(x)$ and $R(x)$ in order to indicate that x can occur free in each of those formulas and $P(a)$, for example, means that a has been substituted for all free occurrences of x in $P(x)$.

1	(1) $\forall x \colon X \bullet (P(x) \Rightarrow Q(x))$	*ass*
1	(2) $P(a) \Rightarrow Q(a)$	1 $\forall$-*elim*
3	(3) $\forall x \colon X \bullet (Q(x) \Rightarrow R(x))$	*ass*
3	(4) $Q(a) \Rightarrow R(a)$	3 $\forall$-*elim*
5	(5) $P(a)$	*ass*
1,5	(6) $Q(a)$	$2,5 \Rightarrow$-*elim*
1,3,5	(7) $R(a)$	$4,6 \Rightarrow$-*elim*
1,3	(8) $P(a) \Rightarrow R(a)$	$7 \Rightarrow$-*int*
1,3	(9) $\forall x \colon X \bullet (P(x) \Rightarrow R(x))$	8 $\forall$-*int*

To illustrate the existential quantifier rules I prove that the sequent

$$\forall x \colon X \bullet (P(x) \Rightarrow Q(x)), \exists x \colon X \bullet \neg Q(x) \;\mapsto\; \exists x \colon X \bullet \neg P(x) \tag{10.12}$$

is valid. This is done as follows:

1	(1) $\forall x \colon X \bullet (P(x) \Rightarrow Q(x))$	*ass*
2	(2) $\exists x \colon X \bullet \neg Q(x)$	*ass*
3	(3) $\neg Q(a)$	*ass*
1	(4) $P(a) \Rightarrow Q(a)$	1 $\forall$-*elim*
5	(5) $P(a)$	*ass*
1,5	(6) $Q(a)$	$4,5 \Rightarrow$-*elim*
1,3,5	(7) *false*	$3,6 \neg$-*elim*
1,3	(8) $\neg P(a)$	$7 \neg$-*int*
1,3	(9) $\exists x \colon X \bullet \neg P(x)$	8 $\exists$-*int*
1,2	(10) $\exists x \colon X \bullet \neg P(x)$	$2,9 \exists$-*elim*

Because the rule $\exists$-*elim* is a bit complicated I explain its operation in this proof in some detail. Recall the rule $\exists$-*elim*:

$$\frac{\Gamma \;\mapsto\; \exists x \colon X \bullet A \quad \Delta, A[a/x] \;\mapsto\; C}{\Gamma, \Delta \;\mapsto\; C.} \; \exists\text{-}elim$$

Here, a is a constant of the same type as x which cannot occur in Γ, Δ, $\exists x \colon X \bullet A$ or C. Line (2) of the above proof is:

$$\overbrace{\exists x \colon X \bullet \neg Q(x)}^{\Gamma} \;\mapsto\; \overbrace{\exists x \colon X \bullet \neg Q(x)}^{\exists x \colon X \bullet A}.$$

And line (9) is:

$$\overbrace{\forall x \colon X \bullet (P(x) \Rightarrow Q(x))}^{\Delta}, \overbrace{\neg Q(a)}^{A[a/x]} \;\mapsto\; \overbrace{\exists x \colon X \bullet \neg P(x)}^{C}.$$

The side conditions are easy to verify, so the output sequent is:

$$\overbrace{\exists x \colon X \bullet \neg Q(x)}^{\Gamma}, \overbrace{\forall x \colon X \bullet (P(x) \Rightarrow Q(x))}^{\Delta} \;\mapsto\; \overbrace{\exists x \colon X \bullet \neg P(x)}^{C}$$

and this is what line (10) of the proof states.

The connection between ∃-*elim* and ∨-*elim* can be brought out clearly by considering the sequent (10.12) in a situation where the set X contains just two elements, say b and c.

1	(1)	$\forall x \colon X \bullet (P(x) \Rightarrow Q(x))$	*ass*
2	(2)	$\neg Q(b) \vee \neg Q(c)$	*ass*
3	(3)	$\neg Q(b)$	*ass*
1	(4)	$P(b) \Rightarrow Q(b)$	1 ∀-*elim*
5	(5)	$P(b)$	*ass*
1, 5	(6)	$Q(b)$	$4, 5 \Rightarrow$-*elim*
1, 3, 5	(7)	*false*	3, 6 ¬-*elim*
1, 3	(8)	$\neg P(b)$	7 ¬-*int*
1, 3	(9)	$\neg P(b) \vee \neg P(c)$	8 ∨-*int*₁
10	(10)	$\neg Q(c)$	*ass*
1	(11)	$P(c) \Rightarrow Q(c)$	1 ∀-*elim*
12	(12)	$P(c)$	*ass*
1, 12	(13)	$Q(c)$	$11, 12 \Rightarrow$-*elim*
1, 10, 12	(14)	*false*	10, 13 ¬-*elim*
1, 10	(15)	$\neg P(c)$	14 ¬-*int*
1, 10	(16)	$\neg P(b) \vee \neg P(c)$	15 ∨-*int*₂
1, 2	(17)	$\neg P(b) \vee \neg P(c)$	2, 9, 16 ∨-*elim*

Recall the rule ∨-*elim*:

$$\frac{\Gamma \mapsto A \vee B \quad \Delta, A \mapsto C \quad \Sigma, B \mapsto C}{\Gamma, \Delta, \Sigma \mapsto C.} \text{ ∨-}elim$$

Line (2) of the above proof is:

$$\overbrace{\neg Qb \vee \neg Qc}^{\Gamma} \mapsto \overbrace{\neg Qb}^{A} \vee \overbrace{\neg Qc}^{B}.$$

Line (9) is:

$$\overbrace{\forall x \colon X \bullet (Px \Rightarrow Qx)}^{\Delta}, \overbrace{\neg Qb}^{A} \mapsto \overbrace{\neg Pb \vee \neg Pc}^{C}.$$

And line (16) is:

$$\overbrace{\forall x \colon X \bullet (Px \Rightarrow Qx)}^{\Sigma}, \overbrace{\neg Qc}^{B} \mapsto \overbrace{\neg Pb \vee \neg Pc}^{C}.$$

Thus, by ∨-*elim* we have:

$$\overbrace{\neg Qb \vee \neg Qc}^{\Gamma}, \overbrace{\forall x \colon X \bullet (Px \Rightarrow Qx)}^{\Delta, \Sigma} \mapsto \overbrace{\neg Pb \vee \neg Pc}^{C}.$$

Because of the analogy between ∨-*elim* and ∃-*elim*, Lemmon (1965), p. 112, calls the formula $A[a/x]$ in the rule ∃-*elim* the *typical disjunct*.

The next sequent of the predicate calculus that I am going to prove to be valid is

$$\exists x\colon X \bullet \forall y\colon Y \bullet P(x,y) \;\mapsto\; \forall y\colon Y \bullet \exists x\colon X \bullet P(x,y), \qquad (10.13)$$

where x and y can both occur free in $P(x,y)$.

$$
\begin{array}{llll}
1 & (1) & \exists x\colon X \bullet \forall y\colon Y \bullet P(x,y) & ass \\
2 & (2) & \forall y\colon Y \bullet P(a,y) & ass \\
3 & (3) & P(a,b) & 2\;\forall\text{-}elim \\
2 & (4) & \exists x\colon X \bullet P(x,b) & 3\;\exists\text{-}int \\
2 & (5) & \forall y\colon Y \bullet \exists x\colon X \bullet P(x,y) & 4\;\forall\text{-}int \\
1 & (6) & \forall y\colon Y \bullet \exists x\colon X \bullet P(x,y) & 1,5\;\exists\text{-}elim
\end{array}
$$

Because the rule $\exists$-*elim* takes a bit of getting used to, I will again explain its application in line (6) in a bit more detail. Recall the tree form of $\exists$-*elim*:

$$\frac{\Gamma \;\mapsto\; \exists x\colon X \bullet A \quad \Delta, A[a/x] \;\mapsto\; C}{\Gamma, \Delta \;\mapsto\; C}\;\exists\text{-}elim$$

Here, $a\colon X$ is a constant which must not occur in Γ, Δ, $\exists x\colon X \bullet A$ or C. Line (1) in the proof is:

$$\overbrace{\exists x\colon X \bullet \forall y\colon Y \bullet P(x,y)}^{\Gamma} \;\mapsto\; \overbrace{\exists x\colon X \bullet \forall y\colon Y \bullet P(x,y).}^{\exists x\colon X \bullet A}$$

Line (5) is:

$$\overbrace{\forall y\colon Y \bullet P(a,y)}^{A[a/x]} \;\mapsto\; \overbrace{\forall y\colon Y \bullet \exists x\colon X \bullet P(x,y)}^{C}$$

and Δ here is empty. The side conditions in the rule $\exists$-*elim* are easy to verify, therefore we can infer:

$$\overbrace{\exists x\colon X \bullet \forall y\colon Y \bullet P(x,y)}^{\Gamma} \;\mapsto\; \overbrace{\forall y\colon Y \bullet \exists x\colon X \bullet P(x,y)}^{C}$$

and this is line (6) in the proof.

It should be noted that the converse of (10.13) is not a valid sequent. It is easy to construct a counterexample. Let $P(x,y)$ be the relation 'x is a parent of y'. Then, although it is true that everybody has a parent, that is to say, $\forall y\colon Y \bullet \exists x\colon X \bullet P(x,y)$, it is false to say that there exists a single[8] person who is a parent of everyone, that is to say, $\exists x\colon X \bullet \forall y\colon Y \bullet P(x,y)$.

The next thing that I prove is that $P(a) \dashv\vdash \exists x\colon X \bullet P(a)$. First, I prove that the sequent $P(a) \mapsto \exists x\colon X \bullet P(a)$ is valid:

$$
\begin{array}{llll}
1 & (1) & P(a) & ass \\
1 & (2) & \exists x\colon X \bullet P(a) & 1\;\exists\text{-}int
\end{array}
$$

In this application of the rule $\exists$-*int* the formula A is taken to be $P(a)$ and t is any constant except a, so that $A[t/x]$ is the same formula as $P(a)$.

---

[8]'Single' in the sense of there being the only one, not in the sense of being unmarried.

Second, I prove that the sequent $\exists x\colon X \bullet P(a) \mapsto P(a)$ is valid:

$$
\begin{array}{lll}
1 & (1) \quad \exists x\colon X \bullet P(a) & ass \\
2 & (2) \quad P(a) & ass \\
1 & (3) \quad P(a) & 1,2\ \exists\text{-}elim
\end{array}
$$

In this application of $\exists$-*elim* both of the formulas A and C are taken to be $P(a)$. This means that $A[b/x]$ is the same as $P(a)$. Note that Δ is the empty set.

The next thing I prove is that $P(y) \dashv\vdash \exists z\colon X \bullet z = y \wedge P(z)$. The proofs make use of the start sequent and the thema for identity. First, I show that the sequent $P(y) \mapsto \exists z\colon X \bullet z = y \wedge P(z)$ is valid:

$$
\begin{array}{lll}
1 & (1) \quad P(y) & ass \\
  & (2) \quad y = y & =\text{-}int \\
1 & (3) \quad y = y \wedge P(y) & 1,2\ \wedge\text{-}int \\
1 & (4) \quad \exists z\colon X \bullet z = y \wedge P(z) & 3\ \exists\text{-}int
\end{array}
$$

In this application of the rule $\exists$-*int* the formula A is taken to be $z = y \wedge P(z)$ and so $A[y/z]$ is the same formula as $y = y \wedge P(y)$.

Second, I show that $\exists z\colon X \bullet z = y \wedge P(z) \mapsto P(y)$ is valid:

$$
\begin{array}{lll}
1 & (1) \quad \exists z\colon X \bullet z = y \wedge P(z) & ass \\
2 & (2) \quad a = y \wedge P(a) & ass \\
2 & (3) \quad a = y & 2\ \wedge\text{-}elim_1 \\
2 & (4) \quad P(a) & 2\ \wedge\text{-}elim_2 \\
2 & (5) \quad P(y) & 3,4\ =\text{-}elim \\
1 & (6) \quad P(y) & 1,5\ \exists\text{-}elim
\end{array}
$$

In this application of $\exists$-*elim* the formula C is taken to be $P(y)$ and A is $z = y \wedge P(z)$, so $A[a/z]$ is the same as $a = y \wedge P(a)$. The set Δ is empty and Γ consist of the single formula $\exists z\colon X \bullet z = y \wedge P(z)$.

10.2.4   Useful Laws

In the following laws x can occur free in P:

$$
\forall x\colon X \bullet P \dashv\vdash \neg\exists x\colon X \bullet \neg P,
$$
$$
\neg\forall x\colon X \bullet P \dashv\vdash \exists x\colon X \bullet \neg P,
$$
$$
\exists x\colon X \bullet P \dashv\vdash \neg\forall x\colon X \bullet \neg P,
$$
$$
\neg\exists x\colon X \bullet P \dashv\vdash \forall x\colon X \bullet \neg P.
$$

In the following group of laws there is no restriction on which variables can or cannot occur free in P and Q:

$$
\forall x\colon X; y\colon Y \bullet P \dashv\vdash \forall y\colon Y; x\colon X \bullet P,
$$
$$
\exists x\colon X; y\colon Y \bullet P \dashv\vdash \exists y\colon Y; x\colon X \bullet P,
$$

$$(\forall x\colon X \bullet P) \vee (\forall x\colon X \bullet Q) \;\vdash\; \forall x\colon X \bullet P \vee Q,$$
$$\forall x\colon X \bullet (P \wedge Q) \;\dashv\vdash\; (\forall x\colon X \bullet P) \wedge (\forall x\colon X \bullet Q),$$
$$\forall x\colon X \bullet (P \Rightarrow Q) \;\vdash\; (\forall x\colon X \bullet P) \Rightarrow (\forall x\colon X \bullet Q),$$
$$\exists x\colon X \bullet (P \vee Q) \;\dashv\vdash\; (\exists x\colon X \bullet P) \vee (\exists x\colon X \bullet Q),$$
$$\exists x\colon X \bullet (P \wedge Q) \;\vdash\; (\exists x\colon X \bullet P) \wedge (\exists x\colon X \bullet Q),$$
$$\exists x\colon X \bullet \forall y\colon Y \bullet P \;\vdash\; \forall y\colon Y \bullet \exists x\colon X \bullet P.$$

In the following laws x cannot occur free in P, but it can occur free in Q:

$$\forall x\colon X \bullet P \;\dashv\vdash\; P,$$
$$\exists x\colon X \bullet P \;\dashv\vdash\; P,$$
$$\forall x\colon X \bullet (P \vee Q) \;\dashv\vdash\; P \vee \forall x\colon X \bullet Q,$$
$$\forall x\colon X \bullet (P \wedge Q) \;\dashv\vdash\; P \wedge \forall x\colon X \bullet Q,$$
$$\forall x\colon X \bullet (P \Rightarrow Q) \;\dashv\vdash\; P \Rightarrow \forall x\colon X \bullet Q,$$
$$(\forall x\colon X \bullet Q) \Rightarrow P \;\dashv\vdash\; \exists x\colon X \bullet (Q \Rightarrow P),$$
$$\exists x\colon X \bullet (P \vee Q) \;\dashv\vdash\; P \vee \exists x\colon X \bullet Q,$$
$$\exists x\colon X \bullet (P \wedge Q) \;\dashv\vdash\; P \wedge \exists x\colon X \bullet Q,$$
$$\exists x\colon X \bullet (P \Rightarrow Q) \;\dashv\vdash\; P \Rightarrow \exists x\colon X \bullet Q,$$
$$(\exists x\colon X \bullet Q) \Rightarrow P \;\dashv\vdash\; \forall x\colon X \bullet (Q \Rightarrow P).$$

In the next two laws x cannot occur free in P and y cannot occur free in Q:

$$\forall y\colon Y \bullet \exists x\colon X \bullet (P \wedge Q) \;\dashv\vdash\; (\forall y\colon Y \bullet P) \wedge (\exists x\colon X \bullet Q),$$
$$\forall y\colon Y \bullet \exists x\colon X \bullet (P \vee Q) \;\dashv\vdash\; (\forall y\colon Y \bullet P) \vee (\exists x\colon X \bullet Q).$$

Next, I give some examples of laws involving identity:

$$\vdash\; \forall x\colon X \bullet x = x,$$
$$\vdash\; \forall x, y\colon X \bullet (x = y \Rightarrow y = x),$$
$$\vdash\; \forall x, y, z\colon X \bullet (x = y \wedge y = z \Rightarrow x = z),$$
$$P[t/x] \;\dashv\vdash\; \exists x\colon X \bullet x = t \wedge P, \tag{10.14}$$
$$P[t/x] \;\dashv\vdash\; \forall x\colon X \bullet x = t \Rightarrow P. \tag{10.15}$$

In (10.14) and (10.15) x can occur free in P, t must be a term of the same type as x and x cannot occur free in t. The two laws (10.14) and (10.15) are called *one-point laws*. They are closely related to the following two theorems:

$$P[t/x] \iff \exists x\colon X \bullet x = t \wedge P,$$
$$P[t/x] \iff \forall x\colon X \bullet x = t \Rightarrow P.$$

The relation between such laws and such theorems is one of the topics of the next section.

10.3   Theorems, Sequents and Themata

In this section I establish the following connections between theorems, valid sequents and correct themata and I give some examples of their usefulness:

$P \dashv\vdash Q$ iff $P \Longleftrightarrow Q$ is a theorem and $P \dashv\vdash Q$ iff both of the themata

$$\frac{\Gamma \mapsto P}{\Gamma \mapsto Q,} \; thema_1 \qquad\qquad \frac{\Gamma \mapsto Q}{\Gamma \mapsto P,} \; thema_2$$

are correct, that is to say, they both transmit validity.

To establish these claims I first show that if $P \dashv\vdash Q$, then $P \Longleftrightarrow Q$ is a theorem. The following incomplete tree proof establishes this:

$$\cfrac{\cfrac{P \mapsto Q}{\mapsto P \Rightarrow Q} \;\Rightarrow\text{-}int \qquad \cfrac{Q \mapsto P}{\mapsto Q \Rightarrow P} \;\Rightarrow\text{-}int}{\mapsto P \Longleftrightarrow Q.} \;\Longleftrightarrow\text{-}int$$

This is incomplete because the leaf nodes are not start sequents. It is, however, made up only out of instances of correct thematic rules, thus it transmits validity from its leaf nodes to its root. By hypothesis the leaf nodes are valid, hence the sequent $\mapsto P \Longleftrightarrow Q$ is valid and by the definition of what a theorem is it follows that $P \Longleftrightarrow Q$ is a theorem.

Next, I show that if $P \Longleftrightarrow Q$ is a theorem, then $P \dashv\vdash Q$. This is done by means of the following incomplete tree proofs:

$$\cfrac{P \mapsto P \qquad \cfrac{\cfrac{\mapsto P \Longleftrightarrow Q}{\mapsto P \Rightarrow Q} \;\Longleftrightarrow\text{-}elim_1}{} \;\Rightarrow\text{-}elim}{P \mapsto Q,} \qquad\qquad \cfrac{Q \mapsto Q \qquad \cfrac{\cfrac{\mapsto P \Longleftrightarrow Q}{\mapsto Q \Rightarrow P} \;\Longleftrightarrow\text{-}elim_2}{} \;\Rightarrow\text{-}elim}{Q \mapsto P.}$$

These are both constructed only out of instances of correct themata, thus they both transmit validity from their leaf nodes to their roots. By hypothesis $P \Longleftrightarrow Q$ is a theorem, therefore the sequent $\mapsto P \Longleftrightarrow Q$ is valid. Thus, both the sequents $P \mapsto Q$ and $Q \mapsto P$ are valid. Hence, $P \dashv\vdash Q$.

Next, I show that if $P \dashv\vdash Q$, then both $thema_1$ and $thema_2$ are correct. The following incomplete tree proofs establish this:

$$\frac{\Gamma \mapsto P \quad P \mapsto Q}{\Gamma \mapsto Q,} \; cut \qquad\qquad \frac{\Gamma \mapsto Q \quad Q \mapsto P}{\Gamma \mapsto P.} \; cut$$

These are both constructed only out of instances of correct thematic rules, therefore they both transmit validity from their leaf nodes to their roots. Consider the tree proof on the left first. By hypothesis, the sequent $P \mapsto Q$ is valid and—as the tree proof transmits validity—if $\Gamma \mapsto P$ is valid, then so is $\Gamma \mapsto Q$. Hence, $thema_1$ is correct. A similar argument concerning the tree proof on the right establishes that $thema_2$ is correct if the sequent $Q \mapsto P$ is valid and this sequent is valid by hypothesis. (Recall that $P \dashv\vdash Q$ iff both of the sequents $P \mapsto Q$ and $Q \mapsto P$ are valid.)

Finally, I show that if *thema₁* and *thema₂* are both correct, then $P \dashv\vdash Q$. The following tree proofs establish this:

$$\frac{P \mapsto P}{P \mapsto Q,} \; thema_1 \qquad \frac{Q \mapsto Q}{Q \mapsto P.} \; thema_2$$

By hypothesis, these are both correctly constructed tree proofs, therefore both $P \mapsto Q$ and $Q \mapsto P$ are valid. Hence, $P \dashv\vdash Q$.

Similarly, it can be shown that $P(x) \dashv\vdash Q(x)$ iff $\forall x: X \bullet P(x) \Longleftrightarrow Q(x)$ is a theorem and that $P(x) \dashv\vdash Q(x)$ iff both of the following themata are correct:

$$\frac{\Gamma \mapsto P(x)}{\Gamma \mapsto Q(x),} \qquad \frac{\Gamma \mapsto Q(x)}{\Gamma \mapsto P(x).}$$

Similar results can also be established when there is a string of universal quantifiers preceding the bi-implication.

These results are used extensively in the next chapter in order to obtain thematic rules that can be used to reason about the various set-theoretic operators that are defined in Z. In the remainder of this section I show how they can be used to obtain thematic analogues of one de Morgan's laws and of the one-point law involving the existential quantifier and also elimination and introduction rules for the restricted universal quantifier and the restricted existential quantifier.

The following de Morgan's law was proved above:

$$\neg(P \vee Q) \dashv\vdash \neg P \wedge \neg Q.$$

Transforming this into themata as explained earlier in this section results in the following rules:

$$\frac{\Gamma \mapsto \neg(P \vee Q)}{\Gamma \mapsto \neg P \wedge \neg Q,} \; deM \qquad \frac{\Gamma \mapsto \neg P \wedge \neg Q}{\Gamma \mapsto \neg(P \vee Q),} \; deM$$

which can be called (*one pair of*) de Morgan's themata. One of these is used twice in the following proof of the law of the excluded middle:

$$\frac{\dfrac{\dfrac{\neg(P \vee \neg P) \mapsto \neg(P \vee \neg P)}{\neg(P \vee \neg P) \mapsto \neg P \wedge \neg\neg P} \; deM}{\neg(P \vee \neg P) \mapsto \neg P} \; {\wedge\text{-}elim_1} \qquad \dfrac{\dfrac{\neg(P \vee \neg P) \mapsto \neg(P \vee \neg P)}{\neg(P \vee \neg P) \mapsto \neg P \wedge \neg\neg P} \; deM}{\dfrac{\neg(P \vee \neg P) \mapsto \neg\neg P}{} } \; {\wedge\text{-}elim_2}}{\dfrac{\dfrac{\neg(P \vee \neg P) \mapsto false}{\mapsto \neg\neg(P \vee \neg P)} \; {\neg\text{-}int}}{\mapsto P \vee \neg P.} \; {\neg\neg\text{-}elim}} \; {\neg\text{-}elim}$$

The one-point law involving the existential quantifier was displayed above as (10.14). Transforming this into themata as explained earlier results in the following rules:

$$\frac{\Gamma \mapsto \exists x: X \bullet x = t \wedge P}{\Gamma \mapsto P[t/x],} \; {\exists\text{-}one\text{-}elim} \qquad \frac{\Gamma \mapsto P[t/x]}{\Gamma \mapsto \exists x: X \bullet x = t \wedge P,} \; {\exists\text{-}one\text{-}int}$$

where x is a variable that occurs free in P and t is a term of the same type in which x does not occur free.

In chapter 2 the following law was displayed:

$$(\forall D \mid P \bullet Q) \Longleftrightarrow (\forall D \bullet P \Rightarrow Q).$$

This can be treated as an axiom. All axioms are theorems, therefore we can transform this law into the following pair of thematic rules:

$$\frac{\Gamma \mapsto \forall D \mid P \bullet Q}{\Gamma \mapsto \forall D \bullet P \Rightarrow Q,} \ \forall\text{-res-elim} \qquad\qquad \frac{\Gamma \mapsto \forall D \bullet P \Rightarrow Q}{\Gamma \mapsto \forall D \mid P \bullet Q.} \ \forall\text{-res-int}$$

In chapter 2 the following law was displayed:

$$(\exists D \mid P \bullet Q) \Longleftrightarrow (\exists D \bullet P \wedge Q).$$

This can be treated as an axiom. All axioms are theorems, therefore using the above transformations which allow us to obtain thematic rules from a theorem whose main connective is $\Longleftrightarrow$ results in the following:

$$\frac{\Gamma \mapsto \exists D \mid P \bullet Q}{\Gamma \mapsto \exists D \bullet P \wedge Q,} \ \exists\text{-res-elim} \qquad\qquad \frac{\Gamma \mapsto \exists D \bullet P \wedge Q}{\Gamma \mapsto \exists D \mid P \bullet Q.} \ \exists\text{-res-int}$$

10.4   Exercises

10.1) Establish, by constructing proofs, that each of the following is true:

a) $P \wedge (Q \wedge R) \dashv\vdash (P \wedge Q) \wedge R$.

b) $P \vee (Q \vee R) \dashv\vdash (P \vee Q) \vee R$.

c) $P \wedge Q \dashv\vdash (P \vee \neg Q) \wedge Q$.

d) $P \Rightarrow Q \dashv\vdash \neg P \vee Q$.

e) $Q \Rightarrow R \vdash (P \vee Q) \Rightarrow (P \vee R)$.

f) $P_1 \Rightarrow P_2, P_3 \Rightarrow P_4 \vdash (P_1 \vee P_3) \Rightarrow (P_2 \vee P_4)$.

10.2) Establish, by constructing proofs, that each of the following is true:

a) $\forall x \colon X \bullet (P(x) \wedge Q(x)) \dashv\vdash (\forall x \colon X \bullet P(x)) \wedge (\forall x \colon X \bullet Q(x))$.

b) $\exists x \colon X \bullet (P(x) \vee Q(x)) \dashv\vdash (\exists x \colon X \bullet P(x)) \vee (\exists x \colon X \bullet Q(x))$.

c) $\forall x \colon X \bullet P(x) \dashv\vdash \neg \exists x \colon X \bullet \neg P(x)$.

d) $\forall x \colon X \bullet (P(x) \Rightarrow Q(x)), \forall x \colon X \bullet P(x) \vdash \forall x \colon X \bullet Q(x)$.

e) $\exists x \colon X \bullet (P(x) \wedge Q(x)) \vdash (\exists x \colon X \bullet P(x)) \wedge (\exists x \colon X \bullet Q(x))$.

10.3) Establish the syntactic equivalence of the formulas $A \Rightarrow false$ and $\neg A$. That is to say, prove that $A \Rightarrow false \dashv\vdash \neg A$.

11

Rigorous Proof

11.1 Introduction

In the previous chapter I developed a proof-theory for first-order logic. Mathematicians rarely, however, construct fully formal proofs of the theorems that interest them. Almost all of the time they make use of *rigorous* proofs. There is, however, a fairly widespread belief among mathematicians that every correct rigorous proof can be transformed into a fully formal one. First-order logic can be thought of as the machine language of mathematics and then rigorous proofs can be compared to programs written in a high-level programming language.[1] In the next section I explain how set theory can be fitted into the framework of a single-conclusion sequent calculus and I give a few examples of formal proofs of set-theoretic results, but towards the end of that section I begin to use informal but rigorous proofs of theorems in set theory. In section 11.3 I present the additional axioms that are needed in order to reason about Cartesian products in Z. In sections 11.4 and 11.5 I turn to the topic of induction—first for the non-negative numbers and then for sequences.

11.2 Reasoning about Sets

In order to reason about sets we need to add some principles to the deductive machinery developed in the previous chapter. There are various ways in which this could be done, but I have decided to include these principles by adding various axioms to the proof-theory of first-order logic. In the context of a sequent calculus an *axiom* is a formula A that forms start sequents of the form $\varnothing \mapsto A$.

The *set equality axiom* is the following formula:

$$\forall U, V : \mathbf{P}\, X \bullet U = V \iff \forall x : X \bullet x \in U \iff x \in V.$$

---

[1] Several books have been published recently which introduce the idea of a rigorous, but not fully formal, mathematical proof. See, for example, (Morash 1987), (Franklin and Daoud 1988) and (Cupillari 1989). It is also a good idea to read (Lakatos 1976) to get an idea of the real role of proof in mathematics.

The *set enumeration axiom* is the following formula:

$$\forall x, y_1, y_2, \ldots, y_n \colon X \bullet (x \in \{y_1, y_2, \ldots, y_n\} \iff (x = y_1 \vee x = y_2 \vee \ldots \vee x = y_n)).$$

The *set comprehension axiom* is the formula:

$$\forall x \colon X \bullet (x \in \{D \mid P \bullet t\} \iff \exists D \mid P \bullet t = x),$$

where D is a declaration, P a formula, x is not declared in D and t is a term of the same type as x which does not contain any free occurrences of x.

The *empty set axiom* is the formula $\forall x \colon X \bullet x \notin \varnothing[X]$. Because the empty set is defined in Z to be the same as $\{x \colon X \mid false\}$ it would, in fact, be possible to prove the formula $\forall x \colon X \bullet x \notin \varnothing[X]$ to be a theorem from the set comprehension axiom. All that shows is that the axioms given here are not independent. There is no harm in that.

The *power set axiom* is the formula:

$$U \in \mathbf{P} V \iff (\forall x \colon X \bullet x \in U \Rightarrow x \in V).$$

Using the results of section 10.3 in the last chapter it is possible to transform all of these—except the empty set axiom—into thematic rules. The elimination and introduction rules relating to set equality are:

$$\frac{\Gamma \mapsto U = V}{\Gamma \mapsto \forall x \colon X \bullet x \in U \iff x \in V,} \; \textit{seteq-elim}$$

$$\frac{\Gamma \mapsto \forall x \colon X \bullet x \in U \iff x \in V}{\Gamma \mapsto U = V.} \; \textit{seteq-int}$$

The elimination and introduction rules relating to set enumeration are:

$$\frac{\Gamma \mapsto x \in \{y_1, y_2, \ldots, y_n\}}{\Gamma \mapsto x = y_1 \vee x = y_2 \vee \ldots \vee x = y_n,} \; \textit{setenum-elim}$$

$$\frac{\Gamma \mapsto x = y_1 \vee x = y_2 \vee \ldots \vee x = y_n}{\Gamma \mapsto x \in \{y_1, y_2, \ldots, y_n\}.} \; \textit{setenum-int}$$

The elimination and introduction rules relating to set comprehension are:

$$\frac{\Gamma \mapsto x \in \{D \mid P \bullet t\}}{\Gamma \mapsto \exists D \mid P \bullet t = x,} \; \textit{setcomp-elim} \qquad \frac{\Gamma \mapsto \exists D \mid P \bullet t = x}{\Gamma \mapsto x \in \{D \mid P \bullet t\},} \; \textit{setcomp-int}$$

where D is a declaration, P a formula, x is not declared in D and t is a term of the same type as x which does not contain any free occurrences of x. The elimination and introduction rules relating to the power set operator are:

$$\frac{\Gamma \mapsto U \in \mathbf{P} V}{\Gamma \mapsto \forall x \colon X \bullet x \in U \Rightarrow x \in V,} \; \mathbf{P}\textit{-elim} \qquad \frac{\Gamma \mapsto \forall x \colon X \bullet x \in U \Rightarrow x \in V}{\Gamma \mapsto U \in \mathbf{P} V.} \; \mathbf{P}\textit{-int}$$

Most of the results that we want to prove about sets involve defined operators. For example, we may want to prove that the formula $\forall U : \mathbf{P}\, X \bullet \varnothing[X] \subseteq U$ is a theorem. This makes use of the symbol $\subseteq$. The formal definition of this is:[2]

$$
\begin{array}{|l}
\hline
=\!=[X]\!=\!=\!=\!=\!=\!=\!=\!=\!=\!=\!= \\
\hline
\_ \subseteq \_ : \mathbf{P}\, X \leftrightarrow \mathbf{P}\, X \\
\hline
\forall U, V : \mathbf{P}\, X \bullet \\
\quad U \subseteq V \iff (\forall x : X \bullet x \in U \Rightarrow x \in V) \\
\hline
\end{array}
$$

Because the formula

$$\forall U, V : \mathbf{P}\, X \bullet (U \subseteq V \iff (\forall x : X \bullet x \in U \Rightarrow x \in V)) \tag{11.1}$$

is used to define the subset relation symbol it can be used as an axiom in proofs, that is to say, as a formula whose correctness is assumed without proof. Using model-theoretic terminology, the formula (11.1) is *true by definition*. Using the results proved in section 10.3 we can transform the formula (11.1) into the following thematic rules:

$$\frac{\Gamma \;\mapsto\; U \subseteq V}{\Gamma \;\mapsto\; \forall x : X \bullet x \in U \Rightarrow x \in V,} \; \subseteq\text{-}elim$$

$$\frac{\Gamma \;\mapsto\; \forall x : X \bullet x \in U \Rightarrow x \in V}{\Gamma \;\mapsto\; U \subseteq V.} \; \subseteq\text{-}int$$

To prove that the formula $\forall U : \mathbf{P}\, X \bullet \varnothing[X] \subseteq U$ is a theorem we reason as follows:

$$
\cfrac{
  \cfrac{
    \cfrac{\mapsto\; \forall x : X \bullet x \notin \varnothing[X]}{\mapsto\; a \notin \varnothing[X]} \; \forall\text{-}elim
    \qquad a \notin \varnothing[X] \;\mapsto\; a \in \varnothing[X] \Rightarrow a \in U
  }{
    \cfrac{
      \cfrac{
        \cfrac{\mapsto\; a \in \varnothing[X] \Rightarrow a \in U}{\mapsto\; \forall x : X \bullet x \in \varnothing[X] \Rightarrow x \in U} \; \forall\text{-}int
      }{\mapsto\; \varnothing[X] \subseteq U} \; \subseteq\text{-}int
    }{\mapsto\; \forall U : \mathbf{P}\, X \bullet \varnothing[X] \subseteq U.} \; \forall\text{-}int
  } \; cut
}{}
$$

The rightmost leaf node is a substitution instance of a valid sequent from the propositional calculus involving $\Rightarrow$ and the conclusion of the sequent which forms the leftmost leaf node is the empty set axiom.

Getting thematic rules from some definitions is more difficult than the way in which the rules $\subseteq$-*elim* and $\subseteq$-*int* were obtained. For example, the definition of the set intersection operator is as follows:

$$
\begin{array}{|l}
\hline
=\!=[X]\!=\!=\!=\!=\!=\!=\!=\!=\!=\!=\!= \\
\hline
\_ \cap \_ : \mathbf{P}\, X \times \mathbf{P}\, X \longrightarrow \mathbf{P}\, X \\
\hline
\forall U, V : \mathbf{P}\, X \bullet \\
\quad U \cap V = \{\, y : X \mid y \in U \wedge y \in V \,\} \\
\hline
\end{array}
$$

---

[2]Formal definitions of almost all of the operators to be found in standard Z are contained in chapter 21. The symbol $\subseteq$ is defined on p. 285.

In order to obtain elimination and introduction rules from this we first need to show that $x \in U \cap V \dashv\vdash x \in U \wedge x \in V$. First, I show that the sequent

$$x \in U \cap V \;\mapsto\; x \in U \wedge x \in V$$

is valid. The following proof achieves this:

$$
\begin{array}{lll}
(1) & \forall U, V : \mathbf{P}\,X \bullet U \cap V = \{\, y \colon X \mid y \in U \wedge y \in V \,\} & \text{definition } \cap \\
(2) & \forall V : \mathbf{P}\,X \bullet U \cap V = \{\, y \colon X \mid y \in U \wedge y \in V \,\} & 1 \;\forall\text{-}elim \\
(3) & U \cap V = \{\, y \colon X \mid y \in U \wedge y \in V \,\} & 2 \;\forall\text{-}elim \\
4 \quad (4) & x \in U \cap V & ass \\
4 \quad (5) & x \in \{\, y \colon X \mid y \in U \wedge y \in V \,\} & 3, 4 \; =\text{-}elim \\
4 \quad (6) & \exists y \colon X \mid y \in U \wedge y \in V \bullet y = x & 5 \; setcomp\text{-}elim \\
4 \quad (7) & \exists y \colon X \bullet y \in U \wedge y \in V \wedge y = x & 6 \; \exists\text{-}res\text{-}elim \\
4 \quad (8) & x \in U \wedge x \in V & 7 \; \exists\text{-}one\text{-}elim
\end{array}
$$

The following proof establishes that the sequent $x \in U \wedge x \in V \;\mapsto\; x \in U \cap V$ is valid:

$$
\begin{array}{lll}
(1) & \forall U, V : \mathbf{P}\,X \bullet U \cap V = \{\, y \colon X \mid y \in U \wedge y \in V \,\} & \text{definition } \cap \\
(2) & \forall V : \mathbf{P}\,X \bullet U \cap V = \{\, y \colon X \mid y \in U \wedge y \in V \,\} & 1 \;\forall\text{-}elim \\
(3) & U \cap V = \{\, x \colon X \mid x \in U \wedge x \in V \,\} & 2 \;\forall\text{-}elim \\
4 \quad (4) & x \in U \wedge x \in V & ass \\
4 \quad (5) & \exists y \colon X \bullet y \in U \wedge y \in V \wedge y = x & 4 \; \exists\text{-}one\text{-}int \\
4 \quad (6) & \exists y \colon X \mid y \in U \wedge y \in V \bullet y = x & 5 \; \exists\text{-}res\text{-}int \\
4 \quad (7) & x \in \{\, y \colon X \mid y \in U \wedge y \in V \,\} & 6 \; setcomp\text{-}int \\
4 \quad (8) & x \in U \cap V & 3, 7 \; =\text{-}elim
\end{array}
$$

Having established that $x \in U \cap V \dashv\vdash x \in U \wedge x \in V$, we can use the results of section 10.3 to obtain the following elimination and introduction rules:

$$
\frac{\Gamma \;\mapsto\; x \in U \cap V}{\Gamma \;\mapsto\; x \in U \wedge x \in V,} \;\cap\text{-}elim
\qquad
\frac{\Gamma \;\mapsto\; x \in U \quad \Delta \;\mapsto\; x \in V}{\Gamma, \Delta \;\mapsto\; x \in U \cap V.} \;\cap\text{-}int
$$

In fact, the results of section 10.3 by themselves do not permit us to obtain $\cap\text{-}int$. In order to get that in the form displayed above we need to use $\wedge\text{-}int$ as follows, where $\cap\text{-}thema\text{-}int$ is what the results of section 10.3 allow us to obtain:

$$
\dfrac{\dfrac{\Gamma \;\mapsto\; x \in U \quad \Delta \;\mapsto\; x \in V}{\Gamma, \Delta \;\mapsto\; x \in U \wedge x \in V} \;\wedge\text{-}int}{\Gamma, \Delta \;\mapsto\; x \in U \cap V.} \;\cap\text{-}thema\text{-}int
$$

Before doing some set-theoretic proofs, I want to derive some thematic rules that make many proofs easier. Often the best way in which to prove that two sets U and V are equal is by proving that U is a subset of V and that V is a subset of U. The following 'conversion' rules justify this proof strategy:

$$
\frac{\Gamma \;\mapsto\; U = V}{\Gamma \;\mapsto\; U \subseteq V \wedge V \subseteq U,} \;=\text{-}to\text{-}\subseteq
\qquad
\frac{\Gamma \;\mapsto\; U \subseteq V \quad \Delta \;\mapsto\; V \subseteq U}{\Gamma, \Delta \;\mapsto\; U = V.} \;\subseteq\text{-}to\text{-}=
$$

These follow from the law

$$\forall U, V: \mathbf{P}\, X \bullet (U = V \Longleftrightarrow (U \subseteq V \wedge V \subseteq U))$$

using methods that have already been discussed and illustrated.

As an example of the use of many of the rules developed so far I prove that set intersection is idempotent. The proof is as follows:

1	(1)	$x \in U \cap U$	ass
1	(2)	$x \in U \wedge x \in U$	1 $\cap$-elim
1	(3)	$x \in U$	2 $\wedge$-elim
	(4)	$x \in U \cap U \Rightarrow x \in U$	3 $\Rightarrow$-int
	(5)	$\forall x: X \bullet x \in U \cap U \Rightarrow x \in U$	4 $\forall$-int
	(6)	$U \cap U \subseteq U$	5 $\subseteq$-int
7	(7)	$x \in U$	ass
7	(8)	$x \in U \cap U$	7,7 $\cap$-int
	(9)	$x \in U \Rightarrow x \in U \cap U$	8 $\Rightarrow$-int
	(10)	$\forall x: X \bullet x \in U \Rightarrow x \in U \cap U$	9 $\forall$-int
	(11)	$U \subseteq U \cap U$	10 $\subseteq$-int
	(12)	$U = U \cap U$	6, 11 $\subseteq$-to-$=$

Mathematicians rarely present set-theoretic proofs so formally. A mathematician is likely to argue as follows. From the definition of set intersection we have that $x \in U \cap U \Longleftrightarrow (x \in U \wedge x \in U)$. Let us assume that $x \in U \cap U$. Then $x \in U$, as from the definition of intersection it follows that $x \in U \wedge x \in U$. So, we have that $x \in U \cap U$ implies that $x \in U$ and by the definition of the subset relation we have that $U \cap U \subseteq U$. Now let us assume that $x \in U$. Thus, $x \in U \wedge x \in U$ and by the definition of set intersection this means that $x \in U \cap U$. Thus, we have shown that $x \in U$ implies that $x \in U \cap U$ and by the definition of $\subseteq$ it follows that $U \subseteq U \cap U$. Combining the two results yields the conclusion that $U = U \cap U$.

To further illustrate the method of rigorous proof I prove that set intersection distributes backwards through set union:

$$(U \cup V) \cap W = (U \cap W) \cup (V \cap W). \tag{11.2}$$

This proof illustrates a different proof strategy from the one used in the proof that set intersection is idempotent. Formula (11.2) makes use of set union, from whose definition we can extract the following law:

$$x \in U \cup V \Longleftrightarrow (x \in U \vee x \in V). \tag{11.3}$$

The proof of (11.2) goes as follows, where each step follows from the previous one because it is an application of (11.3) or the law that $x \in U \cap V \Longleftrightarrow (x \in U \wedge x \in V)$, unless otherwise indicated:

$$x \in (U \cup V) \cap W \Longleftrightarrow (x \in U \cup V) \wedge x \in W,$$
$$\Longleftrightarrow (x \in U \vee x \in V) \wedge x \in W,$$
$$\Longleftrightarrow (x \in U \wedge x \in W) \vee (x \in V \wedge x \in W),$$

by using the tautology $(P \vee Q) \wedge R \Longleftrightarrow (P \wedge R) \vee (Q \wedge R)$,

$$\Longleftrightarrow (x \in U \cap W) \vee (x \in V \cap W),$$
$$\Longleftrightarrow x \in (U \cap W) \cup (V \cap W).$$

This proof makes use of the fact that in the propositional calculus $\wedge$ distributes backwards through $\vee$.

The next thing that I am going to prove in order to illustrate the notion of a rigorous proof is that set difference distributes backwards through set union:

$$(U \cup V) \setminus W = (U \setminus W) \cup (V \setminus W). \tag{11.4}$$

From the definition of set difference we obtain the law:

$$x \in U \setminus V \Longleftrightarrow x \in U \wedge x \notin V. \tag{11.5}$$

The proof of (11.4) goes as follows, where each step follows from the previous one because it is an application of (11.3) or (11.5), unless otherwise indicated:

$$x \in (U \cup V) \setminus W \Longleftrightarrow (x \in U \cup V) \wedge x \notin W,$$
$$\Longleftrightarrow (x \in U \wedge x \in V) \wedge x \notin W,$$
$$\Longleftrightarrow (x \in U \wedge x \notin W) \wedge (x \in V \wedge x \notin W),$$
by using the tautology $(P \wedge Q) \wedge R \Longleftrightarrow (P \wedge R) \wedge (Q \wedge R)$,
$$\Longleftrightarrow (x \in U \setminus W) \wedge (x \in V \setminus W),$$
$$\Longleftrightarrow x \in (U \setminus W) \cup (V \setminus W).$$

11.3   Reasoning about Tuples

In order to reason about tuples and Cartesian products we need two more axioms. The first of these is an axiom relating to *tuple equality*:

$$\forall x_1, y_1 : X_1; x_2, y_2 : X_2; \ldots; x_n, y_n : X_n \bullet$$
$$(x_1, x_2, \ldots, x_n) = (y_1, y_2, \ldots, y_n) \Longleftrightarrow (x_1 = y_1 \wedge x_2 = y_2 \wedge \ldots x_n = y_n).$$

Using the results of section 10.3 and some rules of the propositional calculus this can be transformed into the following two themata:

$$\frac{\Gamma \;\mapsto\; (x_1, x_2, \ldots, x_n) = (y_1, y_2, \ldots, y_n)}{\Gamma \;\mapsto\; x_1 = y_1 \wedge x_2 = y_2 \wedge \ldots \wedge x_n = y_n,} \; \textit{tup-eq-elim}$$

$$\frac{\Gamma_1 \;\mapsto\; x_1 = y_1 \quad \Gamma_2 \;\mapsto\; x_2 = y_2 \quad \ldots \quad \Gamma_n \;\mapsto\; x_n = y_n}{\Gamma_1, \Gamma_2, \ldots, \Gamma_n \;\mapsto\; (x_1, x_2, \ldots, x_n) = (y_1, y_2, \ldots, y_n).} \; \textit{tup-eq-int}$$

The second axiom relates to *tuple membership*:

$$t \in X_1 \times X_2 \times \cdots \times X_n \Longleftrightarrow \exists x_1 : X_1; x_2 : X_2; \ldots; x_n : X_n \bullet t = (x_1, x_2, \ldots, x_n).$$

Using the results of section 10.3 we can derive the following two themata:

$$\frac{\Gamma \;\mapsto\; t \in X_1 \times X_2 \times \cdots \times X_n}{\Gamma \;\mapsto\; \exists x_1 : X_1; x_2 : X_2; \ldots; x_n : X_n \bullet t = (x_1, x_2, \ldots, x_n),} \; \textit{tup-mem-elim}$$

$$\frac{\Gamma \;\mapsto\; \exists x_1 : X_1; x_2 : X_2; \ldots; x_n : X_n \bullet t = (x_1, x_2, \ldots, x_n)}{\Gamma \;\mapsto\; t \in X_1 \times X_2 \times \cdots \times X_n.} \; \textit{tup-mem-int}$$

11.4   Mathematical Induction

The principle of mathematical induction is a rule of inference that allows us to prove things about all numbers. There are various forms of this principle. I present one of these in this section which allows us to prove that certain things are true of all the non-negative numbers. It says that in order to show that $P(n)$ holds for all natural numbers, all we have to show is:

(1) $P(0)$ holds.

(2) $\forall i\colon \mathbf{N} \bullet P(i) \Rightarrow P(i+1)$.

Here, part (1) is known as the *base case* and part (2) is known as the *inductive step*.

   In order to illustrate how this version of the principle of mathematical induction is used I prove that the formula

$$\sum_{i=0}^{i=n} i^2 = \frac{n(n+1)(2n+1)}{6} \tag{11.6}$$

is true for all non-negative numbers n. For convenience, I abbreviate (11.6) as $P(n)$, thus:

$$P(n) == \sum_{i=0}^{i=n} i^2 = \frac{n(n+1)(2n+1)}{6}.$$

Base Case   First, I have to show that $P(0)$ holds. When $n = 0$, we have that:

$$LHS \text{ of } (11.6) = \sum_{i=0}^{i=0} i^2 = 0.$$

Also when $n = 0$,

$$RHS \text{ of } (11.6) = \frac{0(0+1)(0+1)}{6} = 0.$$

Thus, the base case has been established, since the *LHS* and *RHS* of (11.6) are both equal to 0.

Inductive Step   I need to show that the formula

$$\sum_{i=0}^{i=n+1} i^2 = \frac{(n+1)(n+2)(2(n+1)+1)}{6} \tag{11.7}$$

is true on the assumption that the inductive hypothesis (11.6) holds.

$$LHS \text{ of } (11.7) = \sum_{i=0}^{i=n} i^2 + (n+1)^2,$$
$$= \frac{n(n+1)(2n+1)}{6} + (n+1)^2,$$

by the inductive hypothesis,

$$= \frac{(n+1)(n(2n+1)+6(n+1))}{6},$$
$$= \frac{(n+1)(2n^2+7n+6)}{6},$$
$$= \frac{(n+1)(n+2)(2n+3)}{6},$$
$$= RHS \text{ of } (11.7).$$

Thus, the inductive step has been established. Since both the base case and the inductive step have been established, the property that (11.6) is true for all non-negative numbers follows by mathematical induction.

11.5   Induction for Sequences

Sequence induction is similar to mathematical induction. One version of it says that in order to show that some property $P(\sigma)$ holds for all sequences σ all we have to show is that:[3]

(1) $P(\langle\,\rangle)$ holds.

(2) If $P(\sigma)$ holds for any sequence σ, then so does $P(\langle x\rangle \,\widehat{}\, \sigma)$. In symbols:

$$\forall x\colon X; \sigma\colon \text{seq}\, X \bullet P(\sigma) \Rightarrow P(\langle x\rangle \,\widehat{}\, \sigma).$$

Here, part (1) is known as the *base case* and part (2) is known as the *inductive step*.

To illustrate sequence induction I shall prove that concatenation is associative, that is to say, that the property

$$\sigma \,\widehat{}\, (\tau \,\widehat{}\, v) = (\sigma \,\widehat{}\, \tau) \,\widehat{}\, v$$

holds for all sequences σ, τ and v. The proof makes use of the fact that $\langle\,\rangle \,\widehat{}\, \sigma = \sigma$ and also of the following property:

$$(\langle x\rangle \,\widehat{}\, \sigma) \,\widehat{}\, \tau = \langle x\rangle \,\widehat{}\, (\sigma \,\widehat{}\, \tau). \tag{11.8}$$

Both of these results are straightforwardly derived from the formal definition of the concatenation operator.

Base Case   We have to prove that:

$$\langle\,\rangle \,\widehat{}\,(\tau \,\widehat{}\, v) = (\langle\,\rangle \,\widehat{}\, \tau) \,\widehat{}\, v.$$

Since $\langle\,\rangle \,\widehat{}\, \sigma = \sigma$ for all sequences σ, we have:

$$\langle\,\rangle \,\widehat{}\,(\tau \,\widehat{}\, v) = \tau \,\widehat{}\, v,$$
$$= (\langle\,\rangle \,\widehat{}\, \tau) \,\widehat{}\, v.$$

This establishes the base case.

---

[3] Just as there are several variants of mathematical induction for numbers—see, for example, (Spivey 1992), p. 114—there are also several variants of sequence induction; see section 22.5.2 below for more information and also (Spivey 1992), p. 123.

Inductive Step We have to prove that:

$$((x) \widehat{\ } \sigma) \widehat{\ } (\tau \widehat{\ } v) = (((x) \widehat{\ } \sigma) \widehat{\ } \tau) \widehat{\ } v, \tag{11.9}$$

on the assumption that:

$$\sigma \widehat{\ } (\tau \widehat{\ } v) = (\sigma \widehat{\ } \tau) \widehat{\ } v, \tag{11.10}$$

holds, for all sequences σ, τ and v. This is proved in the following way:

$$LHS \text{ of } (11.9) = ((x) \widehat{\ } \sigma) \widehat{\ } (\tau \widehat{\ } v),$$
$$= (x) \widehat{\ } (\sigma \widehat{\ } (\tau \widehat{\ } v)),$$

by the property (11.8),

$$= (x) \widehat{\ } ((\sigma \widehat{\ } \tau) \widehat{\ } v),$$

by the inductive hypothesis (11.10),

$$= ((x) \widehat{\ } (\sigma \widehat{\ } \tau)) \widehat{\ } v,$$

by the property (11.8),

$$= (((x) \widehat{\ } \sigma) \widehat{\ } \tau) \widehat{\ } v,$$

again by the property (11.8),

$$= RHS \text{ of } (11.9).$$

This establishes the inductive step. Thus, by sequence induction it follows that concatenation is associative.

11.6   Exercises

11.1) Let $U, V, W : \mathbf{P} X$. Prove the following formulas to be theorems:

a) $U = X \setminus (X \setminus U)$.

b) $X \setminus (U \cap V) = (X \setminus U) \cup (X \setminus V)$.

11.2) Prove the following results using mathematical induction:

a) $\displaystyle\sum_{i=0}^{i=n} i = \frac{n(n+1)}{2}$.

b) $\displaystyle\sum_{i=0}^{i=n} i^3 = \left(\frac{n(n+1)}{2}\right)^2$.

12

Immanent Reasoning

12.1   Introduction

One of the major advantages of using a formal language like Z is that it is easy to reason about the specifications written in it. In part I of this book I gave a tutorial introduction to the topic of how to use Z *descriptively* to specify various kinds of system and in chapters 10 and 11 I explained how to carry out formal and rigorous proofs, respectively. In this chapter I combine these two topics and give examples of proofs explicitly concerned with specifications. The title of this chapter, namely 'Immanent Reasoning', refers to the fact that the things I am going to prove relate to a single specification.[1] In the next chapter I look at proofs which relate two specifications. It is also possible to construct proofs which seek to relate specifications and programs and that is the topic of chapters 14 and 15.

12.2   Specifying a Classroom

In order to illustrate the sort of thing that you can prove about a specification I use a simple example of a classroom.[2] The specification uses the type *Person* of all people and the constant *Max*, which is the maximum number of people that can fit into the classroom that is being modelled. The state of the classroom system is given by the following schema:

$$\begin{array}{|l}\hline \_\,Class1 \,_____ \\ d \colon \mathbf{P}\, Person \\ \hline \#d \le Max \\ \hline \end{array}$$

---

[1] My use of the word 'immanent' is derived from the way in which some philosophers use it. See, for example, (Popper 1975), p. 34, who distinguishes between immanent and transcendent criticism.

[2] This is a fairly common example. Jones (1980), pp. 136–138 and 142–143, uses it and Sørensen used it in lectures at Oxford University's Programming Research Group that I attended in 1984–1985.

The schemas $\Delta Class1$ and $\Xi Class1$ are defined in the standard way:

$$\Delta Class1 \triangleq Class1 \wedge Class1',$$

$$\Xi Class1 \triangleq [\Delta Class1 \mid d' = d].$$

The initial state schema is $InitClass1'$, where the schema $InitClass1$ is defined as follows:

$$InitClass1 \triangleq [Class1 \mid d = \varnothing].$$

Only two operations will be defined on this state. The first is of someone entering the classroom:

___Enter1_____
$\Delta Class1$
$p?: Person$
_____
$\#d < Max$
$p? \notin d$
$d' = d \cup \{p?\}$
_____

Clearly, someone can only enter the classroom if it is not full already and this precondition is captured by means of the formula $\#d < Max$.

The next operation specifies what happens when someone leaves the classroom:

___Leave1_____
$\Delta Class1$
$p?: Person$
_____
$p? \in d$
$d' = d \setminus \{p?\}$
_____

Clearly, someone can only leave the classroom if he or she is present in it and this requirement is captured by means of the formula $p? \in d$.

12.3   Schemas and Formulas

Before I can give some examples of proofs about specifications, I have to say something about the way in which schema names can occur as parts of formulas. I introduce this topic by means of some examples.

Consider the classroom specification given above. We might want to state various properties about the system being described. For example, we might want to express the fact that sometimes the classroom is empty. This is represented as follows:

$$\exists d: \mathbf{P}\, Person \mid \#d \leq Max \bullet d = \varnothing. \tag{12.1}$$

Alternatively, we might want to express the possibility that the classroom never contains any women. Using *male*: **P** *Person* to represent the set of all men, this would be represented as:

$$\forall d: \mathbf{P}\, Person \mid \#d \leq Max \bullet d \subseteq male. \qquad (12.2)$$

This is, in general, false for most classrooms.

There might be occasions on which we want to know the actual number of people in the classroom. The function

$$\lambda d: \mathbf{P}\, Person \mid \#d \leq Max \bullet \#d \qquad (12.3)$$

returns the size of a classroom.

If you look at the formulas (12.1) and (12.2) and also at the expression (12.3), you should notice that each of them contains the declaration and formula combination $d: \mathbf{P}\, Person \mid \#d \leq Max$ as a part and this combination should remind you of the schema *Class1*, which is made up out of the same declaration and formula. Because of this, it is possible to represent (12.1) as $\exists Class1 \bullet d = \varnothing$ and to represent (12.2) as $\forall Class1 \bullet d \subseteq male$ and to represent (12.3) as $\lambda Class1 \bullet \#d$. In fact, this is how schemas came about historically.[3]

As well as occurring after the symbols $\exists$, $\forall$ and λ, schema names in Z can also occur where you would expect a formula. In this case it is just as if you had written down the formula that occurs in the predicate-part of the schema involved. Thus, the formula

$$\exists d': \mathbf{P}\, Person \mid \#d' \leq Max \bullet InitClass1'$$

is equivalent to

$$\exists d': \mathbf{P}\, Person \mid \#d' \leq Max \bullet \#d' \leq Max \wedge d' = \varnothing.$$

Using both of the conventions discussed in the section it is possible to express this very concisely as $\exists Class1' \bullet InitClass1'$.

12.4   The Initialization Proof Obligation

One of the things that you have either to prove, or to convince yourself of in some other way, about every specification that you write is that the initial state exists. In the case of the classroom system this proof obligation is expressed by the formula $\exists Class1' \bullet InitClass1'$. As explained in the previous section, this is equivalent to

$$\exists d': \mathbf{P}\, Person \mid \#d' \leq Max \bullet \#d' \leq Max \wedge d' = \varnothing.$$

As explained in chapter 2, this restricted existential quantification is equivalent to the unrestricted form

$$\exists d': \mathbf{P}\, Person \bullet \#d' \leq Max \wedge \#d' \leq Max \wedge d' = \varnothing.$$

---

[3]It is also possible to include a schema name as part of a set comprehension and also as part of a μ-term.

Because conjunction is idempotent, this is equivalent to the formula

$$\exists d' : \mathbf{P}\, Person \bullet \# d' \leq Max \wedge d' = \varnothing.$$

You may think that this formula is so obviously true—because the empty set of people exists—that it does not require proof, but in general this will not be the case. The way we prove this result is by means of the rule of existential quantifier introduction discussed on p. 142 above. This states that from $A[t/x]$ we can infer $\exists x : X \bullet A$, if x is a variable of type X and t is a term of type X. (The notation $A[t/x]$ refers to that formula formed from A by substituting t for all free occurrences of x.) From the definition of the cardinality operator $\#$ it follows that $\#\varnothing = 0$. 0 is the least element of $\mathbf{N}$, so $0 \leq Max$. From the properties of identity it follows that $\varnothing = \varnothing$. These considerations allow us to conclude that $\#\varnothing \leq Max \wedge \varnothing = \varnothing$. This is equivalent to the formula

$$\# d' \leq Max \wedge d' = \varnothing[\varnothing/d'],$$

where the variable d' is of type $\mathbf{P}\, Person$. The rule of existential quantifier introduction therefore allows us to infer

$$\exists d' : \mathbf{P}\, Person \bullet \# d' \leq Max \wedge d' = \varnothing.$$

This proves that for the classroom system the initial state exists.

12.5   Constructing Theories about Specifications

Given a specification there are usually lots of things that we can prove about it and so it is possible to construct a *theory* about that specification. Such a theory increases our understanding of the specification and reinforces our faith in its correctness. In this section I want to give a simple example of the sort of thing that we can prove about the classroom specification.

The property of the classroom specification that I am going to consider is that if someone leaves the classroom and then re-enters it, the state of the classroom is unaltered (but, of course, the person in question must be in the classroom in the first place). This can be represented in Z by means of the formula:

$$(Leave1 \,\mathbin{\raise0.3ex\hbox{\scriptsize;}}\, Enter1) \Longleftrightarrow (\Xi Class1 \mid p? \in d). \tag{12.4}$$

The formula on the right of the bi-implication sign of (12.4) is:

$$\# d \leq Max \wedge \# d' \leq Max \wedge d' = d \wedge p? \in d. \tag{12.5}$$

Thus, to establish the truth of (12.4) I just have to show that the formula on the left of the bi-implication sign is equivalent to this. Let $Alpha \stackrel{\wedge}{=} Leave1 \,\mathbin{\raise0.3ex\hbox{\scriptsize;}}\, Enter1$. Then, $Alpha$ is the following schema:

```
┌─ Alpha ────────────────────────────────────
│ d, d': P Person
│ p?: Person
├────────────────────────────────────────────
│ #d ≤ Max
│ #d' ≤ Max
│ p? ∈ d
│ d' = d
└────────────────────────────────────────────
```

The conjunction of the four formulas in the predicate-part of this is identical to (12.5), as required.

12.6 Investigating Preconditions

Throughout this book I talk about the *preconditions* of a schema specifying some state transformation. Such language is justified in this section.

Z contains a precondition operator (pre) which makes a schema out of a schema by hiding all the after and output variables of the given schema. Thus, since *Enter1* is a schema, so is pre *Enter1*. Z also contains the convention that *PreS* ≙ pre *S*, for all schema names *S*.[4] Thus, *PreEnter1* is just another way of referring to the schema pre *Enter1*.

Given a schema *S* which specifies some operation or state transformation, what *PreS* does is to indicate those states on which the operation *S* can be successfully carried out. In other words, if a state satisfies *PreS*, then the operation specified by *S* can be carried out on that state. So, *PreEnter1* tells us on which states *Enter1* can be performed. What *PreEnter1* actually amounts to is this:

```
┌─ PreEnter1 ────────────────────────────────
│ d: P Person
│ p?: Person
├────────────────────────────────────────────
│ ∃d': P Person •
│       (#d ≤ Max ∧
│        #d' ≤ Max ∧
│        #d < Max ∧
│        p? ∉ d ∧
│        d' = d ∪ {p?})
└────────────────────────────────────────────
```

Usually the formula in the predicate-part of a precondition schema can be considerably simplified and in most cases the existential quantifier can be removed. I now show how *PreEnter1* can be simplified.

By means of the one-point law involving the existential quantifier we have that the formula in the predicate-part of *PreEnter1* is equivalent to

$$\#d \leq Max \land \#(d \cup \{p?\}) \leq Max \land \#d < Max \land p? \notin d.$$

---

[4] See (Spivey 1992), p. 72, for more information.

(This is obtained by substituting the term $d \cup \{p?\}$ for d' in the formula $\#d \leq Max \land$ $\#d' \leq Max \land \#d < Max \land p? \notin d$.) Because $p? \notin d$, we have $\#(d \cup \{p?\}) = \#d + 1$. Therefore, $\#d < Max$ and as $\#d < Max$ implies $\#d \leq Max$, we can simplify *PreEnter1* to the following:

```
┌─ PreEnter1 ──────────────────────────────────────
│  d: P Person
│  p?: Person
├──────────────────────────────────────────────────
│  #d < Max
│  p? ∉ d
└──────────────────────────────────────────────────
```

This can be rewritten as

```
┌─ PreEnter1 ──────────────────────────────────────
│  Class1
│  p?: Person
├──────────────────────────────────────────────────
│  #d < Max
│  p? ∉ d
└──────────────────────────────────────────────────
```

The two formulas in the predicate-part of this way of writing *PreEnter1*—*excluding* the formulas that come from the state schema *Class1*—are the two preconditions of the schema *Enter1*. This is, in fact, the terminology that I use throughout this book. For example, on p. 48 I said that the preconditions of the schema *AddEntry* are the formulas:

$$name? \in members,$$

$$name? \mapsto newnumber? \notin telephones.$$

I justify that here. The expanded version of *AddEntry* is:

```
┌─ AddEntry ───────────────────────────────────────
│  members, members': P Person
│  telephones, telephones': Person ↔ Phone
│  name?: Person
│  newnumber?: Phone
├──────────────────────────────────────────────────
│  dom telephones ⊆ members
│  dom telephones' ⊆ members'
│  name? ∈ members
│  name? ↦ newnumber? ∉ telephones
│  telephones' = telephones ∪ {name? ↦ newnumber?}
│  members' = members
└──────────────────────────────────────────────────
```

The schema pre *AddEntry* or *PreAddEntry* is, therefore:

```
┌─ PreAddEntry ────────────────────────────────────────────
│ members: P Person
│ telephones: Person ↮ Phone
│ name?: Person
│ newnumber?: Phone
├──────────────────────────────────────────────────────────
│ ∃members': P Person; telephones': Person ↮ Phone •
│     (dom telephones ⊆ members ∧
│     dom telephones' ⊆ members' ∧
│     name? ∈ members ∧
│     name? ↦ newnumber? ∉ telephones ∧
│     telephones' = telephones ∪ {name? ↦ newnumber?} ∧
│     members' = members)
└──────────────────────────────────────────────────────────
```

Using the one-point law involving the existential quantifier twice on the formula in the predicate-part of the schema *PreAddEntry* results in the formula:

$$
\begin{aligned}
&\text{dom } telephones \subseteq members \ \wedge \\
&\text{dom}(telephones \cup \{name? \mapsto newnumber?\}) \subseteq members \ \wedge \\
&name? \in members \ \wedge \\
&name? \mapsto newnumber? \notin telephones.
\end{aligned}
\tag{12.6}
$$

By the properties of the domain operator the second conjunct of (12.6) is equivalent to dom *telephones* ∪ {*name?*} ⊆ *members*, and this is a syntactic consequence of

$$\text{dom } telephones \subseteq members \wedge name? \in members.$$

Therefore, the formula (12.6) is syntactically equivalent to:

$$
\begin{aligned}
&\text{dom } telephones \subseteq members \ \wedge \\
&name? \in members \ \wedge \\
&name? \mapsto newnumber? \notin telephones.
\end{aligned}
$$

The schema pre *AddEntry*, therefore, simplifies to:

```
┌─ PreAddEntry ────────────────────────────────────────────
│ members: P Person
│ telephones: Person ↮ Phone
│ name?: Person
│ newnumber?: Phone
├──────────────────────────────────────────────────────────
│ dom telephones ⊆ members
│ name? ∈ members
│ name? ↦ newnumber? ∉ telephones
└──────────────────────────────────────────────────────────
```

This can also be written as:

```
┌─ PreAddEntry ──────────────────────────────────────────────
│ PhoneDB
│ name?: Person
│ newnumber?: Phone
├────────────────────────────────────────────────────────────
│ name? ∈ members
│ name? ↦ newnumber? ∉ telephones
└────────────────────────────────────────────────────────────
```

So, the preconditions of the schema *AddEntry* are the two formulas *name?* ∈ *members* and *name?* ↦ *newnumber?* ∉ *telephones*.

12.7 Totality

Another useful thing to know about a specification is which operations are *total* and which are not. An operation is *total* if it is defined on every state which satisfies the state invariant.[5] The operation *Enter1* is not total, because it does not say what happens when $\#d = Max$, and it does not state what happens when $p? \in d$. In order to specify a total operation corresponding to someone entering the classroom we need some additional schemas. The schema *Full1* specifies what happens when $\#d = Max$.

```
┌─ Full1 ────────────────────────────────────────────────────
│ ΞClass1
│ p?: Person
│ rep!: Report
├────────────────────────────────────────────────────────────
│ #d = Max
│ rep! = 'Class full'
└────────────────────────────────────────────────────────────
```

The schema *AlreadyPresent1* specifies what happens when $p? \in d$, that is to say, when the person $p?$ who is trying to enter the classroom is already in the classroom.

```
┌─ AlreadyPresent1 ──────────────────────────────────────────
│ ΞClass1
│ p?: Person
│ rep!: Report
├────────────────────────────────────────────────────────────
│ p? ∈ d
│ rep! = 'Already here'
└────────────────────────────────────────────────────────────
```

The schema *Success* just outputs the message 'Okay'. It is used to tell us that the operation *Enter1* has been successfully carried out.

```
┌─ Success ──────────────────────────────────────────────────
│ rep!: Report
├────────────────────────────────────────────────────────────
│ rep! = 'Okay'
└────────────────────────────────────────────────────────────
```

---

[5]This means that the precondition of a total operation need not be the always true formula.

It is now possible to specify the total operation of someone attempting to enter the classroom:

$$DoEnter1 \stackrel{\triangle}{=} (Enter1 \wedge Success) \vee Full1 \vee AlreadyPresent1.$$

To show that *DoEnter1* is total I work out what the precondition schema *PreDoEnter1* is:

```
┌─ PreDoEnter1 ─────────────────────────────────────────
│  d: P Person
│  p?: Person
│ ─────────────────────────
│  #d ≤ Max
└───────────────────────────────────────────────────────
```

An alternative way of writing this is:

```
┌─ PreDoEnter1 ─────────────────────────────────────────
│  Class1
│  p?: Person
└───────────────────────────────────────────────────────
```

The schema *DoEnter1* is total because it specifies what happens no matter what values its inputs and before variables have. (The values of the before variables have to, however, satisfy the before state invariant.)

12.8 Operation Refinement

The final topic that I deal with in this chapter is that of *operation refinement*. This takes place within a single specification in that only one kind of state space is involved. It is a way of relating operations defined on the same data.

The concrete operation *OpC* is a refinement of the abstract operation *OpA*, both defined on the same state space, iff both of the following formulas can be proved to be theorems:

$$\text{pre } OpA \Rightarrow \text{pre } OpC,$$
$$\text{pre } OpA \wedge OpC \Rightarrow OpA.$$

The first of these specifies that the concrete operation succeeds whenever the abstract one does, although there might be situations in which the concrete state succeeds but the abstract one does not. The second formula specifies that the abstract and concrete operations produce the same results on the same starting states.

13

Reification and Decomposition

13.1   Introduction

The reader should, by now, understand the structure of a formal specification written in Z. One of the first things that has to be done is to define the state of the system being described. For example, the state of a classroom could be specified like this, where *Person* is the type of all people:

```
┌─ Class1 ──────────────────────────────────────────────
│ d: P Person
├───────────────────────────────────────────────────────
│ #d ≤ Max
└───────────────────────────────────────────────────────
```

Here, d is the set of all the people currently in the classroom and *Max* is a number representing the capacity of the classroom. After the state has been defined, various operations are then specified. For example, the operation of someone leaving the classroom can be specified in this way:

```
┌─ Leave1 ──────────────────────────────────────────────
│ Δ Class1
│ p?: Person
├───────────────────────────────────────────────────────
│ p? ∈ d
│ d' = d \ {p?}
└───────────────────────────────────────────────────────
```

The purpose of a formal specification is to help us in the writing of programs and to enable us to prove that a particular program either does or does not meet its specification. Because Z contains many very high-level abstract mathematical data types and because operations are specified by giving their preconditions and postconditions, the 'distance' between the specification and available programming language constructs may sometimes seem far too great to bridge. Thus, in these cases, it is often a good idea to write another specification which uses less abstract data types and more 'algorithmic' constructs in it. This second specification can then be thought of as being intermediate between the original specification and the eventual program. (I call this intermediate specification the *design* in this chapter.) Clearly, the specification and the design have to be related in some way. What we require is that any program which is a correct implementation of the design is also a correct implementation of the specification. When this requirement obtains we say that the state of the design is a *reification* or *refinement* of the state of the specification and that the operations in the specification have been *decomposed* into those of the design or that the operations in the design *model* those in the specification.[1]

Even in the case of the classroom specification a design would be useful. We might decide to implement the set d of people by means of a linked list or an array, but any proofs relating specification and program would be very complicated. By writing a design involving sequences rather than sets, we divide the large distance between specification and program into two manageable parts and the resulting proofs are individually much less complicated.

So, to summarize, the process of taking an abstract mathematical data type, like a set, and representing it by a sequence, say, is called *data reification*. This is the process of transforming one data type into another one. It transforms an abstract data type into a more concrete one. It is possible to carry out data refinement in Z by using appropriate schemas, and I do that in the latter part of this chapter, but because the ideas involved are fairly complex I begin this chapter by explaining the important notion of a retrieve function and how to establish the correctness of a proposed retrieve function without using schemas. When the ideas involved are understood, it is then easier to see how a schema can be used instead of a retrieve function and to appreciate the proof obligations involved.

13.2   Modelling Sets by Sequences

Although sets are available in some programming languages, in this section I consider the reification of sets into sequences in order to illustrate the ideas involved. For illustrative purposes I consider sets of people and, as usual, *Person* is the type of all people. Let $U : \mathbf{P}\, Person$ be a set of people. For example, U might be the set $\{fry, dove, cox\}$. We want to represent the set U by means of an appropriate sequence of people $\sigma : \operatorname{seq} Person$, where $\operatorname{seq} Person$ is the set of all finite sequences of elements drawn from the type *Person*. So, for example, we might have $\sigma = \langle fry, cox, dove \rangle$. In this example, the abstract data type consists of the elements of $\mathbf{P}\, Person$ and the operations defined on those sets and the concrete data type consists of the elements of $\operatorname{seq} Person$ and the operations defined on those sequences. (Recall that a member of $\mathbf{P}\, Person$ is a subset of *Person* and a member of $\operatorname{seq} Person$ is a sequence of elements drawn from *Person*.)

The way we relate the abstract and concrete data types is by means of a *retrieve*

---

[1] Sometimes the refined specification may itself require further reification. Thus, there may be situations in which it is necessary to have several intermediate specifications between the original abstract specification and the final computer program.

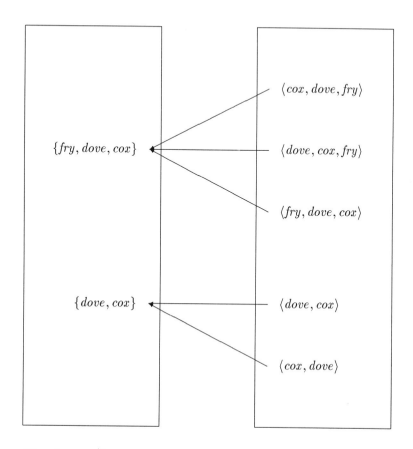

The abstract data type   The concrete data type

Figure 13.1: The retrieve function.

function. The retrieve function maps the concrete data type into the abstract one:

$$ret: \text{seq } Person \rightarrow \mathbf{P} \ Person.$$

In the case of sets being modelled as sequences a suitable retrieve function is *ret*, where *ret* $\sigma = \text{ran } \sigma$. The retrieve function has to be from the concrete data type to the abstract one because many sequences correspond to the same set. This is illustrated in Fig. 13.1.

13.2.1   Correctness of Operation Modelling

In relating abstract and concrete data types we have to relate operations defined on the abstract data type, like set union, intersection and difference, to operations defined on the concrete data type. For an operation $\heartsuit$ in the concrete world to correctly model an operation $\triangle$ in the abstract world the diagram in Fig. 13.2 must commute; that is to say, the following result must be provable:

$$ret(\sigma \heartsuit \tau) = (ret\,\sigma)\,\triangle\,(ret\,\tau). \tag{13.1}$$

In order to model set union, let us try the function *append*, which is defined like this:[2]

$=[X]=$

$\quad append\colon \mathrm{seq}\,X \times \mathrm{seq}\,X \to \mathrm{seq}\,X$

$\quad \forall x\colon X;\sigma,\tau\colon \mathrm{seq}\,X \;\bullet$
$\qquad (append\,(\langle\;\rangle,\tau) = \tau)\;\wedge$
$\qquad (x \in \mathrm{ran}\,\tau$
$\qquad\qquad \Rightarrow append\,(\langle x\rangle \,^\frown\, \sigma,\tau) = append\,(\sigma,\tau))\;\wedge$
$\qquad (x \notin \mathrm{ran}\,\tau$
$\qquad\qquad \Rightarrow append\,(\langle x\rangle \,^\frown\, \sigma,\tau) = \langle x\rangle \,^\frown\, append\,(\sigma,\tau))$

In the case of the proposed model of set union in the world of sequences, namely *append*, we have to prove the following in order to show that it is correct:

$$ret(append(\sigma,\tau)) = (ret\,\sigma) \cup (ret\,\tau). \tag{13.2}$$

One standard way of proving things about sequences is by using *sequence induction* as explained in section 11.5. Recall that one way of showing that some property $P(\sigma)$ holds for all sequences σ is to establish both the following results:

(1) $P(\langle\;\rangle)$ holds.

(2) If $P(\sigma)$ holds for any sequence σ, then so does $P(\langle x\rangle \,^\frown\, \sigma)$. In symbols, this is:

$$\forall x\colon X;\sigma\colon \mathrm{seq}\,X \;\bullet\; P(\sigma) \Rightarrow P(\langle x\rangle \,^\frown\, \sigma).$$

Here, part (1) is known as the *base case* and part (2) is known as the *inductive step*. In the case of the formula (13.2) that we want to prove, the property $P(\sigma)$ is:

$$ret(append\,(\sigma,\tau)) = (ret\,\sigma) \cup (ret\,\tau).$$

First, I prove the base case and then the inductive step.

---

[2]The reason why I use *append* to model set union rather than, say, sequence concatenation is because the *append* function has the property that if σ and τ do not contain any duplicate elements, then neither does *append*(σ,τ).

The abstract world

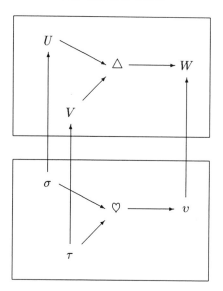

The concrete world

Figure 13.2: Correctness condition for operation modelling.

Base Case We need to prove that the property is true for the empty sequence $\langle\ \rangle$; that is to say, we need to prove the following:

$$ret(append\ (\langle\ \rangle, \tau)) = (ret\langle\ \rangle) \cup (ret\ \tau).$$

I do this by showing that both sides are equal to the same thing.

$$LHS = ret\ \tau,$$

by the first clause of the definition of *append*.

$$RHS = \varnothing \cup ret\ \tau,$$

since $ret\ \tau = \operatorname{ran}\tau$ and $\operatorname{ran}\langle\ \rangle = \varnothing$,

$$= ret\ \tau,$$

by properties of set union. So, *LHS* = *RHS* and the base case is proved.

Inductive Step To prove the inductive step we have to prove that

$$ret(append\ (\langle x \rangle \frown \sigma, \tau)) = (ret(\langle x \rangle \frown \sigma)) \cup (ret\ \tau) \qquad (13.3)$$

holds on the assumption that

$$ret(append\ (\sigma, \tau)) = (ret\ \sigma) \cup (ret\ \tau). \tag{13.4}$$

The formula (13.4) is known as the *inductive hypothesis.*

To prove the inductive step there are two cases to consider, namely when $x \in \text{ran } \tau$ and when $x \notin \text{ran } \tau$. Taking the first case first:

$$LHS \text{ of } (13.3) = ret(append(\sigma, \tau)),$$

by the second clause of the definition of *append,*

$$= ret\ \sigma \cup ret\ \tau,$$

by the inductive hypothesis (13.4).

$$RHS \text{ of } (13.3) = ret\langle x \rangle \cup ret\ \sigma \cup ret\ \tau,$$

because $ret\ \sigma = \text{ran } \sigma$ and $\text{ran}(\sigma \frown \tau) = \text{ran } \sigma \cup \text{ran } \tau$,

$$= \{x\} \cup ret\ \sigma \cup ret\ \tau,$$
$$= ret\ \sigma \cup ret\ \tau,$$

as $x \in ret\ \tau$. The result is proved as both the *LHS* and *RHS* of (13.3) are equal to the same thing.

Now we look at the second case:

$$LHS \text{ of } (13.3) = ret(\langle x \rangle \frown append(\sigma, \tau)),$$

by the third clause of the definition of *append,*

$$= ret\langle x \rangle \cup ret(append(\sigma, \tau)),$$

since $ret\ \sigma = \text{ran } \sigma$ and $\text{ran}(\sigma \frown \tau) = \text{ran } \sigma \cup \text{ran } \tau$,

$$= ret\langle x \rangle \cup ret\ \sigma \cup ret\ \tau.$$
$$RHS \text{ of } (13.3) = ret\langle x \rangle \cup ret\ \sigma \cup ret\ \tau.$$

The result is proved as both the *LHS* and *RHS* of (13.3) are equal to the same thing.

Having proved both the base case and the inductive step, it follows by the principle of sequence induction that the formula (13.2) holds for all sequences σ and τ. So, I have proved that *append* correctly models the behaviour of $\cup$ in the concrete realm.

13.2.2 Modelling Set Intersection

The next thing that I am going to do is to show how set intersection and set difference can be modelled in the world of sequences by means of the functions *inter* and *subtract*. Both of these have the property that if σ and τ do not contain any duplicate elements, then neither does $inter(\sigma, \tau)$ nor $subtract(\sigma, \tau)$. The function *inter* is defined as follows:

$=[X]$
$inter: \operatorname{seq} X \times \operatorname{seq} X \rightarrow \operatorname{seq} X$

$\forall x: X; \sigma, \tau: \operatorname{seq} X \bullet$
$\quad (inter(\langle\,\rangle, \tau) = \langle\,\rangle) \wedge$
$\quad (x \in \operatorname{ran} \tau$
$\quad\quad \Rightarrow inter(\langle x \rangle \frown \sigma, \tau) = \langle x \rangle \frown inter(\sigma, \tau)) \wedge$
$\quad (x \notin \operatorname{ran} \tau$
$\quad\quad \Rightarrow inter(\langle x \rangle \frown \sigma, \tau) = inter(\sigma, \tau))$

To prove that *inter* correctly models $\cap$ we have to prove that

$$ret(inter(\sigma, \tau)) = ret\,\sigma \cap ret\,\tau. \tag{13.5}$$

This is done by using induction on the sequence σ. As usual, the proof is split into the base case and the inductive step.

Base Case   For the base case we have to prove that (13.5) holds when $\sigma = \langle\,\rangle$.

$$LHS \text{ of } (13.5) = ret(inter(\langle\,\rangle, \tau)),$$
$$= ret\langle\,\rangle,$$

by the first clause of the definition of *inter*,

$$= \emptyset.$$

The next thing that I show is that the *RHS* of (13.5) is also equal to the empty set.

$$RHS \text{ of } (13.5) = ret\langle\,\rangle \cap ret\,\tau,$$
$$= \emptyset \cap ret\,\tau,$$
$$= \emptyset.$$

The base case is established, since the *LHS* and *RHS* of (13.5) are both equal to the same thing, namely the empty set.

Inductive Step   We need to prove:

$$ret(inter(\langle x \rangle \frown \sigma, \tau)) = ret(\langle x \rangle \frown \sigma) \cap ret\,\tau, \tag{13.6}$$

on the assumption that $ret(inter(\sigma, \tau)) = ret\,\sigma \cap ret\,\tau$. We do this by case analysis, treating the situation in which $x \in \operatorname{ran} \tau$ first and then the situation in which $x \notin \operatorname{ran} \tau$.

   Case 1   In this situation we have that $x \in \operatorname{ran} \tau$. I look at the *LHS* and *RHS* of (13.6) in turn.

$$LHS \text{ of } (13.6) = ret(\langle x \rangle \frown inter(\sigma, \tau)),$$
$$= ret\langle x \rangle \cup ret(inter(\sigma, \tau)),$$
$$= \{x\} \cup (ret\,\sigma \cap ret\,\tau),$$

by the inductive hypothesis.

$$RHS \text{ of } (13.6) = (ret\langle x\rangle \cup ret\,\sigma) \cap ret\,\tau,$$
$$= (\{x\} \cup ret\,\sigma) \cap ret\,\tau,$$
$$= (\{x\} \cap ret\,\tau) \cup (ret\,\sigma \cap ret\,\tau),$$

because $\cap$ distributes backwards through $\cup$,

$$= \{x\} \cup (ret\,\sigma \cap ret\,\tau).$$

As both the *LHS* and *RHS* of (13.6) are equal to the same thing, I have established that (13.6) is true in the case when $x \in ran\,\tau$.

Case 2   In this case we have that $x \notin ran\,\tau$. Again, I look at the *LHS* and *RHS* of (13.6) in turn.

$$LHS \text{ of } (13.6) = ret(inter(\sigma,\tau)),$$

by the third clause of the definition of *inter*,

$$= ret\,\sigma \cap ret\,\tau,$$

by the inductive hypothesis.

$$RHS \text{ of } (13.6) = (ret\langle x\rangle \cup ret\,\sigma) \cap ret\,\tau,$$
$$= (\{x\} \cup ret\,\sigma) \cap ret\,\tau,$$
$$= (\{x\} \cap ret\,\tau) \cup (ret\,\sigma \cap ret\,\tau),$$
$$= \varnothing \cup (ret\,\sigma \cap ret\,\tau),$$
$$= ret\,\sigma \cap ret\,\tau.$$

As both the *LHS* and *RHS* of (13.6) are equal to the same thing, I have established that (13.6) is true in the case when $x \notin ran\,\tau$. Since $x \in ran\,\tau \lor x \notin ran\,\tau$ is a theorem of classical logic it follows that the inductive step has been established.

Since both the base case and the inductive step have been proved, formula (13.5) follows by the principle of sequence induction.

13.2.3   Modelling Set Difference

The function *subtract* is defined in this way:

$$
\begin{array}{|l}
\hline
[X] \\\hline
subtract \colon \mathrm{seq}\,X \times \mathrm{seq}\,X \to \mathrm{seq}\,X \\\hline
\forall x \colon X; \sigma, \tau \colon \mathrm{seq}\,X \bullet \\
\quad (subtract(\langle\,\rangle, \tau) = \langle\,\rangle) \land \\
\quad (x \in ran\,\tau \\
\quad\quad\quad \Rightarrow subtract(\langle x\rangle \,\widehat{}\, \sigma, \tau) = subtract(\sigma, \tau)) \land \\
\quad (x \notin ran\,\tau \\
\quad\quad\quad \Rightarrow subtract(\langle x\rangle \,\widehat{}\, \sigma, \tau) = \langle x\rangle \,\widehat{}\, subtract(\sigma, \tau)) \\\hline
\end{array}
$$

To prove that *subtract* correctly models \ we have to prove:

$$ret(subtract(\sigma, \tau)) = ret\ \sigma \setminus ret\ \tau. \tag{13.7}$$

This is done using sequence induction. First, I prove the base case and then the inductive step.

Base Case For the base case we have to prove that (13.7) holds when $\sigma = \langle\ \rangle$. I show that in that situation both the *RHS* and *LHS* of (13.7) are equal to the empty set. First, I look at the *LHS* of (13.7).

$$
\begin{aligned}
LHS \text{ of } (13.7) &= ret(subtract(\langle\ \rangle, \tau)), \\
&= ret\ \langle\ \rangle, \\
&= \varnothing.
\end{aligned}
$$

Having established that the *LHS* of (13.7) is equal to the empty set, I turn my attention to the *RHS* of (13.7).

$$
\begin{aligned}
RHS \text{ of } (13.7) &= ret\ \langle\ \rangle \setminus ret\ \tau, \\
&= \varnothing \setminus ret\ \tau, \\
&= \varnothing.
\end{aligned}
$$

Having shown that the *LHS* and *RHS* of (13.7) are both equal to the empty set, I have established the base case.

Inductive Step We need to prove:

$$ret(subtract(\langle x \rangle \frown \sigma, \tau)) = ret(\langle x \rangle \frown \sigma) \setminus ret\ \tau, \tag{13.8}$$

on the assumption that $ret(subtract(\sigma, \tau)) = ret\ \sigma \setminus ret\ \tau$. We do this by case analysis, treating the situations in which $x \in ran\ \tau$ and $x \notin ran\ \tau$ separately. First, I look at the situation in which $x \in ran\ \tau$.

Case 1 In this case we have that $x \in ran\ \tau$. First, I look at the *LHS* of (13.8).

$$LHS \text{ of } (13.8) = ret(subtract(\sigma, \tau)),$$

by the definition of *subtract*,

$$= ret\ \sigma \setminus ret\ \tau,$$

by the inductive hypothesis. Now, I look at the *RHS* of (13.8).

$$
\begin{aligned}
RHS \text{ of } (13.8) &= (ret\langle x \rangle \cup ret\ \sigma) \setminus ret\ \tau, \\
&= (\{x\} \cup ret\ \sigma) \setminus ret\ \tau, \\
&= ret\ \sigma \setminus ret\ \tau,
\end{aligned}
$$

since $x \in ran\ \tau$ and $ret\ \tau = ran\ \tau$. Thus, I have shown that (13.8) holds when $x \in ran\ \tau$, since both the *LHS* and *RHS* of it are equal to the same thing.

Case 2 In this case we have that $x \notin \operatorname{ran} \tau$. First, I look at the *LHS* of (13.8).

$$\textit{LHS of } (13.8) = ret((\langle x \rangle ^\frown subtract(\sigma, \tau))),$$
$$= ret\langle x \rangle \cup ret(subtract(\sigma, \tau)),$$
$$= ret\langle x \rangle \cup (ret\,\sigma \setminus ret\,\tau),$$

by the inductive hypothesis,

$$= \{x\} \cup (ret\,\sigma \setminus ret\,\tau).$$

Now I am going to consider the *RHS* of (13.8).

$$\textit{RHS of } (13.8) = (ret\langle x \rangle \cup ret\,\sigma) \setminus ret\,\tau,$$
$$= (\{x\} \cup ret\,\sigma) \setminus ret\,\tau,$$
$$= (\{x\} \setminus ret\,\tau) \cup (ret\,\sigma \setminus ret\,\tau),$$

because $\setminus$ distributes backwards through $\cup$,

$$= \{x\} \cup (ret\,\sigma \setminus ret\,\tau).$$

as $x \notin \operatorname{ran} \tau$. Thus, I have shown that (13.8) is true when $x \notin \operatorname{ran} \tau$. Since we must have that either $x \in \operatorname{ran} \tau$ or $x \notin \operatorname{ran} \tau$, it follows that the inductive step has been established.

Since both the base case and the inductive step have been shown to be true, it follows by the principle of sequence induction that the formula (13.7) holds for all sequences σ and τ.

13.3   Reification and Decomposition using Schemas

13.3.1   Introduction

When I introduced schemas in chapter 4 I explained how they are used to define the state space of some problem domain and also how they are used to specify various operations on that state space. In the earlier part of this chapter I explained the important notion of a retrieve function which relates objects in a concrete world to those objects in an abstract realm which they are modelling. In this section I explain how a schema can be used to perform the work done by a retrieve function and also how the correctness criterion (13.1) appears when we are using a schema to relate an abstract and a more concrete specification.[3] In order to illustrate the use of a schema to relate a concrete and an abstract specification I make use of the classroom example again.

13.3.2   Example Specification and Design

To save space in this section I refer to the abstract specification simply as the *specification* and the more concrete specification I shall call the *design*. The example

---

[3]It is possible to model an abstract specification by a concrete one even if there is no *function* from the concrete objects to the abstract ones. Sometimes a *relation* between abstract and concrete objects suffices. I say more about this in section 13.3.5 below.

specification and design that I discuss are shown in Fig. 13.3. Note that although the schemas *InitClass1* and *InitClass2* are defined in Fig. 13.3, the initial state schemas of the specification and the design are *InitClass1'* and *InitClass2'*, respectively.

Because the functions *append* and *subtract* used in the design have the property that if σ and τ do not contain any duplicate members then neither does $append(\sigma, \tau)$ nor $subtract(\sigma, \tau)$, we can be certain that any state obtained from the initial state by the application of the operations *Enter2* and *Leave2* has the property that the sequence l that is part of it does not contain any duplicate elements.

13.3.3 Relating Specification and Design

The next thing that needs to be done is to relate the abstract and concrete states. This is done in Z by means of the following schema:

$$
\begin{array}{l}
\underline{\quad Class1Class2 \quad} \\
\quad Class1 \\
\quad Class2 \\
\overline{} \\
\quad d = \operatorname{ran} l \\
\end{array}
$$

In full this schema is:

$$
\begin{array}{l}
\underline{\quad Class1Class2 \quad} \\
\quad d : \mathbf{P}\, Person \\
\quad l : \operatorname{seq} Person \\
\overline{} \\
\quad \#d \leq Max \\
\quad \#l \leq Max \\
\quad d = \operatorname{ran} l \\
\end{array}
$$

Recall that when I was explaining the retrieve function *ret*, which allows us to model a set U by a sequence σ, I said that $U = ret\,\sigma$. (For this example $ret\,\sigma = \operatorname{ran}\sigma$.) That is the reason why the formula $d = \operatorname{ran} l$ is included in *Class1Class2*.

13.3.4 Correctness of Design

In order to prove that the design is a correct reification of the specification we have to prove a number of things. In the first place we have to prove that the initial states correspond to one another and then—for each operation in the design—we have to prove both that it is correct and also that it is applicable. Proving correctness and applicability for an operation defined using schemas corresponds to proving the correctness criterion (13.1) for the retrieve function.

Correspondence of Initial States

The schema *Class1Class2* is like the retrieve function I described earlier. In order to show that initial states correspond in the abstract and concrete worlds we have to

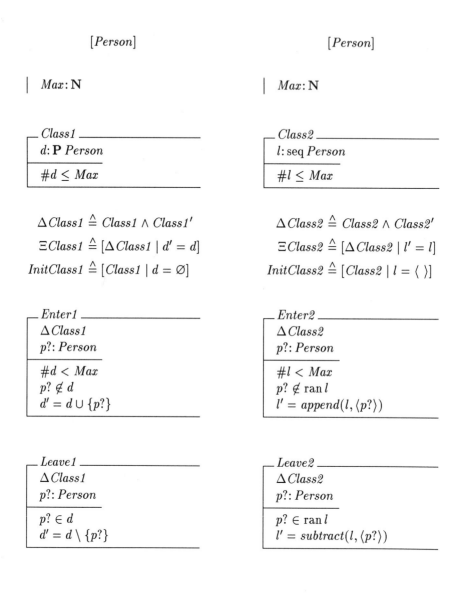

$$[Person]$$

$$[Person]$$

$$| \; Max : \mathbf{N}$$

$$| \; Max : \mathbf{N}$$

$$\begin{array}{l} \underline{\quad Class1 \quad\quad\quad\quad\quad\quad\quad} \\ \; d : \mathbf{P}\ Person \\ \overline{} \\ \; \#d \le Max \end{array}$$

$$\begin{array}{l} \underline{\quad Class2 \quad\quad\quad\quad\quad\quad\quad} \\ \; l : \operatorname{seq}\ Person \\ \overline{} \\ \; \#l \le Max \end{array}$$

$$\Delta\,Class1 \;\hat{=}\; Class1 \wedge Class1'$$
$$\Xi\,Class1 \;\hat{=}\; [\Delta\,Class1 \mid d' = d]$$
$$InitClass1 \;\hat{=}\; [Class1 \mid d = \varnothing]$$

$$\Delta\,Class2 \;\hat{=}\; Class2 \wedge Class2'$$
$$\Xi\,Class2 \;\hat{=}\; [\Delta\,Class2 \mid l' = l]$$
$$InitClass2 \;\hat{=}\; [Class2 \mid l = \langle\,\rangle]$$

$$\begin{array}{l} \underline{\quad Enter1 \quad\quad\quad\quad\quad\quad} \\ \; \Delta\,Class1 \\ \; p? : Person \\ \overline{} \\ \; \#d < Max \\ \; p? \notin d \\ \; d' = d \cup \{p?\} \end{array}$$

$$\begin{array}{l} \underline{\quad Enter2 \quad\quad\quad\quad\quad\quad} \\ \; \Delta\,Class2 \\ \; p? : Person \\ \overline{} \\ \; \#l < Max \\ \; p? \notin \operatorname{ran} l \\ \; l' = append(l, \langle p?\rangle) \end{array}$$

$$\begin{array}{l} \underline{\quad Leave1 \quad\quad\quad\quad\quad\quad} \\ \; \Delta\,Class1 \\ \; p? : Person \\ \overline{} \\ \; p? \in d \\ \; d' = d \setminus \{p?\} \end{array}$$

$$\begin{array}{l} \underline{\quad Leave2 \quad\quad\quad\quad\quad\quad} \\ \; \Delta\,Class2 \\ \; p? : Person \\ \overline{} \\ \; p? \in \operatorname{ran} l \\ \; l' = subtract(l, \langle p?\rangle) \end{array}$$

The specification

The design

Figure 13.3: Classroom specification and design.

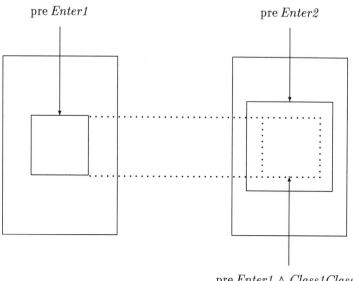

Figure 13.4: Applicability.

prove that $InitClass2' \land Class1Class2' \Rightarrow InitClass1'$ is a theorem of first-order logic. Expanding this we get the formula:

$$
\begin{aligned}
&\#l' \leq Max \land l' = \langle\,\rangle \land \\
&\#d' \leq Max \land \#l' \leq Max \land d' = \text{ran } l' \\
\Rightarrow \\
&\#d' \leq Max \land d' = \varnothing.
\end{aligned}
\tag{13.9}
$$

As is conventional in mathematics we assume that all the free variables in this formula are universally quantified over. The formula (13.9) is a theorem iff (13.10) is a valid sequent.

$$
\begin{aligned}
&\#l' \leq Max, l' = \langle\,\rangle, \#d' \leq Max, d' = \text{ran } l' \\
\longmapsto \\
&\#d' \leq Max \land d' = \varnothing.
\end{aligned}
\tag{13.10}
$$

The first conjunct in the conclusion of (13.10) occurs amongst the premises and the second conjunct is a consequence of the two formulas $l' = \langle\,\rangle$ and $d' = \text{ran } l'$, therefore (13.10) is a valid sequent.

Applicability of *Enter2*

In order to prove that the operation *Enter2* is applicable we have to prove that the formula

$$\text{pre } Enter1 \wedge Class1Class2 \Rightarrow \text{pre } Enter2 \qquad (13.11)$$

is a theorem of first-order logic. (13.11) states that if we start from a state in the state space of the abstract world which satisfies the preconditions of *Enter1* (that is to say, a state in which the operation *Enter1* can be performed successfully), then any concrete state corresponding to that abstract state by means of *Class1Class2* can also be performed successfully. Fig. 13.4 presents this graphically. Expanding (13.11) we get the formula:

$$
\begin{aligned}
&\#d < Max \wedge p? \notin d \wedge \\
&\#d \leq Max \wedge \#l \leq Max \wedge d = \text{ran } l \\
&\Rightarrow \\
&\#l < Max \wedge p? \notin \text{ran } l.
\end{aligned}
\qquad (13.12)
$$

(13.12) is a theorem iff (13.13) is a valid sequent.

$$
\begin{aligned}
&\#d < Max, p? \notin d, \#d \leq Max, \#l \leq Max, d = \text{ran } l \\
&\longmapsto \\
&\#l < Max \wedge p? \notin \text{ran } l.
\end{aligned}
\qquad (13.13)
$$

The first conjunct in the conclusion of (13.13) follows from the formulas $\#d < Max$, $d = \text{ran } l$ and $\#l = \# \text{ran } l$. The first two of these occur amongst the premises of (13.13) and the third one follows from the fact that l does not contain any duplicate elements. The second conjunct in the conclusion of (13.13) follows from the two formulas $p? \notin d$ and $d = \text{ran } l$. Thus, (13.13) is valid and so (13.12) is a theorem.

Correctness of *Enter2*

The correctness of *Enter2* is expressed by means of the formula:

$$\text{pre } Enter1 \wedge \Delta Class1Class2 \wedge Enter2 \Rightarrow Enter1. \qquad (13.14)$$

The significance of the proof obligation (13.14) is best explained with reference to Fig. 13.5. The formula (13.14) expresses symbolically the following requirement. Let a be a state in the specification which satisfies pre *Enter1*, that is to say, it is a state which allows the operation *Enter1* to be carried out, and let c be the concrete state in the design which corresponds to a through the schema *Class1Class2*. Since I have already proved that *Enter1* is applicable, we know that c satisfies pre *Enter2*; therefore, we know that there is an after state c' which is the result of carrying out the operation *Enter2* starting from the before state c. Furthermore, let a' be the state back in the specification which is related through *Class1Class2'* to c'. Given all these states— which is conveyed by the antecedent of (13.14)—then what the consequent of (13.14) says is that a' is the result of applying *Enter1* to the state a. In other words, the diagram in Fig. 13.5 commutes.

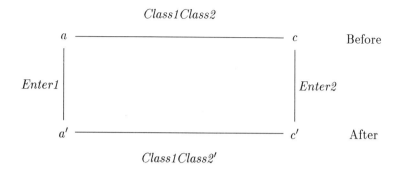

The abstract state   The concrete state

Figure 13.5: Correctness.

Now I am going to convince you that (13.14) is a theorem. Expanding it we get:

$\#d < Max \land p? \notin d \land$
$\#d \leq Max \land \#l \leq Max \land d = \text{ran } l \land \#d' \leq Max \land \#l' \leq Max \land d' = \text{ran } l' \land$
$\#l < Max \land \#l' \leq Max \land p? \notin \text{ran } l \land l' = append(l, \langle p? \rangle)$
$\Rightarrow$
$\#d < Max \land \#d' \leq Max \land p? \notin d \land d' = d \cup \{p?\}.$

This may seem exceedingly complicated at first sight; however, it becomes easier to take in and manipulate when represented as a sequent:

$$\#d < Max, p? \notin d, d = \text{ran } l, \#d' \leq Max, \#l' \leq Max,$$
$$d' = \text{ran } l', \#l < Max, p? \notin \text{ran } l, l' = append(l, \langle p? \rangle)$$
$$\longmapsto$$
$$\#d < Max \land \#d' \leq Max \land p? \notin d \land d' = d \cup \{p?\}.$$

Note that the formulas $\#d \leq Max$ and $\#l \leq Max$ do not appear in the set of assumptions because they are implied by $\#d < Max$ and $\#l < Max$, respectively. Of the four conjuncts in the conclusion of the above sequent only the last one, namely $d' = d \cup \{p?\}$, does not occur in the set of assumptions or premises. Hence, it is the only one that we need to show follows from the premises. This is done as follows:

> From the formulas $d' = \text{ran } l'$ and $l' = append(l, \langle p? \rangle)$ it follows that $d' = \text{ran}(append(l, \langle p? \rangle))$. By the properties of the range operator and the *append* function we can infer that $d' = \text{ran } l \cup \{p?\}$. Combining this with the formula $d = \text{ran } l$ gives us $d' = d \cup \{p?\}$, as required.

Discussion

The proof obligations just discussed are not as general as they could be. They are simplified because the formula

$$\forall Class2 \bullet \exists_1 Class1 \bullet Class1Class2 \qquad (13.15)$$

is a theorem. The formula (13.15) states that one and only one abstract state corresponds to any given concrete state. A sequence of people, whose length is less than or equal to *Max*, corresponds to one and only one set made up out of those self-same people, though—of course—many sequences correspond to that set. It is possible—and at times necessary—to make use of retrieve schemas which do not have this property. In this case the initialization proof obligation and the correctness requirement are more complicated, although the proof of applicability remains the same. I illustrate these more general proof obligations with the same classroom example.

13.3.5 General Correctness of Design

Correspondence of Initial States

Given a specification and a design linked by a schema which does not necessarily satisfy the property exemplified by (13.15) the first thing we have to prove is that the initial states of the specification and the design correspond to one another. (Remember that *Class1Class2* is like the retrieve function I described earlier.) So, what we have to establish is the following formula:

$$InitClass2' \Rightarrow \exists Class1' \bullet (InitClass1' \wedge Class1Class2').$$

In words this says that if we have an initial state in the design, then there exists a state in the specification which is an initial state and which is related to the initial state of the design by means of *Class1Class2'*. Expanding this formula we get:

$$\#l' \leq Max \wedge l' = \langle \, \rangle$$
$$\Rightarrow$$
$$\exists d' \colon \mathbf{P} \, Person \mid \#d' \leq Max \; \bullet \qquad (13.16)$$
$$\#d' \leq Max \wedge d' = \varnothing \wedge$$
$$\#d' \leq Max \wedge \#l' \leq Max \wedge d' = \operatorname{ran} l'.$$

The formula (13.16) is a theorem iff (13.17) is a valid sequent.

$$\#l' \leq Max, l' = \langle \, \rangle$$
$$\longmapsto$$
$$\exists d' \colon \mathbf{P} \, Person \; \bullet \qquad (13.17)$$
$$\#d' \leq Max \wedge d' = \varnothing \wedge \#l' \leq Max \wedge d' = \operatorname{ran} l'.$$

(In transforming (13.16) into (13.17) the restricted existential quantification has been changed into an unrestricted one and duplicate conjuncts inside the scope of the existential quantifier have been deleted.) By one of the one-point laws the conclusion of (13.17) is equivalent to the formula $\#\varnothing \leq Max \wedge \#l' \leq Max \wedge \varnothing = \operatorname{ran} l'$, which follows from the premises of (13.17), therefore (13.17) is valid and so (13.16) is a theorem.

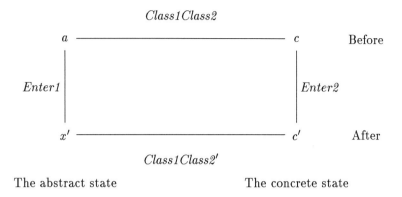

Figure 13.6: Correctness in the general case.

Correctness of *Enter2*

For each operation we have to prove *correctness* and *applicability*. The proof of applicability in the general case is proved in exactly the same way as discussed on p. 184 above. In order to prove that the operation *Enter2* is correct in the general case we have to prove that the formula

$$\text{pre } \textit{Enter1} \wedge \textit{Class1Class2} \wedge \textit{Enter2} \Rightarrow \exists \textit{Class1}' \bullet (\textit{Class1Class2}' \wedge \textit{Enter1})$$

is a theorem. In order to understand this proof obligation let a be an abstract state, let c be a concrete state corresponding to a by means of *Class1Class2* and let c' be a concrete state that results from c by the application of *Enter2*. Then, this proof obligation states that given a, c and c' as mentioned, there exists an abstract state x' which is the result of applying *Enter1* to a and it is also related to c' by means of *Class1Class2'*. The diagram in Fig. 13.6 might help to clarify this proof obligation. The above formula states that there exists an x' which satisfies the diagram in Fig. 13.6. Expanding the formula that we have to prove results in

$$
\begin{aligned}
&\#d < \textit{Max} \wedge p? \notin d \wedge \\
&\#d \leq \textit{Max} \wedge \#l \leq \textit{Max} \wedge d = \mathrm{ran}\, l \wedge \\
&\#l \leq \textit{Max} \wedge \#l' \leq \textit{Max} \wedge \#l < \textit{Max} \wedge p? \notin \mathrm{ran}\, l \wedge l' = \textit{append}(l, \langle p? \rangle) \\
&\Rightarrow \qquad\qquad\qquad\qquad\qquad\qquad\qquad\qquad\qquad\qquad\qquad\qquad (13.18)\\
&\exists d' : \mathbf{P}\, \textit{Person} \mid \#d' \leq \textit{Max} \bullet \\
&\qquad \#d' \leq \textit{Max} \wedge \#l' \leq \textit{Max} \wedge d' = \mathrm{ran}\, l' \wedge \\
&\qquad \#d \leq \textit{Max} \wedge \#d' \leq \textit{Max} \wedge \#d < \textit{Max} \wedge p? \notin d \wedge d' = d \cup \{p?\}.
\end{aligned}
$$

This is a theorem iff (13.19) is a valid sequent. In transforming (13.18) into a sequent the one-point law involving the existential quantifier was used and also duplicate formulas were removed.

$$\begin{aligned}
&\#d < Max, p? \notin d, d = \operatorname{ran} l, \\
&\#l' \leq Max, \#l < Max, p? \notin \operatorname{ran} l, l' = append(l, \langle p? \rangle)
\end{aligned}$$

$$\mapsto \tag{13.19}$$

$$\begin{aligned}
&\#(d \cup \{p?\}) \leq Max \wedge \#l' \leq Max \wedge \\
&d \cup \{p?\} = \operatorname{ran} l' \wedge \#d < Max \wedge p? \notin d.
\end{aligned}$$

The sequent (13.19) is valid, as the reader can easily confirm for himself or herself.

14

Floyd–Hoare Logic

14.1 Introduction

In this chapter I present the basic ideas of Floyd–Hoare logic. There are several varieties of this kind of logic, but all of them are formal systems in which it is possible to reason mathematically about computer programs and their specifications and, in some cases in this type of logic, it can be established conclusively that a particular program does indeed meet its specification. In such a case the program is said to have been *verified* relative to that specification. The form in which a specification is presented in a Floyd–Hoare logic is different from how it would be presented in Z, but in the next chapter I show how a Z specification can be transformed into the kind of specification that is characteristic of a Floyd–Hoare logic.

As already mentioned there are several varieties of Floyd–Hoare logic. The differences relate to the choice of programming language constructs that can be handled in a particular logic. If ever I do speak in this book about *the* Floyd–Hoare logic, then I mean the specific one that is described in this chapter.

Floyd–Hoare logic was introduced into computer science by Hoare (1969) who was influenced to a considerable extent by the work of Floyd (1967). In such a short chapter as this one it is impossible to do very much. There are, however, a growing number of books that go into the subject much more deeply than is possible here and the reader is encouraged to read one of these if he or she is not already familiar with the ways in which Floyd–Hoare logics are used not only to verify programs but also to help construct them from their specifications in the first place. I have found the following to be useful: (Gries 1981), (Backhouse 1986), (Baber 1987), (Gumb 1989), (Dromey 1989), (Kaldewaij 1990) and (Cohen 1990).

Floyd–Hoare logic is a kind of logic and its proof-theory makes use of some of the same basic ideas that were introduced in chapter 10 where I dealt with the proof-theory of first-order logic. In particular, it uses the same notions of a sequent, a start sequent and a thema and the definitions of *tree proof*, *validity* and *theorem* are the same. The class of formulas it deals with is, however, extended—as are the set of primitive start sequents and the collection of primitive themata. One of the consequences of these extensions is that in a Floyd–Hoare logic it is possible to introduce programming language constructs into a tree proof by means of their respective introduction rules or start sequents. In the next two sections I make explicit how the class of formulas, the set of primitive start sequents and the collection of primitive themata are to be extended. In section 14.4 I explain what total correctness is and how it is related to partial correctness and in section 14.5 I explain the difference between program variables and mathematical variables. In section 14.6 I introduce the notion of a verification condition and there I explain its role in program verification.

14.2   Hoare Triples

The characteristic formulas of a Floyd–Hoare logic are of the form $\{P\}\ \gamma\ \{Q\}$, where P and Q are formulas of first-order logic and γ is a command belonging to some programming language or other. A formula $\{P\}\ \gamma\ \{Q\}$ is known variously as a *Hoare formula*, a *Hoare triple*, a *partial correctness specification*, a *partial correctness assertion* (sometimes contracted simply to *assertion*) or as an *asserted program*.[1] In this book I call such a formula either a *(Hoare) triple* or a *formula (of Floyd–Hoare logic)*. The formula P is known as the *precondition* or the *input assertion* and Q is known as the *postcondition* or the *output assertion* or as the *result assertion*. The terms *precondition* and *postcondition* are used in this book.

To explain the meaning of a Hoare triple $\{P\}\ \gamma\ \{Q\}$ I need to introduce the notion of a state.[2] A *state* is an association between program variables and their values.[3] It is, in fact, a function which maps variables to abstract mathematical entities like numbers, sets, tuples, sequences and so on. For example, the state *sta* might associate the program variable XX with the number 1 and the program variable YY with the number 7. Thus, $sta = \{\,'XX' \mapsto 1, 'YY' \mapsto 7\,\}$. A formula P is *true in a state sta* if P is true when the variables in P are given the meaning that they have in *sta*. For example, with *sta* as given above the formula $XX = YY$ is false, but the formula $XX + 6 = YY$ is true. The meaning of a Hoare triple can now be given. First, I explain what it is for a triple to be true in a state and then I say what it means for a triple to be true (in all states). The formula $\{P\}\ \gamma\ \{Q\}$ is *true in a state sta* iff, for all states *sta'*, if P is true in *sta* and the execution of γ transforms *sta* into *sta'* and the execution of γ terminates, then Q is true in *sta'*. The formula $\{P\}\ \gamma\ \{Q\}$ is *true (in all states)* iff, for all states *sta* and *sta'*, if P is true in *sta* and the execution of γ transforms *sta* into *sta'* and the execution of γ terminates, then Q is true in *sta'*.[4]

---

[1] A selection of the sources where these various designations may be found is: 'Hoare formula' (Sperschneider and Antoniou 1991, p. 360), 'Hoare triple' (O'Donnell 1982, p. 927), 'partial correctness specification' (Gordon 1988, p. 8), 'partial correctness assertion' (Sperschneider and Antoniou 1991, p. 360), 'assertion' (Nielson and Nielson 1992, p. 175) and 'asserted program' (Mason 1987, p. 2).

[2] The notion of a state needed to explain the meaning of a Hoare triple is different from the notion of a state used in Z, for example, when we talk about the state space of some specification.

[3] This notion of a state suffices for the simple programming language considered in this chapter. For more complicated languages a more sophisticated notion may be required. See (Gordon 1979) for more information.

[4] This account is based on that of Sperschneider and Antoniou (1991), p. 360, to which the reader is referred for a more formal treatment of these notions.

14.3 Start Sequents and Themata

14.3.1 Introduction

In this section the various primitive start sequents and primitive themata are given for the constructs of a small programming language whose abstract syntax is

$$\gamma ::= skip$$
$$| \quad x := t$$
$$| \quad \gamma_1; \gamma_2$$
$$| \quad \textbf{while } P \textbf{ do } \gamma$$
$$| \quad \textbf{if } P \textbf{ then } \gamma_1 \textbf{ else } \gamma_2$$
$$| \quad \textbf{for } x := t \textbf{ to } u \textbf{ do } \gamma$$

where γ, γ_1 and γ_2 are commands, x is a variable and t and u are terms. In order to illustrate some of the start sequents and themata a proof will be constructed which shows that the following formula is a theorem:

$$\{true\}$$

$$REM := END; QUO := 0;$$
$$\textbf{while } SOR \leq REM \textbf{ do} \qquad\qquad (14.1)$$
$$REM := REM - SOR; QUO := QUO + 1$$

$$\{END = SOR * QUO + REM \wedge REM < SOR\},$$

where the program variables QUO, REM, END and SOR are all integer-valued ones. Note that program variables consist entirely of capital letters and they are always made up out of more than one letter. The command in (14.1) carries out division by repeated subtraction with END being the dividend and SOR the divisor. If the command terminates, then the variable QUO will contain the quotient and REM the remainder when END is divided by SOR. (The circumstances in which this command does actually terminate are discussed in section 14.4 below.) Before giving the primitive start sequents and the primitive themata for the constructs of the small programming language introduced above a number of general purpose structural rules are presented.

14.3.2 Structural Rules

If $P \mapsto Q$ is valid, then P is said to be *stronger* than Q and Q is said to be *weaker* than P. The first structural rule is called *precondition strengthening*:

$$\frac{\Gamma, P \mapsto Q \quad \Delta \mapsto \{Q\} \gamma \{R\}}{\Gamma, \Delta \mapsto \{P\} \gamma \{R\}.} \quad pre\text{-}strength$$

The next structural rule is *postcondition weakening*:

$$\frac{\Gamma \mapsto \{P\} \gamma \{Q\} \quad \Delta, Q \mapsto R}{\Gamma, \Delta \mapsto \{P\} \gamma \{R\}.} \quad post\text{-}weak$$

The next structural rule is *specification conjunction*:

$$\frac{\Gamma_1 \mapsto \{P_1\}\, \gamma\, \{Q_1\} \quad \Gamma_2 \mapsto \{P_2\}\, \gamma\, \{Q_2\}}{\Gamma_1, \Gamma_2 \mapsto \{P_1 \wedge P_2\}\, \gamma\, \{Q_1 \wedge Q_2\}.} \quad spec\text{-}conj$$

14.3.3   The *skip* Command

The start sequent for the *skip* command, which does nothing, is $\mapsto \{P\}\, skip\, \{P\}$. In constructing tree proofs in a Floyd–Hoare logic this start sequent can be used to construct leaf nodes. In chapter 10 I said that if it is postulated that a start sequent can have the form $\varnothing \mapsto A$, then the formula A is known as an *axiom*. Thus, Hoare triples of the form $\{P\}\, skip\, \{P\}$ are axioms of the Floyd–Hoare logic being proposed.

14.3.4   Substitution

The notation $P[t/x]$ is used to represent the formula that results when every free occurrence of the variable x in P is replaced by the term t. $P[t/x]$ can be read as 'P with t substituted for x'. Some examples of substitution should make clear how it works. The symbol $\equiv$ in the following examples represents syntactic identity. That is to say, $P \equiv Q$ means that P and Q are exactly the same linguistic expression.

$$END = SOR * QUO + REM\ [(QUO + 1)/QUO] \quad (14.2)$$
$$\equiv END = SOR * (QUO + 1) + REM.$$

14.3.5   Assignment

The start sequent for assignment is $\mapsto \{P[t/x]\}\, x := t\, \{P\}$. In constructing tree proofs in a Floyd–Hoare logic this start sequent can be used to construct leaf nodes. In other words, every Hoare triple of the form $\{P[t/x]\}\, x := t\, \{P\}$ is an axiom of the logic being developed and such an axiom is known as *the assignment axiom*. Using the substitution (14.2) the use of the start sequent for assignment can be illustrated like this:

$$\mapsto \{END = SOR * (QUO + 1) + REM\}$$
$$QUO := QUO + 1 \quad (14.3)$$
$$\{END = SOR * QUO + REM\}.$$

Typically, the assignment axiom is used to solve the following kind of problem. Given the Hoare triple

$$\{P\}\, REM := REM - SOR\, \{END = SOR * (QUO + 1) + REM\}, \quad (14.4)$$

what is a suitable choice for the formula P which will make (14.4) into a theorem? Using the assignment axiom to calculate P results in the formula

$$END = SOR * (QUO + 1) + REM\ [(REM - SOR)/REM].$$

That is to say, the formula $END = SOR * (QUO + 1) + (REM - SOR)$ and this is equivalent to $END = SOR * QUO + REM$. We thus know that the following is valid:

$$\mapsto \{END = SOR * QUO + REM\}$$
$$REM := REM - SOR \qquad (14.5)$$
$$\{END = SOR * (QUO + 1) + REM\}.$$

It should be noted, however, that $END = SOR * QUO + REM$ is not the only formula that P could be. If we are given what Q is—but not what P is—in the Hoare triple $\{P\}\ x := t\ \{Q\}$, then there are infinitely many formulas that P could be. However, if we use the assignment axiom to calculate P, the formula we obtain is the *weakest* precondition that exists in the sense that every other precondition R that makes the Hoare triple $\{R\}\ x := t\ \{Q\}$ a theorem entails P. In other words, if R is any formula that makes $\{R\}\ x := t\ \{Q\}$ a theorem, then $R \mapsto Q[t/x]$ is valid.

14.3.6   Sequencing

The rule governing the introduction of the semicolon is

$$\frac{\Gamma \mapsto \{P\}\,\gamma\,\{Q\} \quad \Delta \mapsto \{Q\}\,\delta\,\{R\}}{\Gamma, \Delta \mapsto \{P\}\,\gamma;\delta\,\{R\}.}\ \text{;-}int$$

This rule can be illustrated by means of two of the sequents that were used to show how the start sequent for assignment works. Note that the precondition of the Hoare triple in (14.3) is the same as the postcondition of the Hoare triple in (14.5). They can, therefore, be combined by means of ;-*int* in this way:

$$\frac{\begin{array}{cc} \mapsto \{END = SOR * QUO + REM\} & \mapsto \{END = SOR * (QUO + 1) + REM\} \\ REM := REM - SOR & QUO := QUO + 1 \\ \{END = SOR * (QUO + 1) + REM\} & \{END = SOR * QUO + REM\} \end{array}}{\begin{array}{c} \mapsto \{END = SOR * QUO + REM\} \\ REM := REM - SOR; QUO := QUO + 1 \\ \{END = SOR * QUO + REM\}. \end{array}}\ \text{;-}int$$

From this we know that

$$\mapsto \{END = SOR * QUO + REM\}$$
$$REM := REM - SOR; QUO := QUO + 1 \qquad (14.6)$$
$$\{END = SOR * QUO + REM\}$$

is a valid sequent. Notice that the precondition of the Hoare triple in (14.6) is the same as its postcondition. Such a formula is known as an *invariant* of the command in question, which in this case is $REM := REM - SOR; QUO := QUO + 1$.

14.3.7   The while-loop

The thematic rule governing the introduction of the **while**-loop is

$$\frac{\Gamma \;\mapsto\; \{P \wedge Q\}\, \gamma\, \{P\}}{\Gamma \;\mapsto\; \{P\}\, \textbf{while}\; Q\; \textbf{do}\; \gamma\, \{P \wedge \neg Q\}.}\;\; \textbf{while-}int$$

From the validity of the sequents

$$END = SOR * QUO + REM \wedge SOR \leq REM \;\mapsto\; END = SOR * QUO + REM$$

and (14.6) we can, by means of the rule of precondition strengthening, obtain

$$\mapsto \{END = SOR * QUO + REM \wedge SOR \leq REM\}$$
$$REM := REM - SOR; QUO := QUO + 1 \qquad\qquad (14.7)$$
$$\{END = SOR * QUO + REM\}.$$

This can be used to illustrate the way in which the rule for introducing the **while**-loop works. The following is a correct instance of this rule:

$$\frac{\begin{array}{c}\mapsto \{END = SOR * QUO + REM \wedge SOR \leq REM\} \\ REM := REM - SOR; QUO := QUO + 1 \\ \{END = SOR * QUO + REM\}\end{array}}{\begin{array}{c}\mapsto \{END = SOR * QUO + REM\} \\ \textbf{while}\; SOR \leq REM\; \textbf{do}\; REM := REM - SOR; QUO := QUO + 1 \\ \{END = SOR * QUO + REM \wedge \neg(SOR \leq REM)\}.\end{array}}\;\; \textbf{while-}int$$

Thus, the following sequent is valid:

$$\mapsto \{END = SOR * QUO + REM\}$$
$$\textbf{while}\; SOR \leq REM\; \textbf{do}\; REM := REM - SOR; QUO := QUO + 1 \qquad (14.8)$$
$$\{END = SOR * QUO + REM \wedge REM < SOR\}.$$

(Note that the formula $\neg(SOR \leq REM)$ has been replaced by the syntactically equivalent formula $REM < SOR$ in the postcondition of the Hoare triple in (14.8).)

   It is now straightforward to complete the proof of the sequent whose set of premises is the empty set and whose conclusion is the Hoare triple (14.1). Using the start sequent for assignment twice it is possible to establish the validity of both the input sequents of the tree proof (14.9).

$$\frac{\begin{array}{cc}\begin{array}{c}\mapsto \{true\} \\ REM := END \\ \{END = REM\}\end{array} & \begin{array}{c}\mapsto \{END = REM\} \\ QUO := 0 \\ \{END = SOR * QUO + REM\}\end{array}\end{array}}{\begin{array}{c}\mapsto \{true\} \\ REM := END; QUO := 0 \\ \{END = SOR * QUO + REM\}.\end{array}}\;\; ;\text{-}int \qquad (14.9)$$

The output sequent of the tree proof (14.9) can be combined with the sequent (14.8) by means of the rule of introducing the semicolon to obtain

$$\mapsto \{true\}$$

$$
\begin{aligned}
&REM := END;\, QUO := 0;\\
&\textbf{while } SOR \leq REM \textbf{ do}\\
&\quad REM := REM - SOR;\, QUO := QUO + 1
\end{aligned}
\tag{14.10}
$$

$$\{END = SOR * QUO + REM \land REM < SOR\}.$$

When a sequent is valid and its set of premises is the empty set, then its conclusion is a theorem. The sequent (14.10) has no premises, thus its conclusion is a theorem. Thus, the Hoare triple (14.1) has been shown to be a theorem of Floyd–Hoare logic.

14.3.8 The Conditional

The rule governing the introduction of the conditional is

$$\frac{\Gamma \mapsto \{P \land Q\}\, \gamma\, \{R\} \quad \Delta \mapsto \{P \land \neg Q\}\, \delta\, \{R\}}{\Gamma, \Delta \mapsto \{P\} \textbf{ if } Q \textbf{ then } \gamma \textbf{ else } \delta\, \{R\}.} \quad \textbf{if-}int$$

It is often more convenient to use a variant of the rule **if-**int and I call this alternative **if-**int-v, where the letter vee comes from the first letter in the word 'variant'.

$$\frac{\Gamma \mapsto \{P \land Q\}\, \gamma\, \{R_1\} \quad \Delta \mapsto \{P \land \neg Q\}\, \delta\, \{R_2\}}{\Gamma, \Delta \mapsto \{P\} \textbf{ if } Q \textbf{ then } \gamma \textbf{ else } \delta\, \{R_1 \lor R_2\}.} \quad \textbf{if-}int\text{-}v$$

This derived rule is established by using postcondition weakening twice and the standard rule for introducing the conditional. The following tree proof

$$
\frac{
\begin{array}{ll}
\mapsto \{II < 0\} & \qquad \mapsto \{II \geq 0\}\\
\quad ABS := -II & \qquad\quad ABS = II\\
\{II < 0 \land ABS = -II\} & \quad \{II \geq 0 \land ABS = II\}
\end{array}
}{
\begin{array}{l}
\mapsto \{true\}\\
\quad \textbf{if } II < 0 \textbf{ then } ABS := -II \textbf{ else } ABS := II\\
\{(II < 0 \land ABS = -II) \lor (II \geq 0 \land ABS = II)\}
\end{array}
} \quad \textbf{if-}int\text{-}v
$$

illustrates the use of the variant rule for introducing the conditional. Both the leaf nodes are instances of the start sequent for assignment.

14.3.9 The for-loop

There is both a start sequent and a thematic rule governing the **for**-loop. First, I state the start sequent:

$$\mapsto \{P \land (u < t)\} \textbf{ for } x := t \textbf{ to } u \textbf{ do } \gamma\, \{P\}.$$

Next, I state the thematic rule:

$$\frac{\Gamma \;\mapsto\; \{P \wedge (t \leq x \leq u)\}\; \gamma\; \{P[x+1/x]\}}{\Gamma \;\mapsto\; \{P[t/x] \wedge (t \leq u)\}\; \textbf{for } x := t \textbf{ to } u \textbf{ do } \gamma\; \{P[u+1/x]\}.} \quad \textbf{for-}\textit{int}$$

The side condition for the thematic rule **for-**$\textit{int}$ is that neither x nor any variable occurring in either t or u can occur on the left-hand side of an assignment in γ.

14.4   Total Correctness

Above I demonstrated that the triple (14.1) is a theorem of Floyd–Hoare logic. However, if $SOR < END < 0$, then the command in (14.1) fails to terminate. If $\{P\}\, \gamma\, \{Q\}$ is a theorem, then whenever the formula P is true before γ is executed and the execution of γ *terminates*, then Q is true after γ has *terminated*. Nothing is said here about Q if γ fails to terminate. The reason why the word 'partial' is used in the phrase 'partial correctness' is because in order to show that a formula $\{P\}\, \gamma\, \{Q\}$ is a theorem we do not have to prove that the execution of the command γ terminates. If this were an additional requirement, then we would be dealing with *total* correctness. Total correctness, however, is what we are really interested in and a good way of demonstrating that a formula $\{P\}\, \gamma\, \{Q\}$ is totally correct is by first demonstrating that it is partially correct and then working out the circumstances in which γ terminates. In the case of the formula (14.1) it terminates at least in those circumstances where $SOR > 0$ and $END \geq 0$.

14.5   Using Mathematical Variables

Above I demonstrated that the formula (14.1) is a theorem of Floyd–Hoare logic. Although the proof is correct, the way in which the postcondition is written in the Hoare triple (14.1) is not entirely satisfactory. The reason for this is that often in using a Floyd–Hoare logic we are concerned with the following kind of problem: Given two formulas P and Q of first-order logic find a suitable command γ which makes $\{P\}\, \gamma\, \{Q\}$ a theorem of Floyd–Hoare logic. Let us consider a specific example of this problem, namely that of finding a command γ which makes the Hoare triple

$$\{\textit{true}\}$$
$$\gamma \qquad\qquad\qquad\qquad\qquad\qquad (14.11)$$
$$\{END = SOR * QUO + REM \wedge REM < SOR\}$$

a theorem of Floyd–Hoare logic. Of course, faced with this problem someone might devise the command

$$REM := END;\, QUO := 0;$$
$$\textbf{while } SOR \leq REM \textbf{ do}$$
$$REM := REM - SOR;\, QUO := QUO + 1$$

but if he or she proposed instead the command

$$END := 1; SOR := 1; QUO := 1; REM := 0$$

as a suitable choice for γ, then he or she would also have found a command Γ which makes (14.11) a theorem. It is unlikely, however, to be a solution in the range of solutions expected by the person who set the problem. This is why only using program variables in the postcondition of a Hoare triple is not entirely satisfactory if we treat the command γ in a Hoare triple as the unknown quantity that we are trying to find.

It is not difficult to get round this difficulty. All that is needed is to introduce some *mathematical* (or *specification* or *logical*) variables into the precondition and postcondition of a Hoare triple which give initial values to some of the program variables and which 'remember' those values. One way of doing this is shown in the following Hoare triple:

$$\{END = end \wedge SOR = sor\}$$

$$REM := END; QUO := 0;$$
while $SOR \leq REM$ **do**
$$\quad REM := REM - SOR; QUO := QUO + 1 \qquad (14.12)$$

$$\{END = end \wedge SOR = sor \wedge$$
$$QUO = quo \wedge REM = rem \wedge$$
$$END = SOR * QUO + REM \wedge REM < SOR\}.$$

Another way of doing it is to express that part of the postcondition which wears the trousers entirely in terms of logical or specification variables, thus

$$\{END = end \wedge SOR = sor\}$$

$$REM := END; QUO := 0;$$
while $SOR \leq REM$ **do**
$$\quad REM := REM - SOR; QUO := QUO + 1$$

$$\{END = end \wedge SOR = sor \wedge$$
$$QUO = quo \wedge REM = rem \wedge$$
$$end = sor * quo + rem \wedge rem < sor\}.$$

In either case we need to keep the collection of program variables and that of specification variables separate. They must be disjoint sets and, furthermore, no specification variable can be allowed to occur in a program.

14.6 Verification Conditions

14.6.1 Introduction

A consistent set of formulas Γ—none of which are themselves Hoare triples—is a set of *verification conditions* for the formula $\{P\} \gamma \{Q\}$ if the sequent $\Gamma \mapsto \{P\} \gamma \{Q\}$ is valid. This has the consequence that if each formula in the set Γ can be proved to be a theorem of first-order logic, then the Hoare triple $\{P\}\,\gamma\,\{Q\}$ is a theorem of Floyd–Hoare logic. Clearly, there are—in general—many different sets of verification conditions for one and the same theorem. Later on in this section I give a series of recipes for generating verification conditions from each of the programming language constructs already introduced. These recipes, in fact, generate the weakest set of formulas that are sufficient to establish $\{P\}\,\gamma\,\{Q\}$. It would be out of place to say more about this topic here, but the interested reader is referred to (Dijkstra 1976). In order to give these recipes I need to introduce some more technical terms.

An *annotated command* is a command with formulas—known as *annotations*—embedded within it. A *properly annotated command* is a command in which annotations have been inserted at the following points:

(1) before each command γ_i, for $2 \leq i \leq n$, in a sequence of commands $\gamma_1; \gamma_2; \ldots; \gamma_n$ which is *not* an assignment command and

(2) after the word **do** in a **while**-loop and in a **for**-loop.

In (1) the sequence $\gamma_1; \gamma_2; \ldots; \gamma_n$ must not be a sub-sequence of a longer sequence of commands. A *properly annotated (Hoare) triple* is a formula $\{P\}\,\gamma\,\{Q\}$ where γ is a properly annotated command.

14.6.2   The *skip* Command

The single verification condition for the Hoare triple $\{P\}\;skip\;\{Q\}$ is the formula $P \Rightarrow Q$. That this is indeed a verification condition for $\{P\}\;skip\;\{Q\}$ can be demonstrated by means of the following incomplete tree proof:

$$\cfrac{\mapsto \{P\}\;skip\;\{P\} \qquad \cfrac{P \mapsto P \quad \mapsto P \Rightarrow Q}{P \mapsto Q}\;\Rightarrow\text{-}elim}{\mapsto \{P\}\;skip\;\{Q\}.}\;post\text{-}weak$$

14.6.3   Assignment

The single verification condition for the Hoare triple $\{P\}\;x := t\;\{Q\}$ is the formula $P \Rightarrow (Q[t/x])$. That this is indeed a verification condition can be established by means of the following incomplete tree proof:

$$\cfrac{\cfrac{P \mapsto P \quad \mapsto P \Rightarrow (Q[t/x])}{P \mapsto Q[t/x]}\;\Rightarrow\text{-}elim \qquad \mapsto \{Q[t/x]\}\;x := t\;\{Q\}}{\mapsto \{P\}\;x := t\;\{Q\}.}\;pre\text{-}strength$$

14.6.4   The Conditional

The verification conditions for $\{P\}$ **if** Q **then** γ **else** δ $\{R\}$ are the verification conditions for $\{P \wedge Q\}\,\gamma\,\{R\}$ and those for $\{P \wedge \neg Q\}\,\delta\,\{R\}$. That this is so follows straightforwardly from the rule **if**-*int*.

14.6.5 Sequencing

The following fact about a properly annotated sequence of commands is needed in order to explain what the verification conditions are for such a command. Let $\gamma_1; \gamma_2; \ldots; \gamma_n$, where $n \geq 2$, be a properly annotated command. Then it has to be one of the following two forms:

(1) $\gamma_1; \gamma_2; \ldots; \gamma_{n-1}; \{A\} \gamma_n$, where γ_n is not an assignment command or

(2) $\gamma_1; \gamma_2; \ldots; \gamma_{n-1}; x := t$.

In both of these cases $\gamma_1; \gamma_2; \ldots; \gamma_{n-1}$ must be a properly annotated command. Generating verification conditions is different depending on what form the sequence of commands takes:

(1) The verification conditions for $\{P\} \gamma_1; \gamma_2; \ldots; \gamma_{n-1} \{A\} \gamma_n \{Q\}$ where γ_n is not an assignment are

 (a) the verification conditions for $\{P\} \gamma_1; \gamma_2; \ldots; \gamma_{n-1} \{A\}$ and

 (b) the verification conditions for $\{A\} \gamma_n \{Q\}$.

(2) The verification conditions for $\{P\} \gamma_1; \gamma_2; \ldots; \gamma_{n-1}; x := t \{Q\}$ are the verification conditions for $\{P\} \gamma_1; \gamma_2; \ldots; \gamma_{n-1} \{Q[t/x]\}$.

14.6.6 The while-loop

The verification conditions for $\{P\}$ **while** Q **do** $\{A\} \gamma \{R\}$ are

(1) $P \Rightarrow A$,

(2) $A \wedge \neg Q \Rightarrow R$ and

(3) the verification conditions for $\{A \wedge Q\} \gamma \{A\}$.

14.6.7 The for-loop

The verification conditions for $\{P\}$ **for** $x := t$ **to** u **do** $\{A\} \gamma \{Q\}$, where neither x nor any variable occurring in either t or u occurs on the left-hand side of an assignment in γ, are

(1) $P \Rightarrow A[t/x]$,

(2) $A[u + 1/x] \Rightarrow Q$,

(3) $P \wedge u < t \Rightarrow Q$ and

(4) the verification conditions for $\{A \wedge t \leq x \leq u\} \gamma \{A[x + 1/x]\}$.

14.6.8   An Example

As an example consider the following command

$$FF := 0; \, GG := 1; \, II := 0;$$
$$\textbf{while } NN \neq II \textbf{ do} \qquad\qquad (14.13)$$
$$(GG := FF + GG; FF := GG - FF; II := II + 1)$$

which calculates Fibonacci numbers. If the initial value of the program variable NN is n, where n is a non-negative whole number, then on termination the value of FF is $fib(n)$, where the function fib is defined like this:

$$fib: \mathbb{N} \longrightarrow \mathbb{N}$$
$$\forall i: \mathbb{N} \bullet$$
$$fib(0) = 0 \,\wedge$$
$$fib(1) = 1 \,\wedge$$
$$fib(i+2) = fib(i+1) + fib(i)$$

The following is the result of properly annotating the command (14.13):

$$FF := 0; \, GG := 1; \, II := 0; \; \{FF = 0 \wedge GG = 1 \wedge II = 0\}$$
$$\textbf{while } NN \neq II \textbf{ do } \{FF = fib(II) \wedge GG = fib(II+1)\}$$
$$(GG := FF + GG; FF := GG - FF; II := II + 1)$$

and the following is an example of a properly annotated triple:

$$\{NN = n\}$$

$$FF := 0; \, GG := 1; \, II := 0; \; \{FF = 0 \wedge GG = 1 \wedge II = 0\}$$
$$\textbf{while } NN \neq II \textbf{ do } \{FF = fib(II) \wedge GG = fib(II+1)\}$$
$$(GG := FF + GG; FF := GG - FF; II := II + 1)$$

$$\{NN = n \wedge FF = fib(n)\}.$$

It is a straightforward—but tedious—task to work out what the verification conditions are for this properly annotated triple.

14.7   Conclusion

In the next chapter I explain how several different kinds of schema can be mechanically transformed into Hoare triples of the form $\{P\} \, \gamma \, \{Q\}$, where γ is the unknown quantity that we are trying to find. To conclude this chapter I just want to say a few things about the way in which the unknown command γ in a Hoare triple can be found—given that we know what P and Q are.

In many areas of intellectual activity, human beings solve problems by a process of trial and error-elimination.[5] Faced with the problem of finding γ in a Hoare triple

---

[5]See, for example, (Popper 1992), pp. 44–53, where it is stressed that the trials are not to be understood as *random* trials (for example, on p. 45).

$\{P\}\ \gamma\ \{Q\}$ the means that are used to find γ are not of paramount importance. In fact, in some cases simply guessing may be the best way to proceed.[6] Once a command has been proposed it is essential to check whether or not it is correct and it is here that verification conditions come into their own. Given the precondition and postcondition of a Hoare triple and a putative command that satisfies that triple, it is possible to automatically generate the set of verification conditions for that triple. If these can be shown to be theorems, then we know that the original guess was correct.[7] If one or more of the verification conditions are not theorems, then the guess may still be correct, but its correctness has to be shown in some other way. This way of going about the task of finding a command that satisfies the precondition and postcondition of a particular Hoare triple fits in very well with one of the main ways in which human beings solve problems.[8]

---

[6] In some of the books that discuss Floyd–Hoare logics in detail—such as (Backhouse 1986) and (Gries 1981)—various heuristics are proposed which help in the process of guessing commands that may be correct.

[7] Much of this can be automated. Much of the book (Gordon 1988) is devoted to the topic of automating those parts of this procedure that can be mechanized.

[8] Even in informal mathematics the method of trial and error-elimination plays a big role. See (Lakatos 1976) for a very entertaining exposition of this.

15

Getting to Program Code

15.1   The Transformation Recipe

In this chapter I show how a Z specification can be related to a programming language by means of a Floyd–Hoare logic. Given a Z specification of a sequential system I show how the initial state schema and the operation and error schemas can be transformed into formulas of a Floyd–Hoare logic in which the middle component, namely the command, is the unknown quantity that we are trying to find. For an operation or error schema the guts of the transformation recipe are as follows:[1]

(1) Program variables must be chosen that are different from all the variables used in the Z specification we are trying to implement.[2] No specification variable can occur as a program variable.[3]

(2) Let Op be a Z schema which describes some operation or is an error schema and which conforms to the standard Z conventions concerning before and after variables and also those concerning input and output variables. Then the Hoare triple corresponding to Op is

$$\{PreOp \wedge \textit{pre-ident}\}\ \gamma\ \{Op\ \chi \wedge \textit{post-ident}\}, \tag{15.1}$$

where γ is a command belonging to some programming language, χ is a substitution and both *pre-ident* and *post-ident* are conjunctions of zero or more identity statements. In the Hoare triple (15.1) the command γ is the unknown quantity and represents what we are trying to determine. Given a schema Op and a choice of program variables everything else in the Hoare triple can be derived automatically. The substitution χ and the two formulas *pre-ident* and *post-ident* are built up as follows:

---

[1]This is an improved version of the translation procedure proposed in (Diller 1992).

[2]The need to clearly distinguish between program variables and specification variables in a Floyd–Hoare logic is well explained by Nielson and Nielson (1992), p. 176, where specification variables are called *logical* variables. Concerning them they say, 'The role of these variables is to "remember" the initial values of the program variables.'

[3]This does not apply to *bound* specification variables like i in $(\exists i{:}1 \mathbin{..} NUM \bullet CL(i) = S)$.

(a) For every input variable *in?* in *Op*, whose corresponding program variable
is *IN?*, both the formulas *pre-ident* and *post-ident* must contain a conjunct
$IN? = in?$

(b) For every variable having both a before (*st*) and an after (*st'*) form in
the schema *Op* the formula *pre-ident* must contain a conjunct $ST = st$
and χ must contain a substitution $[ST/st']$, where *ST* is the corresponding
program variable.

(c) For every output variable *out!* in *Op*, whose corresponding program variable
is *OUT!*, the formula *post-ident* must contain a conjunct $OUT! = out!$

One of the functions of the formula *pre-ident* in (15.1) is to give an initial value to
program variables like *ST* which correspond to specification variables having both a
before and an after form.

In the situation where we want to obtain a Hoare triple from an initial state schema
the transformation procedure is much simpler. In this case step (2) needs to be replaced
by the following:

(2′) Let *InitState'* be an initial state schema containing neither input variables, nor
before state variables nor output variables. Then the Hoare triple corresponding
to *InitState'* is

$$\{true\}\ \gamma\ \{InitState'\ \chi\},$$

where χ is a substitution that contains a substitution $[ST/st']$ for each after state
variable *st'* in *InitState'* whose corresponding program variable is *ST*.

The reason for the separation that I make between specification and program variables
is that they are very different kinds of thing. A specification variable is a mathematical
variable whose meaning remains constant in any scope in which it occurs, whereas a
program variable can have many values inside a single scope.

15.2   Modelling a Simple Bank Account

In order to illustrate the process of constructing a Hoare triple (containing a command
γ as an unknown quantity) from a schema I use the specification of a simple bank
account. The state schema of this specification is called *Account*:

```
┌─ Account ──────────────────────────────────────────
│ bal, odl: Z
├────────────────────────────────────────────────────
│ odl ≥ 0
│ odl + bal ≥ 0
└────────────────────────────────────────────────────
```

Two integer-valued variables are declared in the schema *Account*, namely *bal* and *odl*.
The variable *odl* represents the overdraft limit of the person whose account this is
and *bal* represents the balance in the account. This is a sterling bank account, so the
integers *bal* and *odl* represent new pence. (There are 100 new pence to the pound.)

The state invariant tells us that the overdraft limit is a non-negative number and that the account holder cannot overstep his or her overdraft limit. Note that *bal* can have as its value a negative number. For example, if $bal = -500$, this means that the account is overdrawn to the tune of £500. This would only be possible if $odl \geq 500$.

The operation of withdrawing money from this account is specified by means of the schema *Withdraw*:

```
┌─ Withdraw ─────────────────────────────────
│ ΔAccount
│ with?: Z
│ ───────────────────────────
│ 0 < with? ≤ odl + bal
│ bal' = bal − with?
│ odl' = odl
└────────────────────────────────────────────
```

The integer-valued variable *with?* is the amount of money that is being withdrawn. It may seem strange to treat *with?* as an input variable, but clearly when you are withdrawing money from a bank account you have to inform the bank of the amount that you want to withdraw. The giving of this information to the bank is what the input variable *with?* represents. Imagine, for example, standing at a cash dispenser and keying in the amount of money you want to withdraw from your account. This is what *with?* represents.

In order to apply the translation described in section 15.1 above we need to calculate what *Pre Withdraw* is. It turns out to be the following schema:

```
┌─ Pre Withdraw ─────────────────────────────
│ Account
│ with?: Z
│ ───────────────────────────
│ 0 < with? ≤ odl + bal
└────────────────────────────────────────────
```

Stage (1) of the translation phase tells us to choose fresh program variables. For this purpose I use the identifiers $WITH?$, BAL and ODL. These correspond to the specification variables *with?*, *bal* and *odl*, respectively. According to stage (2) of the translation recipe, the Hoare triple that we are after is

$$\{Pre\,Withdraw \wedge \text{pre-ident}\} \; \gamma \; \{Withdraw \; \chi \wedge \text{post-ident}\},$$

where the substitution χ and the two formulas *pre-ident* and *post-ident* are as follows:

$$\chi \equiv [BAL/bal', ODL/odl'],$$
$$\text{pre-ident} \equiv WITH? = with? \wedge BAL = bal \wedge ODL = odl,$$
$$\text{post-ident} \equiv WITH? = with?$$

Expanding the Hoare triple and carrying out the substitutions results, after some rearrangement of sub-formulas, in

$$\{Account \wedge 0 < with? \leq odl + bal \wedge$$
$$WITH? = with? \wedge BAL = bal \wedge ODL = odl\}$$

$$\gamma$$

(15.2)

$$\{Account \wedge 0 < with? \leq odl + bal \wedge$$
$$WITH? = with? \wedge BAL = bal - with? \wedge ODL = odl \wedge$$
$$ODL \geq 0 \wedge ODL + BAL \geq 0\}.$$

It is not difficult to work out that one possibility for the command γ is the assignment $BAL := BAL - WITH?$ and that this is indeed a correct solution to the initial problem of finding the unknown γ can be confirmed by working out the verification condition for (15.2) with the command $BAL := BAL - WITH?$ as γ. This turns out to be

$$Account \wedge 0 < with? \leq odl + bal \wedge$$
$$WITH? = with? \wedge BAL = bal \wedge ODL = odl$$

$$\Rightarrow$$

$$Account \wedge 0 < with? \wedge$$
$$WITH? = with? \wedge BAL - WITH? = bal - with? \wedge ODL = odl \wedge$$
$$ODL \geq 0 \wedge ODL + BAL - WITH? \geq 0,$$

which can straightforwardly be proved to be a theorem.

15.2.1 Adding Messages

When specifying total operations in Z some sort of message is added which either reports that the operation has been successful or else outputs some sort of error message. I use the schema *WithdrawOkay* to represent the successful completion of the operation specified by *Withdraw* together with the outputting of a suitable message.

$$WithdrawOkay \stackrel{\wedge}{=} Withdraw \wedge Success,$$

where *Success* is the schema:

```
┌─ Success ──────────────────────────────────────────
│ rep!: Report
│ ───────────────────────────────────────────────────
│ rep! = 'Okay'
└─────────────────────────────────────────────────────
```

The operation specified by *Withdraw* can go wrong in two ways, namely when an attempt is made to withdraw a non-positive amount of money and also when an attempt is made to withdraw an amount of money that would lead to the overdraft limit being exceeded. The first of these possibilities is captured by means of the schema *NonPositiveWithdrawal*:

```
┌─ NonPositiveWithdrawal ──────────────────────────────────
│ ΞAccount
│ with?: Z
│ rep!: Report
├──────────────────────────────────────────────────────────
│ with? ≤ 0
│ rep! = 'Cannot withdraw non-positive amounts'
└──────────────────────────────────────────────────────────
```

It may seem strange to include the possibility of *with?* being negative, but recall that we are modelling the *information* component of a bank account. A bank teller, for example, may be keying in information to the bank's computer and by mistake he or she may hit the minus key before hitting the digits representing the amount to be withdrawn. It is to trap this kind of error that we need the schema *NonPositiveWithdrawal*.

The second of the ways in which *Withdraw* can go wrong is captured by means of the schema *NotEnoughMoney*:

```
┌─ NotEnoughMoney ─────────────────────────────────────────
│ ΞAccount
│ with?: Z
│ rep!: Report
├──────────────────────────────────────────────────────────
│ with? > odl + bal
│ rep! = 'Not enough money in account'
└──────────────────────────────────────────────────────────
```

The total specification of attempting to withdraw money from a bank account can now be given:

$$DoWithdraw \triangleq WithdrawOkay$$
$$\vee$$
$$NonPositiveWithdrawal$$
$$\vee$$
$$NotEnoughMoney.$$

One of the advantages of using the method for obtaining program code described earlier in this chapter is that it allows a large task to be split up into a number of smaller ones. For example, if our goal were to obtain a command corresponding to the schema *DoWithdraw*, we could first of all obtain commands corresponding to the three schemas *WithdrawOkay*, *NonPositiveWithdrawal* and *NotEnoughMoney* and then combine them in order to achieve our original goal. I now show how this can be done.

Using the method for obtaining program code described earlier it is possible to show that the command

$$BAL := BAL - WITH?; REP! := \text{'Okay'}$$

implements the schema *WithdrawOkay*, that the command

$$REP! := \text{'Cannot withdraw non-positive amounts'}$$

implements the schema *NonPositiveWithdrawal* and that the command

$$REP! := \text{'Not enough money in account'}$$

implements *NotEnoughMoney*. The command which implements *DoWithdraw* is, therefore,

if $0 < WITH? \leq ODL + BAL$ **then**
    $BAL := BAL - WITH?; REP! := \text{'Okay'}$
else if $WITH? \leq 0$ **then**
    $REP! := \text{'Cannot withdraw non-positive amounts'}$
else if $WITH? > ODL + BAL$ **then**
    $REP! := \text{'Not enough money in account'}$
else
    skip

Note that the only reason for including the *skip* command is that the small programming language introduced in the previous chapter only contains a two-armed conditional. It does not have a one-armed conditional.

15.3   A Sales Database

15.3.1   Informal Account

In this section I apply the method of getting program code from a Z specification described earlier to a larger example. The system to be specified can be described informally as follows:[4]

> A company employs a team of salespeople. For reasons of security and privacy these salespeople are known by their reference numbers which form an initial segment of the positive whole numbers. Every month each salesperson is eligible for both a commission on the amount he or she has sold and also a bonus. A database is, therefore, required which will keep track of the total value of the sales made by each person. The system is also expected to calculate the value of the commission and the bonus if these are due to any salesperson. At the beginning of each month the records are initialized to zero, that is to say, the value of each person's sales is changed to zero pounds. The manager is responsible for initializing the database each month and for deciding when the commission and bonus are to be paid, so the system specified should not do these things automatically at the beginning and end of each month. The manager is also responsible for keeping track of the sales made by his or her team and so records are kept. He or she needs to be able to update these records so that he or she knows the current value of the sales made by any member of the team. However, a check should be made to ensure that the value of a sale is entered correctly by insisting that the value of each sale be input twice

---

[4]This problem was suggested by one described by Welsh and Elder (1988), p. 140.

and the two values compared. Only if they agree should the amount be added to the quantity representing the running total of the sales made by the salesperson in question.

At the end of each month the manager needs to know who is eligible for either a commission or a bonus and also the value of that bonus or commission. Thus, it must be possible for the manager to interrogate the database. On inputting a salesperson's reference number, the system must output the value of the total sales made by that salesperson and also the amount of commission and bonus that they are due (both of which may be zero). The size of the team is quite small, so this is the only way in which it is necessary to interrogate the database. (If the size of the team was quite large, it would make more sense for some sort of report to be produced.) A salesperson only gets a commission if the value of his or her sales exceeds two-thirds of the average value of all the sales made by the team. If this happens, then the value of the bonus is 10 percent of the amount by which that person's sales exceeds the threshold value, which is two-thirds of the average value of all the sales made by the team. If the value of a salesperson's sales exceeds 115 per cent of the average value of the sales made by the team, then that person gets a bonus whose value is half a per cent of the total value of the sales made by the whole team.

15.3.2   The State Space

As, later on, I specify a user-interface for this system the specification makes use of a single basic type, namely *Command*, whose meaning will be explained in due course. The specification also makes use of a global constant *TeamSize* which represents the number of people in the sales team. This is introduced into the specification by means of an axiomatic description

$$\mid \ \textit{TeamSize} : \mathbf{N}$$

A number of messages are needed and these are all members of the set *Report*:

$$\textit{Report} ::= \text{`Okay'}$$
$$\mid \ \text{`Unknown salesperson'}$$
$$\mid \ \text{`Input not confirmed'}$$
$$\mid \ \text{`Unknown command'}.$$

The state of the system is defined by means of the schema *SalesDB*:

SalesDB
_____

$sales, comm, bonus : 1 .. \textit{TeamSize} \longrightarrow \mathbf{N}$
$tot, ave, thresh : \mathbf{N}$

_____

$tot = sumarray(sales)$
$ave = tot \ \mathbf{div} \ \textit{TeamSize}$
$thresh = (2 * ave) \ \mathbf{div} \ 3$

The array *sales* keeps track of the running total of the sales made by each team member and the arrays *comm* and *bonus* contain, respectively, the amount of commission and the bonus that each team member has earned.[5] The variable *tot* keeps track of the combined value of all the sales made by the team and *ave* is the result of dividing *tot* by the size of the team. The variable *thresh* represents the value of the sales made by a salesperson on which he or she does not receive commission. Note that the function *sumarray* occurs in the predicate-part of the schema *SalesDB*. When applied to an array of numbers this function returns the sum of all those numbers.

The Δ and Ξ schemas have their usual meaning and the initial state is given by *InitSalesDB'*, where *InitSalesDB* is defined in this way:

$$
\begin{array}{|l}
\_\,\textit{InitSalesDB}\,\_\!\_\!\_\!\_\!\_\!\_\!\_\!\_\!\_\!\_\!\_\!\_\!\_\!\_\!\_\!\_ \\
\;\; \textit{SalesDB} \\
\hline
\;\; \forall i : 1 \,..\, \textit{TeamSize} \bullet \\
\;\;\;\;\;\; \textit{sales}(i) = \textit{comm}(i) = \textit{bonus}(i) = 0 \\
\end{array}
$$

Note that in the schema *InitSalesDB'* there is no need to state explicitly that the variables *tot'*, *ave'* and *thresh'* are all equal to zero. As *InitSalesDB'* includes the schema *SalesDB'* these three variables have to be equal to zero because of their connection—through the state invariant of *SalesDB'*—with the array *sales'*.

15.3.3   The Operations

Adding Information

Four operations are provided: one of these updates the database when a salesperson makes a sale, another calculates the commission that is due to those salespeople who have earned it, another works out the value of the bonus that is due to those who have earned it and the final one allows the database to be interrogated by the reference number of a particular salesperson. The first of these operations is specified by the schema *AddSales*, which is defined in this way:

$$
\begin{array}{|l}
\_\,\textit{AddSales}\,\_\!\_\!\_\!\_\!\_\!\_\!\_\!\_\!\_\!\_\!\_\!\_\!\_\!\_\!\_\!\_ \\
\;\; \Delta\,\textit{SalesDB} \\
\;\; \textit{ref?}, \textit{amnt?}, \textit{conf?} : \mathbb{N} \\
\hline
\;\; \textit{ref?} \in 1 \,..\, \textit{TeamSize} \\
\;\; \textit{amnt?} = \textit{conf?} \\
\;\; \textit{sales'} = \textit{sales} \oplus \{\textit{ref?} \mapsto \textit{sales}(\textit{ref?}) + \textit{amnt?}\} \\
\;\; \textit{tot'} = \textit{tot} + \textit{amnt?} \\
\;\; \textit{comm'} = \textit{comm} \\
\;\; \textit{bonus'} = \textit{bonus} \\
\end{array}
$$

---

[5]The use of total functions, whose from-set is an initial segment of the positive whole numbers, in order to model arrays in Z is explained in more detail in section 6.5.

The variable *ref?* is the reference number of the team member whose records are being updated. The variables *amnt?* and *conf?* represent the value of the sales that that person has made. To prevent some errors being made this number has to be input twice and the two values compared. The schema *AddSalesOkay* is the same as *AddSales* except that a suitable message is output indicating the successful completion of the operation.

$$AddSalesOkay \triangleq AddSales \wedge Success.$$

As usual, the schema *Success* is defined in this way:

$$
\begin{array}{|l}
\hline
Success \underline{\hspace{6cm}} \\
rep! : Report \\
\hline
rep! = \text{`Okay'} \\
\hline
\end{array}
$$

The operation *AddSales* can go wrong in two different ways. When *ref?* is not a member of the set $1 .. TeamSize$ the schema *UnknownSalesperson* specifies what happens:

$$
\begin{array}{|l}
\hline
UnknownSalesperson \underline{\hspace{4cm}} \\
\Xi SalesDB \\
ref? : \mathbb{N} \\
rep! : Report \\
\hline
ref? \notin 1 .. TeamSize \\
rep! = \text{`Unknown salesperson'} \\
\hline
\end{array}
$$

The second way in which the operation specified by means of the schema *AddSales* can go wrong is when *amnt?* differs from *conf?* What happens in these circumstances is specified by means of the schema *NotConfirmed*:

$$
\begin{array}{|l}
\hline
NotConfirmed \underline{\hspace{5cm}} \\
\Xi SalesDB \\
amnt?, conf? : \mathbb{N} \\
rep! : Report \\
\hline
amnt? \neq conf? \\
rep! = \text{`Input not confirmed'} \\
\hline
\end{array}
$$

The specification of the total operation is given by the schema *DoAddSales*:

$$DoAddSales \triangleq AddSalesOkay$$
$$\vee$$
$$UnknownSalesperson$$
$$\vee$$
$$NotConfirmed.$$

Calculating Commission

The schema *Commission* represents the operation by means of which commission is calculated.

```
┌─ Commission ──────────────────────────────────────────
│ ΔSalesDB
├───────────────────────────────────────────────────────
│ ∀i : 1 .. TeamSize •
│       comm' = comm ⊕
│              {i ↦ (if  sales(i) > thresh
│                    then (sales(i) − thresh) div 10 else 0)}
│ sales' = sales
│ bonus' = bonus
│ tot' = tot
│ ave' = ave
│ thresh' = thresh
└───────────────────────────────────────────────────────
```

One of the formulas in the predicate-part of this schema makes use of Z's conditional expression. The general form of this expression is

$$\textbf{if } P \textbf{ then } t \textbf{ else } u.$$

When P is true this conditional expression is equivalent to t and when P is false it is equivalent to u.

The operation specified by means of the schema *Commission* always succeeds, therefore *CommissionOkay* and *DoCommission* are defined to be the same schema:

$$CommissionOkay \mathrel{\hat=} Commission \wedge Success,$$

$$DoCommission \mathrel{\hat=} CommissionOkay.$$

Working Out the Bonus

The schema *Bonus* represents the operation by means of which the value of the bonus is worked out that each salesperson who has earned it is to receive.

```
┌─ Bonus ───────────────────────────────────────────────
│ ΔSalesDB
├───────────────────────────────────────────────────────
│ ∀i : 1 .. TeamSize •
│       bonus' = bonus ⊕
│              {i ↦ (if  sales(i) > (115 * ave) div 100
│                    then tot div 200 else 0)}
│ sales' = sales
│ comm' = comm
│ tot' = tot
│ ave' = ave
│ thresh' = thresh
└───────────────────────────────────────────────────────
```

The operation specified by *Bonus* always succeeds, so *BonusOkay* and *DoBonus* are defined to be the same schema:

$$BonusOkay \;\hat{=}\; Bonus \wedge Success,$$

$$DoBonus \;\hat{=}\; BonusOkay.$$

Interrogating the Database

Schema *FindCAB* ('find commission and bonus') is used to interrogate the database by inputting the reference number of a salesperson.

FindCAB
$\Xi SalesDB$
$ref?: \mathbf{N}$
$inform!: \mathbf{N} \times \mathbf{N} \times \mathbf{N}$

$ref? \in 1 \,.\,.\, TeamSize$
$inform! = (sales(ref?), comm(ref?), bonus(ref?))$

The operation *FindCAB* goes wrong if the input reference number is not that of one of the salespeople.

$$FindCABOkay \;\hat{=}\; FindCAB \wedge Success,$$

$$DoFindCAB \;\hat{=}\; FindCABOkay$$
$$\vee$$
$$UnknownSalesperson.$$

15.3.4   The User-interface

The basic type *Command* is the set of all possible commands that might be needed in order to implement the sales database. It contains at least the five commands *in*, *as*, *cc*, *cb* and *fi*. The command *in* is used to initialize the system, *as* ('add sales') is used when information is going to be added to the database, *cc* is used in order to get the system to calculate each salesperson's commission, *cb* gets the system to calculate each salesperson's bonus and *fi* ('find information') is used to interrogate the database.

The schema *InitSalesDBCommand* is used to check whether or not the input command is *in*. Similarly, the schema *DoAddSalesCommand* checks whether or not the input command is *as*, *DoCommissionCommand* checks whether or not the input command is *cc*, *DoBonusCommand* checks whether or not the input command is *cb* and

DoFindCABCommand checks whether or not the input command is *fi*.

$$InitSalesDBCommand \mathrel{\hat=} [cmd?: Command \mid cmd? = in],$$

$$DoAddSalesCommand \mathrel{\hat=} [cmd?: Command \mid cmd? = as],$$

$$DoCommissionCommand \mathrel{\hat=} [cmd?: Command \mid cmd? = cc],$$

$$DoBonusCommand \mathrel{\hat=} [cmd?: Command \mid cmd? = cb],$$

$$DoFindCABCommand \mathrel{\hat=} [cmd?: Command \mid cmd? = fi].$$

The schema *COInitSalesDB* combines the schema which tests whether or not the input command is *in* with the schema *InitSalesDB'* which initializes the database and the schemas *CODoAddSales*, *CODoCommission*, *CODoBonus* and *CODoFindCAB* are formed in a similar way:

$$COInitSalesDB \mathrel{\hat=} InitSalesDBCommand \wedge InitSalesDB',$$

$$CODoAddSales \mathrel{\hat=} DoAddSalesCommand \wedge DoAddSales,$$

$$CODoCommission \mathrel{\hat=} DoCommissionCommand \wedge DoCommission,$$

$$CODoBonus \mathrel{\hat=} DoBonusCommand \wedge DoBonus,$$

$$CODoFindCAB \mathrel{\hat=} DoFindCABCommand \wedge DoFindCAB.$$

The letters *CO*, by the way, come from the initial letters of the phrase 'carry out'.

The complete specification of the sales database including the specification of the user-interface can now be given. It is *SalesDatabase*, which is defined like this:

$$SalesDatabase \mathrel{\hat=} COInitSalesDB$$
$$\vee$$
$$CODoAddSales$$
$$\vee$$
$$CODoCommission$$
$$\vee$$
$$CODoBonus$$
$$\vee$$
$$CODoFindCAB$$
$$\vee$$
$$UnknownCommand,$$

where the schema *UnknownCommand* is defined like this:

```
┌─ UnknownCommand ─────────────────────────────────
│ ΞSalesDB
│ cmd?: Command
│ rep!: Report
├──────────────────────────────────────────────────
│ cmd? ∉ {in, as, cc, cb, fi}
│ rep! = 'Unknown command'
└──────────────────────────────────────────────────
```

15.3.5 Calculating Preconditions

In deriving Hoare triples from the operation and error schemas defined above we will need to know what their precondition schemas are. The precondition schema corresponding to *AddSalesOkay* is:

┌─ *PreAddSalesOkay* ─────────────────────────────
│ *SalesDB*
│ *ref?*, *amnt?*, *conf?*: $\mathbb{N}$
│ ─────────────────────────────
│ *ref?* $\in$ 1 .. *TeamSize*
│ *amnt?* = *conf?*
└─────────────────────────────

The precondition schemas corresponding to the error schemas *UnknownSalesperson* and *NotConfirmed* are:

┌─ *PreUnknownSalesperson* ──────
│ *SalesDB*
│ *ref?*: $\mathbb{N}$
│ ──────────────
│ *ref?* $\notin$ 1 .. *TeamSize*
└──────────────

┌─ *PreNotConfirmed* ──────────
│ *SalesDB*
│ *amnt?*, *conf?*: $\mathbb{N}$
│ ──────────────
│ *amnt?* $\neq$ *conf?*
└──────────────

The precondition schemas corresponding to *CommissionOkay* and *BonusOkay* are both the same as the state schema *SalesDB*:

┌─ *PreCommissionOkay* ────────
│ *SalesDB*
└──────────────

┌─ *PreBonusOkay* ──────────
│ *SalesDB*
└──────────────

15.3.6 The Implementation

Implementing *InitSalesDB'*

First of all we need to choose some fresh program variables corresponding to the specification variables that are used in *InitSalesDB'*:

program variables	specification variables
SALES	*sales'*
COMM	*comm'*
BONUS	*bonus'*
TOT	*tot'*
AVE	*ave'*
THRESH	*thresh'*

Following the recipe given above for transforming an initial state schema into a Hoare triple results in

$$\{true\} \; \gamma \; \{InitSalesDB' \; \chi\}, \tag{15.3}$$

where the substitution χ is as follows:

$$\chi \equiv [SALES/sales', COMM/comm', BONUS/bonus',$$
$$TOT/tot', AVE/ave', THRESH/thresh'].$$

Expanding this Hoare triple results in

$\{true\}$

γ

$\{\forall i \colon 1 \mathbin{..} TeamSize \bullet SALES(i) = COMM(i) = BONUS(i) = 0 \land$
$TOT = sumarray(SALES) \land AVE = TOT \; \textbf{div} \; TeamSize \land$
$THRESH = (2 * AVE) \; \textbf{div} \; 3\}.$

A suitable command to take the place of γ in this is

```
for II := 1 to TeamSize do
    (SALES[II] := 0; COMM[II] := 0; BONUS[II] := 0);
TOT := sumarray(SALES);
AVE := TOT div TeamSize;
THRESH := (2 * AVE) div 3
```

and that this does indeed implement the Hoare triple (15.3) can be confirmed by generating a set of verification conditions for this command and then proving that each of those verification conditions is indeed a theorem (of first-order logic).

Implementing *DoAddSales*

To begin with I show how *AddSalesOkay* can be implemented. First of all we need to choose some program variables corresponding to the specification variables that are used in the schema *AddSalesOkay*:

program variables	specification variables
REF?	*ref?*
AMNT?	*amnt?*
CONF?	*conf?*
SALES	*sales*
COMM	*comm*
BONUS	*bonus*
TOT	*tot*
AVE	*ave*
THRESH	*thresh*
REP!	*rep!*

The substitution χ and the formulas *pre-ident* and *post-ident* are as follows:

$$\chi \equiv [SALES/sales', COMM/comm', BONUS/bonus',$$
$$TOT/tot', AVE/ave', THRESH/thresh'],$$

$$pre\text{-}ident \equiv REF? = ref? \wedge AMNT? = amnt? \wedge CONF? = conf? \wedge$$
$$SALES = sales \wedge COMM = comm \wedge BONUS = bonus \wedge$$
$$TOT = tot \wedge AVE = ave \wedge THRESH = thresh,$$

$$post\text{-}ident \equiv REF? = ref? \wedge AMNT? = amnt? \wedge CONF? = conf? \wedge$$
$$REP! = rep!$$

The Hoare triple that is obtained by following the recipe given above is

$$\{PreAddSalesOkay \wedge pre\text{-}ident\}$$
$$\gamma \tag{15.4}$$
$$\{AddSalesOkay \; \chi \wedge post\text{-}ident\}$$

and when partially expanded this becomes:

$$\{SalesDB \wedge ref? \in 1 \,..\, TeamSize \wedge amnt? = conf? \wedge$$
$$REF? = ref? \wedge AMNT? = amnt? \wedge CONF? = conf? \wedge$$
$$SALES = sales \wedge COMM = comm \wedge BONUS = bonus \wedge$$
$$TOT = tot \wedge AVE = ave \wedge THRESH = thresh\}$$
$$\gamma$$
$$\{SalesDB \wedge ref? \in 1 \,..\, TeamSize \wedge amnt? = conf? \wedge$$
$$rep! = \text{'Okay'} \wedge$$
$$SALES = sales \oplus \{ref? \mapsto sales(ref?) + amnt?\} \wedge$$
$$TOT = tot + amnt? \wedge TOT = sumarray(SALES) \wedge$$
$$AVE = TOT \text{ div } TeamSize \wedge$$
$$THRESH = (2 * AVE) \text{ div } 3 \wedge$$
$$REF? = ref? \wedge AMNT? = amnt? \wedge CONF? = conf? \wedge$$
$$COMM = comm \wedge BONUS = bonus \wedge REP! = rep!\}.$$

A suitable command for implementing this is

$$SALES[REF?] := SALES[REF?] + AMNT?;$$
$$TOT := TOT + AMNT?;$$
$$AVE := TOT \text{ div } TeamSize;$$
$$THRESH := (2 * AVE) \text{ div } 3;$$
$$REP! := \text{'Okay'}$$

and that this does indeed implement the Hoare triple (15.4) can be confirmed by generating a set of verification conditions from it and then proving that each of those verification conditions is actually a theorem. This command can now be made into the body of a procedure called *ADD_SALES_OKAY*.

The above process can be repeated for the schemas *UnknownSalesperson* and *NotConfirmed* and we could prove that the two commands

$$REP! := \text{'Unknown salesperson'}$$
$$REP! := \text{'Input not confirmed'}$$

implement, respectively, those two schemas. The command that implements the schema *DoAddSales* is, therefore:

if $REF? \in 1 .. TeamSize \wedge AMNT? = CONF?$ **then**
    $ADD\_SALES\_OKAY(params)$
else if $REF? \notin 1 .. TeamSize$ **then**
    $REP! := \text{'Unknown salesperson'}$
else if $AMNT? \neq CONF?$ **then**
    $REP! := \text{'Input not confirmed'}$
else
    skip

and this can be made into the body of a procedure called DO_ADD_SALES. The identifier *params* here represents some suitable choice of actual parameters. (In a genuine implementation using a real programming language this procedure might also contain the code for outputting a suitable prompt in order to get the user to input the reference number of a salesperson and also the value of the amount that he or she has sold and the confirmation of this amount.)

Implementing *DoCommission* and *DoBonus*

The method used for showing how *DoAddSales* can be implemented can be applied to the schema *DoCommission* and the result would be that the command

for $II := 1$ **to** *TeamSize* **do**
    if $SALES[II] > THRESH$ **then**
        $COMM[II] := (SALES[II] - THRESH)$ **div** 10
    else
        $COMM[II] := 0;$
    $REP! := \text{'Okay'}$

is a suitable choice for a correct implementation. It is a good idea to make this into a procedure that can be called $DO\_COMMISSION$.

Similarly, it can be shown that the command

for $II := 1$ **to** *TeamSize* **do**
    if $SALES[II] > (115 * AVE)$ **div** 100 **then**
        $BONUS[II] := TOT$ **div** 200
    else
        $BONUS[II] := 0;$
    $REP! := \text{'Okay'}$

implements the schema *DoBonus* and this can be made into the body of a procedure called DO_BONUS.

Implementing *DoFindCAB*

The schema *FindCABOkay* is implemented by means of the command

$$INFORM! := (SALES(REF?), COMM(REF?), BONUS(REF?));$$
$$REP! := \text{'Okay'}$$

and this could be made into the body of a procedure called *FIND_CAB*. The schema *DoFindCAB* would then be implemented by means of the command

> **if** *REF?* $\in 1 \mathinner{.\,.} TeamSize$ **then**
>   *FIND_CAB_OKAY(params)*
> **else**
>   *REP!* := 'Unknown salesperson'

which can be made into the body of a procedure *DO_FIND_CAB*.

Implementing the User-interface

Using the ideas and techniques introduced so far in this chapter the implementation of the user-interface should be entirely obvious.

> **if** *CMD?* = *in* **then**
>   *INIT_SALES_DB(params)*
> **else if** *CMD?* = *as* **then**
>   *DO_ADD_SALES(params)*
> **else if** *CMD?* = *cc* **then**
>   *DO_COMMISSION(params)*
> **else if** *CMD?* = *cb* **then**
>   *DO_BONUS(params)*
> **else if** *CMD?* = *fi* **then**
>   *DO_FIND_CAB(params)*
> **else if** *CMD?* $\notin \{in, as, cc, cb, fi\}$ **then**
>   *UNKNOWN_COMMAND*
> **else**
>   *skip*

15.4   Conclusion

Further examples of the use of Floyd–Hoare logic to relate a Z specification to a program can be found in (Diller 1992). Some of the following conclusions are expanded versions of the conclusions of that paper to be found on pp. 72–73. Compared to some other ways that have been proposed of relating Z specifications and program code the method described here has several things in its favour.

(1) The method of relating a Z specification to program code used in this chapter works perfectly well with the current standard version of Z. No changes need to

be made to Z in order to make it combine smoothly with a Floyd–Hoare logic. King (1990) uses the refinement calculus developed by Morgan (1990) to get program code from a Z specification, but he is compelled to make changes to the Z language in order to enable it to mesh with Z.

(2) The specification and implementation languages used are kept separate. I think that this is important because specification and implementation are separate concerns requiring different skills and having different goals. When writing a formal specification in Z a good specifier puts the techniques of procedural and representational abstraction into practice. Operations are specified by describing their input-output behaviour and high-level abstract mathematical data types are employed. The Z language is well suited to this task. It would be inappropriate, I believe, to try to extend Z by including programming language constructs in it or to try to implement Z directly.

(3) Floyd–Hoare logics are well understood and widely taught. They are well understood in the sense that they and their mathematical foundations have been thoroughly investigated. See, for example, (Cousot 1990) for an excellent summary of the theoretical work that has been done on them. Having been around for over 20 years they are part of the intellectual toolbox of the modern programmer. Furthermore, Floyd–Hoare logics have been devised that can cope with every kind of construct found in a modern high-level programming language. For example, Alagić and Arbib (1978) describe a Floyd–Hoare logic for the whole of Pascal—based on the work of Hoare and Wirth (1973)—and Sperschneider and Antoniou (1991), chapter 18, present a way of dealing with modules in the context of a Floyd–Hoare logic. By way of contrast, the refinement calculus presented in (Morgan 1990) is indeed an elegant formal system, but it will take a long time for it to become part of our intellectual furniture.

(4) As is well known it is impossible to write an algorithm—which always succeeds—whose input is a specification of a programming task and whose output is an algorithm that meets that specification, but verification condition generators can be written for Floyd–Hoare logics. These enable the process of program verification to be partially automated. Such tools would make the techniques introduced in this chapter easier to use in practice. (Some of the remarks made at the end of the previous chapter are also relevant here.)

Part III

Case Studies

16

Two Small Case Studies

16.1 The Bill of Materials Problem

16.1.1 Introduction

In this chapter I develop two small case studies. The first is a Z version of the bill of materials problem and the second is the specification of a route planner. Jones (1980), pp. 125–126 and 201–203, discusses the bill of materials problem. Imagine that a manufacturing company maintains a database which keeps information on the immediate constituents of the various articles that it makes. These immediate constituents may themselves be made up out of other components and so on, but clearly there must be some primitive components which are not made up out of any simpler components. All this information is kept in the database as well.

Given such a database—known as a *bill of materials*—there are various pieces of information that we are interested in extracting from it, such as (a) all the components that are used in the construction of a particular item and (b) all the items in the construction of which one particular component is used.

16.1.2 Representing the Database

An example of a bill of materials is pictured in Fig. 16.1.[1] In this diagram if a part x is joined by a line to a part y and x is to the left of y, then that is to be understood as meaning that y is an immediate constituent of x. Thus, p_7, p_3 and p_2 are immediate constituents of p_1. Lines are terminated by small filled-in circles, so p_3 is an immediate constituent of p_5, but neither p_6 nor p_7 are. The primitive non-composite parts are p_4, p_6 and p_7.

There are various ways in which a bill of materials can be represented in Z. We can, for example, represent it as a partial function $bom: Part \nrightarrow \mathbf{F}\ Part$ from parts to finite sets of parts. Here, $Part$ is the type of all parts, both primitive and composite, and for a given part x, $bom\ x$ is the set of all the immediate constituents of x. If x is non-

---

[1]This is exactly the same example that Jones (1980) discusses. See his Fig. 28 on p. 125. I have used his example so that it is easy for the reader to compare our discussions of this problem.

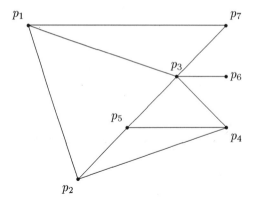

Figure 16.1: An example of a bill of materials.

composite, then *bom x = ∅*.[2] Using this representation, the information contained in Fig. 16.1 is expressed in the function *bom* which is shown in Fig. 16.2. It is not difficult to define a relation which holds between two things iff the first is a constituent—not necessarily immediate—of the second.[3]

$$
\begin{array}{l}
\underline{[X]} \\
\quad isconstit\colon (X \twoheadrightarrow \mathbf{F}\,X) \longrightarrow (X \leftrightarrow X) \\
\hline
\quad \forall f\colon X \twoheadrightarrow \mathbf{F}\,X;\, x,y\colon X \bullet \\
\qquad x \mapsto y \in isconstit\,f \iff \\
\qquad\qquad (y \in fx \vee \exists z\colon X \mid z \in fx \bullet z \mapsto y \in isconstit\,f)
\end{array}
$$

We have that $x \mapsto y \in isconstit(bom)$ iff y is a constituent of x.

We are only interested in bills of materials that are free of cycles, that is to say, no part can be a constituent of itself. The set of all cycle-free bills of materials is *cyclefree[Part]*, where *cyclefree* is defined as follows:

$$
\begin{array}{l}
\underline{[X]} \\
\quad cyclefree\colon \mathbf{P}(X \twoheadrightarrow \mathbf{F}\,X) \\
\hline
\quad \forall f\colon X \twoheadrightarrow \mathbf{F}\,X \bullet \\
\qquad f \in cyclefree \iff \neg\exists x\colon X \bullet x \mapsto x \in isconstit\,f
\end{array}
$$

16.1.3 Specifying Parts Explosion

The first thing that I am going to specify is the set of all constituents—both immediate and non-immediate—of a particular part x with respect to a given bill of

---

$$bom = \{p_1 \mapsto \{p_2, p_3, p_7\},$$
$$p_2 \mapsto \{p_4, p_5\},$$
$$p_3 \mapsto \{p_4, p_6, p_7\},$$
$$p_4 \mapsto \varnothing,$$
$$p_5 \mapsto \{p_3, p_4\},$$
$$p_6 \mapsto \varnothing,$$
$$p_7 \mapsto \varnothing\}.$$

Figure 16.2: An example of the function *bom*.

materials *bom*. The part itself is to figure amongst its constituents. The required set is $expl1[Part](bom, x)$, where $expl1$ is defined like this:[4]

$$\boxed{\begin{array}{l} =[X] = \\ \hline expl1 : (X \nrightarrow \mathbf{F}\,X) \times X \longrightarrow \mathbf{F}\,X \\ \hline \forall f : X \nrightarrow \mathbf{F}\,X; x : X \bullet \\ \qquad expl1(f, x) = \{x\} \cup \bigcup \{y : X \mid y \in fx \bullet expl1(f, y)\} \end{array}}$$

The next thing that we want to specify is the set of all parts in the construction of which a particular part x figures, with respect to a bill of materials *bom*. The part x is to appear in the set returned. The required set is $figs1[Part](bom, x)$, where $figs1$ is defined as follows:

$$\boxed{\begin{array}{l} =[X] = \\ \hline figs1 : (X \nrightarrow \mathbf{F}\,X) \times X \longrightarrow \mathbf{F}\,X \\ \hline \forall f : X \nrightarrow \mathbf{F}\,X; x : X \bullet \\ \qquad figs1(f, x) = \{x\} \cup \{y : X; U : \mathbf{F}\,X \mid y \mapsto U \in f \wedge x \in U \bullet y\} \end{array}}$$

16.1.4 Another Specification

Given any problem to specify there are usually several ways of representing the information or data involved. In this subsection I am going to illustrate this by giving another specification of the parts explosion problem. Rather than representing a bill of materials as a function belonging to the set $Part \nrightarrow \mathbf{F}\,Part$, I shall represent it by means of a relation belonging to the set $Part \leftrightarrow Part$. The information contained in Fig. 16.1 is now represented by the relation $moo : Part \leftrightarrow Part$, defined as shown in Fig. 16.3. An ordered pair $x \mapsto y$ is an element of moo iff y is an immediate constituent of x. The part y is a constituent of x iff $x \mapsto y \in moo^+$, that is to say, the transitive closure[5] of moo, and moo is cycle-free iff $\neg \exists x : Part \bullet x \mapsto x \in moo^+$. Using this

---

[4]This is just a translation into Z of Jones's solution. See (Jones 1980), p. 126.

[5]The transitive closure of a relation—and also its reflexive-transitive closure—are explained in section 5.1.2 and defined formally in section 21.2.8.

$$moo = \{p_1 \mapsto p_2,$$
$$p_1 \mapsto p_3,$$
$$p_1 \mapsto p_7,$$
$$p_2 \mapsto p_4,$$
$$p_2 \mapsto p_5,$$
$$p_3 \mapsto p_4,$$
$$p_3 \mapsto p_6,$$
$$p_3 \mapsto p_7,$$
$$p_5 \mapsto p_3,$$
$$p_5 \mapsto p_4\}.$$

Figure 16.3: The relation *moo*.

representation of the bill of materials the definition of the set of all constituents—both immediate and non-immediate—of a particular part x with respect to a given bill of materials *moo* is $moo^*(\{x\})$, where F^* is the reflexive-transitive closure of F.

The definition of the set of all parts in the construction of which a particular part x figures, with respect to a bill of materials *moo*, is given by $(moo^*)^{\sim}(\{x\})$. It is possible to introduce definitions of functions *expl2* and *figs2* like this:

$$\boxed{\begin{array}{l} \underline{[X]} \\ expl2 : (X \leftrightarrow X) \times X \longrightarrow \mathbf{F}\,X \\ \hline \forall f : X \leftrightarrow X ; x : X \bullet \\ \quad expl2(f, x) = f^*(\{x\}) \end{array}}$$

$$\boxed{\begin{array}{l} \underline{[X]} \\ figs2 : (X \leftrightarrow X) \times X \longrightarrow \mathbf{F}\,X \\ \hline \forall f : X \leftrightarrow X ; x : X \bullet \\ \quad figs2(f, x) = (f^*)^{\sim}(\{x\}) \end{array}}$$

Doing this, the required specifications become, respectively, $expl2[Part](moo, x)$ and $figs2[Part](moo, x)$. Because the terms used in the definition of *expl2* and *figs2* are so simple, there is little point, however, in introducing these definitions.

Using this representation of the bill of materials it is easy to express the set of all primitive components. A *primitive* component is one which does not have any immediate constituents. The set of all such components is ran *moo* \ dom *moo*. One of the connections that exist between these two representations is given by the following formula:

$$\forall x : Part \bullet bom\ x = moo(\{x\}).$$

State and Operations

Using the functions defined it is a fairly straightforward exercise to develop a Z specification of the bill of materials problem. In doing this I will use the simpler representation of such a bill. The state is represented by means of the schema *Materials*:

```
┌─ Materials ────────────────────────────────────
│  moo: Part ↔ Part
├────────────────────────────────────────────────
│  ¬∃x: Part • x ↦ x ∈ moo⁺
```

The single formula in the predicate-part of this schema states that the relation *moo* does not contain any cycles.

The schemas Δ*Materials* and Ξ*Materials* are defined in the usual way:

$$\Delta Materials \;\hat{=}\; Materials \wedge Materials',$$

$$\Xi Materials \;\hat{=}\; [\Delta Materials \mid moo' = moo].$$

The initial state schema is *InitMaterials'*, where the schema *InitMaterials* is defined like this:

$$InitMaterials \;\hat{=}\; [Materials \mid moo = \varnothing].$$

Many operations could be defined on this state, such as adding new components to the database, but I will just specify two ways of interrogating the database, namely finding out the components of a particular item and finding out all the items in the manufacture of which a particular thing is used.

```
┌─ SubComponents ────────────────────────────────
│  Ξ Materials
│  in?: Part
│  out!: P Part
├────────────────────────────────────────────────
│  in? ∈ ran moo ∪ dom moo
│  out! = moo*(|{in?}|)
```

```
┌─ SuperComponents ──────────────────────────────
│  Ξ Materials
│  in?: Part
│  out!: P Part
├────────────────────────────────────────────────
│  in? ∈ ran moo ∪ dom moo
│  out! = (moo*)~(|{in?}|)
```

16.2 A Route Planner

16.2.1 Introduction

In this section I am going to develop the formal specification of a route planner. I start by discussing the problem informally. Fig. 16.4 shows a schematic map of an imaginary geographical region. The letters A, B, C, D, E, F, G, H and I represent places. The important thing about a place is that it occurs at a road junction. A place is just a location where two or more roads meet.

The symbols r_i, for $1 \leq i \leq 16$, represent roads or road-segments. r_3 and r_{12} might be the same road—the A38, for example—but for our purposes they have to be considered distinct because if you travel on r_3 you are not forced to travel on r_{12}. I will, however, call the r_i *roads* for the sake of brevity.

For this problem we have to associate every road with two attributes, namely its length and the kind of road it is. For simplicity, I will just consider three kinds of road, namely motorways, A-roads and B-roads. The length in kilometres and the kind of each road in Fig. 16.4 is given in the following table:

Road	Length	Kind
r_1	15	motorway
r_2	11	A-road
r_3	17	B-road
r_4	12	B-road
r_5	18	A-road
r_6	20	A-road
r_7	19	B-road
r_8	19	motorway
r_9	17	A-road
r_{10}	21	B-road
r_{11}	13	B-road
r_{12}	19	B-road
r_{13}	22	A-road
r_{14}	6	B-road
r_{15}	19	A-road
r_{16}	10	A-road

Note that the map in Fig. 16.4 is not drawn to scale. It has, rather, to be understood by analogy with the map of the London Underground. It only shows the 'topology' of the situation it purports to depict.

The sort of operation that we want to define is one in which the user inputs the starting point and the finishing point of his journey and any constraints that he might want to put on the roads on which he travels—for example, that he does not want to travel on a motorway—and the system outputs the shortest route that satisfies those constraints. (It is possible for there to be several routes of the same length which are each shorter than any other possible route. In that case the system should output all these shortest routes.)

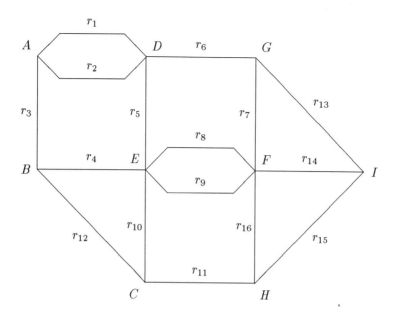

Figure 16.4: An imaginary geographical region.

As an example, consider a user who wants to go from A to E. There are a large number of possible routes. The best way to represent a route is as a sequence of roads. So, some of the possible routes from A to E are:

$$\sigma_1 = \langle r_3, r_4 \rangle,$$
$$\sigma_2 = \langle r_1, r_5 \rangle,$$
$$\sigma_3 = \langle r_2, r_5 \rangle,$$
$$\sigma_4 = \langle r_1, r_6, r_7, r_{14}, r_{15}, r_{11}, r_{10} \rangle,$$
$$\sigma_5 = \langle r_3, r_{12}, r_{11}, r_{15}, r_{14}, r_{16}, r_{11}, r_{10} \rangle.$$

Route σ_1 only uses B-roads, whereas σ_2 and σ_3 avoid using B-roads. Route σ_2 chooses a motorway if one is available. Routes σ_4 and σ_5 are very circuitous and σ_5 contains a cycle. In this case there are two routes shorter than all the others, namely σ_1 and σ_3, and these are both 29 kilometres long. If the user puts no constraints on the kind of road on which he wants to travel, then the system should output both of these routes. If he wants to travel only on B-roads, then the system should output σ_1, and so on.

16.2.2   The State Space

This specification uses three basic types:

$$[Place, Road, RoadType]$$

Place is the type of all possible locations, *Road* is the type of all possible roads and *RoadType* is the type of all possible kinds of road.

The state space of the route planner is given by means of the schema *Map*:

```
┌─ Map ────────────────────────────────────────────
│ joins: Road ⇸ F Place
│ kind: Road ⇸ RoadType
│ length: Road ⇸ N
│ knownplaces: F Place
│ knownroads: F Road
├──────────────────────────────────────────────────
│ knownplaces = ⋃ ran joins
│ knownroads = dom joins
│ ∀U: ran joins • #U = 2
│ dom joins = dom kind = dom length
└──────────────────────────────────────────────────
```

The set *knownplaces* is the set of places that are actually on the map and the set *knownroads* is the set of roads that are on the map. The reason for including these two sets is that we want to allow for the possibility of adding information to the database about new roads that have been constructed and new places that can be reached by road. The function *joins* yields a set of places linked by the road given to it as an argument and the formula $\forall U: \text{ran} \, joins \bullet \#U = 2$ tells us that every road links two and only two places. The function *kind* yields a road type as value for a road given to it as an argument and the function *length* returns the length of a road in kilometres.

The formula:

$$\text{dom} \, joins = \text{dom} \, kind = \text{dom} \, length, \tag{16.1}$$

informs us that every road on the map which links two places must be of a specific kind and also must have a definite length.

16.2.3   The Operations

In order to help me to specify operations on the state of the route planner I will first define two functions, namely *allroutes* and *shortestroutes*. First, I define *allroutes*:

```
│ allroutes: F Road ⟶ (Road ⇸ P Place)
│            ⟶ (Place × Place) ⟶ P(seq Road)
├──────────────────────────────────────────────────
│ ∀U: F Road; f: Road ⇸ P Place; x, y: Place; σ: seq Road •
│ σ ∈ allroutes U f (x, y) ⟺
│     (ran σ ⊆ U ∧
│     (∀i: dom σ | i ≠ #σ •
│         (σ ⨟ f)(i) ∩ (σ ⨟ f)(i + 1) ≠ ∅) ∧
│     ((x ∈ (σ ⨟ f)(1) ∧ y ∈ (σ ⨟ f)(#σ)) ∨ (x ∈ (σ ⨟ f)(#σ) ∧ y ∈ (σ ⨟ f)(1))))
```

The definition of *allroutes* works as follows. When it is used we have to supply arguments $U\colon \mathbf{F}\ Road$, $f\colon Road \nrightarrow \mathbf{P}\ Place$ and $(x,y)\colon Place \times Place$. It has to be parameterized to a set U of roads because we only want roads that are members of *knownroads* to figure in the routes we output to the user and it has to be parameterized to a function f, since we only want the routes we output to pass through places that are on the map. The places x and y are the starting and finishing point of the journey our user is making and the set *allroutes* $U\ f\ (x,y)$ is the set of all routes which join x and y.

Let σ be an arbitrary route. Then the formula ran $\sigma \subseteq U$ constrains the route to only use roads drawn from the set U. To understand the next formula in the definition, recall that as σ is a sequence we can write it as $\langle x_1, x_2, \ldots, x_n \rangle$. When we come to use *allroutes* the actual parameters corresponding to f will be *joins*, thus $\sigma \, \sqeq \, joins$ is a sequence of sets—each of cardinality 2—of places $\langle U_1, U_2, \ldots, U_n \rangle$. For σ to be a route we want there to be at least one element in common between each two elements of $\sigma \, \sqeq \, joins$ that are next to one another. We allow $U_i = U_{i+1}$, since there is no need to disallow cycles in our routes at this stage.

The final formula in the definition just says that x and y are the first and last members of σ, not necessarily in that order. Clearly, someone who asks for routes from x to y will receive exactly the same response as someone who asks for all the routes from y to x. All the roads on our map are assumed to be two-way.

Before defining *shortestroutes* I need to define a function *sumseq* which takes a sequence of non-negative numbers and returns their sum. It is necessary to do this because Z, unfortunately, does not contain a summation operator.

$$
\begin{array}{|l}
\hline
sumseq\colon \operatorname{seq} \mathbf{N} \longrightarrow \mathbf{N} \\
\hline
\forall i\colon \mathbf{N}; \sigma\colon \operatorname{seq} \mathbf{N} \bullet \\
\quad sumseq\ \langle\ \rangle = 0 \wedge \\
\quad sumseq\ (\langle i \rangle \frown \sigma) = i + sumseq\ \sigma \\
\end{array}
$$

It is now possible to define *shortestroutes* in terms of *allroutes*:

$$
\begin{array}{|l}
\hline
shortestroutes\colon \mathbf{F}\ Road \longrightarrow (Road \nrightarrow \mathbf{P}\ Place) \\
\quad\quad \longrightarrow (Road \nrightarrow \mathbf{N}) \longrightarrow (Place \times Place) \longrightarrow \mathbf{P}(\operatorname{seq} Road) \\
\hline
\forall U\colon \mathbf{F}\ Road; f\colon Road \nrightarrow \mathbf{P}\ Place; g\colon Road \nrightarrow \mathbf{N}; x,y\colon Place; \sigma \operatorname{seq} Road \bullet \\
\quad \sigma \in shortestroutes\ U\ f\ g\ (x,y) \Longleftrightarrow \\
\quad\quad (\sigma \in allroutes\ U\ f\ (x,y) \wedge \\
\quad\quad (\forall \tau\colon \operatorname{seq} Road \mid \tau \in allroutes\ U\ f\ (x,y) \bullet \\
\quad\quad\quad sumseq\ (\sigma \, \sqeq \, g) \leq sumseq\ (\tau \, \sqeq \, g))) \\
\end{array}
$$

Using the function *shortestroutes* it is now possible to specify the operation *Routes*. This accepts as input the starting point and the finishing point of the journey being undertaken—these are represented by *start?* and *finish?*, respectively—and produces as output the set *out!* of all routes between *start?* and *finish?*

```
┌─ Routes ─────────────────────────────────────────────────┐
│ ΞMap                                                      │
│ start?, finish?: Place                                    │
│ out!: P(seq Road)                                         │
├───────────────────────────────────────────────────────── │
│ {start?, finish?} ⊆ knownplaces                           │
│ out! = shortestroutes knownroads joins length (start?, finish?) │
└───────────────────────────────────────────────────────────┘
```

The schema *Routes* gives no opportunity for the user to indicate what kinds of road he wants to travel on. In order to give him that opportunity we use the schema *ChoosyRoutes*, in which the variable *acc?* ('acceptable') contains all the types of road the user does not mind travelling on.

```
┌─ ChoosyRoutes ───────────────────────────────────────────┐
│ ΞMap                                                      │
│ start?, finish?: Place                                    │
│ acc?: F RoadType                                          │
│ out!: P(seq Road)                                         │
├───────────────────────────────────────────────────────── │
│ {start?, finish?} ⊆ knownplaces                           │
│ out! = shortestroutes knownroads                          │
│            ((dom(kind ▷ acc?)) ◁ joins) length (start?, finish?) │
└───────────────────────────────────────────────────────────┘
```

17

Wing's Library Problem

17.1 Introduction

In this chapter I present a Z specification of a library system which is informally described by Wing (1988), p. 67, as follows:[1]

> Consider a small library database with the following transactions:
>
> 1. Check out a copy of a book. Return a copy of a book.
>
> 2. Add a copy of a book to the library. Remove a copy of a book from the library.
>
> 3. Get the list of books by a particular author or in a particular subject area.
>
> 4. Find out the list of books currently checked out by a particular borrower.
>
> 5. Find out what borrower last checked out a particular copy of a book.
>
> There are two types of users: staff users and ordinary borrowers. Transactions 1, 2, 4 and 5 are restricted to staff users, except that ordinary borrowers can perform transaction 4 to find out the list of books currently borrowed by themselves. The database must also satisfy the following constraints:
>
> - All copies in the library must be available for check-out or be checked out.
>
> - No copy of a book may be both available and checked out at the same time.
>
> - A borrower may not have more than a predefined number of books checked out at one time.

---

[1] Several people have given me valuable feedback on the version of this specification that appeared in the first edition of this book, but I would like to express my gratitude here in particular to Lindsay Groves and Rosemary Docherty both of whom made many helpful comments and suggestions for improvement. I have incorporated some of these, but have decided not to alter the main structure of the specification.

17.2 Basic Types and User-defined Sets

This specification makes use of the following basic types:

$$[Book, Copy, Person, Author, Subject]$$

The type *Book* is the set of all possible books and *Copy* is the type of all possible copies of books. Books are considered to be abstract objects, whereas copies are physical objects. It is necessary to make this distinction in order to deal with the possibility that the library may contain several distinct copies of the same book. This happens, for example, when a book is popular and in much demand or when several editions of the same book have been published.

The reason why I talk of 'all *possible* books' and 'all *possible* copies' is that we need to allow for the production of books and copies in the future. If I just said 'all books', someone might think that I was restricting the specification to books which actually exist at the present time.

The type *Person* is the set of all possible people. Staff users of the library database and ordinary borrowers will be drawn from the type *Person*. The type *Author* is the set of all possible authors and *Subject* is the type of all conceivable subjects, that is to say, the things that books can be about. The types *Author* and *Person* are distinguished because some books are considered to have been written by institutions. Some manuals and some standards fall into this category.

We also need a set of all necessary messages. It is defined by enumeration like this:

Report ::= 'Okay'
       | 'Unauthorized requestor'
       | 'Not registered'
       | 'Copy checked out'
       | 'Cannot borrow any more copies'
       | 'Copy available'
       | 'This book is not new to the library'
       | 'This book is new to the library'
       | 'This copy is owned by the library'
       | 'This copy is not owned by the library'
       | 'This is the only copy in the library'
       | 'This is not the only copy in the library'
       | 'The library has no books by this author'
       | 'The library has no books on this subject'
       | 'Unknown borrower'
       | 'Not authorized requestor'
       | 'Copy not previously borrowed'.

We also need a constant *MaxCopiesAllowed* which is the maximum number of copies that anyone can borrow. The correct way in which to introduce such a constant into a Z specification document is by means of an axiomatic description with no formula occurring in its predicate-part as follows:

$$| \quad MaxCopiesAllowed: \mathbb{N}$$

17.3 The State of the System

I shall describe the state of the library database in several stages. To begin with, the schema *BookInfo* contains information relating to the books in the library. Recall that a book is an abstract object, whereas a copy is a physical object. The library may contain several copies of the same book.[2]

$$
\begin{array}{|l}
\hline
\underline{\quad BookInfo\ } \\
instanceof: Copy \nrightarrow Book \\
writtenby: Book \nrightarrow \mathbb{F}\,Author \\
about: Book \nrightarrow \mathbb{F}\,Subject \\
\hline
\mathrm{dom}\ writtenby \subseteq \mathrm{ran}\ instanceof \\
\mathrm{dom}\ about \subseteq \mathrm{ran}\ instanceof \\
\hline
\end{array}
$$

The function *instanceof* tells us which book a copy is an instance of. There may be several copies of the same book, but a copy can only be an instance of one book. Hence, *instanceof* is a function. I am going to assume that the information component of the database does not contain any information about books which are not in the library.[3] How this assumption is captured in the specification will be explained later.[4] Because of this assumption every book in the library and known to the database must have at least one copy associated with it. The set ran *instanceof* is the set of all the books in the library and dom *instanceof* is the set of all the copies in the library. Given a book x the number of copies of that book in the library is $\#instanceof^{\sim}(\!(\{x\})\!)$.

The function *writtenby* tells us who wrote a particular book. It returns a set of authors which may be empty. Some books—like bound copies of journals—are associated with the empty set of authors.[5] Similarly, the function *about* tells us what a book is about. It returns a set of subjects, which again may be empty.[6]

The formula dom *writtenby* $\subseteq$ ran *instanceof*, in conjunction with (17.1) on p. 237, tells us that the database does not contain author information about books that are not in the library and the formula dom *about* $\subseteq$ ran *instanceof*, again in conjunction

---

[2]In the first edition of this book this schema was called *ParaLibrary*. The name *BookInfo* was suggested by Lindsay Groves.

[3]In a real-life situation it would be a good idea to check whether this is acceptable to the client for whom the software based on this specification will be produced. Needless to say, such consultation should take place as early as possible, since much of the following specification depends on it.

[4]It is captured by means of formula (17.1) on p. 237.

[5]In a real-life situation it would be a good idea to find out whether this is acceptable to the client.

[6]Here again—in a real-life situation—it would be advisable to consult the client to see if this interpretation of the informal requirements is acceptable.

with (17.1) on page 237, tells us that the database does not contain subject information about books which are not in the library.[7]

The schema *LibraryDB* contains the rest of the information needed by the library.

```
┌─ LibraryDB ─────────────────────────────────────────────────────────┐
│  borrower, staff: F Person                                           │
│  available, checkedout: F Copy                                       │
│  previouslyborrowedby, borrowedby: Copy ⇸ Person                     │
├─────────────────────────────────────────────────────────────────────┤
│  borrower ∩ staff = ∅                                                │
│  available ∩ checkedout = ∅                                          │
│  dom borrowedby = checkedout                                         │
│  ran borrowedby ⊆ borrower                                           │
│  dom previouslyborrowedby ⊆ available ∪ checkedout                   │
│  ran previouslyborrowedby ⊆ borrower                                 │
│  ∀x: borrower • #borrowedby~(|{x}|) ≤ MaxCopiesAllowed               │
└─────────────────────────────────────────────────────────────────────┘
```

Six identifiers are declared in this schema. The finite sets *borrower* and *staff* contain the people who can use the library and those who administer it, respectively. A member of the set *borrower* is known either as a borrower or as a registered user. The formula *borrower* ∩ *staff* = ∅ tells us that the set of ordinary borrowers and that of staff users are disjoint. This means that staff cannot borrow books from the library.[8]

The finite sets *available* and *checkedout* contain, respectively, all the copies of books that either are available for check-out or have actually been checked out. The formula *available* ∩ *checkedout* = ∅ captures the following constraint from the statement of requirements:

- No copy of a book may be both available and checked out at the same time.

The function *borrowedby* tells us who is currently borrowing a particular copy of a book and *previouslyborrowedby* tells us who, if anyone, was the last person to borrow a copy of a book. For example, let x be a particular copy of a book that is currently on loan. Then, *borrowedby*(x) is the current borrower of x and *previouslyborrowedby*(x) is the person, if any, who borrowed x immediately before the person *borrowedby*(x).

The formula dom *borrowedby* = *checkedout* tells us that the set of copies that have been borrowed by someone or other is the same as the set of copies that are checked out and the formula ran *borrowedby* ⊆ *borrower* states that every checked out copy must have been borrowed by a registered user, that is to say, a borrower.

The formula dom *previouslyborrowedby* ⊆ *available* ∪ *checkedout* states that previously borrowed copies either are available for check-out or have been checked out again

---

[7]Using the subset relation in these two formulas, rather than set equality, allows for the possibility that the library contains books about which it has either no author information or no subject information. I think it is desirable to allow for this. In setting up a library database, first, information relating to the borrowing of copies is input and then—possibly at a later stage—subject and author information is introduced.

[8]In a real-life situation it would be a good idea to find out whether this is acceptable to the customer.

and the formula ran *previouslyborrowedby* ⊆ *borrower* states that the last borrower of every copy borrowed must have been a registered user.

The final formula in the schema, namely

$$\forall x: borrower \bullet \#borrowedby^\sim(\!\!\{\{x\}\}\!\!) \leq MaxCopiesAllowed$$

captures the constraint:

- A borrower may not have more than a predefined number of books checked out at one time.

In some libraries borrowers are partitioned into several categories and different regulations apply to members of each category. For example, members of one category may be allowed to borrow more copies than members of another category. The constraint just quoted is consistent with that possibility, but it is also consistent with the situation I have assumed in which there is only a single ceiling on the number of copies of books that any user can borrow. In a real-life situation it would probably be a good idea to consult the client over this matter.

The complete state of the library is given by means of *LibraryState*:

```
┌─ LibraryState ─────────────────────────────
│ BookInfo
│ LibraryDB
├─────────────────────────────────────────────
│ dom instanceof = available ∪ checkedout
└─────────────────────────────────────────────
```

The formula that occurs in the predicate-part of the schema *LibraryState*, namely

$$\text{dom } instanceof = available \cup checkedout \qquad (17.1)$$

tells us that the database does not contain information about copies of books which are not in stock.

The schemas Δ*BookInfo*, Δ*LibraryDB* and Δ̇*LibraryState* are defined in the usual way:

$$\Delta BookInfo \triangleq BookInfo \wedge BookInfo',$$

$$\Delta LibraryDB \triangleq LibraryDB \wedge LibraryDB',$$

$$\Delta LibraryState \triangleq LibraryState \wedge LibraryState'.$$

Similarly, the schemas Ξ*BookInfo*, Ξ*LibraryDB* and Ξ*LibraryState* are defined in the standard way:

$$\Xi BookInfo \triangleq [\Delta BookInfo \mid \theta BookInfo' = \theta BookInfo],$$

$$\Xi LibraryDB \triangleq [\Delta LibraryDB \mid \theta LibraryDB' = \theta LibraryDB],$$

$$\Xi LibraryState \triangleq [\Delta LibraryState \mid \theta LibraryState' = \theta LibraryState].$$

Note that Ξ*LibraryState* could also have been defined to be the conjunction of the schemas Ξ*BookInfo* and Ξ*LibraryDB* as no new variables were introduced in the schema *LibraryState*. The initial state schemas are *InitBookInfo'*, *InitLibraryDB'* and *InitLibraryState'*, where *InitBookInfo*, *InitLibraryDB* and *InitLibraryState* are defined as follows:

$$InitBookInfo \triangleq [BookInfo \mid$$
$$instanceof = \varnothing \wedge$$
$$writtenby = \varnothing \wedge$$
$$about = \varnothing],$$

$$InitLibraryDB \triangleq [LibraryDB \mid$$
$$borrower = \varnothing \wedge$$
$$staff = \varnothing \wedge$$
$$available = \varnothing \wedge$$
$$checkedout = \varnothing \wedge$$
$$previouslyborrowedby = \varnothing \wedge$$
$$borrowedby = \varnothing],$$

$$InitLibraryState \triangleq InitBookInfo \wedge InitLibraryDB.$$

17.4   The Operations

17.4.1   Checking Out and Returning Copies of Books

Checking Out Copies of Books

First of all I will specify the transaction of a borrower *reg?* successfully checking out a copy *vol?* from the library. I shall ignore for the time being who is requesting the transaction to be carried out and what happens if the transaction is unsuccessful.

CheckOutCopy
$\Delta LibraryState$
$\Xi BookInfo$
$reg?: Person$
$vol?: Copy$

$reg? \in borrower$
$vol? \in available$
$\#borrowedby^{\sim}(\!|\{reg?\}|\!) < MaxCopiesAllowed$

$available' = available \setminus \{vol?\}$
$checkedout' = checkedout \cup \{vol?\}$
$borrowedby' = borrowedby \cup \{vol? \mapsto reg?\}$

$previouslyborrowedby' = previouslyborrowedby$
$borrower' = borrower$
$staff' = staff$

I do mean that the two schemas $\Delta LibraryState$ and $\Xi BookInfo$ should be included in the schema *CheckOutCopy*. This means that some variables—like *writtenby*—occur in both, but this does not cause any harm.

Note that I have introduced two blank lines into the predicate-part of this schema. The purpose of these is to separate the formulas that occur in the predicate-part into three groups. The top group comprises the preconditions of the schema. The middle group of formulas actually records what happens when the operation being carried out is successful and the bottom group of formulas contains information about those variables that are left unaltered by this operation.[9]

The preconditions of the schema *CheckOutCopy* are the three formulas:

$$reg? \in borrower,$$

$$vol? \in available,$$

$$\# borrowedby^{\sim}(\!|\{reg?\}|\!) < MaxCopiesAllowed.$$

The first of these states that only registered users can borrow copies and the second states that only available copies can be borrowed. The third formula says that a borrower can only borrow copies if the number of copies he currently has out on loan is strictly less than the maximum number allowed. An alternative way of expressing the same thing is by means of the formula

$$\#(borrowedby \rhd \{reg?\}) < MaxCopiesAllowed.$$

The schema *CheckOutCopy* only records the successful borrowing of a copy and the three formulas:

$$available' = available \setminus \{vol?\},$$

$$checkedout' = checkedout \cup \{vol?\},$$

$$borrowedby' = borrowedby \cup \{vol? \mapsto reg?\},$$

record what happens when a copy has been successfully borrowed. The first two of these state that the copy *vol?* is transferred from being available for loan to actually being borrowed. The third formula records the information that borrower *reg?* has now copy *vol?* on loan.

Every variable other than *available'*, *checkedout'* and *borrowedby'* is left unchanged by this operation. In particular the variable *previouslyborrowedby'* is unaltered. If someone borrows a copy of a book, that in no way alters the previous borrower of that copy.

Having explained what happens when a copy is successfully borrowed, I now need to take into account the status of the person who requests this transaction. This is because in the informal description of the library it is stated that only staff members can check out copies of books. The schema *AuthorizedRequestor* is used to record the

---

[9]This schema also has additional formulas in its predicate-part, namely the three formulas which collectively form the state invariant of the schema *LibraryState* and also the formulas introduced in the definition of $\Xi BookInfo$.

fact that the person *requestor?* is allowed to perform those transactions that only staff
members of the library can perform.

```
┌─ AuthorizedRequestor ─────────────────────────────────
│ staff : F Person
│ requestor? : Person
├───────────────────────────────────────────────────────
│ requestor? ∈ staff
└───────────────────────────────────────────────────────
```

The successful operation of a borrower *reg?* checking out a copy *vol?* from the library—
taking into account who is requesting the transaction—is specified by the schema

$$AuthorizedRequestor \land CheckOutCopy.$$

Now I am going to show you how errors are dealt with. The conjoined schema just
mentioned has four preconditions, but it can go wrong in five distinct ways. This is
because there are two different situations in which *vol?* $\notin$ *available* can be true, namely

$$vol? \notin available \cup checkedout,$$
$$vol? \notin available \land vol? \in checkedout.$$

The first of these is true when the library does not possess the copy *vol?* and the second
of these is true when the library does own the copy *vol?* but it is currently on loan. I
shall specify each of these by means of its own schema.

The schema *UnauthorizedRequestor* specifies what happens when an unauthorized
person tries to perform the transaction of checking out a copy of a book. The state of
the database is unchanged, but an error message is displayed.

```
┌─ UnauthorizedRequestor ───────────────────────────────
│ ΞLibraryState
│ requestor? : Person
│ rep! : Report
├───────────────────────────────────────────────────────
│ requestor? ∉ staff
│ rep! = 'Unauthorized requestor'
└───────────────────────────────────────────────────────
```

The schema *Unregistered* specifies what happens when someone tries to borrow a copy
who is not a registered borrower of the library.

```
┌─ Unregistered ────────────────────────────────────────
│ ΞLibraryState
│ reg? : Person
│ rep! : Report
├───────────────────────────────────────────────────────
│ reg? ∉ borrower
│ rep! = 'Not registered'
└───────────────────────────────────────────────────────
```

The schema *CopyNotOwned* specifies what happens when someone tries to borrow a copy which is not in the library, meaning that the library does not own a copy.

```
┌─ CopyNotOwned ─────────────────────────────────────
│ ΞLibraryState
│ vol?: Copy
│ rep!: Report
├────────────────────────────────────────────────────
│ vol? ∉ available ∪ checkedout
│ rep! = 'This copy is not owned by the library'
└────────────────────────────────────────────────────
```

The schema *CopyCheckedOut* specifies what happens when someone tries to borrow a copy which is owned by the library but currently has been checked out.

```
┌─ CopyCheckedOut ───────────────────────────────────
│ ΞLibraryState
│ vol?: Copy
│ rep!: Report
├────────────────────────────────────────────────────
│ vol? ∈ checkedout
│ rep! = 'Copy checked out'
└────────────────────────────────────────────────────
```

The schema *TooManyCopies* specifies what happens when someone tries to borrow a copy of a book when they have already borrowed as many copies as they are allowed to.

```
┌─ TooManyCopies ────────────────────────────────────
│ ΞLibraryState
│ reg?: Person
│ rep!: Report
├────────────────────────────────────────────────────
│ reg? ∈ borrower
│ #borrowedby~(|{reg?}|) = MaxCopiesAllowed
│ rep! = 'Cannot borrow any more copies'
└────────────────────────────────────────────────────
```

Thus, the complete specification of the transaction of borrowing a copy of a book is captured by the schema *DoCheckOutCopy*:

$$DoCheckOutCopy \triangleq AuthorizedRequestor \land CheckOutCopy \land Success$$
$$\lor$$
$$UnauthorizedRequestor$$
$$\lor$$
$$Unregistered$$
$$\lor$$
$$CopyNotOwned$$
$$\lor$$
$$CopyCheckedOut$$
$$\lor$$
$$TooManyCopies.$$

The schema *Success* just outputs a confirmatory message that the operation being performed has been successfully completed:

```
┌─ Success ─────────────────────────────────────────────
│ rep!: Report
├───────────────────────────────────────────────────────
│ rep! = 'Okay'
└───────────────────────────────────────────────────────
```

Returning a Copy of a Book

The specification of the transaction of returning a copy of a book is captured by means of the schema *Return*. This assumes that the transaction is successful and it ignores who is requesting the transaction.

```
┌─ Return ──────────────────────────────────────────────
│ ΔLibraryState
│ ΞBookInfo
│ vol?: Copy
├───────────────────────────────────────────────────────
│ vol? ∈ checkedout
│
│ available' = available ∪ {vol?}
│ checkedout' = checkedout \ {vol?}
│ borrowedby' = {vol?} ◁ borrowedby
│ previouslyborrowedby' =
│        previouslyborrowedby ⊕ {vol? ↦ borrowedby(vol?)}
│
│ borrower' = borrower
│ staff' = staff
└───────────────────────────────────────────────────────
```

The inclusion of the schema $\Xi BookInfo$ in *Return* tells us that the information component of the library system is unaffected by someone returning a copy of a book.

The precondition of the schema *Return* is the formula $vol? \in checkedout$. What happens when a copy is successfully returned is captured by the middle group of four formulas in *Return*. The first two of these state that the copy $vol?$ is transferred from actually being borrowed to just being available for loan. The third removes the information relating to $vol?$ from $borrowedby'$ and the fourth formula records the information that the last person to borrow $vol?$ was $borrowedby\ (vol?)$, overriding any information about who previously borrowed $vol?$

The formula $vol? \in checkedout$ can be false in two distinct situations, namely when the copy $vol?$ is not owned by the library and when the copy $vol?$ is owned by the library but has not been borrowed. These two cases are captured by the schemas *CopyNotOwned* and *CopyAvailable*, respectively. The definition of the first of these has already been given, in connection with the specification of the transaction of borrowing a copy, and the definition of the second follows here:

```
┌─ CopyAvailable ─────────────────────────────────────────
│ ΞLibraryState
│ vol?: Copy
│ rep!: Report
├─────────────────────────────────────────────────────────
│ vol? ∈ available
│ rep! = 'Copy available'
└─────────────────────────────────────────────────────────
```

Thus, the total specification of the transaction of returning a copy of a book is given by means of the schema *DoReturn*, defined as follows:

$$DoReturn \,\hat{=}\, AuthorizedRequestor \wedge Return \wedge Success$$
$$\vee$$
$$UnauthorizedRequestor$$
$$\vee$$
$$CopyAvailable$$
$$\vee$$
$$CopyNotOwned.$$

17.4.2 Adding and Removing Copies of Books

Adding a Copy of a Book to the Library

In adding a copy of a book to the library we need to consider two cases, namely that in which the book is new to the library and that in which the library already owns a copy of the book being added. The first of these is captured by the schema *DoAddNewBook* and the second by *DoAddAnotherCopy*.

The reason why I split the operation of adding a copy of a book into two cases is because I have made the assumption that the library database does not contain information about books which are not in the library. So, if a copy of a book not in the library is added to the library, we also have to add information about the author or authors of the book and the subjects it is about. Whereas, if the library has one or more copies of a particular book and we are just adding another copy of this book to the library, then it is not necessary to add author or subject information.

Adding a New Book to the Library   One of the reasons why the operation of adding a new book to the library is so complicated is that as well as adding the book we also have to add information about its author or authors and also about what its subject matter is. It would be possible to define an operation which just adds a book to the library and does not add any information about it. That this is possible is due to the fact that the subset relation—and not set equality—was used in the state invariant of *BookInfo*.

```
┌─ AddNewBook ──────────────────────────────────────────────┐
│ Δ LibraryState                                             │
│ vol?: Copy                                                 │
│ book?: Book                                               │
│ who?: F Author                                            │
│ about?: F Subject                                         │
├───────────────────────────────────────────────────────────┤
│ book? ∉ ran instanceof                                    │
│ vol? ∉ available ∪ checkedout                             │
│                                                           │
│ available' = available ∪ {vol?}                          │
│ instanceof' = instanceof ∪ {vol? ↦ book?}                │
│ writtenby' = writtenby ∪ {book? ↦ who?}                  │
│ about' = about ∪ {book? ↦ about?}                        │
│                                                           │
│ checkedout' = checkedout                                 │
│ previouslyborrowedby' = previouslyborrowedby             │
│ borrowedby' = borrowedby                                 │
│ borrower' = borrower                                     │
│ staff' = staff                                          │
└───────────────────────────────────────────────────────────┘
```

One of the preconditions of *AddNewBook* is *book?* $\notin$ ran *instanceof*. This states that we can only add an entirely new book to the library if the library does not contain this book already. The situation in which it is attempted to add a book to the library, which is not new to the library, is captured by the schema *NotNewBook*.

```
┌─ NotNewBook ──────────────────────────────────────────────┐
│ Ξ LibraryState                                            │
│ book?: Book                                              │
│ rep!: Report                                             │
├───────────────────────────────────────────────────────────┤
│ book? ∈ ran instanceof                                   │
│ rep! = 'This book is not new to the library'             │
└───────────────────────────────────────────────────────────┘
```

The other precondition is *vol?* $\notin$ *available* $\cup$ *checkedout*. This states that the copy *vol?*—corresponding to book *book?*—that we are adding to the library must not already be owned by the library. This situation is captured by the schema *CopyOwned* which is defined thus:

```
┌─ CopyOwned ───────────────────────────────────────────────┐
│ Ξ LibraryState                                            │
│ vol?: Copy                                               │
│ rep!: Report                                             │
├───────────────────────────────────────────────────────────┤
│ vol? ∈ available ∪ checkedout                            │
│ rep! = 'This copy is owned by the library'               │
└───────────────────────────────────────────────────────────┘
```

Thus, the total specification of the transaction of adding a book entirely new to the library is given by the schema *DoAddNewBook*:

$$DoAddNewBook \; \hat{=} \; AuthorizedRequestor \wedge AddNewBook \wedge Success$$
$$\vee$$
$$UnauthorizedRequestor$$
$$\vee$$
$$NotNewBook$$
$$\vee$$
$$CopyOwned.$$

Adding Another Copy of a Book   The successful transaction of adding a copy of a book to the library—in the case when the library already has at least one copy of that book—is defined by means of the schema *AddAnotherCopy*. This ignores what happens if the transaction is unsuccessful.

```
┌─ AddAnotherCopy ────────────────────────────────
│ Δ LibraryState
│ vol?: Copy
│ book?: Book
├─────────────────────────────────────────────────
│ vol? ∉ available ∪ checkedout
│ book? ∈ ran instanceof
│
│ available' = available ∪ {vol?}
│ instanceof' = instanceof ∪ {vol? ↦ book?}
│
│ checkedout' = checkedout
│ previouslyborrowedby' = previouslyborrowedby
│ borrowedby' = borrowedby
│ borrower' = borrower
│ staff' = staff
│ writtenby' = writtenby
│ about' = about
└─────────────────────────────────────────────────
```

The schema *BookNewToLibrary* and the schema *CopyOwned* capture what happens when the preconditions of the operation *AddAnotherCopy* are violated.

```
┌─ BookNewToLibrary ──────────────────────────────
│ Ξ LibraryState
│ book?: Book
│ rep!: Report
├─────────────────────────────────────────────────
│ book? ∉ ran instanceof
│ rep! = 'This book is new to the library'
└─────────────────────────────────────────────────
```

The total specification of adding a copy of a book to the library—in the case when that book is not new to the library—is given by the schema *DoAddAnotherCopy*:

$$DoAddAnotherCopy \,\hat{=}\, AuthorizedRequestor \wedge AddAnotherCopy \wedge Success$$
$$\vee$$
$$UnauthorizedRequestor$$
$$\vee$$
$$BookNewToLibrary$$
$$\vee$$
$$CopyOwned.$$

Removing a Copy of a Book from the Library

The operation of removing a copy of a book from the library is split into two cases, namely that of removing a copy of a book while leaving other copies of the same book in the library and that of removing the only copy of a book from the library. The reason for this is similar to the reason why I split the operation of adding a copy of a book to the library into two cases. If the library has two or more copies of a particular book and one of them is removed, then we want to retain author and subject information about that book. However, if the library has only a single copy of a book and we remove that copy, then we also have to remove all the author and subject information relating to that book.

Removing One of Several Copies   The schema *RemoveOther* specifies what happens when a copy of a book is removed from the library, but the copy that is removed is not the only copy of that book possessed by the library.

RemoveOther
$\Delta LibraryState$
$vol?: Copy$

$vol? \in available$
$\#(instanceof^{\sim} (\!|\{instanceof(vol?)\}|\!)) > 1$

$available' = available \setminus \{vol?\}$
$previouslyborrowedby' = \{vol?\} \vartriangleleft previouslyborrowedby$
$instanceof' = \{vol?\} \vartriangleleft instanceof$

$checkedout' = checkedout$
$borrowedby' = borrowedby$
$borrower' = borrower$
$staff' = staff$
$writtenby' = writtenby$
$about' = about$

We need the precondition *vol?* $\in$ *available* because we cannot remove a copy that is currently checked out. The formula

$$\#(instanceof^{\sim}(\!|\{instanceof(vol?)\}|\!)) > 1$$

tells us that there is more than one copy of the book one of whose instances is *vol?*. This interpretation can be built up from its structure. The expression *instanceof(vol?)* is that book which has *vol?* as one of its instances, therefore,

$$instanceof^{\sim}(\!|\{instanceof(vol?)\}|\!)$$

is the set of all the copies that are instances of *instanceof(vol?)*.

The operation *RemoveOther* can go wrong in several ways, namely

(1) *vol?* $\in$ *checkedout*,

(2) *vol?* $\notin$ *available* $\wedge$ *vol?* $\notin$ *checkedout*,

(3) $\#(instanceof^{\sim}(\!|\{instanceof(vol?)\}|\!)) = 1$.

Case (1) is captured by *CopyCheckedOut*, case (2) by the schema *CopyNotOwned* and case (3) by the schema *OnlyCopy*. The first two of these schemas have already been defined. The definition of *OnlyCopy* follows:

```
┌─ OnlyCopy ──────────────────────────────────
│ Ξ LibraryState
│ vol?: Copy
│ rep!: Report
├─────────────────────────────────────────────
│ #(instanceof~(|{instanceof(vol?)}|)) = 1
│ rep! = 'This is the only copy in the library'
└─────────────────────────────────────────────
```

Thus, the total specification of the operation of removing one of several copies of a book from the library is given by the schema *DoRemoveOther*:

$$DoRemoveOther \ \hat{=} \ AuthorizedRequestor \wedge RemoveOther \wedge Success$$
$$\vee$$
$$UnauthorizedRequestor$$
$$\vee$$
$$CopyCheckedOut$$
$$\vee$$
$$CopyNotOwned$$
$$\vee$$
$$OnlyCopy.$$

Removing the Only Copy of a Book   When we remove the last copy of a book
from the library, we also have to remove all mention of that book from the information
part of the library state. The book in question does not have to be separately input,
since it is *instanceof(vol?)*.

┌─ *RemoveLast* ──
│ Δ*LibraryState*
│ *vol?*: *Copy*
├──
│ *vol?* $\in$ *available*
│ $\#(instanceof^\sim(\!\{instanceof(vol?)\}\!)) = 1$
│
│ *available'* = *available* \ {*vol?*}
│ *previouslyborrowedby'* = {*vol?*} $\lhd$ *previouslyborrowedby*
│ *instanceof'* = {*vol?*} $\lhd$ *instanceof*
│ *writtenby'* = {*instanceof(vol?)*} $\lhd$ *writtenby*
│ *about'* = {*instanceof(vol?)*} $\lhd$ *about*
│
│ *checkedout'* = *checkedout*
│ *borrowedby'* = *borrowedby*
│ *borrower'* = *borrower*
│ *staff'* = *staff*
└──

The operation *RemoveLast* can go wrong in the following ways:

(1) *vol?* $\in$ *checkedout*,

(2) *vol?* $\notin$ *available* $\wedge$ *vol?* $\notin$ *checkedout*,

(3) $\#(instanceof^\sim(\!\{instanceof(vol?)\}\!)) > 1.$

Case (1) is captured by *BookCheckedOut*, case (2) by the schema *CopyNotOwned*—
both of which have already been defined—and case (3) is dealt with by the following
schema:

┌─ *NotOnlyCopy* ───
│ Ξ*LibraryState*
│ *vol?*: *Copy*
│ *rep!*: *Report*
├──
│ $\#(instanceof^\sim(\!\{instanceof(vol?)\}\!)) > 1$
│ *rep!* = 'This is not the only copy in the library'
└──

The total specification is captured by the following schema:

$$DoRemoveLast \ \hat{=} \ AuthorizedRequestor \wedge RemoveLast \wedge Success$$
$$\vee$$
$$UnauthorizedRequestor$$
$$\vee$$
$$CopyCheckedOut$$
$$\vee$$
$$CopyNotOwned$$
$$\vee$$
$$NotOnlyCopy.$$

17.4.3 Interrogating the Library Database

The library system described so far can be interrogated in various ways. We need to describe an operation which outputs all the books written or co-authored by a particular author and we need to describe a transaction which lists all the books about a particular subject. Unlike the transactions specified so far, these operations can be performed by anyone.

Interrogation by Author

```
┌─ ByAuthor ─────────────────────────────────
│ ΞLibraryState
│ writer?: Author
│ out!: F Book
├────────────────────────────────────────────
│ writer? ∈ ⋃{ x: Book • writtenby(x) }
│ out! = { x: Book | writer? ∈ writtenby(x) }
└────────────────────────────────────────────
```

The precondition of the schema *ByAuthor* contains the term

$$\bigcup\{ x \colon Book \bullet writtenby(x) \}.$$

This represents a set of authors and an author is a member of this set if the library has at least one of his or her books. It would have been possible to leave out the precondition of the schema *ByAuthor*, because when the library has no books by an author *writer?*, then the set *out!* is the empty set. In the first edition of this book, on p. 190, I did leave out this precondition, but on reflection it seems to me more sensible to have it in. The reason for this is that it allows us to output a meaningful message when the precondition is violated. When the precondition is contravened the schema *UnknownAuthor* specifies what happens:

```
┌─ UnknownAuthor ─────────────────────────────────────────
│ ΞLibraryState
│ writer?: Author
│ rep!: Report
├─────────────────────────────────────────────────────────
│ writer? ∉ ⋃{ x: Book • writtenby(x) }
│ rep! = 'The library has no books by this author'
└─────────────────────────────────────────────────────────
```

The total specification of the operation of interrogating the library database by author is given by means of the schema *DoByAuthor*:

$$DoByAuthor \; \hat{=} \; ByAuthor \wedge Success$$
$$\vee$$
$$UnknownAuthor.$$

Note that the operation of interrogating the database is available to everyone, so there is no need to include a schema which checks to see who is attempting to carry out the transaction.

Interrogation by Subject

Interrogating the library system by subject is analogous to interrogating it by author. In neither case do we need to take into account who is requesting the transaction, because these operations are available to all.

```
┌─ BySubject ─────────────────────────────────────────────
│ ΞLibraryState
│ what?: Subject
│ out!: F Book
├─────────────────────────────────────────────────────────
│ what? ∈ ⋃{ x: Book • about(x) }
│ out! = { x: Book | what? ∈ about(x) }
└─────────────────────────────────────────────────────────
```

Just as in the case of the schema *BySubject* it would have been possible to leave out the precondition—and that is what, in fact, I did on p. 191 of the first edition of this book—but I now think that it is better to output a sensible message when *out!* is the empty set. The schema *UnknownSubject* takes care of the situation in which the precondition is false:

```
┌─ UnknownSubject ────────────────────────────────────────
│ ΞLibraryState
│ what?: Subject
│ rep!: Report
├─────────────────────────────────────────────────────────
│ what? ∉ ⋃{ x: Book • about(x) }
│ rep! = 'The library has no books on this subject'
└─────────────────────────────────────────────────────────
```

The total specification of the operation of interrogating the library database by subject is given by means of the schema *DoBySubject*:

$$DoBySubject \stackrel{\triangle}{=} BySubject \land Success$$
$$\lor$$
$$UnknownSubject.$$

Who has Borrowed What?

The schema *BooksBorrowedBy* defines the transaction of finding out what copies someone has borrowed.

BooksBorrowedBy ─────────────────────────
$\Xi LibraryState$
$reg?: Person$
$out!: \mathbf{F}\ Copy$

$reg? \in borrower$

$out! = borrowedby^\sim (\!|\{reg?\}|\!)$

This transaction can be performed by a staff user for any borrower or by a borrower for himself or herself; hence we need the schema *SelfRequestor*:

SelfRequestor ─────────────────────────
$reg?, requestor?: Person$

$reg? = requestor?$

This transaction is unsuccessful if you try to get information about someone's borrowings if they are not registered users:

UnknownBorrower ─────────────────────────
$\Xi LibraryState$
$reg?: Person$
$rep!: Report$

$reg? \notin borrower$
$rep! =$ 'Unknown borrower'

Another way in which this transaction can go wrong is if it is neither requested by a staff member of the library nor requested by an ordinary borrower for himself or herself:

```
┌─ NotAuthorizedRequestor ────────────────────────────
│ ΞLibraryState
│ reg?, requestor?: Person
│ rep!: Report
├─────────────────────────────────────────────────────
│ requestor? ∉ staff
│ reg? ≠ requestor?
│ rep! = 'Not authorized requestor'
└─────────────────────────────────────────────────────
```

The total specification is given by the following schema:

$$DoBooksBorrowedBy \;\hat{=}\; AuthorizedRequestor \land BooksBorrowedBy \land Success$$
$$\lor$$
$$SelfRequestor \land BooksBorrowedBy \land Success$$
$$\lor$$
$$UnknownBorrower$$
$$\lor$$
$$NotAuthorizedRequestor.$$

Who last Borrowed a Given Copy?

The next transaction that I am going to specify is that of finding out who was the last person to borrow a particular copy of a book.

```
┌─ PreviousBorrower ──────────────────────────────────
│ ΞLibraryState
│ reg!: Person
│ vol?: Copy
├─────────────────────────────────────────────────────
│ vol? ∈ available ∪ checkedout
│ reg! = previouslyborrowedby(vol?)
└─────────────────────────────────────────────────────
```

This transaction fails either if the copy *vol?* is not owned by the library or if the copy *vol?* has never been borrowed.

```
┌─ CopyNotPreviouslyBorrowed ─────────────────────────
│ ΞLibraryState
│ vol?: Copy
│ rep!: Report
├─────────────────────────────────────────────────────
│ vol? ∉ dom previouslyborrowedby
│ rep! = 'Copy not previously borrowed'
└─────────────────────────────────────────────────────
```

Thus, the total specification of the operation of finding out who last borrowed a particular copy of a book is given like this:

$$DoPreviousBorrower \; \hat{=} \; PreviousBorrower \wedge AuthorizedRequestor \wedge Success$$
$$\vee$$
$$UnauthorizedRequestor$$
$$\vee$$
$$CopyNotOwned$$
$$\vee$$
$$CopyNotPreviouslyBorrowed.$$

Note that this is a transaction that can only be performed by a staff member of the library.

18

Partial Specification of a Text-editor

18.1 Introduction

In this chapter I present part of the specification of a display-oriented text-editor. It is based on the specification of the VED and QED editors given in (Sufrin 1981)—a revised version of which appears as (Sufrin 1982). More recently Neilson (1990), part 3, has presented a specification of a full-screen text-editor using a version of Z that differs from the standard one in only minor details. (Sufrin's specification made use of an early version of Z that is now obsolete.) Furthermore, Neilson goes on to refine his specification into a program written in C. The source code of this implementation is included as appendix C of his technical monograph. I do not take the specification very far and the reader is very strongly urged to look up the original papers by Sufrin and the technical monograph by Neilson.

18.2 Basic Types

This specification makes use of a single given set or basic type:

$$[Char]$$

The type *Char* is the set of all the characters that we might need. In this chapter elements belonging to the type *Char* will be set in typewriter font. The type *Char* includes the newline character, which is symbolized as ↓. *Report* is the set of all necessary messages:

$$Report ::= \text{'Okay'}$$
$$| \text{'At top of document'}$$
$$| \text{'At bottom of document'}.$$

18.3   The State Space

The first model of an editor uses a very simple state space which just consists of two sequences of characters. The schema which defines this state space is called *Doc1*:

```
┌─ Doc1 ──────────────────────────────────────────────────
│ left, right: seq Char
│
```

The sequence *left* contains all the characters in the document being edited which lie to the left of the cursor and the sequence *right* contains all the characters in the document being edited which lie to the right of the cursor.

The schemas $\Delta Doc1$ and $\Xi Doc1$ are defined in the standard way:

$$\Delta Doc1 \triangleq Doc1 \wedge Doc1',$$

$$\Xi Doc1 \triangleq [\Delta Doc1 \mid \theta Doc1' = \theta Doc1].$$

The initial state schema is *InitDoc1'*, where *InitDoc1* is defined as follows:

$$InitDoc1 \triangleq [Doc1 \mid left = \langle\,\rangle; right = \langle\,\rangle].$$

18.4   The Operations

In this section I consider some of the basic editing operations that we demand of an editor and how they can be formally specified. I will look at the operations of deleting a character from the document, moving the cursor one character and inserting a character. To begin with I will specify these operations as they apply to the left of the cursor and then as they apply to the right of the cursor.

18.4.1   Operations to the Left of the Cursor

Deleting One Character to the Left of the Cursor

The operation of deleting a single character which is immediately to the left of the cursor—that is to say, the last character of the sequence *left*—is graphically depicted in Fig. 18.1 and it is specified like this:

```
┌─ DeleteLeftDoc1 ────────────────────────────────────────
│ ΔDoc1
│────────────────────────────────────────────────────────
│ left ≠ ⟨ ⟩
│ left' = front left
│ right' = right
│
```

The precondition of the operation *DeleteLeftDoc1* is the formula $left \neq \langle\,\rangle$. We cannot delete the character to the left of the cursor when the sequence *left* is empty. In order

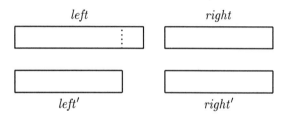

Figure 18.1: Deleting one character to the left of the cursor.

to provide a total specification of this operation we need to specify what happens when the sequence *left* is empty. This is done by the schema *ErrorAtTop*:

```
┌─ ErrorAtTop ──────────────────────────────
│ ΞDoc1
│ rep!: Report
├────────────────────────────────────────────
│ left = ⟨ ⟩
│ rep! = 'At top of document'
└────────────────────────────────────────────
```

The total specification is given by the schema *DoDeleteLeftDoc1*, which is defined as follows:

$$DoDeleteLeftDoc1 \stackrel{\triangle}{=} DeleteLeftDoc1 \wedge Success$$
$$\vee$$
$$ErrorAtTop.$$

The schema *Success* used here just reports that an operation has been successfully performed:

```
┌─ Success ──────────────────────────────────
│ rep!: Report
├────────────────────────────────────────────
│ rep! = 'Okay'
└────────────────────────────────────────────
```

Moving One Character to the Left of the Cursor

The operation of moving the cursor one character to the left is graphically depicted in Fig. 18.2. It just involves taking the last character from the sequence *left* and putting it at the front of the sequence *right*.

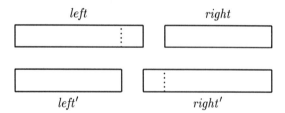

Figure 18.2: Moving one character to the left of the cursor.

─── *MoveLeftDoc1* ──────────────────────────────────
  $\Delta Doc1$
  ────────────────────────────────────
  $left \neq \langle\,\rangle$
  $left' = front\ left$
  $right' = \langle last\ left \rangle \frown right$
──

In giving the total specification of the operation *DoMoveLeftDoc1* we again need to take into account what happens when *left* is empty:

$$DoMoveLeftDoc1 \overset{\wedge}{=} MoveLeftDoc1 \wedge Success$$
$$\vee$$
$$ErrorAtTop.$$

Inserting One Character to the Left of the Cursor

The operation of inserting a single character immediately to the left of the cursor is graphically depicted in Fig. 18.3. It just involves adding the input character to the end of the sequence *left*.

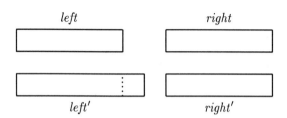

Figure 18.3: Inserting one character to the left of the cursor.

```
┌─ InsertLeftDoc1 ────────────────────────────────────────
│  ΔDoc1
│  ch?: Char
├──────────────────
│  left' = left ⌢ ⟨ch?⟩
│  right' = right
└─────────────────────────────────────────────────────────
```

The operation of inserting a character always succeeds, so there is no need to add an error condition in its total specification:

$$DoInsertLeftDoc1 \triangleq InsertLeftDoc1 \wedge Success.$$

Observation

It would be possible—and entirely straightforward—to specify operations like deleting a word to the left of the cursor or moving to the beginning of the word immediately to the left of the cursor and so on. For more details see the papers by Sufrin mentioned in the introduction to this chapter and also the technical monograph by Neilson.

18.4.2   Operations to the Right of the Cursor

Character operations to the right of the cursor are similar to those to the left of the cursor, so they are described more succinctly.

Deleting One Character to the Right of the Cursor

The operation of deleting one character to the right of the cursor is graphically depicted in Fig. 18.4 and it is formally specified like this:

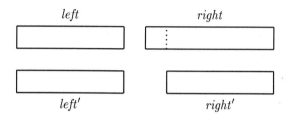

Figure 18.4: Deleting one character to the right of the cursor.

$\_\_$ *DeleteRightDoc1* $_____$

$\Delta Doc1$

$right \neq \langle \, \rangle$

$right' = tail\ right$

$left' = left$

We cannot delete a character to the right of the cursor when the sequence *right* is empty. When that happens we want to output an appropriate error message.

$\_\_$ *ErrorAtBottom* $_____$

$\Xi Doc1$

rep!: *Report*

$right = \langle \, \rangle$

$rep! = $ 'At bottom of document'

It is now possible to specify the total operation of deleting a single character to the right of the cursor:

$$DoDeleteRightDoc1 \stackrel{\wedge}{=} DeleteRightDoc1 \wedge Success$$
$$\vee$$
$$ErrorAtBottom.$$

Moving One Character to the Right of the Cursor

The operation of moving one character to the right of the cursor is graphically depicted in Fig. 18.5. It involves taking the character at the extreme left of the sequence *right* and putting it at the extreme right of the sequence *left*. The formal specification of this operation is captured by means of the schema *MoveRightDoc1*, which is defined like this:

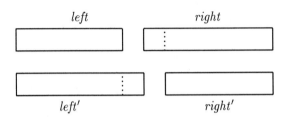

Figure 18.5: Moving one character to the right of the cursor.

```
┌─ MoveRightDoc1 ──────────────────────────────
│ ΔDoc1
├──────────────────────────────────────────────
│ right ≠ ⟨ ⟩
│ left' = left ⌢ ⟨head right⟩
│ right' = tail right
└──────────────────────────────────────────────
```

The operation of moving right one character position cannot succeed if the cursor is at the end of the document, thus this possibility has to be catered for in giving the total specification:

$$DoMoveRightDoc1 \;\hat{=}\; MoveRightDoc1 \land Success$$
$$\lor$$
$$ErrorAtBottom.$$

Inserting One Character to the Right of the Cursor

The operation of inserting a single character to the right of the cursor is graphically depicted in Fig. 18.6. It is formally specified in this way:

```
┌─ InsertRightDoc1 ────────────────────────────
│ ΔDoc1
│ ch?: Char
├──────────────────────────────────────────────
│ left' = left
│ right' = ⟨ch?⟩ ⌢ right
└──────────────────────────────────────────────
```

As in the case of inserting a character to the left of the cursor, the operation of inserting a character to the right of the cursor cannot fail. Thus, its complete specification is defined like this:

$$DoInsertRightDoc1 \;\hat{=}\; InsertRightDoc1 \land Success.$$

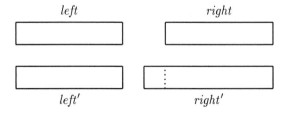

Figure 18.6: Inserting one character to the right of the cursor.

Observation

It would be possible—and entirely straightforward—to specify operations like deleting a word to the right of the cursor or moving to the beginning of the word immediately to the right of the cursor and so on.

18.5   The *Doc2* State

The *Doc1* model of an editor is very simple and it is very easy to specify operations like deleting characters, inserting them and moving through the document. It was developed for that very reason, but now it is necessary to show how the *Doc1* model can be related to the familiar editor displays that we see on our terminals. The first step in this direction is to develop a *Doc2* model in which we specify an unbounded display. This is thought of as a non-empty sequence of lines, where a line is a sequence of characters *excluding* the newline character ↓. Thus, the set *Line* is defined like this:

$$Line == \mathrm{seq}(\mathit{Char} \setminus \{↓\}).$$

An *unbounded display* is a sequence of lines which we think of as displayed one below the other—with the first displayed at the top and the second immediately below it and so on—and aligned at their left edge, that is to say, they are left justified. An example of such an unbounded display is given in Fig. 18.7, where a line is represented as a rectangle. In formally specifying an unbounded display we need to take into account the cursor position.

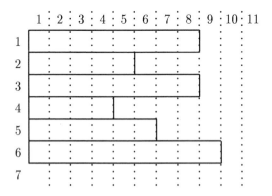

Figure 18.7: An example of an unbounded display.

```
┌─ UnboundedDisplay ──────────────────────────────────
│ doclines: seq₁ Line
│ line, col: N₁
├──────────────────────────────────────────
│ line ≤ #doclines
│ col ≤ #(doclines(line)) + 1
└──────────────────────────────────────────
```

The numbers *line* and *col* refer to the cursor position. Co-ordinates are given in the form $(line, col)$, where *line* is the line number—that is to say, the number on the left of the display in Fig. 18.7—and *col* is the column number—that is to say, the number at the top of the display in Fig. 18.7. The formulas in the predicate-part of the schema *UnboundedDisplay*, namely

$$line \leq \#doclines,$$
$$col \leq \#(doclines(line)) + 1,$$

ensure that the cursor lies either inside the document or just to the right of the right-most character position on any given line. This is because if there are n characters on a line, then there are $n + 1$ cursor positions. When we come to implement the editor the cursor on a terminal will actually appear at a character position. I use the convention that the logical cursor position—that is to say, the 'gap' between the two sequences *left* and *right* in *Doc1*—corresponds to the 'gap' between the character position where the physical cursor appears and the character position immediately to its left.

In order to relate the *Doc1* state to the *Doc2* state we need the function *flatten*:

```
│ flatten: seq₁ Line ⟶ seq Char
├──────────────────────────────────────────
│ ∀xs: Line; xss: seq₁ Line •
│     flatten⟨xs⟩ = xs ∧
│     flatten(⟨xs⟩ ⌢ xss) = xs ⌢ ⟨↓⟩ ⌢ (flatten xss)
```

The function *flatten* takes a non-empty sequence of lines and concatenates all the members of that sequence into a single sequence of characters, while at the same time inserting newline characters between each pair of lines. An example of its use should make its operation clearer:

$$flatten \ \langle\langle a, b, c\rangle, \langle d, e, f, g\rangle, \langle h, i\rangle\rangle = \langle a, b, c, ↓, d, e, f, g, ↓, h, i\rangle.$$

The function *flatten* is, in fact, a one-to-one and onto function, so it has an inverse which is also a total function. This means that given an arbitrary sequence of characters, say xs, there exists one and only one non-empty sequence of lines, say xss, such that $flatten \ xss = xs$. (In Z a one-to-one and onto total function is known as a *bijection*.) The *Doc2* state can now be specified as follows:

```
┌─ Doc2 ──────────────────────────────────────────────
│ Doc1
│ UnboundedDisplay
├─────────────────────────────────────────────────────
│ left ⌢ right = flatten doclines
│ line = #(left ▷ {↵}) + 1
│ col = #left − #(flatten(doclines for (line − 1)))
└─────────────────────────────────────────────────────
```

The symbol $\triangleright$ is range restriction and, so, the value of $\#(left \triangleright \{↵\})$ is the number of newline characters in the sequence *left*. The function *for* was described in chapter 7. Given a sequence σ and a number i, σ *for* i is the sequence obtained by taking the first i elements of σ in the order in which they occur in σ.

If we expand the schema *Doc2* we get the following:

```
┌─ Doc2 ──────────────────────────────────────────────
│ left, right: seq Char
│ doclines: seq₁ Line
│ line, col: N₁
├─────────────────────────────────────────────────────
│ line ≤ #doclines
│ col ≤ #(doclines line) + 1
│ left ⌢ right = flatten doclines
│ line = #(left ▷ {↵}) + 1
│ col = #left − #(flatten(doclines for (line − 1)))
└─────────────────────────────────────────────────────
```

To see how the final formula, namely

$$col = \#left - \#(flatten(doclines \; for \; (line - 1))),$$

calculates the value of *col* given *line* consider the following simple example. Let *left* and *right* be the following sequences:

$$left = \langle a, b, ↵, c, d, e, ↵, f \rangle,$$
$$right = \langle g, h, ↵, i, j \rangle.$$

The value of $flatten^{\sim}(left \frown right)$ looks like this:

$$\langle$$
$$\langle a, b \rangle,$$
$$\langle c, d, e \rangle,$$
$$\langle f, \boxed{g}, h \rangle,$$
$$\langle i, j \rangle$$
$$\rangle.$$

Here the frame around the letter **g** represents the cursor position. This sequence of sequences is *doclines*, since $left \frown right = flatten \; doclines$ and *flatten*, being a bijection, has an inverse which is a total function.

The value of *line* is easy to determine; it is 3. Now let us consider the formula:

$$col = \#left - \#(\mathit{flatten}\ (\mathit{doclines\ for}\ (line - 1))).$$

The value of the term *doclines for* $(line - 1)$ is the sequence of lines $\langle\langle \mathsf{a}, \mathsf{b}\rangle, \langle \mathsf{c}, \mathsf{d}, \mathsf{e}\rangle\rangle$, that is to say, the sequence consisting of the first two items of the sequence *doclines*. Applying *flatten* to this results in the sequence $\langle \mathsf{a}, \mathsf{b}, \downarrow, \mathsf{c}, \mathsf{d}, \mathsf{e}\rangle$ and the length of this is 6. The length of *left* is 8; therefore the calculated value of *col* is 2, as it should be.

18.5.1 Promoting *Doc1* Operations to *Doc2* Ones

It is entirely straightforward to promote *Doc1* operations to *Doc2* ones. We just form the conjunction of each *Doc1* operation with $\Delta Doc2$, thus:

$$DoDeleteLeftDoc2 \triangleq DoDeleteLeftDoc1 \wedge \Delta Doc2,$$
$$DoMoveLeftDoc2 \triangleq DoMoveLeftDoc1 \wedge \Delta Doc2,$$
$$DoInsertLeftDoc2 \triangleq DoInsertLeftDoc1 \wedge \Delta Doc2,$$
$$DoDeleteRightDoc2 \triangleq DoDeleteRightDoc1 \wedge \Delta Doc2,$$
$$DoMoveRightDoc2 \triangleq DoMoveRightDoc1 \wedge \Delta Doc2,$$
$$DoInsertRightDoc2 \triangleq DoInsertRightDoc1 \wedge \Delta Doc2.$$

Each of the *Doc2* operations is quite complicated if expanded. For example, the expanded version of *DoDeleteLeftDoc2* is:

DoDeleteLeftDoc2
$left, left', right, right'$: seq $Char$
$doclines, doclines'$: seq_1 $Line$
$line, line', col, col'$: $\mathbf{N}_1$
$rep!$: $Report$

$line \leq \#doclines$
$col \leq \#(doclines\ line) + 1$
$left \frown right = flatten\ doclines$
$line = \#(left \rhd \{\downarrow\}) + 1$
$col = \#left - \#(flatten\ (doclines\ for\ (line - 1)))$
$line' \leq \#doclines'$
$col' \leq \#(doclines'\ line') + 1$
$left' \frown right' = flatten\ doclines'$
$line' = \#(left' \rhd \{\downarrow\}) + 1$
$col' = \#left' - \#(flatten\ (doclines'\ for\ (line' - 1)))$
$((left \neq \langle\ \rangle\ \wedge$
$left' = front\ left\ \wedge$
$right' = right\ \wedge$
$rep! = \text{'Okay'})$

   $\vee$

$(left = \langle\ \rangle\ \wedge$
$left' = left\ \wedge$
$right' = right\ \wedge$
$rep! = \text{'At top of document'}))$

18.6 The *Doc3* Model

18.6.1 Putting a Window on the Unbounded Display

In the *Doc3* version of the editor we put a window on the unbounded display. This window will represent what we actually see on a computer terminal when the specification is implemented. An example of such a window is shown in Fig. 18.8. The portion of the unbounded display lying below line 1, above line 2, to the left of line 3 and to the right of line 4 corresponds to a particular window.

In order to model such a window I need the function *truncate*:

$truncate$: $(\mathbf{N}_1 \times \mathbf{N}_1 \times \mathbf{N} \times \mathbf{N}) \longrightarrow \text{seq}_1\ Line \longrightarrow \text{seq}\ Line$

$\forall wid, hei$: $\mathbf{N}_1$; $vert, hor$: $\mathbf{N}$; xss: $\text{seq}_1\ Line\ \bullet$
   $truncate\ (wid, hei, vert, hor)\ xss =$
      $(take\ hei\ (drop\ vert\ xss))\ \mathbin{;}\ (drop\ hor)\ \mathbin{;}\ (take\ wid)$

The effect of *truncate* is easier to understand than at first appears. The component *drop vert xss*, corresponds to the portion of the unbounded display below the horizontal

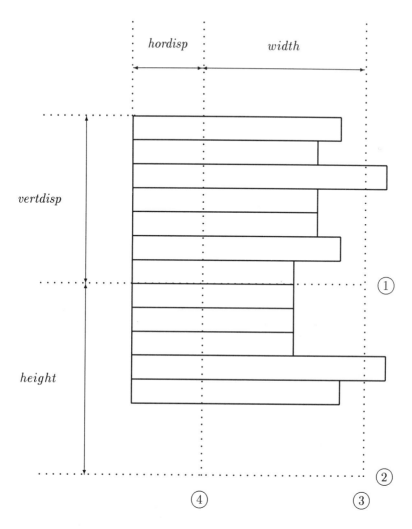

Figure 18.8: Putting a window on the unbounded display.

line marked 1 in Fig. 18.8. The expression *take hei* (*drop vert xss*) corresponds to the portion of the unbounded display between the horizontal lines marked 1 and 2 in Fig. 18.8. I will call this expression σ for ease of reference:

$$\sigma == take\ hei\ (drop\ vert\ xss).$$

Note that σ represents a sequence. Getting the portion of the unbounded display that lies between the vertical lines marked 3 and 4 in Fig. 18.8 is a bit more complicated. The portion to the right of the vertical line 4 is $\sigma \,\natural\, (drop\ hor)$. This has the effect of removing the first *hor* characters from each item in σ. Given an arbitrary sequence σ: seq X and a total function $f : X \longrightarrow Y$, $\sigma \,\natural\, f$ is a sequence of the same length as σ in which f has been applied to each element of σ.[1] Informally, we have

$$\sigma \,\mathring{,}\, f = \langle f(\sigma(1)), f(\sigma(2)), \ldots, f(\sigma(\#\sigma)) \rangle.$$

The portion between the vertical lines 3 and 4 is $\sigma \,\mathring{,}\, (\textit{drop hor}) \,\mathring{,}\, (\textit{take wid})$.

Now it is possible to define the *Doc3* state:

─── *Doc3* ──────────────────────────────
  Doc2
  window: seq *Line*
  width, *height*: $\mathbb{N}_1$
  hordisp, *vertdisp*: $\mathbb{N}$
─────────────────────────────────────
  window = *truncate* (*width*, *height*, *hordisp*, *vertdisp*) *doclines*
  line $\leq$ *height*
  col $\leq$ *width* + 1
─────────────────────────────────────

The parameters *width* and *height* represent the width and height, respectively, of the window on the unbounded display. The final two formulas here ensure that the cursor lies inside the window. It is now possible to promote all the previously defined operations to the *Doc3* model, but things begin to get slightly more complicated because we want to ensure that if we move either right or left then the cursor stays inside the window, so a movement of the cursor might involve a shift in the window as well. One operation that cannot cause a movement of the window—in order to ensure that the cursor lies within the window—is that of inserting a character to the right of the cursor. This is specified as follows:

$$DoInsertRightDoc3 \,\hat{=}\, [\,DoInsert RightDoc2 \,\mathring{,}\, \Delta Doc3$$
$$|\ width' = width;\ height' = height\,].$$

We have to add the formulas so that the window stays the same throughout the operation. In this editor no line wrap-around takes place; thus the portion of the eleventh line of text—that is to say, the penultimate line—in Fig. 18.8 which lies to the right of the vertical line labelled 3 does not appear in the window.

18.7 Conclusion

The specification contained in this chapter is far from complete. One of the reasons for including it was that the specification by Sufrin (1981) was one of the earliest large examples of the use of Z and it is often referred to in the literature on Z, so I thought that it was important to give the reader some idea of its nature and character. If I have whetted anybody's appetite, then I would advise that person to read and study (Neilson 1990). This technical monograph contains a complete specification of a full-screen text-editor as well as a refinement and a full implementation of it.

───────────────────────

[1] Functional programmers will recognize $\sigma \,\mathring{,}\, f$ to be *map f σ*.

Part IV

Specification Animation

19

Animation using Miranda

19.1   Introduction

In this chapter I show how a Z specification can be animated using Miranda. The specification that I have chosen to use as an illustration of the method to be described is that of the internal telephone directory described in chapter 4.

Miranda is a functional programming language designed by David Turner and it is described by him in (Turner 1986). I assume that the reader of this chapter is familiar with Miranda and so I do not explain every feature of it that I use. (Holyer 1991) is a good introduction to Miranda and also to functional programming in general.

In this chapter typewriter font is used for expressions and declarations belonging to Miranda. In addition, in order to avoid confusion between the different type systems of Z and Miranda the word *datatype* in this chapter is used to denote a type in the Miranda language and the word *type* refers to a type in Z.

19.2   The Animation

19.2.1   Overall Structure

The Miranda animation is written in the form of an interactive program. The overall structure of this program—and some of the actual functions used—are taken from the excellent book by Bird and Wadler (1988). The definitions of the functions `read1`, `read2`, `write`, `end`, `before` and `after` are to be found on pp. 199–203 of that book. (The function I call `read1` Bird and Wadler call `read`.) These definitions are not repeated here. The reader unfamiliar with (Bird and Wadler 1988) is strongly urged to read the section of that book dealing with 'Interactive Programs', namely section 7.8, pp. 196–203, before reading the remainder of this chapter.

19.2.2   Basic Types

The specification of the internal telephone directory makes use of three basic types, namely *Person*, *Phone* and *Command*, and it also uses the set *Report* of messages that are output by the system. The members of each of these sets are represented in the Miranda animation as lists of characters or strings. Miranda does not contain a primitive **string** datatype, so this has to be defined:

```
string == [char]
person == string
phone  == string
```

Two equals signs next to one another == are used in Miranda to define type synonyms. For example, **string == [char]** defines the identifier **string** to be a synonym for the type **[char]**. Note that I have defined neither the datatype **command** nor **report**. This is because commands and messages are treated differently in the animation from **person** and **phone**. The reason why the identifiers **person** and **phone** do not have initial capital letters is that in Miranda only identifiers representing type constructors can start with a capital letter.

19.2.3 The State Space

The state schema for the internal telephone directory specification is *PhoneDB*, which was defined like this:

> ┌─ *PhoneDB* ──────────────────────────────
> │ *members*: **P** *Person*
> │ *telephones*: *Person* ↔ *Phone*
> ├──
> │ dom *telephones* ⊆ *members*
> └──

Objects belonging to the state space are represented in the Miranda animation as 2-tuples belonging to the datatype **phonedb**, which is defined like this:

```
phonedb == ([person], [(person, phone)])
```

An element of the datatype **phonedb** is a 2-tuple whose first component is a list of members of the datatype **person** and whose second component is a list of 2-tuples each of which consists of a member of **person** and a member of **phone**. The first component of an element of **phonedb** corresponds to the set *members* in *PhoneDB* and the second component corresponds to the relation *telephones*. So, a set of things drawn from the type *Person* is represented in the Miranda script as a list of things belonging to the datatype **person** and a relation between the sets *Person* and *Phone* is represented by an association list of 2-tuples.

Note that an element of the datatype **phonedb** need not satisfy the state invariant of the schema *PhoneDB*. The way in which I have chosen to treat the state invariant is by having a boolean-valued function **invar** that returns **False** if the state invariant is violated. Of course, if the Miranda functions corresponding to the operation schemas defined in the specification of the internal telephone directory have been correctly implemented, then it is impossible for the state invariant ever to be broken. The function **invar** is called by the function **phdb**, which is invoked every time an operation is performed on the database. The definitions of these two functions are:

```
phdb :: phonedb -> string -> string
phdb db = tndb db, if invar db
        = write "Invariant violated\n" (tndb db), otherwise

invar :: phonedb -> bool
invar (mem, tel) = and [ member mem n | (n, e) <- tel ]
```

To indicate that an entity `ent` belongs to the datatype `dat` in Miranda the notation `ent :: dat` is used. The reason why there are two colons in this declaration is because a single colon represents the infix *cons* operation which forms a new list out of an old one by sticking a single element to the front of the old list.

19.2.4   The Initial State

The initial state is represented in the Miranda animation by the constant `empty`, which belongs to the datatype `phonedb`. It is defined like this:

```
empty :: phonedb
empty = ([ ], [ ])
```

19.2.5   The Operations

Introduction

Six operations were defined in the specification of the internal telephone directory, but I will only explain how one of them is 'translated' into a Miranda function. The animation of the other five operations is done in a similar manner. The operation that I use in order to illustrate the method is that of adding an entry to the system.

Adding an Entry

The schema *AddEntry* specifies what happens when an entry is added to the database:

```
┌─ AddEntry ─────────────────────────────────────────
│ ΔPhoneDB
│ name?: Person
│ newnumber?: Phone
├────────────────────────────────────────────────────
│ name? ∈ members
│ name? ↦ newnumber? ∉ telephones
│ telephones' = telephones ∪ {name? ↦ newnumber?}
│ members' = members
└────────────────────────────────────────────────────
```

This is translated straightforwardly into the Miranda function `addEntry`, which is only going to be invoked when the preconditions of the operation are satisfied.

```
addEntry n e (mem, tel) = (mem, tel ++ [(n, e)])
```

The identifiers **n**, **e**, **mem** and **tel** correspond, respectively, to *name?*, *newnumber?*, *members* and *telephones*. The list addition operator **++** has been used to represent set union. This makes the correspondence between the Miranda function and the schema very clear, but a more efficient version of **addEntry** would use the infix *cons* operator like this:

```
addEntry n e (mem, tel) = (mem, (n, e) : tel)
```

The operation specified by *AddEntry* is a partial one. The total version of this operation is defined by means of the schema *DoAddEntry*:

$$DoAddEntry \overset{\wedge}{=} AddEntry \wedge Success$$
$$\vee$$
$$NotMember$$
$$\vee$$
$$EntryAlreadyExists.$$

The schema *Success* used in this definition of *DoAddEntry* outputs a message indicating that operation has been performed successfully:

Success
rep!: *Report*
___
rep! = 'Okay'

When the precondition *name?* ∈ *members* of the schema *AddEntry* is violated what happens is defined by means of the schema *NotMember*:

NotMember
Ξ*PhoneDB*
name?: *Person*
rep!: *Report*
___
name? ∉ *members*
rep! = 'Not a member'

When the precondition *name?* ↦ *newnumber?* ∉ *telephones* of the schema *AddEntry* is infringed what happens is defined by means of the schema *EntryAlreadyExists*:

EntryAlreadyExists
Ξ*PhoneDB*
name?: *Person*
newnumber?: *Phone*
rep!: *Report*
___
name? ↦ *newnumber?* ∈ *telephones*
rep! = 'Entry already exists'

The precondition *name?* ∈ *members* in the schema *AddEntry* becomes the Miranda expression `member mem n` and the precondition *name?* ↦ *newnumber?* ∉ *telephones* becomes the Miranda expression `~ member tel (n, e)`. The function `member` is a predefined Miranda function which tests whether its second argument is an element of the list which is its first argument. The Miranda function `addEntry` is invoked only when the two boolean-valued expressions `member mem n` and `~ member tel (n, e)` are true. When either is false, the appropriate error message is output. The function `doAddEntry` corresponds to the Z schema *DoAddEntry*.

```
doAddEntry (n, e)
= write "Okay\n" (phdb (addEntry n e (mem, tel))),
    if member mem n & ~ member tel (n, e)
= write "Not a member\n" (phdb (mem, tel)),
    if ~ member mem n
= write "Entry already exists\n" (phdb (mem, tel)),
    if member tel (n, e)
```

The function `write` that is used in the definition of `doAddEntry` is defined in (Bird and Wadler 1988, p. 200), where the way in which it works is also explained.

19.2.6   The Miranda Script

Apart from the definitions of the functions `read1`, `read2`, `write`, `end`, `before` and `after`, the Miranda script of the animation of the internal telephone directory specification is included here. The program is invoked by giving the command `go $-` to the Miranda interpreter. The function `tndb` reads a command from the keyboard—after giving the prompt `Command:`—and then, depending on which command is entered, calls the relevant function to process that command. The command `end` terminates the program and if something is typed that is not a valid command, then a suitable error message is produced. The function `cocmd` ('carry out command') corresponds to what Bird and Wadler (1988), p. 202, call `tcommand`.

```
string   == [char]
person   == string
phone    == string
phonedb  == ([person], [(person, phone)])

go :: string -> string
go = phdb empty

phdb :: phonedb -> string -> string
phdb db = tndb db, if invar db
        = write "Invariant violated\n" (tndb db), otherwise

invar :: phonedb -> bool
invar (mem, tel) = and [ member mem n | (n, e) <- tel ]
```

```
empty :: phonedb
empty = ([ ], [ ])

tndb :: phonedb -> string -> string

tndb (mem, tel)
= read1 "Command: " cocmd
  where
  cocmd "end" = write "Exit program\n" end
  cocmd "ae"  = read2 ("Name? ", "Extension? ") doAddEntry
  cocmd "fp"  = read1 "Name? " doFindPhones
  cocmd "fn"  = read1 "Extension? " doFindNames
  cocmd "re"  = read2 ("Name? ", "Extension? ") doRemoveEntry
  cocmd "am"  = read1 "Name? " doAddMember
  cocmd "rm"  = read1 "Name? " doRemoveMember
  cocmd other = write "Unknown command\n" donothing

  addEntry n e (mem, tel) = (mem, tel ++ [(n, e)])
  doAddEntry (n, e)
  = write "Okay\n" (phdb (addEntry n e (mem, tel))),
      if member mem n & ~ member tel (n, e)
  = write "Not a member\n" (phdb (mem, tel)),
      if ~ member mem n
  = write "Entry already exists\n" (phdb (mem, tel)),
      if member tel (n, e)

  findPhones n (mem, tel) = disp (image tel [n])
  doFindPhones n
  = write (findPhones n (mem, tel) ++ "\n\n") (phdb (mem, tel)),
      if member (domain tel) n
  = write "Unknown name\n" (phdb (mem, tel)),
      otherwise

  findNames e (mem, tel) = disp (image (inverse tel) [e])
  doFindNames e
  = write (findNames e (mem, tel) ++ "\n\n") (phdb (mem, tel)),
      if member (range tel) e
  = write "Unknown extension\n" (phdb (mem, tel)),
      otherwise

  removeEntry n e (mem, tel) = (mem, tel -- [(n, e)])
  doRemoveEntry (n, e)
  = write "Okay\n" (phdb (removeEntry n e (mem, tel))),
```

```
      if member tel (n, e)
  = write "Unknown entry\n" (phdb (mem, tel)),
      otherwise

  addMember n (mem, tel) = (mem ++ [n], tel)
  doAddMember n
  = write "Okay\n" (phdb (addMember n (mem, tel))),
      if ~ member mem n
  = write "Already member\n" (phdb (mem, tel)),
      otherwise

  removeMember n (mem, tel) = (mem -- [n], ndres [n] tel)
  doRemoveMember n
  = write "Okay\n" (phdb (removeMember n (mem, tel))),
      if member mem n
  = write "Not a member\n" (phdb (mem, tel)),
      otherwise

  donothing = write "\n\n" (phdb (mem, tel))

domain :: [(*, **)] -> [*]
domain f = [ x | (x, y) <- f ]

range :: [(*, **)] -> [**]
range f = [ y | (x, y) <- f ]

image :: [(*, **)] -> [*] -> [**]
image f u = [ y | (x, y) <- f ; member u x ]

inverse :: [(*, **)] -> [(**,*)]
inverse f = [ (y, x) | (x, y) <- f ]

ndres :: [*] -> [(*, **)] -> [(*, **)]
ndres u f = [ (x, y) | (x, y) <- f ; ~ member u x ]

disp :: [string] -> string
disp x = "Empty\n", x = [ ]
       = hd x, # x = 1
       = hd x ++ "\n" ++ disp (tl x), otherwise
```

General-purpose Functions

The animation makes use of a number of general-purpose functions, namely domain, range, image, inverse, ndres and disp, which are likely to crop up over and over again if you are involved in animating several Z specifications. The function disp is slightly different from the others, so I will explain it first. It takes a list of strings and turns it into a string. If the list consists of more than one string, then newline characters are inserted between the components before it is turned into a string. This function is used in displaying a list of strings on the terminal. The other functions correspond to standard Z operators as shown in the table below, where the association list **as** corresponds to the relation F and the list **us** corresponds to the set U.

Miranda	Z
`domain as`	$\mathrm{dom}\ F$
`range as`	$\mathrm{ran}\ F$
`image as us`	$F(\!| U |\!)$
`inverse as`	$F^{\sim}$
`ndres us as`	$U \triangleleft F$

If a large number of animations were being done, it would make sense to define further general-purpose Miranda functions corresponding to the remaining standard Z operators.

Part V

Reference Manual

20

Methods of Definition

20.1 Axiomatic Description

One form that an *axiomatic description* in Z can take is

$$
\begin{array}{|l}
D \\
\hline
P
\end{array}
$$

where D is a declaration which introduces one or more global variables and P is a formula that constrains the values that can be taken by the variables introduced in D. For example, the function used in Z to construct a number range can be defined like this:

$$
\begin{array}{|l}
\_\ldots\_ : \mathbf{Z} \times \mathbf{Z} \longrightarrow \mathbf{P}\,\mathbf{Z} \\
\hline
\forall i, j : \mathbf{Z} \bullet \\
\quad i\,..\,j = \{\, n : \mathbf{Z} \mid i \leq n \wedge n \leq j \,\}
\end{array}
$$

If P is absent, the default is the formula *true*. Thus, the axiomatic description

$$
\begin{array}{|l}
Capacity : \mathbf{N}
\end{array}
$$

is equivalent to

$$
\begin{array}{|l}
Capacity : \mathbf{N} \\
\hline
true
\end{array}
$$

It is also possible to have several declarations in the top region of an axiomatic description or several formulas in the bottom region. The following definition of the functions *min* and *max* illustrates the latter possibility:

$$
\begin{array}{|l}
min, max : \mathbf{P}_1\,\mathbf{Z} \nrightarrow \mathbf{Z} \\
\hline
min = \lambda U : \mathbf{P}_1\,\mathbf{Z} \mid m \in U \wedge (\forall i : U \bullet m \leq i) \bullet m \\
max = \lambda U : \mathbf{P}_1\,\mathbf{Z} \mid m \in U \wedge (\forall i : U \bullet i \leq m) \bullet m
\end{array}
$$

The variables declared in the top region cannot have been previously declared globally and their scope extends to the end of the specification. See section 3.2.2 (p. 48) of (Spivey 1992) for more information about the topic of axiomatic description.

20.2   Generic Definition

One form that a *generic definition* can take in Z is

$$
\begin{array}{|l}
\hline\hline
[X_1, \ldots, X_n] \\
D \\
\hline
P \\
\hline
\end{array}
$$

where the X_i are the formal generic parameters which can occur in the types assigned to the identifiers in the declaration D. The formula P defines the identifiers introduced in D. For example, the operator which forms the inverse of a relation can be defined like this:

$$
\begin{array}{|l}
\hline\hline
[X, Y] \\
\_^{\sim} : (X \leftrightarrow Y) \longrightarrow (Y \leftrightarrow X) \\
\hline
\forall F : X \leftrightarrow Y \bullet \\
\quad F^{\sim} = \{\, x : X; y : Y \mid x \mapsto y \in F \bullet y \mapsto x \,\} \\
\hline
\end{array}
$$

It is also possible to have several declarations in the top region of a generic definition or several formulas in the bottom region. The following illustrates one of the possibilities:

$$
\begin{array}{|l}
\hline\hline
[X] \\
\_ \neq \_ : X \leftrightarrow X \\
\_ \notin \_ : X \leftrightarrow \mathbf{P}\, X \\
\hline
\forall x, y : X \bullet x \neq y \Longleftrightarrow \neg(x = y) \\
\forall x : X; U : \mathbf{P}\, X \bullet x \notin U \Longleftrightarrow \neg(x \in U) \\
\hline
\end{array}
$$

A frequently used special case of Z's generic definition construct is the *abbreviation definition* used for introducing—possibly generic—constants. Its general form is $\pi ==$ t where π is a pattern and t is an expression. A pattern is either something of the form $a[X_1, \ldots, X_n]$ or something of the form a, $\rho\, x$ or $x\, \omega\, y$, where a is a constant, x and y are variables, ρ is a unary prefix operator, ω is an infix binary operator and the X_i are formal generic parameters. Some examples should clarify this account. All the following are legitimate abbreviation definitions in Z:

$$\varnothing[X] == \{\, x : X \mid \textit{false} \,\},$$
$$\textit{square} == \lambda i : \mathbf{N} \bullet i * i,$$
$$\mathbf{P}_1\, X == \{\, U : \mathbf{P}\, X \mid U \neq \varnothing \,\},$$
$$X \leftrightarrow Y == \mathbf{P}(X \times Y).$$

See sections 3.2.5 (p. 50) and 3.9.2 (pp. 80–82) of (Spivey 1992) for much more information about the topics of abbreviation definition and the definition of generic constants.

20.3   Schema Definition

One version of the vertical form of a *schema* in Z is

```
┌─ S ────────────────────────────────────────────────
│  D
│  ────────────
│  P
└────────────────────────────────────────────────────
```

where S is the name of the schema, D is a declaration and P a formula. If P is absent, the default is the formula *true*. It is also possible to have several declarations in the top region or several formulas in the bottom region. The top region of the schema box is known as the *declaration-part* and the bottom region is called the *predicate-part* and the two are separated from each other by means of a short horizontal line. Usually, different basic declarations in a schema are written on separate lines—as are the formulas in the predicate-part of the schema—like this:

```
┌─ Example ──────────────────────────────────────────
│  i, j: Z
│  U, V: P Z
│  ────────────
│  i ∈ U
│  j ∈ V
│  U ∩ V = ∅
└────────────────────────────────────────────────────
```

It is possible, however, to combine several declarations and write them on a single line by separating them with semicolons. Similarly, it is possible to combine several formulas and place them on a single line by separating them with semicolons. Doing this with the schema *Example* makes it look like this:

```
┌─ Example ──────────────────────────────────────────
│  i, j: Z; U, V: P Z
│  ────────────
│  i ∈ U; j ∈ V; U ∩ V = ∅
└────────────────────────────────────────────────────
```

There is also a horizontal form of schema definition. Using this a schema T consisting of several declarations and a number of formulas can be defined in this way:

$$T \triangleq [\, D_1; D_2; \ldots; D_n \mid P_1; P_2; \ldots; P_m \,],$$

where the D_i are declarations and the P_j are formulas. Using this horizontal form of schema definition the schema *Example* could be defined like this:

$$Example \triangleq [\, i, j: \mathbf{Z}; U, V: \mathbf{P}\,\mathbf{Z} \mid i \in U; j \in V; U \cap V = \emptyset \,].$$

For more information about schemas see (Spivey 1992), pp. 29 and 49–50.

It is also possible to have *generic schemas*. One of the forms that such a schema can take is:

$$\begin{array}{|l}
\hline S[X_1, \ldots, X_n] \quad\rule{7cm}{0pt} \\
\quad D \\
\hline
\quad P \\
\hline
\end{array}$$

where each X_i can occur either on the right-hand side of a colon in D or as part of an expression which occurs on the right-hand side of a colon in the declaration D. When generic schemas are used actual parameters—which must have values that are sets—have to be substituted for the X_i. If P is absent, the default is *true* and it is also possible for there to be several declarations in the top region or several formulas in the bottom region. For more information about generic schemas see (Spivey 1992), pp. 38–39 and 79.

21

Formal Definitions

21.1 Sets

21.1.1 Relations between Sets

The relations of equality and set membership are represented in Z by means of the symbols $=$ and $\in$, respectively. They are not defined in the reference manual (Spivey 1992), but an informal account of their meaning is given on p. 68: a formula $x = y$ is true if x and y are the same object and $x \in U$ is true if x is a member of the set U. Difference and non-membership are defined straightforwardly like this:

$$
\begin{array}{l}
\underline{[X]} \\
\hline
\_ \neq \_ : X \leftrightarrow X \\
\_ \notin \_ : X \leftrightarrow \mathbf{P}\,X \\
\hline
\forall x, y : X \bullet x \neq y \iff \neg(x = y) \\
\forall x : X;\, U : \mathbf{P}\,X \bullet x \notin U \iff \neg(x \in U)
\end{array}
$$

A set U is a *subset* of a set V iff every member of U is also a member of V. A set U is a *proper subset* of a set V iff every member of U is a member of V but $U \neq V$.

$$
\begin{array}{l}
\underline{[X]} \\
\hline
\_ \subseteq \_ ,\, \_ \subset \_ : \mathbf{P}\,X \leftrightarrow \mathbf{P}\,X \\
\hline
\forall U, V : \mathbf{P}\,X \bullet \\
\qquad (U \subseteq V \iff (\forall x : X \bullet x \in U \Rightarrow x \in V))\ \wedge \\
\qquad (U \subset V \iff (U \subseteq V \wedge U \neq V))
\end{array}
$$

21.1.2 Operators on Sets

The union of two sets U and V, written $U \cup V$, denotes the set consisting of all those elements which are either in U or in V. The intersection of two sets U and V, written

$U \cap V$, denotes the set consisting of all those elements which are both in U and in V. The difference between two sets U and V, written $U \setminus V$, denotes the set consisting of all those elements of U which are not also members of V. The symmetric difference between two sets U and V, written $U \bigtriangleup V$, is the set which consists of all the elements that are in either U or V but not both. Note that symmetric difference is not part of standard Z.

$$
\begin{array}{|l}
\hline
[X] \\
\hline
{\,}_-\cup{\,}_-,{\,}_-\cap{\,}_-,{\,}_-\setminus{\,}_-,{\,}_-\bigtriangleup{\,}_-: \mathbf{P}\,X \times \mathbf{P}\,X \to \mathbf{P}\,X \\
\hline
\forall U, V : \mathbf{P}\,X \bullet \\
\quad U \cup V = \{\, x : X \mid x \in U \vee x \in V \,\} \wedge \\
\quad U \cap V = \{\, x : X \mid x \in U \wedge x \in V \,\} \wedge \\
\quad U \setminus V = \{\, x : X \mid x \in U \wedge x \notin V \,\} \wedge \\
\quad U \bigtriangleup V = \{\, x : X \mid (x \in U \wedge x \notin V) \vee (x \in V \wedge x \notin U) \,\} \\
\hline
\end{array}
$$

21.1.3 Generalized Union and Intersection

The generalized union of a set xss of sets of type $\mathbf{P}\,X$, represented as $\bigcup xss$, is the set which contains all those members of X which are in at least one member of xss. The generalized intersection of a set xss of sets of type $\mathbf{P}\,X$, represented as $\bigcap xss$, is the set which contains all those members of X which are in all of the members of xss.

$$
\begin{array}{|l}
\hline
[X] \\
\hline
\bigcup, \bigcap : \mathbf{P}(\mathbf{P}\,X) \to \mathbf{P}\,X \\
\hline
\forall xss : \mathbf{P}(\mathbf{P}\,X) \bullet \\
\quad \bigcup xss = \{\, x : X \mid (\exists xs : xss \bullet x \in xs) \,\} \wedge \\
\quad \bigcap xss = \{\, x : X \mid (\forall xs : xss \bullet x \in xs) \,\} \\
\hline
\end{array}
$$

21.1.4 Finite Sets

A *finite set* is one which cannot be put into a one-to-one and onto correspondence with a proper subset of itself. The collection of all the finite subsets of a set X is symbolized as $\mathbf{F}\,X$ and the combination of symbols $\mathbf{F}_1\,X$ represents the collection of all the finite, non-empty subsets of X.

$$
\mathbf{F}\,X == \{\, U : \mathbf{P}\,X \mid \neg \exists V : \mathbf{P}\,U \bullet V \neq U \wedge (\exists f : V \rightarrowtail\!\!\!\rightarrow U) \,\},
$$
$$
\mathbf{F}_1\,X == (\mathbf{F}\,X) \setminus \{\varnothing\}.
$$

All finite sets can be put into a one-to-one correspondence with an initial segment of the non-negative numbers, whose largest element is called the *cardinality* (or *size*) of the finite set. The cardinality operator, denoted by $\#$, is defined as follows:

$$
\begin{array}{|l}
\hline
\!\!=\![X]\!\!=\!\!\!\!=\!\!\!\!=\!\!\!\!=\!\!\!\!=\!\!\!\!=\!\!\!\!=\!\!\!\!=\!\!\!\!=\!\!\!\!=\!\!\!\!=\!\!\!\!= \\
\quad \#\colon \mathbf{F}\,X \longrightarrow \mathbf{N} \\
\hline
\quad \forall U\colon \mathbf{F}\,X \bullet \\
\qquad \#U = \mu n\colon \mathbf{N} \mid \exists f\colon U \rightarrowtail\!\!\!\rightarrow 1 \mathinner{\ldotp\ldotp} n \\
\hline
\end{array}
$$

The symbol μ used in this definition is Z's *definite description operator*. Let P be a formula. Then $\mu x\colon X \mid P$ refers to the unique object x belonging to the set X which satisfies P.

The notation $\_ \mathinner{\ldotp\ldotp} \_$ is used for a number range:

$$
\begin{array}{|l}
\hline
\quad \_\mathinner{\ldotp\ldotp}\_\colon \mathbf{Z} \times \mathbf{Z} \longrightarrow \mathbf{P}\,\mathbf{Z} \\
\hline
\quad \forall i, j\colon \mathbf{Z} \bullet \\
\qquad i \mathinner{\ldotp\ldotp} j = \{\, n\colon \mathbf{Z} \mid i \le n \wedge n \le j \,\} \\
\hline
\end{array}
$$

Note that if $i \le j$, then $\#(i \mathinner{\ldotp\ldotp} j) = j - i + 1$ and that if $i > j$, then $i \mathinner{\ldotp\ldotp} j = \varnothing$, so $\#(i \mathinner{\ldotp\ldotp} j) = 0$. These equations hold for all integers i and j—even the negative ones.

21.1.5 Smallest and Largest Elements

Let U be a non-empty set of integers. Then $min\,U$ is that integer which is the least element of U, if such an integer exists. Similarly, $max\,U$ is that integer which is the largest member of U, if such an integer exists.

$$
\begin{array}{|l}
\hline
\quad min, max\colon \mathbf{P}_1\,\mathbf{Z} \rightarrowtail \mathbf{Z} \\
\hline
\quad min = \lambda U\colon \mathbf{P}_1\,\mathbf{Z} \mid m \in U \wedge (\forall i\colon U \bullet m \le i) \bullet m \\
\quad max = \lambda U\colon \mathbf{P}_1\,\mathbf{Z} \mid m \in U \wedge (\forall i\colon U \bullet i \le m) \bullet m \\
\hline
\end{array}
$$

21.2 Relations

21.2.1 Introduction

The set of all relations between the sets X and Y is symbolized as $X \leftrightarrow Y$ and is defined like this:

$$ X \leftrightarrow Y \mathrel{==} \mathbf{P}(X \times Y). $$

Let $F\colon X \leftrightarrow Y$ be a relation. Then, as an alternative to $(x, y) \in F$, we often write $x \mapsto y \in F$. The ordered pair $x \mapsto y$ is also known as a *maplet*. When $(x, y) \in F$, it is also possible to represent this as $x \underline{F} y$, where the symbol for the relation is underlined. This is only allowed when F is an alphanumeric identifier.

21.2.2 Domains and Ranges

Let $F\colon X \leftrightarrow Y$ be a relation. Then the *domain* of F is the set of all those things in X that are related by F to at least one thing in Y and the *range* of F is the set of all those things in Y to which at least one thing in X is related by F.

$$
\begin{array}{|l}
\hline
=\![X,Y]\!=\!=\!=\!=\!=\!=\!=\!=\!=\!=\!=\!=\!= \\
\quad \mathrm{dom} \colon (X \leftrightarrow Y) \longrightarrow \mathbf{P}\,X \\
\quad \mathrm{ran} \colon (X \leftrightarrow Y) \longrightarrow \mathbf{P}\,Y \\
\hline
\quad \forall F \colon X \leftrightarrow Y \; \bullet \\
\qquad\quad \mathrm{dom}\, F = \{\, x \colon X;\, y \colon Y \mid x \mapsto y \in F \bullet x \,\} \wedge \\
\qquad\quad \mathrm{ran}\, F = \{\, x \colon X;\, y \colon Y \mid x \mapsto y \in F \bullet y \,\} \\
\hline
\end{array}
$$

21.2.3 Inversion

Let $F \colon X \leftrightarrow Y$ be a relation. Then $y \mapsto x$ is a member of the *relational inverse* of F—which is symbolized as $F^{\sim}$—iff $x \mapsto y$ is a member of F.

$$
\begin{array}{|l}
\hline
=\![X,Y]\!=\!=\!=\!=\!=\!=\!=\!=\!=\!=\!=\!=\!= \\
\quad \_^{\sim} \colon (X \leftrightarrow Y) \longrightarrow (Y \leftrightarrow X) \\
\hline
\quad \forall F \colon X \leftrightarrow Y \; \bullet \\
\qquad\quad F^{\sim} = \{\, x \colon X;\, y \colon Y \mid x \mapsto y \in F \bullet y \mapsto x \,\} \\
\hline
\end{array}
$$

21.2.4 Domain Restriction and Anti-restriction

Let $F \colon X \leftrightarrow Y$ be a relation and $U \subseteq X$. Then $x \mapsto y$ is a member of the relation which results when F has had its *domain restricted* to U iff x belongs to U and $x \mapsto y$ is a member of F. This relation is written as $U \lhd F$. Also, $x \mapsto y$ is a member of the relation which results when F has had its *domain anti-restricted* to U iff x does not belong to U and $x \mapsto y$ is a member of F. This relation is written as $U \ntriangleleft F$. Sometimes domain anti-restriction is known as *domain subtraction* or *domain corestriction*.

$$
\begin{array}{|l}
\hline
=\![X,Y]\!=\!=\!=\!=\!=\!=\!=\!=\!=\!=\!=\!=\!= \\
\quad \_\lhd\_,\_\ntriangleleft\_ \colon (\mathbf{P}\,X) \times (X \leftrightarrow Y) \longrightarrow (X \leftrightarrow Y) \\
\hline
\quad \forall U \colon \mathbf{P}\,X;\, F \colon X \leftrightarrow Y \; \bullet \\
\qquad\quad U \lhd F = \{\, x \colon X;\, y \colon Y \mid x \mapsto y \in F \wedge x \in U \bullet x \mapsto y \,\} \wedge \\
\qquad\quad U \ntriangleleft F = \{\, x \colon X;\, y \colon Y \mid x \mapsto y \in F \wedge x \notin U \bullet x \mapsto y \,\} \\
\hline
\end{array}
$$

21.2.5 Range Restriction and Anti-restriction

Let $F \colon X \leftrightarrow Y$ be a relation and $V \subseteq Y$. Then $x \mapsto y$ is a member of the relation which results when F has had its *range restricted* to V iff y belongs to V and $x \mapsto y$ is a member of F. This relation is symbolized as $F \rhd V$. Also, $x \mapsto y$ is a member of the relation which results when F has had its *range anti-restricted* to V iff y does not belong to V and $x \mapsto y$ is a member of F. This relation is written as $F \triangleright V$. Sometimes range anti-restriction is known as *range subtraction* or *range corestriction*.

$$\boxed{\begin{array}{l} \rule{0pt}{0pt}[X,Y] \\ \hline \_ \triangleright \_ , \_ \triangleright \_ : (X \leftrightarrow Y) \times (\mathbf{P}\,Y) \longrightarrow (X \leftrightarrow Y) \\ \hline \forall F: X \leftrightarrow Y; V: \mathbf{P}\,Y \bullet \\ \quad F \triangleright V = \{\, x: X; y: Y \mid x \mapsto y \in F \wedge y \in V \bullet x \mapsto y \,\} \wedge \\ \quad F \triangleright V = \{\, x: X; y: Y \mid x \mapsto y \in F \wedge y \notin V \bullet x \mapsto y \,\} \end{array}}$$

21.2.6 Composition

Let $F: X \leftrightarrow Y$ and $G: Y \leftrightarrow Z$. Then an ordered pair $x \mapsto z$ belongs to the *composition* of F with G—which is symbolized as $F \,\mathring{;}\, G$—iff there exists at least one thing in Y to which x is related by F and which, in turn, is related to z by G.

$$\boxed{\begin{array}{l} \rule{0pt}{0pt}[X,Y,Z] \\ \hline \_ \,\mathring{;}\, \_ : (X \leftrightarrow Y) \times (Y \leftrightarrow Z) \longrightarrow (X \leftrightarrow Z) \\ \hline \forall F: X \leftrightarrow Y; G: Y \leftrightarrow Z \bullet \\ \quad F \,\mathring{;}\, G = \{\, x: X; z: Z \mid (\exists y: Y \bullet x \mapsto y \in F \wedge y \mapsto z \in G) \bullet x \mapsto z \,\} \end{array}}$$

We can write $G \circ F$ for $F \,\mathring{;}\, G$. The operator $\circ$ is sometimes known as *backward relational composition*.

21.2.7 Image

Let $F: X \leftrightarrow Y$ and $U \subseteq X$. Then the *relational image* of a set U through the relation F (sometimes called the *F-image* of U), which is written $F(\!|U|\!)$, is the set of all those elements of the range of F to which F maps elements of U. In other words, it is the set of all those objects y to which F relates some member x of U. The notion of the relational image of a set through a relation can be thought of as a generalization of the notion of function application.

$$\boxed{\begin{array}{l} \rule{0pt}{0pt}[X,Y] \\ \hline \_ (\!|\_|\!): (X \leftrightarrow Y) \times (\mathbf{P}\,X) \longrightarrow (\mathbf{P}\,Y) \\ \hline \forall F: X \leftrightarrow Y; U: \mathbf{P}\,X \bullet \\ \quad F(\!|U|\!) = \{\, y: Y \mid \exists x: U \bullet x \mapsto y \in F \,\} \end{array}}$$

21.2.8 Iteration and Closures

Let $F: X \leftrightarrow X$ be a relation. Then *iter* $i\,F$, where i is a positive whole number, is the result of composing F with itself $i - 1$ times. When i is negative, then *iter* $i\,F$ is the result of composing $F^\sim$ with itself $-(i+1)$ times. When i is zero, then $iter\ i\ F$ is id X. It is more common to write F^i for $iter\ i\ F$, where $i \in \mathbf{Z}$.

$$\boxed{\begin{array}{l} \underline{[X]}\\[2pt] iter\colon \mathbf{Z} \longrightarrow (X \leftrightarrow X) \longrightarrow (X \leftrightarrow X)\\[6pt] \hline\\[-6pt] \forall F\colon X \leftrightarrow X \bullet\\ \qquad iter\ 0\ F = \mathrm{id}\ X \wedge\\ \qquad (\forall i\colon \mathbf{N} \bullet iter(i+1)\,F = F\,;(iter\ i\ F)) \wedge\\ \qquad (\forall i\colon \mathbf{N} \bullet iter(-i)\,F = iter\ i\,(F^\sim)) \end{array}}$$

Let $F\colon X \leftrightarrow X$ be a relation. Then F^+ is its *transitive closure* and F^* is its *reflexive-transitive closure*. The ordered pair $x \mapsto y$, where $x, y \in X$, is a member of F^+ if for some positive whole number i the pair $x \mapsto y$ is a member of F^i. The ordered pair $x \mapsto y$, where $x, y \in X$, is a member of F^* if for some non-negative whole number i the pair $x \mapsto y$ is a member of F^i.

$$\boxed{\begin{array}{l} \underline{[X]}\\[2pt] \_^+, \_^*\colon (X \leftrightarrow X) \longrightarrow (X \leftrightarrow X)\\[6pt] \hline\\[-6pt] \forall F\colon X \leftrightarrow X \bullet\\ \qquad F^+ = \bigcap\{\,G\colon X \leftrightarrow X \mid F \subseteq G \wedge G\,;G \subseteq G\,\} \wedge\\ \qquad F^* = \bigcap\{\,G\colon X \leftrightarrow X \mid \mathrm{id}\ X \subseteq G \wedge F \subseteq G \wedge G\,;G \subseteq G\,\} \end{array}}$$

21.2.9   Overriding

Let $F, G\colon X \leftrightarrow Y$ be relations. Then an ordered pair $x \mapsto y$, where $x \in X$ and $y \in Y$, is a member of $F \oplus G$ when either $x \mapsto y$ is in G or when $x \mapsto y$ is in F and $x \mapsto y$ is not in G. $F \oplus G$ can be read as 'F overridden by G'. Note that in the first edition of Spivey's reference manual $\oplus$ was only defined in the case when its arguments were functions, but in the second edition the definition was extended to allow the arguments to $\oplus$ to be relations.

$$\boxed{\begin{array}{l} \underline{[X,Y]}\\[2pt] \_ \oplus \_\colon (X \leftrightarrow Y) \times (X \leftrightarrow Y) \longrightarrow (X \leftrightarrow Y)\\[6pt] \hline\\[-6pt] \forall F, G\colon X \leftrightarrow Y \bullet\\ \qquad F \oplus G = ((\mathrm{dom}\ G) \triangleleft F) \cup G \end{array}}$$

21.3   Functions

21.3.1   Possibly Non-finite Functions

A *partial function* from X to Y is a relation between X and Y which maps each element of its domain to a single element of its range. The set of all partial functions from X to Y is symbolized as $X \nrightarrow Y$ and is defined like this:

$$X \nrightarrow Y == \{\, f : X \leftrightarrow Y \mid (\forall x : X;\, y, z : Y \bullet x \mapsto y \in f \wedge x \mapsto z \in f \Rightarrow y = z)\,\}.$$

An *injective function* is one whose inverse is also a function. A *partial injective function* or a *partial injection* is a partial function whose inverse is also a function. The set of all partial injections from X to Y can be defined like this:

$$X \rightarrowtail\mkern-14mu\nrightarrow Y == \{\, f : X \nrightarrow Y \mid f^{\sim} \in Y \nrightarrow X\,\}.$$

A *surjective function* or a *surjection* from X to Y or a function from X *onto* Y is one whose range is the whole of Y. A *partial surjective function* or *partial surjection* from X to Y is a partial function from X to Y whose range is the whole of Y. The set of all partial surjections from X to Y is defined like this:

$$X \nrightarrow\mkern-14mu\rightarrow Y == \{\, f : X \nrightarrow Y \mid \operatorname{ran} f = Y\,\}.$$

A *partial surjective injection* or a *partial injective surjection* is a partial function which is both one-to-one and onto. There is no standard Z symbol for the collection of all such functions from X to Y, but I suggest symbolizing this as $X \rightarrowtail\mkern-14mu\rightarrow Y$. The following is a possible definition of this:

$$X \rightarrowtail\mkern-14mu\rightarrow Y == \{\, f : X \nrightarrow Y \mid \operatorname{ran} f = Y \wedge f^{\sim} \in Y \nrightarrow X\,\}.$$

A *total function* from X to Y is a partial function from X to Y whose domain is the whole of X. The set of all total functions from X to Y is symbolized as $X \longrightarrow Y$ and is defined like this:

$$X \longrightarrow Y == \{\, f : X \nrightarrow Y \mid \operatorname{dom} f = X\,\}.$$

A *total injective function* is a total function whose inverse is also a function. The set of all total injections from X to Y can be defined in this way:

$$X \rightarrowtail Y == \{\, f : X \longrightarrow Y \mid f^{\sim} \in Y \nrightarrow X\,\}.$$

A *total surjective function* from X to Y is a total function from X to Y whose range is the whole of Y. The set of all total surjections from X to Y can be defined like this:

$$X \longrightarrow\mkern-18mu\rightarrow Y == \{\, f : X \longrightarrow Y \mid \operatorname{ran} f = Y\,\}.$$

A function from X to Y is a *bijection* or is said to be a *one-to-one correspondence* if it is a total surjective function from X to Y which is also a total injective function. The set of all bijections from X to Y can be defined in this way:

$$X \rightarrowtail\mkern-14mu\rightarrow Y == (X \longrightarrow\mkern-18mu\rightarrow Y) \cap (X \rightarrowtail Y).$$

21.3.2 Finite Functions

A *finite partial function* from X to Y is a partial function from X to Y whose domain is a finite subset of X. The set of all finite partial functions from X to Y is symbolized as $X \nrightarrow Y$ and is defined like this:

$$X \nrightarrow Y == \{ f : X \nrightarrow Y \mid \operatorname{dom} f \in \mathbf{F}\, X \},$$

where $\mathbf{F}\, X$ means the set of all the finite subsets of X. A *finite injective function* is a finite function whose inverse is also a function. The set of all finite partial injections from X to Y can be defined like this:

$$X \rightarrowtail\!\!\!\nrightarrow Y == (X \nrightarrow Y) \cap (X \rightarrowtail Y).$$

21.3.3 Lambda Abstraction

Do not confuse Z's λ-notation with the λ-calculus. The λ-notation in Z is just a variant way of defining a function.

$$\lambda x : X \mid P \bullet t == \{ x : X \mid P \bullet x \mapsto t \},$$
$$\lambda x_1 : X_1 ; \ldots ; x_n : X_n \mid P \bullet t == \{ x_1 : X_1 ; \ldots ; x_n : X_n \mid P \bullet (x_1, \ldots, x_n) \mapsto t \},$$

where P is a formula and t is a term.

21.4 Sequences

21.4.1 Basic Definitions

Given a set X, the *finite sequences* made up of elements drawn from X are the finite partial functions from $\mathbf{N}$ to X whose domains are initial segments of the positive natural numbers. The type $\operatorname{iseq} X$ of *injective* sequences consists of all those sequences that do not contain repetitions.

$$\operatorname{seq} X == \{ f : \mathbf{N} \nrightarrow X \mid \operatorname{dom}\, f = 1 \,..\, \#f \},$$
$$\operatorname{seq}_1 X == (\operatorname{seq} X) \setminus \{\varnothing\},$$
$$\operatorname{iseq} X == (\operatorname{seq} X) \cap (\mathbf{N} \rightarrowtail\!\!\!\nrightarrow X).$$

21.4.2 Sequence Constructors

Let σ and τ be sequences. Then $\sigma \frown \tau$ is the sequence that results when all the elements of τ are stuck on the end of σ in the same order as they occur in τ. The sequence $\sigma \frown \tau$ is known as the *concatenation* of σ and τ.

$$
\begin{array}{l}
=\!\![X]\!\!=\!\!=\!\!=\!\!=\!\!=\!\!=\!\!=\!\!=\!\!=\!\!=\!\!= \\
\hline
\_ \frown \_ : (\operatorname{seq} X) \times (\operatorname{seq} X) \longrightarrow (\operatorname{seq} X) \\
\hline
\forall \sigma, \tau : \operatorname{seq} X \bullet \\
\quad\quad \sigma \frown \tau = \sigma \cup \{ n : \operatorname{dom} \tau \bullet n + \#\sigma \mapsto \tau(n) \}
\end{array}
$$

Let xss be a sequence whose elements are themselves sequences. Then $^\frown\!/\,xss$ is the sequence that results when the individual elements of xss are concatenated together. Informally, $^\frown\!/\,xss = xss(1)\,^\frown xss(2)\,^\frown \ldots\, ^\frown xss(\#xss)$. The operator $^\frown\!/$ is known as the *distributed concatenation operator*.

$$
\begin{array}{l}
\rule{0pt}{0pt}[X]\rule{4cm}{0.4pt} \\
\quad ^\frown\!/ : \mathrm{seq}(\mathrm{seq}\,X) \longrightarrow \mathrm{seq}\,X \\
\rule{4cm}{0.4pt} \\
\quad ^\frown\!/\,\langle\,\rangle = \langle\,\rangle \\
\quad \forall \sigma\colon \mathrm{seq}\,X \bullet\ ^\frown\!/\langle\sigma\rangle = \sigma \\
\quad \forall \sigma, \tau\colon \mathrm{seq}(\mathrm{seq}\,X) \bullet \\
\qquad ^\frown\!/(\sigma\,^\frown \tau) = (^\frown\!/\,\sigma)\,^\frown (^\frown\!/\,\tau)
\end{array}
$$

21.4.3 Sequence Destructors

Let σ be a non-empty sequence. Then *head* σ is the first element of σ, *last* σ is the last element of σ, *front* σ is the sequence that results when the last element of σ is removed and *tail* σ is the sequence that results when the first element of σ is removed.

$$
\begin{array}{l}
\rule{0pt}{0pt}[X]\rule{4cm}{0.4pt} \\
\quad head, last\colon \mathrm{seq}_1\,X \longrightarrow X \\
\quad front, tail\colon \mathrm{seq}_1\,X \longrightarrow \mathrm{seq}\,X \\
\rule{4cm}{0.4pt} \\
\quad head = \lambda \sigma\colon \mathrm{seq}_1\,X \bullet \sigma(1)\ \wedge \\
\quad last = \lambda \sigma\colon \mathrm{seq}_1\,X \bullet \sigma(\#\sigma)\ \wedge \\
\quad front = \lambda \sigma\colon \mathrm{seq}_1\,X \bullet (1 \mathrel{..} \#\sigma - 1) \vartriangleleft \sigma\ \wedge \\
\quad tail = \lambda \sigma\colon \mathrm{seq}_1\,X \bullet (\{0\} \vartriangleleft succ)\,\mathbin{\raisebox{0.5pt}{\fontsize{9}{9}\selectfont$\circ$}}\,\sigma
\end{array}
$$

Let σ be a sequence and n a non-negative number. Then σ *after* n is the sequence which results when the first n elements of σ are removed and σ *for* n is the sequence which results when every element in σ after the nth is removed.

$$
\begin{array}{l}
\rule{0pt}{0pt}[X]\rule{4cm}{0.4pt} \\
\quad \_\ after\ \_,\_\ for\ \_\colon (\mathrm{seq}\,X) \times \mathbf{N} \longrightarrow (\mathrm{seq}\,X) \\
\rule{4cm}{0.4pt} \\
\quad \forall \sigma\colon \mathrm{seq}\,X;\, n\colon \mathbf{N} \bullet \\
\qquad \sigma\ after\ n = (\{0\} \vartriangleleft succ^n)\,\mathbin{\raisebox{0.5pt}{\fontsize{9}{9}\selectfont$\circ$}}\,\sigma\ \wedge \\
\qquad \sigma\ for\ n = 1 \mathrel{..} n \vartriangleleft \sigma
\end{array}
$$

It is sometimes useful to have curried versions of *after* and *for*. These are known as *drop* and *take*.

$$
\begin{array}{l}
\rule{0pt}{0pt}[X]\rule{4cm}{0.4pt} \\
\quad drop, take\colon \mathbf{N} \longrightarrow \mathrm{seq}\,X \longrightarrow \mathrm{seq}\,X \\
\rule{4cm}{0.4pt} \\
\quad drop = \lambda n\colon \mathbf{N} \bullet (\lambda \sigma\colon \mathrm{seq}\,X \bullet \sigma\ after\ n)\ \wedge \\
\quad take = \lambda n\colon \mathbf{N} \bullet (\lambda \sigma\colon \mathrm{seq}\,X \bullet \sigma\ for\ n)
\end{array}
$$

Note that none of the functions *after*, *for*, *drop* or *take* are part of standard Z.

Let $\sigma: \text{seq } X$ and $V \subseteq X$. Then $\sigma \upharpoonright V$ is the sequence whose elements occur in the set V and the order in which they occur in $\sigma \upharpoonright V$ is the same as that in which they occur in σ. The symbol $\upharpoonright$ is known as the *filtering operator*.

$$
\begin{array}{l}
\underline{\hspace{0.3em}[X]\hspace{0.3em}} \\
\_ \upharpoonright \_ : \text{seq } X \times \mathbf{P} X \longrightarrow \text{seq } X \\
\hline
\forall V: \mathbf{P} X \bullet \\
\quad \langle\,\rangle \upharpoonright V = \langle\,\rangle \wedge \\
\quad (\forall x: X \bullet \\
\qquad (x \in V \Rightarrow \langle x \rangle \upharpoonright V = \langle x \rangle) \wedge \\
\qquad (x \notin V \Rightarrow \langle x \rangle \upharpoonright V = \langle\,\rangle)) \wedge \\
\quad (\forall \sigma, \tau: \text{seq } X \bullet \\
\qquad (\sigma \,\widehat{}\, \tau) \upharpoonright V = (\sigma \upharpoonright V) \,\widehat{}\, (\tau \upharpoonright V))
\end{array}
$$

Let $U \subseteq \mathbf{N}_1$ and $\sigma: \text{seq } X$. Then $U \uparrow \sigma$ is that sequence of elements of σ which occur at a position in σ whose index occurs in the set U. The symbol $\uparrow$ is known as the *extraction operator*.

$$
\begin{array}{l}
\underline{\hspace{0.3em}[X]\hspace{0.3em}} \\
\_ \uparrow \_ : \mathbf{P} \mathbf{N}_1 \times \text{seq } X \longrightarrow \text{seq } X \\
\hline
\forall U: \mathbf{P} \mathbf{N}_1 \bullet \\
\quad U \uparrow \langle\,\rangle = \langle\,\rangle \wedge \\
\quad (\forall x: X \bullet \\
\qquad (1 \in U \Rightarrow U \uparrow \langle x \rangle = \langle x \rangle) \wedge \\
\qquad (1 \notin U \Rightarrow U \uparrow \langle x \rangle = \langle\,\rangle)) \wedge \\
\quad (\forall \sigma, \tau: \text{seq } X \bullet \\
\qquad U \uparrow (\sigma \,\widehat{}\, \tau) = (U \uparrow \sigma) \,\widehat{}\, (U \uparrow \tau))
\end{array}
$$

21.4.4   Reversing a Sequence

Let σ be a sequence. Then the sequence *rev* σ contains exactly the same elements as does σ, but they occur in reverse order.

$$
\begin{array}{l}
\underline{\hspace{0.3em}[X]\hspace{0.3em}} \\
rev \_ : (\text{seq } X) \longrightarrow (\text{seq } X) \\
\hline
\forall \sigma: \text{seq } X \bullet \\
\quad rev \, \sigma = \lambda n: \text{dom } \sigma \bullet \sigma(\#\sigma - n + 1)
\end{array}
$$

21.4.5   Disjointness and Partitioning

Let f be an indexed set of sets. Then f is a member of **disjoint** f if each pair of sets $f(x)$ and $f(y)$, where x and y are distinct members of dom f, have no elements in common.

$$\boxed{\begin{array}{l} [I, X] \\ \hline \text{disjoint } \_: \mathbf{P}(I \to\!\!\!\!\to \mathbf{P}\,X) \\ \hline \forall f: I \to\!\!\!\!\to \mathbf{P}\,X \bullet \\ \quad (\text{disjoint } f \Longleftrightarrow (\forall x, y: \operatorname{dom} f \mid x \neq y \bullet f(x) \cap f(y) = \varnothing)) \end{array}}$$

Let $f: I \to\!\!\!\!\to \mathbf{P}\,X$ be an indexed set of sets and let $U \subseteq X$. Then f *partitions* U if f is a member of **disjoint** f and the generalized union of the set consisting of all the sets $f(x)$, where $x \in \operatorname{dom} f$, is the partitioned set U.

$$\boxed{\begin{array}{l} [I, X] \\ \hline \_ \text{ partition } \_: (I \to\!\!\!\!\to \mathbf{P}\,X) \leftrightarrow \mathbf{P}\,X \\ \hline \forall f: I \to\!\!\!\!\to \mathbf{P}\,X; U: \mathbf{P}\,X \bullet \\ \quad (f \text{ partition } U \Longleftrightarrow \text{disjoint } f \wedge \bigcup\{\, x: \operatorname{dom} f \bullet f(x)\,\} = U) \end{array}}$$

21.5 Bags

21.5.1 Basic Definitions

A bag is a collection of objects in which the number of times an object occurs is significant. The type of all bags of elements drawn from X is denoted by bag X. This is defined thus:

$$\operatorname{bag} X == X \to\!\!\!\!\to \mathbf{N}_1 \,.$$

21.5.2 Bag Manipulating Operators

Applied to a bag L and an object x the function *count* returns the number of times that x occurs in L. *count* $L\,x$ is also represented as $L \natural x$. The symbol $\otimes$ represents bag scaling. Let i be a non-negative number and L a bag. Then the number of times that an object occurs in the bag $i \otimes L$ is i times the number of times that it occurs in L.

$$\boxed{\begin{array}{l} [X] \\ \hline \textit{count}: \operatorname{bag} X \rightarrowtail\!\!\!\!\to (X \longrightarrow \mathbf{N}) \\ \_ \otimes \_: \mathbf{N} \times \operatorname{bag} X \longrightarrow \operatorname{bag} X \\ \hline \forall x: X; L: \operatorname{bag} X \bullet \\ \quad \textit{count } L = (\lambda x: X \bullet 0) \oplus L \\ \forall i: \mathbf{N}; L: \operatorname{bag} X; x: X \bullet \\ \quad \textit{count}(i \otimes L)\, x = i * \textit{count } L\, x \end{array}}$$

The relation $x \sqsubseteq L$ holds if *count* $L\,x > 0$. It means that x occurs in L at least once. The sub-bag relation is symbolized by the sign $\sqsubseteq$. If the bags L and M are both of the same type, then L is a *sub-bag* of M if each element of L occurs in M and the number of times that it occurs in M is at least the same as the number of times that it occurs in L.

$$\begin{array}{|l}
\hline [X] \\\hline
\_ \mathrel{\mathsf{E}} \_ : X \leftrightarrow \mathrm{bag}\, X \\
\_ \sqsubseteq \_ : \mathrm{bag}\, X \leftrightarrow \mathrm{bag}\, X \\
\hline
\forall x\colon X;\, L\colon \mathrm{bag}\, X \bullet \\
\quad x \mathrel{\mathsf{E}} L \iff x \in \mathrm{dom}\, L \\
\forall L, M\colon \mathrm{bag}\, X \bullet \\
\quad L \sqsubseteq M \iff (\forall x\colon X \bullet count\, L\, x \le count\, M\, x) \\
\hline
\end{array}$$

The union of bags is represented by $\uplus$ and $\biguplus$ represents bag difference. Bag union is also known as *bag sum*. The number of times an object occurs in $L \uplus M$, where L and M are bags of the same type, is the sum of the number of times that it occurs in L and in M. If the number of times that an object occurs in L is greater than or equal to the number of times that it occurs in M, then the number of times it occurs in $L \biguplus M$ is the number of times it occurs L minus the number of times that it occurs in M; otherwise, that object does not occur in $L \biguplus M$.

$$\begin{array}{|l}
\hline [X] \\\hline
\_ \uplus \_,\, \_ \biguplus \_ : \mathrm{bag}\, X \times \mathrm{bag}\, X \longrightarrow \mathrm{bag}\, X \\
\hline
\forall L, M\colon \mathrm{bag}\, X;\, x\colon X \bullet \\
\quad count(L \uplus M)\, x = count\, L\, x + count\, M\, x \land \\
\quad count(L \biguplus M)\, x = max\{(count\, L\, x - count\, M\, x), 0\} \\
\hline
\end{array}$$

The pairwise minimum of two bags is represented by the symbol $\sqcap$ and the symbol $\sqcup$ represents the pairwise maximum of two bags. Let $L, M\colon \mathrm{bag}\, X$ be bags, let x be a member of X and let $l, m\colon \mathbf{N}$ be non-negative numbers such that $l = count\, L\, x$ and $m = count\, M\, x$. Then the number of times that x occurs in $L \sqcap M$ is the lesser of l and m and the number of times that x occurs in $L \sqcup M$ is the greater of l and m. Note that neither $\sqcap$ nor $\sqcup$ is a part of standard Z.

$$\begin{array}{|l}
\hline [X] \\\hline
\_ \sqcap \_,\, \_ \sqcup \_ : \mathrm{bag}\, X \times \mathrm{bag}\, X \longrightarrow \mathrm{bag}\, X \\
\hline
\forall L, M\colon \mathrm{bag}\, X;\, x\colon X \bullet \\
\quad count(L \sqcap M)\, x = min\{count\, L\, x, count\, M\, x\} \land \\
\quad count(L \sqcup M)\, x = max\{count\, L\, x, count\, M\, x\} \\
\hline
\end{array}$$

Let σ be a sequence. Then *items* σ is the bag in which each element x appears exactly as often as x appears in σ.

$$\begin{array}{|l}
\hline [X] \\\hline
items\, \_ : \mathrm{seq}\, X \longrightarrow \mathrm{bag}\, X \\
\hline
\forall \sigma\colon \mathrm{seq}\, X;\, x\colon X \bullet \\
\quad count(items\, \sigma)\, x = \#\{i\colon \mathrm{dom}\, \sigma \mid \sigma i = x\} \\
\hline
\end{array}$$

The symbols ♯, ⊗, ∈, ⊑ and ⊎ were introduced in the second edition of Spivey's reference manual. They do not appear in (Spivey 1989). See (Spivey 1992, pp. 124–126) for additional information about them. Note that the symbol ∈ replaces 'in'.

22

Rules and Obligations

22.1 First-order Logic

There are many ways of formalizing logic. In this book I have used a single-conclusion sequent calculus in order to present formal proofs. A *sequent* in such a calculus is an ordered pair made up out of a set of formulas, known as the *premises* of the sequent, and a single formula which is the *conclusion* of the sequent. Such a sequent is written $\Gamma \mapsto A$, where Γ is the set of premises and A is the conclusion.

22.1.1 Start Sequents

In order for a tree proof to be correctly constructed every leaf node must be an instance of a valid start sequent. Anything of the form $A \mapsto A$ is a primitive start sequent. When we are dealing with identity, then anything of the form $\mapsto t = t$, where t is a term, is also a primitive start sequent.[1]

22.1.2 Themata

A *thema* in the sequent calculus is a structured entity consisting of one or more *input sequents* and an *output sequent*. Themata are also known as *thematic rules* or simply as *rules* when there is little possibility of confusing them with other kinds of rule. Themata are written in the following way:

$$\underbrace{\overbrace{\Gamma_1 \mapsto A_1}^{\text{first input sequent}} \quad \cdots \quad \overbrace{\Gamma_n \mapsto A_n}^{n\text{th input sequent}}}_{} \quad name$$
$$\underbrace{\Delta \mapsto B}_{\text{output sequent}}$$

Think of this as a mini-tree with n leaves and a root. Each leaf is an input sequent and the root is the output sequent. In this book the name of the thematic rule is written to the right of the horizontal line which separates the input sequents from the output

---

[1] Further primitive start sequents will be needed when we come to formalize Floyd–Hoare logic as a single-conclusion sequent calculus.

sequent. Let $\heartsuit$ be an arbitrary two-place connective, then an *elimination* rule for $\heartsuit$ is one in which $\heartsuit$ appears in the conclusion of at least one of the input sequents to the rule and $\heartsuit$ does not occur in the conclusion of the output sequent of the rule. An *introduction* rule for $\heartsuit$ is one in which $\heartsuit$ does not appear in the conclusion of any of the input sequents to the rule, but $\heartsuit$ does occur in the conclusion of the output sequent of the rule.

Conjunction   There are two elimination rules associated with conjunction:

$$\frac{\Gamma \;\mapsto\; A \wedge B}{\Gamma \;\mapsto\; A,} \; \wedge\text{-}elim_1 \qquad \frac{\Gamma \;\mapsto\; A \wedge B}{\Gamma \;\mapsto\; B.} \; \wedge\text{-}elim_2$$

Conjunction has a single introduction rule:

$$\frac{\Gamma \;\mapsto\; A \quad \Delta \;\mapsto\; B}{\Gamma, \Delta \;\mapsto\; A \wedge B.} \; \wedge\text{-}int$$

Disjunction   There is one elimination rule associated with disjunction:

$$\frac{\Gamma \;\mapsto\; A \vee B \quad \Delta, A \;\mapsto\; C \quad \Sigma, B \;\mapsto\; C}{\Gamma, \Delta, \Sigma \;\mapsto\; C.} \; \vee\text{-}elim$$

There are two introduction rules for disjunction:

$$\frac{\Gamma \;\mapsto\; A}{\Gamma \;\mapsto\; A \vee B,} \; \vee\text{-}int_1 \qquad \frac{\Gamma \;\mapsto\; B}{\Gamma \;\mapsto\; A \vee B.} \; \vee\text{-}int_2$$

Implication   There is one elimination rule associated with implication:

$$\frac{\Gamma \;\mapsto\; A \quad \Delta \;\mapsto\; A \Rightarrow B}{\Gamma, \Delta \;\mapsto\; B.} \; \Rightarrow\text{-}elim$$

There is one introduction rule associated with implication:

$$\frac{\Gamma \;\mapsto\; B}{\Gamma \setminus \{A\} \;\mapsto\; A \Rightarrow B.} \; \Rightarrow\text{-}int$$

The formula A can occur in the set of premises Γ, but it does not have to.

Bi-implication   The elimination rules for bi-implication allow us to change them into implications:

$$\frac{\Gamma \;\mapsto\; A \Longleftrightarrow B}{\Gamma \;\mapsto\; A \Rightarrow B,} \; \Longleftrightarrow\text{-}elim_1 \qquad \frac{\Gamma \;\mapsto\; A \Longleftrightarrow B}{\Gamma \;\mapsto\; B \Rightarrow A.} \; \Longleftrightarrow\text{-}elim_2$$

There is a single introduction rule for bi-implication:

$$\frac{\Gamma \;\mapsto\; A \Rightarrow B \quad \Delta \;\mapsto\; B \Rightarrow A}{\Gamma, \Delta \;\mapsto\; A \Longleftrightarrow B.} \; \Longleftrightarrow\text{-}int$$

Negation, *false* **and** *true*   Negation has a single elimination rule:

$$\frac{\Gamma \mapsto A \quad \Delta \mapsto \neg A}{\Gamma, \Delta \mapsto false.} \; \neg\text{-}elim$$

Negation has a single introduction rule:

$$\frac{\Gamma, A \mapsto false}{\Gamma \mapsto \neg A.} \; \neg\text{-}int$$

The introduction and elimination rules for negation are easy to remember if you make use of the fact that $\neg A$ is syntactically equivalent to $A \Rightarrow false$. So, they can be seen as special cases of the introduction and elimination rules for implication.

Associated with negation there is also a double negation elimination rule:

$$\frac{\Gamma \mapsto \neg\neg A}{\Gamma \mapsto A.} \; \neg\neg\text{-}elim$$

The next rule involves the always false proposition *false*. It is known as *false* elimination:

$$\frac{\Gamma \mapsto false}{\Gamma \mapsto A.} \; false\text{-}elim$$

The final two primitive rules of the propositional calculus allow us to eliminate and introduce the constant formula *true*.

$$\frac{\Gamma \mapsto true}{\Gamma \mapsto \neg false,} \; true\text{-}elim \qquad \frac{\Gamma \mapsto \neg false}{\Gamma \mapsto true.} \; true\text{-}int$$

Universal Quantifier   There is one elimination rule associated with the universal quantifier:

$$\frac{\Gamma \mapsto \forall x\!:\! X \bullet A}{\Gamma \mapsto A[t/x].} \; \forall\text{-}elim$$

Here, t is any term of the same type as x. The notation $A[t/x]$ stands for that formula which is obtained by substituting t for all free occurrences of x in A.

There is a single introduction rule for the universal quantifier:

$$\frac{\Gamma \mapsto A}{\Gamma \mapsto \forall x\!:\! X \bullet A[x/a].} \; \forall\text{-}int$$

Here, x is a variable and a a constant of the same type which does not occur in Γ.

Restricted Universal Quantifier   The elimination and introduction rules for the restricted universal quantifier are as follows:

$$\frac{\Gamma \mapsto \forall D \mid P \bullet Q}{\Gamma \mapsto \forall D \bullet P \Rightarrow Q,} \; \forall\text{-}res\text{-}elim \qquad \frac{\Gamma \mapsto \forall D \bullet P \Rightarrow Q}{\Gamma \mapsto \forall D \mid P \bullet Q,} \; \forall\text{-}res\text{-}int$$

where D is a declaration and P and Q are formulas.

Existential Quantifier   There is one elimination rule associated with the existential quantifier:

$$\frac{\Gamma \;\mapsto\; \exists x\colon X \bullet A \quad \Delta, A[a/x] \;\mapsto\; C}{\Gamma, \Delta \;\mapsto\; C.} \;\; \exists\text{-}elim$$

Here, a is a constant—of the same type as x—which must not occur in Γ, Δ, $\exists x\colon X \bullet A$ or C.

There is one introduction rule associated with the existential quantifier:

$$\frac{\Gamma \;\mapsto\; A[t/x]}{\Gamma \;\mapsto\; \exists x\colon X \bullet A.} \;\; \exists\text{-}int$$

Here, t is a term and x a variable of the same type.

Restricted Existential Quantifier   The elimination and introduction rules for the restricted existential quantifier are as follows:

$$\frac{\Gamma \;\mapsto\; \exists D \mid P \bullet Q}{\Gamma \;\mapsto\; \exists D \bullet P \wedge Q,} \;\; \exists\text{-}res\text{-}elim \qquad \frac{\Gamma \;\mapsto\; \exists D \bullet P \wedge Q}{\Gamma \;\mapsto\; \exists D \mid P \bullet Q,} \;\; \exists\text{-}res\text{-}int$$

where D is a declaration and P and Q are formulas.

Identity   The elimination rule for identity is:

$$\frac{\Gamma \;\mapsto\; A \quad \Delta \;\mapsto\; t = u}{\Gamma, \Delta \;\mapsto\; B.} \;\; =\text{-}elim$$

Here, t and u are any terms of the same type and B is like A except that u has been substituted for t one or more times. There is no need to substitute u for *all* occurrences of t.

As already mentioned, the way in which the identity sign is introduced into a tree proof is by allowing leaf nodes to have the form $\mapsto t = t$, where t is any term. This start sequent is known as $=$-*int*.

One-point Rules   The one-point elimination and introduction rules involving the universal quantifier are as follows:

$$\frac{\Gamma \;\mapsto\; \forall x\colon X \bullet x = t \Rightarrow P}{\Gamma \;\mapsto\; P[t/x],} \;\; \forall\text{-}one\text{-}elim \qquad \frac{\Gamma \;\mapsto\; P[t/x]}{\Gamma \;\mapsto\; \forall x\colon X \bullet x = t \Rightarrow P,} \;\; \forall\text{-}one\text{-}int$$

where x is a variable that occurs free in P and t is a term of the same type which does not contain any free occurrences of x.

The one-point elimination and introduction rules involving the existential quantifier are as follows:

$$\frac{\Gamma \;\mapsto\; \exists x\colon X \bullet x = t \wedge P}{\Gamma \;\mapsto\; P[t/x],} \;\; \exists\text{-}one\text{-}elim \qquad \frac{\Gamma \;\mapsto\; P[t/x]}{\Gamma \;\mapsto\; \exists x\colon X \bullet x = t \wedge P,} \;\; \exists\text{-}one\text{-}int$$

where x is a variable that occurs free in P and t is a term of the same type which does not contain any free occurrences of x.

22.2 Reasoning about Sets

Equality   The *set equality axiom* is the formula

$$\forall U, V : \mathbf{P}\, X \bullet U = V \iff \forall x : X \bullet x \in U \iff x \in V$$

and the following are the elimination and introduction rules for set equality:

$$\frac{\Gamma \mapsto U = V}{\Gamma \mapsto \forall x : X \bullet x \in U \iff x \in V,} \; \textit{seteq-elim}$$

$$\frac{\Gamma \mapsto \forall x : X \bullet x \in U \iff x \in V}{\Gamma \mapsto U = V.} \; \textit{seteq-int}$$

Enumeration   The *set enumeration axiom* is the formula

$$\forall x, y_1, y_2, \ldots, y_n : X \bullet (x \in \{y_1, y_2, \ldots, y_n\} \iff (x = y_1 \lor x = y_2 \lor \ldots \lor x = y_n))$$

and the following are the elimination and introduction rules for set enumeration:

$$\frac{\Gamma \mapsto x \in \{y_1, y_2, \ldots, y_n\}}{\Gamma \mapsto x = y_1 \lor x = y_2 \lor \ldots \lor x = y_n,} \; \textit{setenum-elim}$$

$$\frac{\Gamma \mapsto x = y_1 \lor x = y_2 \lor \ldots \lor x = y_n}{\Gamma \mapsto x \in \{y_1, y_2, \ldots, y_n\}.} \; \textit{setenum-int}$$

Comprehension   The *set comprehension axiom* is the formula

$$\forall x : X \bullet (x \in \{D \mid P \bullet t\} \iff \exists D \mid P \bullet t = x),$$

where D is a declaration, P a formula, x is not declared in D and t is a term of the same type as x. The following are the elimination and introduction rules for set comprehension:

$$\frac{\Gamma \mapsto x \in \{D \mid P \bullet t\}}{\Gamma \mapsto \exists D \mid P \bullet t = x,} \; \textit{setcomp-elim} \qquad \frac{\Gamma \mapsto \exists D \mid P \bullet t = x}{\Gamma \mapsto x \in \{D \mid P \bullet t\}.} \; \textit{setcomp-int}$$

Empty Set   The *empty set axiom* is the formula $\forall x : X \bullet x \notin \varnothing[X]$.

Power Set   The *power set axiom* is the formula

$$U \in \mathbf{P}\, V \iff (\forall x : X \bullet x \in U \Rightarrow x \in V)$$

and the following are the elimination and introduction rules for the power set:

$$\frac{\Gamma \mapsto U \in \mathbf{P}\, V}{\Gamma \mapsto \forall x : X \bullet x \in U \Rightarrow x \in V,} \; \textbf{P}\textit{-elim} \qquad \frac{\Gamma \mapsto \forall x : X \bullet x \in U \Rightarrow x \in V}{\Gamma \mapsto U \in \mathbf{P}\, V.} \; \textbf{P}\textit{-int}$$

22.3   Reasoning about Tuples

Equality   The *tuple equality* axiom is the formula

$$\forall x_1, y_1 \colon X_1; x_2, y_2 \colon X_2; \ldots; x_n, y_n \colon X_n \bullet$$
$$(x_1, x_2, \ldots, x_n) = (y_1, y_2, \ldots, y_n) \Longleftrightarrow (x_1 = y_1 \wedge x_2 = y_2 \wedge \ldots x_n = y_n)$$

and the following are the elimination and introduction rules for tuple equality:

$$\frac{\Gamma \;\mapsto\; (x_1, x_2, \ldots, x_n) = (y_1, y_2, \ldots, y_n)}{\Gamma \;\mapsto\; x_1 = y_1 \wedge x_2 = y_2 \wedge \ldots x_n = y_n,} \; \textit{tup-eq-elim}$$

$$\frac{\Gamma_1 \;\mapsto\; x_1 = y_1 \quad \Gamma_2 \;\mapsto\; x_2 = y_2 \quad \ldots \quad \Gamma_n \;\mapsto\; x_n = y_n}{\Gamma_1, \Gamma_2, \ldots, \Gamma_n \;\mapsto\; (x_1, x_2, \ldots, x_n) = (y_1, y_2, \ldots, y_n).} \; \textit{tup-eq-int}$$

Membership   The *tuple membership* axiom is the formula

$$t \in X_1 \times X_2 \times \cdots \times X_n \Longleftrightarrow \exists x_1 \colon X_1; x_2 \colon X_2; \ldots; x_n \colon X_n \bullet t = (x_1, x_2, \ldots, x_n)$$

and the following are the elimination and introduction rules for tuple membership:

$$\frac{\Gamma \;\mapsto\; t \in X_1 \times X_2 \times \cdots \times X_n}{\Gamma \;\mapsto\; \exists x_1 \colon X_1; x_2 \colon X_2; \ldots; x_n \colon X_n \bullet t = (x_1, x_2, \ldots, x_n),} \; \textit{tup-mem-elim}$$

$$\frac{\Gamma \;\mapsto\; \exists x_1 \colon X_1; x_2 \colon X_2; \ldots; x_n \colon X_n \bullet t = (x_1, x_2, \ldots, x_n)}{\Gamma \;\mapsto\; t \in X_1 \times X_2 \times \cdots \times X_n.} \; \textit{tup-mem-int}$$

22.4   Floyd–Hoare Logic

The *skip* Command   In a Floyd–Hoare logic it is legitimate to have leaf nodes that are instances of the start sequent for the *skip* command:

$$\mapsto \{P\} \; \gamma \; \{P\}.$$

Assignment   In a Floyd–Hoare logic it is legitimate to have leaf nodes that are instances of the start sequent for assignment:

$$\mapsto \{P[t/x]\} \; x := t \; \{P\},$$

where $P[t/x]$ stands for the result of substituting the term t for all the free occurrences of the variable x in P.

Sequencing   The following is the thema which allows us to introduce the semicolon into a formula of Floyd–Hoare logic:

$$\frac{\Gamma \;\mapsto\; \{P\} \; \gamma \; \{Q\} \quad \Delta \;\mapsto\; \{Q\} \; \delta \; \{R\}}{\Gamma, \Delta \;\mapsto\; \{P\} \; \gamma; \delta \; \{R\}.} \; \textit{;-int}$$

The Conditional The following thema allows us to introduce the conditional into a formula:

$$\frac{\Gamma \mapsto \{P \wedge Q\}\, \gamma\, \{R\} \quad \Delta \mapsto \{P \wedge \neg Q\}\, \delta\, \{R\}}{\Gamma, \Delta \mapsto \{P\}\ \textbf{if}\ Q\ \textbf{then}\ \gamma\ \textbf{else}\ \delta\ \{R\}.}\quad \textit{if-int}$$

The while-loop The following thema allows us to introduce the **while**-loop into a formula:

$$\frac{\Gamma \mapsto \{P \wedge Q\}\, \gamma\, \{P\}}{\Gamma \mapsto \{P\}\ \textbf{while}\ Q\ \textbf{do}\ \gamma\ \{P \wedge \neg Q\}.}\quad \textit{while-int}$$

The for-loop There is both a start sequent and a rule governing the **for**-loop. First, the start sequent:

$$\mapsto \{P \wedge (u < t)\}\ \textbf{for}\ x := t\ \textbf{to}\ u\ \textbf{do}\ \gamma\, \{P\}.$$

The rule governing the **for**-loop is as follows:

$$\frac{\Gamma \mapsto \{P \wedge (t \le x \le u)\}\, \gamma\, \{P[x+1/x]\}}{\Gamma \mapsto \{P[t/x] \wedge (t \le u)\}\ \textbf{for}\ x := t\ \textbf{to}\ u\ \textbf{do}\ \gamma\, \{P[u+1/x]\}.}\quad \textit{for-int}$$

The side condition for the **for**-loop is that neither x nor any variable occurring in either t or u can occur on the left-hand side of an assignment in γ.

Structural Rules

There are quite a few structural rules for a Floyd–Hoare logic. In this book I have used the following three. First, there is the rule of precondition strengthening:

$$\frac{\Gamma, P \mapsto Q \quad \Delta \mapsto \{Q\}\, \gamma\, \{R\}}{\Gamma, \Delta \mapsto \{P\}\, \gamma\, \{R\}.}\quad \textit{pre-strength}$$

Second, there is the rule of postcondition weakening:

$$\frac{\Gamma \mapsto \{P\}\, \gamma\, \{Q\} \quad \Delta, Q \mapsto R}{\Gamma, \Delta \mapsto \{P\}\, \gamma\, \{R\}.}\quad \textit{post-weak}$$

Third, there is the rule of specification conjunction:

$$\frac{\Gamma_1 \mapsto \{P_1\}\, \gamma\, \{Q_1\} \quad \Gamma_2 \mapsto \{P_2\}\, \gamma\, \{Q_2\}}{\Gamma_1, \Gamma_2 \mapsto \{P_1 \wedge P_2\}\, \gamma\, \{Q_1 \wedge Q_2\}.}\quad \textit{spec-conj}$$

22.5 Induction

22.5.1 Mathematical Induction

The principle of mathematical induction is a rule of inference that allows us to prove that certain things are true of all the non-negative numbers. It says that in order to show that $P(n)$ holds for all natural numbers, all we have to show is:

(1) $P(0)$ holds.

(2) $\forall i: \mathbb{N} \bullet P(i) \Rightarrow P(i+1)$.

Here, part (1) is known as the *base case* and part (2) is known as the *inductive step*.

22.5.2   Induction for Sequences

Sequence induction is similar to mathematical induction. It comes in several flavours. One version says that in order to show that some property $P(\sigma)$ holds for all sequences σ all we have to show is that:

(1) $P(\langle \, \rangle)$ holds.

(2) If $P(\sigma)$ holds for any sequence σ, then so does $P(\langle x \rangle \frown \sigma)$. In symbols:

$$\forall x: X; \sigma: \operatorname{seq} X \bullet P(\sigma) \Rightarrow P(\langle x \rangle \frown \sigma).$$

Here, part (1) is known as the *base case* and part (2) is known as the *inductive step*.

Another version says that in order to show that some property $P(\sigma)$ holds for all sequences $\sigma: \operatorname{seq} X$ all you have to show is that:

(1) $P(\langle \, \rangle)$ holds.

(2) If $P(\sigma)$ holds for any sequence σ, then so does $P(\sigma \frown \langle x \rangle)$. In symbols:

$$\forall x: X; \sigma: \operatorname{seq} X \bullet P(\sigma) \Rightarrow P(\sigma \frown \langle x \rangle).$$

Yet another version says that in order to prove that $P(\sigma)$ holds for all sequences you just need to prove that:

(1) $P(\langle \, \rangle)$ holds.

(2) $P(\langle x \rangle)$ is true for all $x: X$.

(3) If $P(\sigma)$ and $P(\tau)$ are true for all sequences σ and τ, then so is $P(\sigma \frown \tau)$. In symbols:

$$\forall \sigma, \tau: \operatorname{seq} X \bullet P(\sigma) \wedge P(\tau) \Rightarrow P(\sigma \frown \tau).$$

22.6   Proof Obligations for Refinement

22.6.1   Operation Refinement

Operation refinement takes place within a single specification in that only one kind of state space is involved. It is a way of relating operations defined on the same data. The concrete operation OpC is a refinement of the abstract operation OpA, both defined on the same state space, iff both of the following formulas are theorems:

$$\operatorname{pre} OpA \Rightarrow \operatorname{pre} OpC,$$
$$\operatorname{pre} OpA \wedge OpC \Rightarrow OpA.$$

The first of these states that the concrete operation succeeds whenever the abstract one does, although there might be situations in which the concrete state succeeds but the abstract one does not. The second formula states that the abstract and concrete operations produce the same results on the same starting states.

22.6.2 Data Refinement

Let *Astate* be an abstract state and *Cstate* a concrete one linked by means of the schema AC. $InitA'$ is the abstract initial state and $InitC'$ is the concrete initial state. OpA and OpC are an abstract and a concrete operation respectively.

For Functions

The following proof obligations have to be proved if the schema AC satisfies the following condition:

$$\forall Cstate \bullet \exists_1 Astate \bullet AC.$$

Initialization

$$InitC' \wedge AC' \Rightarrow InitA'.$$

Applicability

$$\text{pre } OpA \wedge AC \Rightarrow \text{pre } OpC.$$

Correctness

$$\text{pre } OpA \wedge \Delta AC \wedge OpC \Rightarrow OpA.$$

In General

The following proof obligations have to be proved if the schema AC does *not* satisfy the following condition:

$$\forall Cstate \bullet \exists_1 Astate \bullet AC.$$

Initialization

$$InitC' \Rightarrow (\exists Astate' \bullet InitA' \wedge AC').$$

Applicability

$$\text{pre } OpA \wedge AC \Rightarrow \text{pre } OpC.$$

Correctness

$$\text{pre } OpA \wedge AC \wedge OpC \Rightarrow (\exists Astate' \bullet AC' \wedge OpA).$$

Part VI

Appendices

A

Variable Conventions

When giving formal definitions or when talking about the general properties of an operator each Roman and Greek letter used in this book has a single meaning. All such letters are included here. The conventions used in this book regarding multi-character identifiers are explained in section 4.11.4.

A			a	
B	formulas		b	constants
C			c	
D	declarations		d	
E			e	unit element
F			f	
G	relations		g	functions
H			h	
I	(index) set		i	
J	unused		j	
K			k	number variables
L			l	
M	bags		m	
N			n	
O	unused		o	unused

P			p	
Q	formulas		q	number variables
R			r	
S			s	
T	schemas		t	
U			u	terms
V			v	
W			w	unused
X	sets		x	
Y			y	variables
Z			z	
Γ			π	pattern
Δ	sets of formulas		ρ	unary prefix operator
Σ			σ	
Φ	data types		τ	sequences
Ψ			υ	
γ	commands		χ	substitution
δ			ω	binary infix operator

Some Greek letters are part of standard Z, namely Δ, Ξ, θ, λ and μ. The letters Δ and Ξ are used to form schema names as explained in section 4.4.2. The letter θ is used to form a binding as explained in section 5.2.7, the letter λ is used to form a λ-term as explained in section 6.4.3 and μ is Z's definite description operator, which is explained in section 2.2.5.

The calligraphic letters $\mathcal{I}$ and $\mathcal{V}$ are used for interpretations in chapter 2 and the letters t and f are also used there for the truth-values truth and falsity, respectively.

B

Answers to Exercises

Chapter 2

2.1) a) $P \wedge P$ is not a tautology. It is false when P is false.

b) $P \wedge \neg Q$ is not a tautology. It is false, for example, when P is false and Q is true.

c) $(P \Rightarrow Q) \Rightarrow P$ is not a tautology. It is false, for example, when P and Q are both false.

d) $P \Rightarrow (Q \Rightarrow P)$ is a tautology. This is shown by the following truth-table:

P	Q	P	$\Rightarrow$	$(Q \Rightarrow P)$
t	t	t	t	t
t	f	t	t	t
f	t	f	t	f
f	f	f	t	t

e) $P \Rightarrow (Q \Rightarrow (P \Rightarrow P))$ is a tautology. This is shown by the following truth-table:

P	Q	P	$\Rightarrow$	$(Q \Rightarrow$	$(P \Rightarrow P))$
t	t	t	t	t	t
t	f	t	t	t	t
f	t	f	t	t	t
f	f	f	t	t	t

f) $(P \wedge Q) \Rightarrow P$ is a tautology. This is shown by the following truth-table:

P	Q	$(P \wedge Q)$	$\Rightarrow$	P
t	t	t	t	t
t	f	f	t	t
f	t	f	t	f
f	f	f	t	f

g) $P \Rightarrow (P \wedge Q)$ is not a tautology. It is false when P is true and Q is false.

h) $((P \wedge Q) \Rightarrow R) \Longleftrightarrow ((P \Rightarrow R) \vee (Q \Rightarrow R))$ is a tautology. This is shown by the following truth-table:

P	Q	R	$((P \wedge Q)$	$\Rightarrow$	$R)$	$\Longleftrightarrow$	$((P \Rightarrow R)$	$\vee$	$(Q \Rightarrow R))$
t	t	t	t	t	t	t	t	t	t
t	t	f	t	f	f	t	f	f	f
t	f	t	f	t	t	t	t	t	t
t	f	f	f	t	f	t	f	t	t
f	t	t	f	t	t	t	t	t	t
f	t	f	f	t	f	t	t	t	f
f	f	t	f	t	t	t	t	t	t
f	f	f	f	t	f	t	t	t	t

2.2)　a) The sequent $\neg P \Rightarrow P \mapsto P$ is valid, as the following truth-table shows:

P	$\neg P$	$\Rightarrow$	P	$\mapsto$	P
t	f	t	t		t
f	t	f	f		f

b) The sequent $P \mapsto Q \Rightarrow (P \wedge Q)$ is valid, as the following truth-table shows:

P	Q	P	$\mapsto$	Q	$\Rightarrow$	$(P \wedge Q)$
t	t	t		t	t	t
t	f	t		f	t	f
f	t	f		t	f	f
f	f	f		f	t	f

c) The sequent $P \Rightarrow Q, P \Rightarrow \neg Q \mapsto \neg P$ is valid, as the following truth-table shows:

P	Q	$P \Rightarrow Q$	$P \Rightarrow \neg Q$	$\mapsto$	$\neg P$
t	t	t	f		f
t	f	f	t		f
f	t	t	t		t
f	f	t	t		t

d) The sequent $(P \wedge Q) \Longleftrightarrow P \mapsto P \Rightarrow Q$ is valid, as the following truth-table shows:

P	Q	$(P \wedge Q)$	$\Longleftrightarrow$	P	$\mapsto$	$P \Rightarrow Q$
t	t	t	t	t		t
t	f	f	f	t		f
f	t	f	t	f		t
f	f	f	t	f		t

e) The sequent $Q \Rightarrow R \;\mapsto\; (P \vee Q) \Rightarrow (P \vee R)$ is valid, as the following truth-table shows:

P	Q	R	$Q \Rightarrow R$	$\mapsto$	$(P \vee Q)$	$\Rightarrow$	$(P \vee R)$
t	t	t	t		t	t	t
t	t	f	f		t	t	t
t	f	t	t		t	t	t
t	f	f	t		t	t	t
f	t	t	t		t	t	t
f	t	f	f		t	f	f
f	f	t	t		f	t	t
f	f	f	t		f	t	f

f) The sequent $P_1 \Rightarrow P_2, P_3 \Rightarrow P_4 \;\mapsto\; (P_1 \vee P_3) \Rightarrow (P_2 \vee P_4)$ is valid, as the following truth-table shows:

P_1	P_2	P_3	P_4	$P_1 \Rightarrow P_2$	$P_3 \Rightarrow P_4$	$\mapsto$	$(P_1 \vee P_3)$	$\Rightarrow$	$(P_2 \vee P_4)$
t	t	t	t	t	t		t	t	t
t	t	t	f	t	f		t	t	t
t	t	f	t	t	t		t	t	t
t	t	f	f	t	t		t	t	t
t	f	t	t	f	t		t	t	t
t	f	t	f	f	f		t	f	f
t	f	f	t	f	t		t	t	t
t	f	f	f	f	t		t	f	f
f	t	t	t	t	t		t	t	t
f	t	t	f	t	f		t	t	t
f	t	f	t	t	t		f	t	t
f	t	f	f	t	t		f	t	t
f	f	t	t	t	t		t	t	t
f	f	t	f	t	f		t	f	f
f	f	f	t	t	t		f	t	t
f	f	f	f	t	t		f	t	f

2.3)

$$P \vee Q == \neg(\neg P \wedge \neg Q),$$

$$P \Rightarrow Q == \neg P \vee Q,$$
$$== \neg(P \wedge \neg Q),$$

$$P \Longleftrightarrow Q == (P \Rightarrow Q) \wedge (Q \Rightarrow P),$$
$$== (\neg(P \wedge \neg Q)) \wedge (\neg(Q \wedge \neg P)).$$

2.4) First, define $\neg P$ and $P \wedge Q$ as follows:

$$\neg P == P \downarrow P,$$
$$P \wedge Q == (P \downarrow P) \downarrow (Q \downarrow Q).$$

Then, use the definitions given in the previous answer.

2.5) a) $\forall i: \mathbf{Z} \mid i \in \{4, 5, 7, 19\} \bullet 2 + 3 = i.$

b) $\exists i: \mathbf{Z} \mid i \in \{4, 5, 7, 19\} \bullet 2 + 3 = i.$

2.6) a) $\forall i: \mathbf{Z} \mid i < 3 \bullet i \neq 7.$

b) $\exists i: \mathbf{Z} \mid i < 3 \bullet i \neq 7.$

c) $\forall i: \mathbf{Z} \mid even\ i \wedge i < 9 \bullet \neg(odd\ i).$

d) $\exists x: Europe \mid ec\ x \bullet x\ borders\ belgium.$

e) $\forall x: Europe \mid ec\ x \bullet \neg(nato\ x).$

The following key is used in giving answers to parts (d) and (e) of this question:

$ec\ \_$	$\_$ is a member of the EC
$nato\ \_$	$\_$ is a member of NATO
$\_\ borders\ \_$	$\_$ borders $\_$

Chapter 3

3.1) a) $\{1, 3, 5, 7, 9, 19, 21, 23, 25, 27\}.$

b) $\{2, 4, 6, 8, 10, 11, 13, 15, 17, 20, 22, 24, 26, 28\}.$

c) $\{11, 13, 15, 17, 29, 31, 33, 35\}.$

d) $\{1, 2, 3, 4, 5, 6, 7, 8, 9, 10, 19, 20, 21, 22, 23, 24, 25, 26, 27, 28\}.$

e) $\{2, 4, 6, 8, 10\}.$

f) $18/37.$

g) $27/37.$

h) $36/37.$

i) $5/37.$

j) $20/37.$

3.2) a)

$$U \cup V = \{0, 1, 2, 3, 4, 5, 7, 11, 13, 17\},$$
$$U \cap V = \{2, 3, 5\},$$
$$U \setminus V = \{7, 11, 13, 17\}.$$

b)

$$10..15 \cup 12..18 = 10..18 = \{10, 11, 12, 13, 14, 15, 16, 17, 18\},$$
$$10..15 \cap 12..18 = 12..15 = \{12, 13, 14, 15\},$$
$$10..15 \setminus 12..18 = 10..11 = \{10, 11\}.$$

c)

$$U \cap \{x: \mathbf{N} \mid x \bmod 3 = 1\} = \{1, 4, 7, 10, 13, 16, 19, 22, 25\},$$
$$U \cap \{x: \mathbf{N} \mid x \operatorname{div} 7 = 2\} = \{14, 15, 16, 17, 18, 19, 20\}.$$

d)

$$\{\varnothing, \{england\}, \{france\}, \{spain\},$$
$$\{england, france\}, \{england, spain\}, \{france, spain\},$$
$$\{england, france, spain\}\}.$$

3.3) a) As Rohl (1983), p. 7, writes, 'A year n is a leap year if it is divisible by 4, but not by 100, unless it is also divisible by 400'.

$$\{n: \mathbf{N} \mid (1900 \leq n \leq 2100) \wedge$$
$$((n \bmod 4 = 0 \wedge n \bmod 100 \neq 0) \vee n \bmod 400 = 0)\}.$$

b) $\{x: Europe \mid ec\ x\}$ and $\{x: Europe \mid pact\ x\}$.

Chapter 4

4.1) a) dom *occupies* = $\{arch, bell, cox, dove, earl, fry\}$.

b) ran *occupies* = $\{m7, m5, g3, m3, g8, g4\}$.

c) It is impossible to write down a legitimate formula of the Z language that states that dom *occupies* and ran *occupies* have no elements in common. The formula dom *occupies* ∩ ran *occupies* = ∅ is illegitimate because the term dom *occupies* ∩ ran *occupies* infringes Z's type discipline. The type of dom *occupies* is **P** *Person* and the type of ran *occupies* is **P** *Room* and the intersection operator can only combine sets which belong to the same type.

d) The term *occupies*⟨|*aigroup*|⟩ represents the collection of rooms occupied by a member of the AI group. It is equivalent to $\{g3, m3, g8, g4\}$.

e) $\forall x: aigroup \bullet \exists y: ground \bullet x \mapsto y \in occupies$. (This answer is due to Anton Eliens who noticed a mistake in earlier printings of this book.)

f)

$$aigroup \triangleleft occupies = \{cox \mapsto g3,$$
$$cox \mapsto m3,$$
$$dove \mapsto g8,$$
$$earl \mapsto g4,$$
$$fry \mapsto g4\}.$$

g) $(aigroup \triangleleft occupies)\langle\!|fmgroup|\!\rangle = \{g3, m3\}$.

h)

$$(aigroup \lhd occupies)^{\sim} = \{g3 \mapsto cox,$$
$$m3 \mapsto cox,$$
$$g8 \mapsto dove,$$
$$g4 \mapsto earl,$$
$$g4 \mapsto fry\}.$$

i) $(aigroup \lhd occupies)^{\sim} \langle\!\langle(aigroup \lhd occupies)\langle\!\langle fmgroup\rangle\!\rangle\rangle\!\rangle = \{cox\}.$

j) $(aigroup \lhd occupies)^{\sim} = \{m5 \mapsto bell, m7 \mapsto arch\}.$

4.2) The basic types or given sets for this specification are:

$$[Person, Film]$$

where *Person* is the set of all people and *Film* is the set of all films, both those that have already been made and also all those that will ever be made in the future.

The state of the filmic database is given by the schema *Films*:

Films

$directedby, writtenby: Person \leftrightarrow Film$

$\text{ran } directedby = \text{ran } writtenby$

The schemas $\Delta Films$ and $\Xi Films$ are defined in the usual way:

$$\Delta Films \mathrel{\hat{=}} Films \wedge Films',$$

$$\Xi Films \mathrel{\hat{=}} [\Delta Films \mid directedby' = directedby; writtenby = writtenby'].$$

$\Xi Films$ could also be defined as $[\Delta Films \mid \theta Films' = \theta Films]$. The initial state schema is *InitFilms'*, where *InitFilms* is defined as follows:

$$InitFilms \mathrel{\hat{=}} [Films \mid directedby = \varnothing; writtenby = \varnothing].$$

The schema *AddFilm* adds information to the database concerning a film with only one director and only one writer. The film is represented by the identifier *movie?* and the director and writer are represented, respectively, by the identifiers *dir?* and *writ?*

AddFilm

$\Delta Films$
$dir?, writ?: Person$
$movie?: Film$

$movie? \notin \text{ran } directedby$
$directedby' = directedby \cup \{dir? \mapsto movie?\}$
$writtenby' = writtenby \cup \{writ? \mapsto movie?\}$

The schema *AddFilm* specifies the successful carrying out of the operation of adding information to the database. The schema *Success* just makes this explicit.

```
┌─ Success ──────────────────────────────────
│ rep!: Report
├────────────────────────────────────────────
│ rep! = 'Okay'
└────────────────────────────────────────────
```

The operation *AddFilm* can only go wrong in one way, namely if the film *movie?* is already in the database. This possibility is captured by means of the schema *AlreadyPresent*. Recall that the film we are adding has only one director and only one writer.

```
┌─ AlreadyPresent ──────────────────────────
│ Ξ Films
│ movie?: Film
│ rep!: Report
├────────────────────────────────────────────
│ movie? ∈ ran directedby
│ rep! = 'Already in database'
└────────────────────────────────────────────
```

The total operation of adding a film to the database is captured by means of the schema *DoAddFilm*.

$$DoAddFilm \mathrel{\hat{=}} AddFilm \wedge Success$$
$$\vee$$
$$AlreadyPresent.$$

The schema *FindFilmsDir* interrogates the database using a person *dir?* as input. The output *oeuvre!* is the set of all the films he has had a hand in directing. It is totalized in the standard way.

```
┌─ FindFilmsDir ────────────────────────────
│ Ξ Films
│ dir?: Person
│ oeuvre!: F Film
├────────────────────────────────────────────
│ dir? ∈ dom directedby
│ oeuvre! = directedby(|{dir?}|)
└────────────────────────────────────────────
```

```
┌─ UnknownDirector ─────────────────────────
│ Ξ Films
│ dir?: Person
│ rep!: Report
├────────────────────────────────────────────
│ dir? ∉ dom directedby
│ rep! = 'Unknown director'
└────────────────────────────────────────────
```

$$DoFindFilmsDir \stackrel{\triangle}{=} FindFilmsDir \wedge Success$$
$$\vee$$
$$UnknownDirector.$$

The schema *FindFilmsWrit* interrogates the database using a person *writ?* as input. The output *oeuvre!* is the set of all the films he has had a hand in writing. It is totalized in the standard way.

```
┌─ FindFilmsWrit ──────────────────────────────────────
│ ΞFilms
│ writ?: Person
│ oeuvre!: F Film
├──────────────────────────────────────────────────────
│ writ? ∈ dom writtenby
│ oeuvre! = writtenby⦇{writ?}⦈
└──────────────────────────────────────────────────────
```

```
┌─ UnknownWriter ──────────────────────────────────────
│ ΞFilms
│ writ?: Person
│ rep!: Report
├──────────────────────────────────────────────────────
│ writ? ∉ dom writtenby
│ rep! = 'Unknown writer'
└──────────────────────────────────────────────────────
```

$$DoFindFilmsWrit \stackrel{\triangle}{=} FindFilmsWrit \wedge Success$$
$$\vee$$
$$UnknownWriter.$$

Chapter 5

5.1) a)

```
│ brother: Person ↔ Person
├──────────────────────────────────────────────────────
│ ∀x, y: Person •
│     x ↦ y ∈ brother ⟺
│         ∃z₁, z₂: Person •
│             x ↦ z₁ ∈ father ∧
│             y ↦ z₁ ∈ father ∧
│             x ↦ z₂ ∈ mother ∧
│             y ↦ z₂ ∈ mother ∧
│             {x, y} ⊆ male ∧ x ≠ y
```

b)

> firstcousin: *Person* $\leftrightarrow$ *Person*
> ___
> $\forall x, y$: *Person* •
> $\quad x \mapsto y \in$ *firstcousin* $\Longleftrightarrow$
> $\qquad \exists v, w$: *Person* •
> $\qquad\quad x \mapsto v \in$ *father* $\cup$ *mother* $\wedge$
> $\qquad\quad y \mapsto w \in$ *father* $\cup$ *mother* $\wedge$
> $\qquad\quad v \mapsto w \in$ *sibling* $\wedge$ $x \neq y$

c)

> grandfather: *Person* $\leftrightarrow$ *Person*
> ___
> $\forall x, y$: *Person* •
> $\quad x \mapsto y \in$ *grandfather* $\Longleftrightarrow$
> $\qquad \exists z$: *Person* •
> $\qquad\quad (x \mapsto z \in$ *father* $\cup$ *mother*$)$ $\wedge$
> $\qquad\quad z \mapsto y \in$ *father*

> grandfather: *Person* $\leftrightarrow$ *Person*
> ___
> *grandfather* $= ($*father* $\cup$ *mother*$)$; *father*

d) The expression *grandfather*$(\!|\{x\}|\!)$ denotes the set of all of x's grandfathers and *grandfather*$^\sim(\!|\{x\}|\!)$ is the set of all of x's grandchildren.

e)

> greatgrandmother: *Person* $\leftrightarrow$ *Person*
> ___
> $\forall x, y$: *Person* •
> $\quad x \mapsto y \in$ *greatgrandmother* $\Longleftrightarrow$
> $\qquad \exists z_1, z_2$: *Person* •
> $\qquad\quad x \mapsto z_1 \in$ *father* $\cup$ *mother* $\wedge$
> $\qquad\quad z_1 \mapsto z_2 \in$ *father* $\cup$ *mother* $\wedge$
> $\qquad\quad z_2 \mapsto y \in$ *mother*

> greatgrandmother: *Person* $\leftrightarrow$ *Person*
> ___
> *greatgrandmother* $= ($*father* $\cup$ *mother*$)$; $($*father* $\cup$ *mother*$)$; *mother*

f) $($*father* $\cup$ *mother*$)^+(\!|\{x\}|\!)$.

5.2) First, we work out what the schema *Alpha* is. This is defined as being equivalent to the schema $AddMember[members^+/members'][telephones^+/telephones']$.

```
┌─ Alpha ─────────────────────────────────────────────────
│ members, members⁺: P Person
│ telephones, telephones⁺: Person ↔ Phone
│ name?: Person
├─────────────────────────────────────────────────────────
│ dom telephones ⊆ members
│ dom telephones⁺ ⊆ members⁺
│ name? ∉ members
│ members⁺ = members ∪ {name?}
│ telephones⁺ = telephones
└─────────────────────────────────────────────────────────
```

Then, we form the schema *Beta*, which is defined to be the conjunction of the schema $AddMember[members^+/members'][telephones^+/telephones']$ and the schema $AddEntry[members^+/members][telephones^+/telephones]$.

```
┌─ Beta ──────────────────────────────────────────────────
│ members, members⁺, members': P Person
│ telephones, telephones⁺, telephones': Person ↔ Phone
│ newnumber?: Phone
│ name?: Person
├─────────────────────────────────────────────────────────
│ dom telephones ⊆ members
│ dom telephones⁺ ⊆ members⁺
│ dom telephones' ⊆ members'
│ name? ∉ members
│ members⁺ = members ∪ {name?}
│ telephones⁺ = telephones
│ name? ∈ members⁺
│ name? ↦ newnumber? ∉ telephones⁺
│ telephones' = telephones⁺ ∪ {name? ↦ newnumber?}
│ members' = members⁺
└─────────────────────────────────────────────────────────
```

The schema $Gamma \stackrel{\wedge}{=} AddMember\,\text{\o}\,AddEntry$ is obtained by existentially quantifying over the variables $members^+$ and $telephones^+$ in the schema *Beta*.

```
┌─ Gamma ─────────────────────────────────────────────────────────
│ ΔPhoneDB
│ newnumber?: Phone
│ name?: Person
├─────────────────────────────────────────────────────────────────
│ name? ∉ members
│ ∃members⁺: P Person; telephones⁺: Person ⟷ Phone •
│        dom telephones⁺ ⊆ members⁺ ∧
│        members⁺ = members ∪ {name?} ∧
│        telephones⁺ = telephones ∧
│        name? ∈ members⁺ ∧
│        name? ↦ newnumber? ∉ telephones⁺ ∧
│        telephones′ = telephones⁺ ∪ {name? ↦ newnumber?} ∧
│        members′ = members⁺
└─────────────────────────────────────────────────────────────────
```

Gamma simplifies to the following schema:

```
┌─ Gamma ─────────────────────────────────────────────────────────
│ ΔPhoneDB
│ name?: Person
│ newnumber?: Phone
├─────────────────────────────────────────────────────────────────
│ name? ∉ members
│ name? ↦ newnumber? ∉ telephones
│ members′ = members ∪ {name?}
│ telephones′ = telephones ∪ {name? ↦ newnumber?}
└─────────────────────────────────────────────────────────────────
```

Chapter 7

7.1) a) $\langle B, L, A, C, K, J, A, C, K \rangle$.

b) B.

c) C.

d) $\langle L, A, C \rangle$.

e) $\langle A, C, K, B, L \rangle$.

f) $\langle L, B, K, C, A \rangle$.

g) $\{1, 2, 3, 4, 5\}$.

h) $\{B, L, A, C, K\}$.

i) $\{A \mapsto 1, C \mapsto 2, K \mapsto 3, B \mapsto 4, L \mapsto 5\}$.

j) $\{C \mapsto A, K \mapsto C, B \mapsto K, L \mapsto B\}$.

k) $\langle A, C, K, E, R \rangle$.

l) $\{1 \mapsto A\}$.

m) $\langle B, L, O, C, K \rangle$.

n) $\langle C, A, B, L, E \rangle$.

Chapter 10

10.1)   a) First, I prove that $P \wedge (Q \wedge R) \vdash (P \wedge Q) \wedge R$:

$$
\begin{array}{lll}
1 & (1)\ \ P \wedge (Q \wedge R) & ass \\
1 & (2)\ \ P & 1\ \wedge\text{-}elim_1 \\
1 & (3)\ \ Q \wedge R & 1\ \wedge\text{-}elim_2 \\
1 & (4)\ \ Q & 3\ \wedge\text{-}elim_1 \\
1 & (5)\ \ R & 3\ \wedge\text{-}elim_2 \\
1 & (6)\ \ P \wedge Q & 2,4\ \wedge\text{-}int \\
1 & (7)\ \ (P \wedge Q) \wedge R & 6,5\ \wedge\text{-}int \\
\end{array}
$$

Next, I prove that $(P \wedge Q) \wedge R \vdash P \wedge (Q \wedge R)$:

$$
\begin{array}{lll}
1 & (1)\ \ (P \wedge Q) \wedge R & ass \\
1 & (2)\ \ P \wedge Q & 1\ \wedge\text{-}elim_1 \\
1 & (3)\ \ P & 2\ \wedge\text{-}elim_1 \\
1 & (4)\ \ Q & 2\ \wedge\text{-}elim_2 \\
1 & (5)\ \ R & 1\ \wedge\text{-}elim_2 \\
1 & (6)\ \ Q \wedge R & 4,5\ \wedge\text{-}int \\
1 & (7)\ \ P \wedge (Q \wedge R) & 3,6\ \wedge\text{-}int \\
\end{array}
$$

b) First, I prove that $P \vee (Q \vee R) \vdash (P \vee Q) \vee R$:

$$
\begin{array}{lll}
1 & (1)\ \ P \vee (Q \vee R) & ass \\
2 & (2)\ \ Q \vee R & ass \\
3 & (3)\ \ Q & ass \\
3 & (4)\ \ P \vee Q & 3\ \vee\text{-}int_2 \\
3 & (5)\ \ (P \vee Q) \vee R & 4\ \vee\text{-}int_1 \\
6 & (6)\ \ R & ass \\
6 & (7)\ \ (P \vee Q) \vee R & 6\ \vee\text{-}int_2 \\
2 & (8)\ \ (P \vee Q) \vee R & 2,5,7\ \vee\text{-}elim \\
9 & (9)\ \ P & ass \\
9 & (10)\ \ P \vee Q & 9\ \vee\text{-}int_1 \\
9 & (11)\ \ (P \vee Q) \vee R & 10\ \vee\text{-}int_1 \\
1 & (12)\ \ (P \vee Q) \vee R & 1,8,11\ \vee\text{-}elim \\
\end{array}
$$

Next, I prove that $(P \vee Q) \vee R \vdash P \vee (Q \vee R)$:

1	(1)	$(P \vee Q) \vee R$	ass
2	(2)	$P \vee Q$	ass
3	(3)	P	ass
3	(4)	$P \vee (Q \vee R)$	3 $\vee$-int_1
5	(5)	Q	ass
5	(6)	$Q \vee R$	5 $\vee$-int_1
5	(7)	$P \vee (Q \vee R)$	6 $\vee$-int_2
2	(8)	$P \vee (Q \vee R)$	$2, 4, 7$ $\vee$-$elim$
9	(9)	R	ass
9	(10)	$Q \vee R$	9 $\vee$-int_2
9	(11)	$P \vee (Q \vee R)$	10 $\vee$-int_2
1	(12)	$P \vee (Q \vee R)$	$1, 8, 11$ $\vee$-$elim$

c) First, I prove that $P \wedge Q \vdash (P \vee \neg Q) \wedge Q$:

1	(1)	$P \wedge Q$	ass
1	(2)	P	1 $\wedge$-$elim_1$
1	(3)	$P \vee \neg Q$	2 $\vee$-int_1
1	(4)	Q	1 $\wedge$-$elim_2$
1	(5)	$(P \vee \neg Q) \wedge Q$	$3, 4$ $\wedge$-int

Next, I prove that $(P \vee \neg Q) \wedge Q \vdash P \wedge Q$:

1	(1)	$(P \vee \neg Q) \wedge Q$	ass
1	(2)	$P \vee \neg Q$	1 $\wedge$-$elim_1$
3	(3)	P	ass
1	(4)	Q	1 $\wedge$-$elim_2$
1,3	(5)	$P \wedge Q$	$3, 4$ $\wedge$-int
6	(6)	$\neg Q$	ass
1,6	(7)	$false$	$4, 6$ $\neg$-$elim$
1,6	(8)	$P \wedge Q$	7 $false$-$elim$
1	(9)	$P \wedge Q$	$2, 5, 8$ $\vee$-$elim$

d) First, I prove that $P \Rightarrow Q \vdash \neg P \vee Q$:

1	(1)	$P \Rightarrow Q$	ass
2	(2)	$\neg(\neg P \vee Q)$	ass
2	(3)	$\neg\neg P \wedge \neg Q$	2 de Morgan
2	(4)	$\neg\neg P$	3 $\wedge$-$elim_1$
2	(5)	P	4 $\neg\neg$-$elim$
1,2	(6)	Q	$1, 5$ $\Rightarrow$-$elim$
2	(7)	$\neg Q$	3 $\wedge$-$elim_2$
1,2	(8)	$false$	$6, 7$ $\neg$-$elim$
1	(9)	$\neg\neg(\neg P \vee Q)$	8 $\neg$-int
1	(10)	$\neg P \vee Q$	9 $\neg\neg$-$elim$

Next, I prove that $\neg P \vee Q \vdash P \Rightarrow Q$:

1	(1)	$\neg P \vee Q$	*ass*
2	(2)	$\neg P$	*ass*
3	(3)	P	*ass*
2,3	(4)	*false*	2,3 $\neg$-*elim*
2,3	(5)	Q	4 *false-elim*
2	(6)	$P \Rightarrow Q$	5 $\Rightarrow$-*int*
7	(7)	Q	*ass*
7	(8)	$P \Rightarrow Q$	7 $\Rightarrow$-*int*
1	(9)	$P \Rightarrow Q$	1,2,7 $\vee$-*elim*

e) That $Q \Rightarrow R \vdash (P \vee Q) \Rightarrow (P \vee R)$ is proved as follows:

1	(1)	$Q \Rightarrow R$	*ass*
2	(2)	$P \vee Q$	*ass*
3	(3)	P	*ass*
3	(4)	$P \vee R$	3 $\vee$-*int*$_1$
5	(5)	Q	*ass*
1,5	(6)	R	1,5 $\Rightarrow$-*elim*
1,5	(7)	$P \vee R$	6 $\vee$-*int*$_2$
1,2	(8)	$P \vee R$	2,4,7 $\vee$-*elim*
1	(9)	$(P \vee Q) \Rightarrow (P \vee R)$	8 $\Rightarrow$-*int*

f) That $P_1 \Rightarrow P_2, P_3 \Rightarrow P_4 \vdash (P_1 \vee P_3) \Rightarrow (P_2 \vee P_4)$ is proved as follows:

1	(1)	$P_1 \Rightarrow P_2$	*ass*
2	(2)	$P_3 \Rightarrow P_4$	*ass*
3	(3)	$P_1 \vee P_3$	*ass*
4	(4)	P_1	*ass*
1,4	(5)	P_2	1,4 $\Rightarrow$-*elim*
1,4	(6)	$P_2 \vee P_4$	5 $\vee$-*int*$_1$
7	(7)	P_3	*ass*
2,7	(8)	P_4	2,7 $\Rightarrow$-*elim*
2,7	(9)	$P_2 \vee P_4$	8 $\vee$-*int*$_2$
1,3,2	(10)	$P_2 \vee P_4$	3,6,9 $\vee$-*elim*
1,2	(11)	$P_1 \vee P_3 \Rightarrow P_2 \vee P_4$	10 $\Rightarrow$-*int*

10.2)   a) First, I prove that $\forall x \colon X \bullet (Px \wedge Qx) \vdash (\forall x \colon X \bullet Px) \wedge (\forall x \colon X \bullet Qx)$.

1	(1)	$\forall x \colon X \bullet (Px \wedge Qx)$	*ass*
1	(2)	$Pa \wedge Qa$	1 $\forall$-*elim*
1	(3)	Pa	2 $\wedge$-*elim*$_1$
1	(4)	$\forall x \colon X \bullet Px$	3 $\forall$-*int*
1	(5)	Qa	2 $\wedge$-*elim*$_2$
1	(6)	$\forall x \colon X \bullet Qx$	5 $\forall$-*int*
1	(7)	$(\forall x \colon X \bullet Px) \wedge (\forall x \colon X \bullet Qx)$	4,6 $\wedge$-*int*

Next, I prove that $(\forall x\colon X \bullet Px) \wedge (\forall x\colon X \bullet Qx) \vdash \forall x\colon X \bullet (Px \wedge Qx)$.

1	(1)	$(\forall x\colon X \bullet Px) \wedge (\forall x\colon X \bullet Qx)$	ass
1	(2)	$\forall x\colon X \bullet Px$	$1 \wedge\text{-}elim_1$
1	(3)	Pa	$2 \; \forall\text{-}elim$
1	(4)	$\forall x\colon X \bullet Qx$	$1 \wedge\text{-}elim_2$
1	(5)	Qa	$4 \; \forall\text{-}elim$
1	(6)	$Pa \wedge Qa$	$3,5 \wedge\text{-}int$
1	(7)	$\forall x\colon X \bullet (Px \wedge Qx)$	$6 \; \forall\text{-}int$

b) First, I prove that $\exists x\colon X \bullet (Px \vee Qx) \vdash (\exists x\colon X \bullet Px) \vee (\exists x\colon X \bullet Qx)$.

1	(1)	$\exists x\colon X \bullet (Px \vee Qx)$	ass
2	(2)	$Pa \vee Qa$	ass
3	(3)	Pa	ass
3	(4)	$\exists x\colon X \bullet Px$	$3 \; \exists\text{-}int$
3	(5)	$(\exists x\colon X \bullet Px) \vee (\exists x\colon X \bullet Qx)$	$4 \; \vee\text{-}int_1$
6	(6)	Qa	ass
6	(7)	$\exists x\colon X \bullet Qx$	$6 \; \exists\text{-}int$
6	(8)	$(\exists x\colon X \bullet Px) \vee (\exists x\colon X \bullet Qx)$	$7 \; \vee\text{-}int_2$
2	(9)	$(\exists x\colon X \bullet Px) \vee (\exists x\colon X \bullet Qx)$	$2,5,8 \; \vee\text{-}elim$
1	(10)	$(\exists x\colon X \bullet Px) \vee (\exists x\colon X \bullet Qx)$	$1,9 \; \exists\text{-}elim$

Next, I prove that $(\exists x\colon X \bullet Px) \vee (\exists x\colon X \bullet Qx) \vdash \exists x\colon X \bullet (Px \vee Qx)$.

1	(1)	$(\exists x\colon X \bullet Px) \vee (\exists x\colon X \bullet Qx)$	ass
2	(2)	$\exists x\colon X \bullet Px$	ass
3	(3)	Pa	ass
3	(4)	$Pa \vee Qa$	$3 \; \vee\text{-}int_1$
3	(5)	$\exists x\colon X \bullet (Px \vee Qx)$	$4 \; \exists\text{-}int$
2	(6)	$\exists x\colon X \bullet (Px \vee Qx)$	$2,5 \; \exists\text{-}elim$
7	(7)	$\exists x\colon X \bullet Qx$	ass
8	(8)	Qa	ass
8	(9)	$Pa \vee Qa$	$8 \; \vee\text{-}int_2$
8	(10)	$\exists x\colon X \bullet (Px \vee Qx)$	$9 \; \exists\text{-}int$
7	(11)	$\exists x\colon X \bullet (Px \vee Qx)$	$7,10 \; \exists\text{-}elim$
1	(12)	$\exists x\colon X \bullet (Px \vee Qx)$	$1,6,11 \; \vee\text{-}elim$

c) That $\forall x\colon X \bullet Px \vdash \neg\exists x\colon X \bullet \neg Px$ is proved as follows:

1	(1)	$\forall x\colon X \bullet Px$	ass
2	(2)	$\exists x\colon X \bullet \neg Px$	ass
3	(3)	$\neg Pa$	ass
1	(4)	Pa	$1 \; \forall\text{-}elim$
1,3	(5)	*false*	$3,4 \; \neg\text{-}elim$
3	(6)	$\neg\forall x\colon X \bullet Px$	$5 \; \neg\text{-}int$
2	(7)	$\neg\forall x\colon X \bullet Px$	$2,6 \; \exists\text{-}elim$
1,2	(8)	*false*	$1,7 \; \neg\text{-}elim$
1	(9)	$\neg\exists x\colon X \bullet \neg Px$	$8 \; \neg\text{-}int$

That $\neg\exists x\colon X \bullet \neg Px \vdash \forall x\colon X \bullet Px$ is proved as follows:

1	(1)	$\neg\exists x\colon X \bullet \neg Px$	ass
2	(2)	$\neg Pa$	ass
2	(3)	$\exists x\colon X \bullet \neg Px$	2 $\exists$-int
1,2	(4)	false	1,3 $\neg$-elim
1	(5)	$\neg\neg Pa$	4 $\neg$-int
1	(6)	Pa	5 $\neg\neg$-elim
1	(7)	$\forall x\colon X \bullet Px$	6 $\forall$-int

d) That $\forall x\colon X \bullet (Px \Rightarrow Qx), \forall x\colon X \bullet Px \vdash \forall x\colon X \bullet Qx$ is proved as follows:

1	(1)	$\forall x\colon X \bullet (Px \Rightarrow Qx)$	ass
2	(2)	$\forall x\colon X \bullet Px$	ass
1	(3)	$Pa \Rightarrow Qa$	1 $\forall$-elim
2	(4)	Pa	2 $\forall$-elim
1,2	(5)	Qa	3,4 $\Rightarrow$-elim
1,2	(6)	$\forall x\colon X \bullet Qx$	5 $\forall$-int

e) That $\exists x\colon X \bullet (Px \wedge Qx) \vdash (\exists x\colon X \bullet Px) \wedge (\exists x\colon X \bullet Qx)$ is proved as follows:

1	(1)	$\exists x\colon X \bullet (Px \wedge Qx)$	ass
2	(2)	$Pa \wedge Qa$	ass
2	(3)	Pa	2 $\wedge$-elim$_1$
2	(4)	$\exists x\colon X \bullet Px$	3 $\exists$-int
2	(5)	Qa	2 $\wedge$-elim$_2$
2	(6)	$\exists x\colon X \bullet Qx$	5 $\exists$-int
2	(7)	$(\exists x\colon X \bullet Px) \wedge (\exists x\colon X \bullet Qx)$	4,6 $\wedge$-int
1	(8)	$(\exists x\colon X \bullet Px) \wedge (\exists x\colon X \bullet Qx)$	1,7 $\exists$-elim

10.3) The following tree proof establishes that the sequent $A \Rightarrow false \;\mapsto\; \neg A$ is syntactically valid:

$$\cfrac{\cfrac{\cfrac{A \Rightarrow false \;\mapsto\; A \Rightarrow false \quad A \mapsto A}{A \Rightarrow false, A \;\mapsto\; false} \Rightarrow\text{-}elim}{A \Rightarrow false \;\mapsto\; \neg A.} \neg\text{-}int}$$

The following tree proof establishes that the sequent $\neg A \;\mapsto\; A \Rightarrow false$ is syntactically valid:

$$\cfrac{\cfrac{\cfrac{\neg A \;\mapsto\; \neg A \quad A \mapsto A}{\neg A, A \;\mapsto\; false} \neg\text{-}elim}{\neg A \;\mapsto\; A \Rightarrow false.} \Rightarrow\text{-}int}$$

Chapter 11

11.1)   a) Apart from the fundamental property of set difference, the following proof also uses a number of properties of the propositional calculus, namely one of de Morgan's laws, double negation, the fact that $\wedge$ distributes forwards through $\vee$ and the laws $P \wedge \neg P \dashv\vdash false$ and $false \vee P \dashv\vdash P$.

$$
\begin{aligned}
x \in X \setminus (X \setminus U) &\Longleftrightarrow x \in X \wedge x \notin X \setminus U, \\
&\Longleftrightarrow x \in X \wedge \neg(x \in X \wedge x \notin U), \\
&\Longleftrightarrow x \in X \wedge (x \notin X \vee x \in U), \\
&\Longleftrightarrow (x \in X \wedge x \notin X) \vee (x \in X \wedge x \in U), \\
&\Longleftrightarrow x \in U.
\end{aligned}
$$

b) Apart from the definitions of set difference, intersection and union, the following proof also uses a number of properties of the propositional calculus, namely one of de Morgan's laws and the fact that $\wedge$ distributes forwards through $\vee$.

$$
\begin{aligned}
x \in X \setminus (U \cap V) &\Longleftrightarrow x \in X \wedge x \notin U \cap V, \\
&\Longleftrightarrow x \in X \wedge \neg(x \in U \wedge x \in V), \\
&\Longleftrightarrow x \in X \wedge (x \notin U \vee x \notin V), \\
&\Longleftrightarrow (x \in X \wedge x \notin U) \vee (x \in X \wedge x \notin V), \\
&\Longleftrightarrow x \in X \setminus U \vee x \in X \setminus V, \\
&\Longleftrightarrow x \in (X \setminus U) \cup (X \setminus V).
\end{aligned}
$$

11.2) a) We want to prove that:

$$
\sum_{i=0}^{i=n} i = \frac{n(n+1)}{2}, \tag{B.1}
$$

holds for all non-negative natural numbers n.

Base Case When $n = 0$, then:

$$
LHS \text{ of (B.1)} = \sum_{i=0}^{i=0} i = 0.
$$

Similarly, when $n = 0$, then:

$$
RHS \text{ of (B.1)} = \frac{0(0+1)}{2} = 0.
$$

As both the LHS and RHS of (B.1) are equal to 0, the base case is established.

Inductive Step We have to prove that:

$$
\sum_{i=0}^{i=n+1} i = \frac{(n+1)(n+2)}{2}, \tag{B.2}
$$

on the assumption that:

$$\sum_{i=0}^{i=n} i = \frac{n(n+1)}{2}, \tag{B.3}$$

is true. This is proved as follows:

$$LHS \text{ of (B.2)} = \sum_{i=0}^{i=n} i + (n+1),$$

$$= \frac{n(n+1)}{2} + (n+1),$$

by the inductive hypothesis (B.3),

$$= \frac{n(n+1) + 2(n+1)}{2},$$

$$= \frac{(n+1)(n+2)}{2},$$

$$= RHS \text{ of (B.2)}.$$

Thus, the inductive step has been established. As both the base case and the inductive step have been established, the prcof of (B.1) for all natural numbers follows by mathematical induction.

b) We want to prove that:

$$\sum_{i=0}^{i=n} i^3 = \left(\frac{n(n+1)}{2}\right)^2, \tag{B.4}$$

holds for all non-negative natural numbers n.

Base Case When $n = 0$, then:

$$LHS \text{ of (B.4)} = \sum_{i=0}^{i=0} i^3 = 0.$$

Similarly, when $n = 0$, then:

$$RHS \text{ of (B.4)} = \left(\frac{0(0+1)}{2}\right)^2 = 0.$$

As both the LHS and RHS of (B.4) are equal to 0, the base case is established.

Inductive Step We have to prove that:

$$\sum_{i=0}^{i=n+1} i^3 = \left(\frac{(n+1)(n+2)}{2}\right)^2, \tag{B.5}$$

on the assumption that:

$$\sum_{i=0}^{i=n} i^3 = \left(\frac{n(n+1)}{2}\right)^2,$$ (B.6)

is true. This is proved like this:

$$LHS \text{ of } (B.5) = \sum_{i=0}^{i=n} i^3 + (n+1)^3,$$

$$= \left(\frac{n(n+1)}{2}\right)^2 + (n+1)^3,$$

by the inductive hypothesis (B.6),

$$= \left(\frac{n+1}{2}\right)^2 (n^2 + 4n + 4),$$

$$= \left(\frac{(n+1)(n+2)}{2}\right)^2,$$

$$= RHS \text{ of } (B.5).$$

Thus, the inductive step has been established. As both the base case and the inductive step have been established, the proof of (B.4) for all natural numbers follows by mathematical induction.

C

Glossary of Terms

abstraction, operational Another name for *procedural abstraction*.

abstraction, procedural When writing a formal specification a person puts *procedural abstraction* into practice if he or she ignores—for the time being—issues relating to the eventual implementation of the system being specified. Thus, for example, operations are specified by describing their input-output behaviour rather than by giving an algorithm that produces the output from the input. Procedural abstraction is sometimes known as *operational abstraction*.

abstraction, representational When writing a formal specification a person puts *representational abstraction* into practice if he or she employs high-level mathematical data types—like sets, relations, functions, sequences and bags—rather than low-level data types characteristic of most imperative programming languages, such as arrays and records.

adequate See under *complete*.

aliorelative Another name for an *irreflexive* relation.

annotated command An *annotated command* is a command with formulas—known as *annotations*—embedded within it. A *properly annotated command*—in the language whose abstract syntax is given on p. 191—is a command in which annotations have been inserted at the following points:

(1) before each command γ_i, for $2 \leq i \leq n$, in a sequence of commands $\gamma_1; \gamma_2; \ldots; \gamma_n$ which is *not* an assignment command and

(2) after the word **do** in a **while**-loop and in a **for**-loop.

In clause (1) the sequence $\gamma_1; \gamma_2; \ldots; \gamma_n$ must not be a sub-sequence of a longer sequence of commands. A *properly annotated (Hoare) triple* is a formula $\{P\} \gamma \{Q\}$ where γ is a properly annotated command.

antecedent Let $P \Rightarrow Q$ be an implicative formula. Then the formula P is known as the *antecedent* of the conditional.

antisymmetric A binary relation $F: X \leftrightarrow X$ is *antisymmetric* if, for all $x, y \in X$, $x \mathrel{F} y$ and $y \mathrel{F} x$ together imply that $x = y$. For example, the subset relation $\subseteq$ is antisymmetric.

apodosis Let $P \Rightarrow Q$ be a conditional formula. Then the formula Q is known as the *apodosis* of the implication.

argument (1) Let $f: X \rightarrow Y$ be a function and let x be an element in its domain. Then x is the *argument* of the function f when f is applied to x. (2) An *argument* is a structured, linguistic entity made up out of a single conclusion and a number of premises. The premises and conclusion are all propositions that can be either true or false. The following is an example of an argument:

> Gray is snoring;
> If Gray is snoring, then she is asleep;
> therefore, Gray is asleep.

The conclusion is individuated by the fact that it is preceded by the word 'therefore', but this is not the only way in which the conclusion can be singled out.

When the propositions in an argument are replaced by variables or schematic letters, then we get what is properly called an *argument schema*, but this is also usually referred to just as an *argument*.

In formal or mathematical logic arguments are represented by sequents. For more information about these see under *sequent*.

asserted program See under *Hoare triple*.

assertion See under *Hoare triple*.

associative (1) A binary operator $\_\,\square\,\_: X \times X \rightarrow X$ is *associative* if, for all $x, y, z: X$, $(x \mathbin{\square} y) \mathbin{\square} z = x \mathbin{\square} (y \mathbin{\square} z)$. (2) A two-place truth-functional connective $\square$ is *associative* if $(P \mathbin{\square} Q) \mathbin{\square} R \dashv\vdash P \mathbin{\square} (Q \mathbin{\square} R)$. By one of the results established in section 10.3 it would be possible to say that $\square$ is associative if the formula

$$(P \mathbin{\square} Q) \mathbin{\square} R \Longleftrightarrow P \mathbin{\square} (Q \mathbin{\square} R)$$

is a theorem. In a logical system that is both sound and complete it is also possible to say that $\square$ is associative if

$$(P \mathbin{\square} Q) \mathbin{\square} R =\!\models P \mathbin{\square} (Q \mathbin{\square} R).$$

When explaining the terms *commutative, backwards distribution, forwards distribution, idempotent, one-point laws* and *unit element* in this glossary, I do so using a syntactic equivalence, even though this could have been done in these other ways.

associative, left (1) Let $\_ \square \_ : X \times X \longrightarrow X$ be a binary operator. Then to say that $\square$ is *left associative* or that it *associates to the left* means that, for all $x, y, z : X$, $x \square y \square z$ is to be understood as $(x \square y) \square z$. (2) A two-place truth-functional connective $\square$ is *left associative* or *associates to the left* if $P \square Q \square R$ is to be parsed as $(P \square Q) \square R$. In Z the connectives $\land$, $\lor$ and $\Longleftrightarrow$ are all left associative.

associative, right (1) Let $\_ \square \_ : X \times X \longrightarrow X$ be a binary operator. Then to say that $\square$ is *right associative* or that it *associates to the right* means that, for all $x, y, z : X$, $x \square y \square z$ is to be understood as $x \square (y \square z)$. (2) A two-place truth-functional connective $\square$ is *right associative* or *associates to the right* if $P \square Q \square R$ is to be parsed as $P \square (Q \square R)$. In Z the connective $\Rightarrow$ associates to the right.

asymmetric A binary relation $F : X \leftrightarrow X$ is *asymmetric* if, for all $x, y \in X$, $x \underline{F} y$ implies that $\neg(y \underline{F} x)$. For example, the relation $\_ < \_ : \mathbf{Z} \leftrightarrow \mathbf{Z}$ is asymmetric.

axiom The word 'axiom' has several meanings. In this book an *axiom* is a formula A which is such that the sequent $\varnothing \mapsto A$ is postulated to be valid. In other words, if A is an axiom, then $\varnothing \mapsto A$ is a primitive start sequent.

axiomatic description See under *description, axiomatic*.

backward relational composition See under *composition, relational*.

bag A *bag* is an unordered collection of things, all of which belong to the same type, in which multiple occurrences of the same thing are significant. In Z a bag is defined to be a function from an arbitrary set X of things to the set of positive whole numbers, thus $\text{bag}\, X == X \nrightarrow \mathbf{N}_1$. Let $L : \text{bag}\, X$ be a bag. Then $x \mapsto i \in L$ iff the thing x occurs i times in the bag L. Bags are also sometimes known as *multisets* or *families*. Hayes (1993), section A.12, pp. 260–261, introduces generalized bags in which an element can occur a negative number of times. The set of all generalized bags, whose elements are drawn from the set X, is represented as $\text{bag}_\pm X$ and is defined as $X \nrightarrow (\mathbf{Z} \setminus \{0\})$.

basic type See under *type, basic*.

biconditional Another name for a *bi-implication*.

bi-implication If P and Q are formulas, then so is $P \Longleftrightarrow Q$ and this is known variously as a *bi-implicative formula*, or as a *bi-implication* or as a *biconditional formula* (or simply as a *biconditional*). The formula $P \Longleftrightarrow Q$ can be read as 'P iff Q'. The reading 'P is equivalent to Q' is best avoided, because the word 'equivalent' has quite a few different meanings and so this reading may lead to confusion. A biconditional is true if both its constituent formulas have the same truth-value and it is false if they have different truth-values. Bi-implication is not idempotent. It is, however, commutative and associative and every logically true formula is a two-sided unit for it.

bijection A *bijection* f from X to Y is a total function which is both injective and surjective. It is sometimes known as a *one-to-one correspondence*. The collection of all bijections from X to Y is symbolized as $X \rightarrowtail\!\!\!\rightarrow Y$.

carrier (of a type) See under *type*.

Cartesian product type See under *type, Cartesian product*.

command, annotated See under *annotated command*.

commutative (1) Let $\_\square\_ : X \times X \longrightarrow X$ be a binary operator. Then $\square$ is *commutative* if, for all $x, y \colon X$, $x \square y = y \square x$. (2) A two-place truth-functional connective $\square$ is *commutative* if $P \square Q \dashv\vdash Q \square P$. (See the entry for the term *associative* for some information about the use of the relation $\dashv\vdash$ in this explanation.)

complete A logical system is *complete* or *adequate* if whenever $\Gamma \models A$, then $\Gamma \vdash A$. In other words, a logical system is *complete* or *adequate* if whenever the sequent $\Gamma \mapsto A$ is semantically valid, then it is also syntactically valid.

composition, relational Let $F \colon X \leftrightarrow Y$ and $G \colon Y \leftrightarrow Z$. Then an ordered pair $x \mapsto z$ belongs to the *composition* of F with G—which is symbolized as $F\,\mathring{,}\,G$—iff there exists at least one thing in Y to which x is related by F and which, in turn, is related to z by G:

$$x \mapsto z \in F\,\mathring{,}\,G \Longleftrightarrow \exists y \colon Y \bullet x \,\underline{F}\, y \wedge y \,\underline{G}\, z,$$

where $x \colon X$ and $y \colon Y$. The symbol $\circ$ is used for *backward relational composition*. Thus, $G \circ F$ is the same as $F\,\mathring{,}\,G$.

conditional Another name for an *implication*.

conjunct See under *conjunction*.

conjunction If P and Q are formulas, then so is $P \wedge Q$ and this is known as the *conjunction* of P and Q. The symbol $\wedge$ can be read as 'and'. The formulas P and Q in a conjunction $P \wedge Q$ are called *conjuncts*. $P \wedge Q$ is true iff both P and Q are true. Conjunction is idempotent, commutative, associative and every logically true formula is a two-sided unit for it.

consequent Let $P \Rightarrow Q$ be an implicative formula. Then the formula Q is known as the *consequent* of the implication.

consistent A set of formulas Γ is *consistent* iff it is not inconsistent.

correct A thema is *correct* iff the output sequent has to be valid when all the input sequents are valid. Thus, in a correct thema validity is transmitted from the input sequents to the output sequent and invalidity is retransmitted from the output sequent to at least one of the input sequents. These properties of a correct thema can be called the principles of *the transmission of validity* and *the retransmission* *of invalidity*, respectively, by analogy with what Lakatos (1978), p. 4, calls the principles of *the transmission of truth* and *the retransmission of falsity* in a valid argument. The analogy is not exact, however, because in my definition of a correct thema the notion of validity that is used is the syntactic one. Geach—in (Lewis 1991), p. 274—talks of thematic rules as being 'validity-preserving', but he is using the semantic notion of validity.

data decomposition See under *refinement, data.*

data refinement See under *refinement, data.*

data reification See under *refinement, data.*

data type A *data type* is a collection of objects together with a number of operations defined on them. Following Jones (1986), p. 281, we can distinguish between a *functional data type* and a *state-based* one. An example of a functional data type is that which consists of all the sets belonging to some type X together with all the standard operations on sets, like intersection, union, difference and so on. These operations are functions. An example of a state-based data type is provided by any Z specification of a sequential system, such as that of the internal telephone directory given in chapter 4.

decomposition, data Another name for *data refinement.*

definiendum In a definition the *definiendum* is the symbol or the combination of symbols being newly introduced. For example, in the abbreviation definition $X \leftrightarrow Y == \mathbf{P}(X \times Y)$ the combination of symbols $X \leftrightarrow Y$ is the *definiendum.*

definiens In a definition the *definiens* is the symbol or the combination of symbols that are used in order to confer meaning on the symbol or combination of symbols being newly introduced. For example, in the abbreviation definition

$$X \leftrightarrow Y == \mathbf{P}(X \times Y)$$

the *definiens* is the combination of symbols $\mathbf{P}(X \times Y)$.

definite description operator In Z the *definite description operator* is represented by the Greek letter μ. The term $\mu D \mid P \bullet t$ refers to the unique thing which is the value of the term t, which may contain variables declared in D. If it does, then their values must satisfy the formula P. For example, $\mu x \colon \mathbf{N}_1 \mid x^2 = x \bullet x$ is a designation for the number one. People with a knowledge of logic will be aware that μ has a different meaning in Z from its usual meaning in mathematical logic. Given a formula P containing free variables $x_1, x_2, \ldots, x_n, y \colon \mathbf{N}$ the usual meaning of $\mu y P(x_1, x_2, \ldots, x_n, y)$ is that it denotes the *least* natural number y which makes P true. See, for example, (Mendelson 1964), p. 121. In formal logic the definite description operator is usually represented by an upside-down, lowercase, Greek letter iota.

description, axiomatic An *axiomatic description* in Z is one of the available methods of definition. It is fully explained in section 20.1.

disjunct See under *disjunction*.

disjunction If P and Q are formulas, then so is $P \vee Q$ and this is known as the *disjunction* of P and Q. The symbol $\vee$ can be read as 'or'. The formulas P and Q in a disjunction $P \vee Q$ are called *disjuncts*. $P \vee Q$ is false iff both P and Q are false. Disjunction is idempotent, commutative, associative and every logically false formula is a two-sided unit for it.

distribution, backwards (1) Let $\_ \square \_, \_ \heartsuit \_ : X \times X \longrightarrow X$ be two binary operators. Then $\square$ *distributes backwards* through $\heartsuit$ if, for all $x, y, z \in X$, the following formula holds:
$$(x \heartsuit y) \square z = (x \square z) \heartsuit (y \square z).$$

(2) A two-place truth-functional connective $\square$ *distributes backwards* through another such connective $\heartsuit$ if $(P \heartsuit Q) \square R \dashv\vdash (P \square R) \heartsuit (Q \square R)$. (See the entry for the term *associative* for some information about the use of the relation $\dashv\vdash$ in this explanation.) People often talk of *left* and *right* distribution, but—as Woodcock and Loomes (1988) point out in footnote 6 on p. 128—such terminology is not used consistently.

distribution, forwards (1) Let $\_ \square \_, \_ \heartsuit \_ : X \times X \longrightarrow X$ be two binary operators. Then $\square$ *distributes forwards* through $\heartsuit$ if, for all $x, y, z \in X$, the following formula holds:
$$x \square (y \heartsuit z) = (x \square y) \heartsuit (x \square z).$$

(2) A two-place truth-functional connective $\square$ *distributes forwards* through another such connective $\heartsuit$ if $P \square (Q \heartsuit R) \dashv\vdash (P \square Q) \heartsuit (P \square R)$. (See the entry for the term *associative* for some information about the use of the relation $\dashv\vdash$ in this explanation.)

domain Let $F : X \leftrightarrow Y$ be a relation. Then the *domain* of F, symbolized as $\operatorname{dom} F$, is the set of all those things in X that are related by F to at least one thing in Y. In other words, the domain of F is the collection of every element x in X which occurs as the first component of an ordered pair $x \mapsto y$ that is a member of F:
$$x \in \operatorname{dom} F \iff (\exists y : Y \bullet x \mapsto y \in F).$$

Note that the set X is *not* known as the domain of the relation F in Z. The terminology of Z allows there to be members of X which are not in $\operatorname{dom} F$.

domain anti-restriction Let $F : X \leftrightarrow Y$ be a relation and $U \subseteq X$. Then $x \mapsto y$ is a member of the relation which results when F has had its *domain anti-restricted* to U iff x does not belong to U and $x \mapsto y$ is a member of F. This relation is written as $U \vartriangleleft F$. Sometimes domain anti-restriction is known as *domain subtraction* or *domain corestriction*.

domain corestriction Another name for *domain anti-restriction*.

domain restriction Let $F: X \leftrightarrow Y$ be a relation and $U \subseteq X$. Then $x \mapsto y$ is a member of the relation which results when F has had its *domain restricted* to U iff x belongs to U and $x \mapsto y$ is a member of F. This relation is written as $U \lhd F$.

domain subtraction Another name for *domain anti-restriction*.

equivalent This is a word that is used in quite a few different ways. In this book *equivalence* is always a relation between formulas, but three different relations can be signified by the word 'equivalent' and these are:

(1) Let *lhs* == *rhs* be an abbreviation definition, where *lhs* is either a single symbol or a combination of symbols and *rhs* is also either a single symbol or a combination of symbols. Then *lhs* is said to be *equivalent (by definition)* to *rhs*.

(2) Two formulas P and Q are (*semantically*) *equivalent* if the sequents $P \mapsto Q$ and $Q \mapsto P$ are both semantically valid.

(3) Two formulas P and Q are (*syntactically*) *equivalent* if the sequents $P \mapsto Q$ and $Q \mapsto P$ are both syntactically valid.

Sometimes a biconditional *formula* $P \iff Q$ is called an *equivalence*—see, for example, (James and James 1976), p. 138, and (Jones 1986), p. 282—but this usage is best avoided as the words 'equivalent' and 'equivalence' have several other meanings and there are alternative ways of referring to a formula whose main connective is $\iff$.

family Another name for a *bag*.

from-set Let $F: X \leftrightarrow Y$ be a relation. Then the set X is known as the *from-set* or the *source* of the relation.

function In Z a *function* or *mapping* f from X to Y is a special kind of relation in which f maps an object x in X to at most one object y in Y. There are many different kinds of function in Z. The least constrained is the *partial function*. The set of all partial functions from X to Y is symbolized as $X \nrightarrow Y$ and is defined thus:

$$X \nrightarrow Y == \{ f: X \leftrightarrow Y \mid (\forall x: X; y, z: Y \bullet x \mapsto y \in f \land x \mapsto z \in f \Rightarrow y = z) \}.$$

function, injective See under *injection*.

function, partial See under *partial function*.

function, surjective See under *surjection*.

function, total See under *total function*.

given set See under *type, basic*.

heterogeneous Let F be a binary relation. Then F is *heterogeneous* if its from-set is different from its to-set.

Hoare formula See under *Hoare triple*.

Hoare triple A (*Hoare*) *triple* is a formula made up out of three components. It is written $\{P\}\,\gamma\,\{Q\}$, where P and Q are formulas of Z and γ is a command belonging to some programming language. The formula $\{P\}\,\gamma\,\{Q\}$ is true in a state *sta* iff, for all states *sta'*, if P is true in *sta* and the execution of γ transforms *sta* into *sta'* and the execution of γ terminates, then Q is true in *sta'*. The formula $\{P\}\,\gamma\,\{Q\}$ is true (in all states) iff, for all states *sta* and *sta'*, if P is true in *sta* and the execution of γ transforms *sta* into *sta'* and the execution of γ terminates, then Q is true in *sta'*. What is called a *Hoare triple* in this book is known elsewhere by a variety of names. Some of these alternative designations are: *asserted program*, *assertion*, *partial correctness assertion* and *partial correctness specification*.

homogeneous Let F be a binary relation. Then F is *homogeneous* if its from-set is the same as its to-set.

idempotent (1) A binary operator $\_\,\square\,\_ : X \times X \longrightarrow X$ is *idempotent* if, for all $x : X$, $x \square x = x$. (2) A two-place truth-functional connective $\square$ is *idempotent* if $P \square P \mathbin{\Vdash\!\!+} P$. (See the entry for the term *associative* for some information about the use of the relation $\mathbin{\Vdash\!\!+}$ in this explanation.)

identity element See under *unit element*.

image, relational Let $F : X \leftrightarrow Y$ and $U \subseteq X$. Then the *relational image* of the set U through the relation F (sometimes called the *F-image* of U), which is written $F(\!|U|\!)$, is the set of all those elements in the range of F to which F maps elements of U. In other words, it is the set of all those objects y to which F relates some member x of U. In symbols,

$$y \in F(\!|U|\!) \iff \exists x : X \bullet x \underline{\,F\,} y \wedge x \in U.$$

implication If P and Q are formulas, then so is $P \Rightarrow Q$ and this is known variously as an *implicative formula*, or as an *implication*, or as a *conditional* (*formula*) or as a *hypothetical* (*formula*). The formula $P \Rightarrow Q$ can be read as 'if P, then Q'. The reading of $P \Rightarrow Q$ as 'P implies (that) Q' is to be avoided. This is because $P \Rightarrow Q$ is a formula and the connective $\Rightarrow$ makes a formula out of two other formulas, whereas to say that P implies Q is to state that a relation holds between the formulas P and Q. To be precise, P implies Q when the formula $P \Rightarrow Q$ is either a theorem or a logical truth. (If it becomes important to distinguish these cases, we can talk of *syntactic* implication and *semantic* implication, respectively. Unfortunately, the use of the word 'implication' for a formula in the object language of the propositional calculus and also for a relation in its meta-language does not aid clarity.) For the formal languages dealt with in this book, to say that P implies Q is the same as saying that P entails Q. The constituent formula P is known as the *antecedent* or the *protasis* of the conditional and Q is known as the *consequent* or the *apodosis* of the conditional. A conditional is false iff its antecedent is true and its consequent is false. Implication is neither idempotent, nor commutative nor associative. Every logically true formula is a left unit for it, but it does not have a right unit.

inconsistent A set of formulas Γ is (*proof-theoretically*) *inconsistent* if there exists a formula P such that both $\Gamma \vdash P$ and $\Gamma \vdash \neg P$.

injection An *injection* or *injective function* f from X to Y is a mapping which is one-to-one, that is to say, if $f(x_1) = f(x_2)$, then $x_1 = x_2$. The collection of all partial injections from X to Y is symbolized as $X \rightarrowtail\mkern-14mu\rightarrow Y$, the collection of all total injections as $X \rightarrowtail Y$, the collection of all bijections as $X \rightarrowtail\mkern-17mu\rightarrow Y$ and the collection of all finite partial injections from X to Y is symbolized as $X \rightarrowtail\mkern-14mu\rightarrow Y$.

injective function See under *injection*.

intransitive Let $F: X \leftrightarrow X$ be a binary relation. Then F is *intransitive* if $x \underline{F} y$ and $y \underline{F} z$ together imply that $\neg(x \underline{F} z)$. For example, the relation *being the father of* is intransitive, because if x is the father of y and y is the father of z, then x cannot be the father of z.

inverse element Let $\_ \Box \_: X \times X \longrightarrow X$ be a binary operator which has the unit element e, that is to say, $x \Box e = x = e \Box x$, for all $x \in X$. Then $y \in X$ is an *inverse element* (or simply *inverse*) of x for the operation $\Box$ if $x \Box y = e = y \Box x$. In the case of addition over the integers 0 is the unit element and the inverse of an integer i is its negative $-i$.

inverse, relational Let $F: X \leftrightarrow Y$ be a relation. Then $y \mapsto x$ is a member of the *relational inverse* of F—which is symbolized as $F^\sim$—iff $x \mapsto y$ is a member of F.

irreflexive A binary relation $F: X \leftrightarrow X$ is *irreflexive* if it does not relate any member of X to itself. In other words, if $\neg \exists x: X \bullet x \underline{F} x$. Equivalently, F is irreflexive if $F \cap \text{id}(X) = \varnothing$. Sometimes an irreflexive relation is known as an *aliorelative* one.

law (1) A *law* of, say, the propositional calculus is a formula that is either a theorem or a logical truth. (The propositional calculus is both sound and complete, therefore a formula is a theorem iff it is a logical truth.) (2) A *law* is a statement in the meta-language expressing some property of the Z symbols. Such a law is often expressed as a semantic or syntactic equivalence.

left associative See under *associative, left*.

left unit See under *unit*.

mapping Another name for a *function*.

multi-set Another name for a *bag*.

negation If P is a formula, then so is $\neg P$ and this is known as the *negation* of P. $\neg P$ can be read as 'not P'. The negation of P is true if P is false and false if P is true.

neutral element See under *unit element*.

non-symmetric A binary relation $F: X \leftrightarrow X$ is *non-symmetric* if $x \underline{F} y$ implies neither that $y \underline{F} x$ nor that $\neg(y \underline{F} x)$. For example, the relation *being a brother of* is non-symmetric, because if x is a brother of y, then y may be either a brother or a sister of x.

non-transitive Let $F: X \leftrightarrow X$ be a binary relation. Then F is *non-transitive* if $x \underline{F} y$ and $y \underline{F} z$ together imply neither that $x \underline{F} z$ nor that $\neg(x \underline{F} z)$. For example, the relation *being a friend of* is non-transitive, because if x is a friend of y and y is a friend of z, then either x may be a friend of z or he or she may not.

one-point laws The following statements are known as *one-point laws*:

$$P[t/x] \dashv\vdash \exists x: X \bullet x = t \wedge P,$$
$$P[t/x] \dashv\vdash \forall x: X \bullet x = t \Rightarrow P.$$

In both of these x can occur free in P and t is a term of the same type as x. (See the entry for the term *associative* for some information about the use of the relation $\dashv\vdash$ in this explanation.)

one-to-one A function f from X to Y is said to be *one-to-one* if $f(x_1) = f(x_2)$ implies that $x_1 = x_2$. In Z a one-to-one function is known as an *injection* or is said to be *injective*. The collection of all partial injections from X to Y is symbolized as $X \rightarrowtail\hspace{-0.5em}\mapsto Y$, the collection of all total injections as $X \rightarrowtail Y$, the collection of all bijections as $X \rightarrowtail\hspace{-0.5em}\twoheadrightarrow Y$ and the collection of all finite partial injections from X to Y is symbolized as $X \rightarrowtail\hspace{-0.5em}+\hspace{-0.5em}+ Y$.

one-to-one correspondence See under *bijection*.

onto A function f from X to Y is said to be *onto* if ran $f = Y$. In Z an onto function is known as a *surjection* or is said to be *surjective*. The collection of all partial surjections from X to Y is symbolized as $X \twoheadrightarrow\hspace{-0.5em}+ Y$, the collection of all total surjections as $X \twoheadrightarrow Y$ and the collection of all bijections as $X \rightarrowtail\hspace{-0.5em}\twoheadrightarrow Y$.

operational abstraction Another name for *procedural abstraction*.

partial correctness assertion See under *Hoare triple*.

partial correctness specification See under *Hoare triple*.

partial function A function f from X to Y is said to be *partial* if $\text{dom } f \subseteq X$. (This has the consequence that the collection of all *total* functions from X to Y is a proper subset of all the *partial* functions from X to Y. The collection of all total functions and the collection of all partial functions are *not* disjoint.) The collection of all partial functions from X to Y is symbolized as $X \nrightarrow Y$, the collection of all partial injections as $X \nrightarrowtail Y$, the collection of all partial surjections as $X \nrightarrow\!\!\!\rightarrow Y$ and the collection of all finite partial functions from X to Y is symbolized as $X \nrightarrow\!\!\!\rightarrow Y$.

partial injection See under *injection*.

partial surjection See under *surjection*.

precedence Let $\_ \square \_, \_ \heartsuit \_ : X \times X \longrightarrow X$ be binary operators. Then $\square$ has *higher precedence* than $\heartsuit$ if $x \square y \heartsuit z$ means $(x \square y) \heartsuit z$ and $x \heartsuit y \square z$ means $x \heartsuit (y \square z)$.

procedural abstraction See under *abstraction, procedural*.

product type See under *type, Cartesian product*.

properly annotated command See under *annotated command*.

properly annotated (Hoare) triple See under *annotated command*.

protasis Let $P \Rightarrow Q$ be a conditional formula. Then the formula P is known as the *protasis* of the implicative formula.

range Let $F : X \leftrightarrow Y$ be a relation. Then the *range* of F, symbolized as $\text{ran } F$, is the set of all those things in Y to which at least one thing in X is related by F. In other words, the range of F is the collection of every element y in Y which occurs as the second component of an ordered pair $x \mapsto y$ that is a member of F:

$$y \in \text{ran } F \iff (\exists x : X \bullet x \mapsto y \in F).$$

range anti-restriction Let $F : X \leftrightarrow Y$ be a relation and $V \subseteq Y$. Then $x \mapsto y$ is a member of the relation which results when F has had its *range anti-restricted* to V iff y does not belong to V and $x \mapsto y$ is a member of F. This relation is written as $U \triangleright F$. Sometimes range anti-restriction is known as *range subtraction* or *range corestriction*.

range corestriction Another name for *range anti-restriction*.

range restriction Let $F : X \leftrightarrow Y$ be a relation and $V \subseteq Y$. Then $x \mapsto y$ is a member of the relation which results when F has had its *range restricted* to V iff y belongs to V and $x \mapsto y$ is a member of F. This relation is written as $U \triangleright F$.

range subtraction Another name for *range anti-restriction*.

refinement, data Let Φ and Ψ be two data types. Then Ψ is a *refinement* of Φ if the objects of Ψ model or implement those of Φ and the operations defined on Ψ model or implement those defined on Φ. Data refinement is also known as *data reification* or *data decomposition*. See chapter 13 for more information about data refinement.

reflexive A binary relation $F: X \leftrightarrow X$ is *reflexive* if, for all $x \in X$, $x \underline{F} x$. Equivalently, F is reflexive if $id(X) \subseteq F$.

reification, data Another name for *data refinement*.

relational composition See under *composition, relational*.

relational image See under *image, relational*.

relational inversion See under *inverse, relational*.

representational abstraction See under *abstraction, representational*.

right associative See under *associative, right*.

right unit See under *unit*.

schema (1) A *schema* in Z is a named, structured, linguistic entity consisting of a collection of declarations and a number of formulas. (The number may well be zero, in which case the default is the constant formula *true*.) See section 20.3 for more information about how schemas can be defined in Z. (2) In logic an argument *schema* is an argument in which the constituent propositions have been replaced by variables or schematic letters. A thema *schema* is to be understood analogously.

schema type See under *type, schema*.

semantic turnstile See under *turnstile*.

semantic validity See under *validity*.

sequent A (*single-conclusion*) *sequent* is an ordered pair consisting of a set of formulas Γ, which are known as the *premises* of the sequent, and a single formula A, which is known as the *conclusion* of the sequent. In this book, such a sequent is represented as $\Gamma \mapsto A$. This choice of notation needs some explanation.

Various symbols are used in the literature on logic to represent a sequent. For example, Paulson (1987), p. 38, uses the notation $\Gamma \vdash A$, Dummett (1977), p. 121, writes $\Gamma : A$ and it is also possible to write $\Gamma \longrightarrow A$, though the arrow is usually used to represent a *multiple-conclusion sequent* which is defined either to be an ordered pair consisting of two sets of formulas or an ordered pair consisting of two sequences of formulas. The creator of the multiple-conclusion sequent calculus, Gentzen (1969), p. 71, uses the arrow, as does Gallier (1986), p. 62, who writes that instead 'of using the notation (Γ, Δ), a sequent is usually denoted as

$\Gamma \longrightarrow \Delta$.' (Shoesmith and Smiley (1978), pp. 33–34, have a useful discussion of how such a sequent has been interpreted.)

It is not a good idea to represent a sequent as $\Gamma \vdash A$, because the symbol $\vdash$ is needed in the metatheory of logic to represent the deducibility relation—see, for example, Dummett (1977), p. 122, and Hunter (1971), pp. 74–75 and 168. In a book on Z, the use of either $\Gamma : A$ or $\Gamma \longrightarrow A$ to represent a sequent would be potentially very confusing, because the symbols : and $\longrightarrow$ already have a definite meaning in Z—the colon is used to give the type of an expression and the arrow is used to denote the set of all total functions between two sets. As a sequent is an ordered pair and as the symbol $\mapsto$ is used to form ordered pairs in Z, it makes sense to write $\Gamma \mapsto A$ for the sequent that consists of the set Γ of formulas and the single formula A. Using $\mapsto$ also has the advantage that—in a sense—it combines the symbols $\vdash$ and $\longrightarrow$ which are probably the commonest symbols used to form a sequent. It only needs to be said that when used in the context $\Gamma \mapsto A$ the symbol $\mapsto$ is different from the symbol that looks the same in Z. Here, $\mapsto$ is a symbol of the meta-language that I use to talk about Z.

As already mentioned, the symbol $\vdash$ is used in this book for the deducibility relation. Thus, $\Gamma \mapsto A \in \_ \vdash \_$ iff A is a syntactic consequence of Γ. I have used a Z-like notation to explain the meaning of $\vdash$, but it needs to be stressed that $\Gamma \mapsto A \in \_ \vdash \_$ (or, equivalently, $\Gamma \vdash A$) is a statement of the meta-language used to talk about Z.

sequent, start A *start sequent* is a sequent that can be used to form a leaf node in a correctly constructed tree proof.

set, given See under *type, basic*.

set type See under *type, set*.

sound A logical system is *sound* if whenever $\Gamma \vdash A$, then $\Gamma \models A$. Equivalently, a logical system is *sound* if whenever the sequent $\Gamma \mapsto A$ is syntactically valid, then it is also semantically valid.

source See under *from-set*.

standard Z See under *Z, standard*.

start sequent See under *sequent, start*.

stronger formula See under *weaker and stronger formulas*.

surjection A *surjection* or *surjective function* f from X to Y is a mapping which is onto, that is to say, ran $f = Y$. The collection of all partial surjections from X to Y is symbolized as $X \nrightarrow\!\!\!\!\rightarrow Y$, the collection of all total surjections as $X \longrightarrow\!\!\!\!\rightarrow Y$ and the collection of all bijections as $X \rightarrowtail\!\!\!\!\rightarrow Y$.

surjective function See under *surjection*.

symmetric A binary relation $F: X \leftrightarrow X$ is *symmetric* if, for all $x, y \in X$, $x \underline{F} y$
implies that $y \underline{F} x$. Equivalently, F is symmetric if $F = F^\sim$.

syntactic turnstile See under *turnstile.*

syntactic validity See under *validity.*

target See under *to-set.*

thema (1) A *thema* is a structured, linguistic entity made up out of a collection of
arguments and a single argument. (Note that the plural of *thema* is *themata.*)
There is no standard terminology for the components of a thema, but I refer to
the collection of arguments as the *input arguments* to the thema and the single
argument as its *output argument.* Whereas an argument is made up out of a
number of premises and a conclusion—all of which are propositions—a thema is
made up out of a number of input arguments and an output argument—all of
which are arguments. The following is an example of a thema:

> If Gray is snoring, then she is asleep;
> Gray is not asleep;
> therefore, Gray is not snoring.
> ─────────────────────────────────
> If Gray is snoring, then she is asleep;
> therefore, if Gray is not asleep, then she is not snoring.

(2) A *thema schema* is a thema in which the constituent propositions of the
arguments involved are replaced by variables or schematic letters. The following
is an example of a thema schema:

$$\frac{P \Rightarrow Q; \neg Q; \text{therefore}, \neg P.}{P \Rightarrow Q; \text{therefore}, \neg Q \Rightarrow \neg P.}$$

The thema displayed above is an *instance* of this thema schema. It is obtained
by substituting propositions for the schematic letters that occur in the thema
schema. When there is little danger of confusion I refer to thema schemas simply
as *themata.* (3) A *thema* is an ordered pair made up out of a set of sequents
and a single sequent. Such a pair is often depicted as a tree. For example, the
following is an example of such a thema:

$$\frac{P \Rightarrow Q, \neg Q \longmapsto \neg P}{P \Rightarrow Q \longmapsto \neg Q \Rightarrow \neg P.}$$

Above the horizontal line occur the *input sequents*—in this case there is only one
of these—and below the line there appears the *output sequent.* Such a thema is
also known as a *thematic rule* or simply as a *rule* when there is little danger of
confusing it with other things that are also known as rules.

theorem Let $\Gamma \longmapsto A$ be a syntactically valid sequent in a given logical system. Then
A is a *theorem* of that logical system if $\Gamma = \emptyset$.

to-set Let $F: X \leftrightarrow Y$ be a relation. Then the set Y is known as the *to-set* or the *target* of the relation.

total function A function f from X to Y is said to be *total* if dom $f = X$. The collection of all total functions from X to Y is symbolized as $X \longrightarrow Y$, that of all total injections as $X \rightarrowtail Y$, that of all total surjections as $X \twoheadrightarrow Y$ and that of all bijections as $X \rightarrowtail\!\!\!\!\twoheadrightarrow Y$.

total injection See under *injection*.

total surjection See under *surjection*.

transitive A binary relation $F: X \leftrightarrow X$ is *transitive* if, for all $x, y, z \in X$, $x \underline{F} y$ and $y \underline{F} z$ together imply that $x \underline{F} z$. Equivalently, F is transitive if $F^2 \subseteq F$.

turnstile The (*semantic*) *turnstile* is the name given to the meta-linguistic symbol $\models$. It represents a relation between sets of formulas and formulas. In other words, $\models$ is a set of sequents. We have that $\Gamma \mapsto A \in \_ \models \_$ or $\Gamma \models A$ iff A is a semantic consequence of the set of formulas Γ. Similarly, the (*syntactic*) *turnstile* is the name given to the meta-linguistic symbol $\vdash$. It represents a relation between sets of formulas and formulas. In other words, $\vdash$ is a set of sequents. We have that $\Gamma \mapsto A \in \_ \vdash \_$ or $\Gamma \vdash A$ iff A is a syntactic consequence of the set of formulas Γ.

type Every expression in a Z document is associated with a unique type. A *type* is just a collection of objects. To be precise, a type—according to Spivey (1992), p. 24—is a special sort of expression, that is to say, something linguistic. It is common, however, also to call the set that a type stands for a *type*—even though a more accurate name for this set is the *carrier* of that type. This slightly inaccurate way of talking is followed in this book. There are two kinds of types in Z, namely *basic types* (also known as *given sets*) and *composite types*. There are three kinds of composite types, namely *set types*, *Cartesian product types* and *schema types*. These are all explained in other parts of this glossary.

type, basic Apart from **Z**, the basic type of all integers, every other basic type used in a specification document must be introduced by means of a *basic type definition*. For example, in the specification of the internal telephone directory, discussed in chapter 4, there occurs on p. 43 the following basic type definition:

$$[Person, Phone]$$

This introduces two basic types, namely *Person* and *Phone*, the internal structure and eventual implementation of which are of no concern to the specification. The given sets introduced in a basic type definition are assumed to be disjoint.

type, Cartesian product One of the three kinds of composite types to be found in Z. Let $X_1, X_2, \ldots, X_n$ be n types, where $n \geq 2$. Then $X_1 \times X_2 \times \cdots \times X_n$ is also a type. It is known as a *Cartesian product type* and it is the set of all the ordered n-tuples $(x_1, x_2, \ldots, x_n)$ such that, for $1 \leq i \leq n$, $x_i \in X_i$. Note that in Z $X \times Y \times Z$, say, is neither the same as $(X \times Y) \times Z$ nor as $X \times (Y \times Z)$. A member of $X \times Y \times Z$ is a triple, whereas a member of $(X \times Y) \times Z$, for example, is an ordered pair $((x, y), z)$ whose first component is itself an ordered pair that belongs to $X \times Y$ and whose second component is a member of Z.

type, data See under *data type*.

type, schema One of the three kinds of composite types to be found in Z. Schema types are explained in section 5.2.6 of this book.

type, set One of the three kinds of composite types to be found in Z. Let X be a type. Then $\mathbf{P}\, X$ is also a type. It is known as a *set type* and it consists of all the subsets of X.

unit element (1) Let $\_\,\square\,\_ : X \times X \longrightarrow X$ be a binary operator. Then e is a *two-sided unit element* for $\square$ if, for all $x \in X$, $x \,\square\, e = x = e \,\square\, x$. This is often shortened to *unit element* or even to *unit*. A unit element for $\square$ is sometimes known either as an *identity element* for $\square$ or a *neutral element* for $\square$. If $x \,\square\, e = x$, for all $x \in X$, then e is known as a *right unit element* (or simply a *right unit*) for $\square$ and if $e \,\square\, x = x$, for all $x \in X$, then e is known as a *left unit element* (or simply a *left unit*) for $\square$. (2) A formula A is a *two-sided unit* (or simply a *unit*) for a two-place truth-functional connective $\square$ if $P \,\square\, A \dashv\vdash P$ and $P \dashv\vdash A \,\square\, P$. A unit element for $\square$ is also known as either an *identity element* for $\square$ or a *neutral element* for $\square$. If $P \,\square\, A \dashv\vdash P$, then A is a *right unit* for $\square$ and if $A \,\square\, P \dashv\vdash P$, then A is a *left unit* for $\square$. (See the entry for the term *associative* for some information about the use of the relation $\dashv\vdash$ in this explanation.)

validity (1) A sequent $\Gamma \longmapsto P$ is (*semantically*) *valid* if there does not exist an interpretation in which P is false and every formula in Γ is true. What constitutes an interpretation varies from one logical system to the next. In the case of the propositional calculus, for example, an interpretation is a function which maps the propositional variables—in this book the letters A, B, C, P, Q and R (sometimes decorated with subscripts)—to the two truth-values. (2) A sequent $\Gamma \longmapsto P$ is (*syntactically*) *valid*—relative to a collection of primitive start sequents and a class of primitive themata—if there exists a correctly constructed tree proof which has it as its root. (Note that this definition of validity applies to a logical system formulated as a single-conclusion sequent calculus. For logical systems formulated differently syntactic validity would have to be defined differently.)

verification condition A consistent set of formulas Γ—none of which are themselves Hoare triples—is a set of *verification conditions* for the triple $\{P\} \, \gamma \, \{Q\}$ if the sequent $\Gamma \longmapsto \{P\} \, \gamma \, \{Q\}$ is syntactically valid. This has the consequence that if each formula in the set Γ can be proved to be a theorem of first-order logic, then the Hoare triple $\{P\} \, \gamma \, \{Q\}$ is a theorem of Floyd–Hoare logic.

weaker and stronger formulas If $P \vdash Q$, then P is said to be *stronger* than Q and Q is said to be *weaker* than P. In first-order logic every theorem or logical truth is weaker than every other formula and every contradiction is stronger than every other formula.

Z, standard In this book *standard Z* is the name given to the dialect of Z that is described in (Spivey 1992). Slightly different versions of Z can be found in appendices A and B of (Hayes 1993) and in (Brien and Nicholls 1992).

D

Glossary of Symbols

Introduction

Unless explicitly stated to the contrary, all the symbols listed in this appendix are part of standard Z. A number in a column headed by the word 'exp' refers to the page on which the meaning of the symbol in question is explained. A number in a column headed by the word 'def' refers to the page on which the symbol in question is defined. Blanks in either of these columns are deliberate. A small number of symbols are defined but not explained. The meaning of a greater number of symbols is explained without a formal definition being given. It is not possible to define everything.

Object Language Logical Symbols

symbol	significance	exp
true	constant true formula	13
false	constant false formula	13
$\neg$	negation	11
$\wedge$	conjunction	11
$\vee$	disjunction	11
$\Rightarrow$	implication	12
$\Longleftrightarrow$	bi-implication	13
$\parallel$	exclusive disjunction	12
$\mid$	alternative denial	14
$\downarrow$	joint denial	29
$\forall$	universal quantifier (restricted)	25
$\forall$	universal quantifier (unrestricted)	26
$\exists$	existential quantifier (restricted)	25
$\exists$	existential quantifier (unrestricted)	26
$\exists_1$	unique quantifier (restricted)	27
$\exists_1$	unique quantifier (unrestricted)	27
let	local definition	28

The symbols $\parallel$, $\mid$ and $\downarrow$ are not part of standard Z.

351

Meta-linguistic Logical Symbols

symbol	significance	exp
$\mapsto$	sequent constructor	15
$\models$	semantic consequence	16
$\models\!\mid$	semantic equivalence	18
$\vdash$	syntactic consequence	131
$\dashv\vdash$	syntactic equivalence	131

The symbol $\mapsto$, when used to form sequents, and the symbols $\models$, $\models\!\mid$, $\vdash$ and $\dashv\vdash$ are not part of standard Z. In this book they are part of the meta-language that is used to talk and reason about Z specifications.

Symbols Related to Numbers

symbol	significance	exp	def
$\mathbb{Z}$	integers	6	
$\mathbb{N}$	natural numbers	32	32
$\mathbb{N}_1$	positive whole numbers	36	36
$=$	equality	7	
$\neq$	difference	7	
$<$	less than	7	
$\leq$	less than or equal to	7	
$>$	greater than	7	
$\geq$	greater than or equal to	7	
$+$	addition	7	
$-$	subtraction	7	
$*$	multiplication	7	
div	integer division	7	
mod	remainder	7	
succ	successor function	101	
..	number range	31	287
min	smallest integer in a set		287
max	largest integer in a set		287
#	cardinality operator	38	286

Term-forming Operators

symbol	significance	exp
μ	definite description operator	27
let	local definition	28
if	conditional term	27

Symbols Related to Sets

symbol	significance	exp	def
$=$	equality	33	
$\in$	set membership	33	
$\neq$	difference		285
$\notin$	set non-membership		285
$\subseteq$	subset	33	285
$\subset$	proper subset	34	285
$\varnothing$	empty set	34	34
$\{\,\}$	empty set	34	34
$\mathbb{P}$	power set	35	
$\mathbb{P}_1$	non-empty subsets	35	35
$\mathbb{F}$	finite subsets	94	286
$\mathbb{F}_1$	non-empty finite subsets		286
$\cup$	set union	35	286
$\cap$	set intersection	35	286
$\setminus$	set difference	36	286
$\triangle$	symmetric set difference	36	286
$\bigcup$	generalized set union	38	286
$\bigcap$	generalized set intersection	38	286
$\times$	Cartesian product	42	

The symbol $\triangle$ is not part of standard Z.

Symbols Related to Relations

symbol	significance	exp	def
$\leftrightarrow$	relations	42	42
$\mapsto$	maplet	42	
dom	domain	44	288
ran	range	45	288
$;$	composition	72	289
$\circ$	backwards composition	72	289
$_-(\!\vert_-\vert\!)$	relational image	56	289
id	identity	72	72
$\lhd$	domain restriction	61	288
$\ntriangleleft$	domain anti-restriction	61	288
$\rhd$	range restriction	74	289
$\ntriangleright$	range anti-restriction	75	289
$\oplus$	overriding	76	290
$_-{}^{\sim}$	inverse of a relation	58	288
$iter,\ _-{}^{n}$	powers of a relation	73	290
$_-{}^{+},\ _-{}^{*}$	closures	73	290

Symbols Related to Functions

symbol	significance	exp	def
⇸	partial functions	91	291
→	total functions	94	291
⤔	partial injections	94	291
⤀	partial surjections	94	291
↣	total injections	94	291
↠	total surjections	94	291
⤖	bijections	94	291
⤗	partial surjective injections	94	291
⇻	finite partial functions	94	292
⤕	finite partial injections	94	292

The symbol ⤗ is not part of standard Z.

Symbols Related to Sequences

symbol	significance	exp	def
seq	sequences	97	292
seq_1	non-empty sequences	98	292
iseq	injective sequences	98	292
⌢	concatenation	98	292
⌢/	distributed concatenation	100	293
rev	reverse	100	294
↾	filtering	99	294
↿	extraction	99	294
head	first element	99	293
tail	subsequence formation	99	293
last	last element	99	293
front	subsequence formation	99	293
after	subsequence formation	99	293
drop	subsequence formation	99	293
for	subsequence formation	100	293
take	subsequence formation	100	293
disjoint	disjointness	100	294
partition	partitioning	100	295

The symbols *after*, *drop*, *for* and *take* are not part of standard Z.

Symbols Related to Bags

symbol	significance	exp	def
bag	bags	103	103
$bag_\pm$	generalized bags	335	335
count	bag counting	103	295
♯	bag counting	104	295
∈	bag membership	104	296
⊎	bag union	104	296
⊌	bag difference		296
⊓	pairwise minimum	105	296
⊔	pairwise maximum	105	296
⊑	sub-bag relationship	104	296
⊗	bag scaling		295
items	items in a sequence	105	296

The symbols $bag_\pm$, ⊓ and ⊔ are not part of standard Z.

Symbols Related to Schemas

symbol	significance	exp
$\widehat{=}$	schema definition	49
⟨...⟩	schema type constructor	86
⇨	ordered pair	86
θ	binding formation	88
⨟	composition	80
≫	piping	84
\	hiding	79
¬	negation	51
∧	conjunction	49
∨	disjunction	49
⇒	implication	49
⟺	bi-implication	49
Δ	Delta	52
Ξ	Xi	53

The symbols ⟨...⟩, ⇨ and θ are used in the meta-language employed by Spivey (1992) to give the meaning of some Z constructs. The symbol ⇨ forms ordered pairs in the meta-language. Thus, *identifier* ⇨ *value* is an ordered pair consisting of an *identifier* and its associated *value*. The Greek letters Δ and Ξ are used to form schema names, but only one of them can appear at most and that has to come first.

Bibliography

Ackermann, R. (1967). *An Introduction to Many-valued Logics*, Monographs in Modern Logic, edited by G. B. Keene, Routledge & Kegan Paul, London.

Alagić, S. and Arbib, M. A. (1978). *The Design of Well-structured and Correct Programs*, Texts and Monographs in Computer Science, edited by F. L. Bauer and David Gries, Springer-Verlag, New York.

Allen, C. and Hand, M. (1992). *Logic Primer*, The MIT Press, Cambridge (Massachusetts).

Baber, R. L. (1987). *The Spine of Software: Designing Provably Correct Software: Theory and Practice, or a Mathematical Introduction to the Semantics of Computer Programs*, Wiley, Chichester.

Backhouse, R. C. (1986). *Program Construction and Verification*, Prentice Hall International Series in Computer Science, edited by C. A. R. Hoare, Prentice Hall, Hemel Hempstead.

Barendregt, H. P. (1984). *The Lambda Calculus: Its Syntax and Semantics*, Vol. 103 of *Studies in Logic and the Foundations of Mathematics*, revised edn, North–Holland, Amsterdam.

Bird, R. and Wadler, P. (1988). *Introduction to Functional Programming*, Prentice Hall International Series in Computer Science, edited by C. A. R. Hoare, Prentice Hall, Hemel Hempstead.

Brien, S. M. and Nicholls, J. E. (1992). Z base standard: Version 1.0, *Technical Monograph PRG–107*, Programming Research Group, Oxford University Computing Laboratory.

Cass, M. and Le Poidevin, R. (1993). *A Logic Primer*, second edn, Vortext, Redbridge (Essex).

Cohen, E. (1990). *Programming in the 1990s: An Introduction to the Calculation of Programs*, Texts and Monographs in Computer Science, edited by David Gries, Springer-Verlag, New York.

Cousot, P. (1990). Methods and logics for proving programs, *in* J. van Leeuwen (ed.), *Handbook of Theoretical Computer Science: Formal Models and Semantics*, Vol. B, Elsevier, Amsterdam, pp. 841–993.

Cupillari, A. (1989). *The Nuts and Bolts of Proofs*, Wadsworth Publishing Company, Belmont (California).

Dijkstra, E. W. (1976). *A Discipline of Programming*, Prentice Hall, London.

Diller, A. (1990). *Z: An Introduction to Formal Methods*, Wiley, Chichester.

Diller, A. (1991). Program verification, Fetzer and Popper's philosophy, *Research Report CSR-91-6*, School of Computer Science, University of Birmingham.

Diller, A. (1992). Z and Hoare logics, *in* J. E. Nicholls (ed.), *Z User Workshop: York 1991*, Springer-Verlag, London, pp. 59–76.

Diller, A. (1993). LaTeX *Line by Line: Tips and Techniques for Document Processing*, John Wiley & Sons, Chichester.

Dromey, R. G. (1989). *Program Derivation: The Development of Programs from Specifications*, Addison-Wesley, Wokingham.

Dummett, M. (1977). *Elements of Intuitionism*, Oxford Logic Guides, general editor: Dana Scott, Oxford University Press, Oxford.

Fetzer, J. H. (1988). Program verification: The very idea, *Communications of the ACM* **31**: 1048–1063.

Floyd, R. W. (1967). Assigning meanings to programs, *in* J. T. Schwartz (ed.), *Mathematical Aspects of Computer Science*, Vol. XIX of *Proceedings of Symposia in Applied Mathematics*, American Mathematical Society, Providence (Rhode Island), pp. 19–32.

Franklin, J. and Daoud, A. (1988). *Introduction to Proofs in Mathematics*, Prentice Hall, Sydney.

Gallier, J. H. (1986). *Logic for Computer Science: Foundations of Automatic Theorem Proving*, Harper & Row Computer Science and Technology Series, Harper & Row, New York.

Geach, P. T. (1976). *Reason and Argument*, Blackwell, Oxford.

Gentzen, G. (1969). Investigations into logical deduction, *The Collected Papers of Gerhard Gentzen*, Studies in Logic and the Foundations of Mathematics, edited by A. Heyting, A. Mostowski, A. Robinson and P. Suppes, North-Holland, Amsterdam, pp. 68–131. Volume edited by M. E. Szabo.

Gordon, M. J. C. (1979). *The Denotational Description of Programming Languages: An Introduction*, Springer-Verlag, New York.

Gordon, M. J. C. (1988). *Programming Language Theory and its Implementation: Applicative and Imperative Paradigms*, Prentice Hall International Series in Computer Science, edited by C. A. R. Hoare, Prentice Hall, Hemel Hempstead.

Gries, D. (1981). *The Science of Programming*, Texts and Monographs in Computer Science, edited by David Gries, Springer-Verlag, New York.

Gumb, R. D. (1989). *Programming Logics: An Introduction to Verification and Semantics*, Wiley, Chichester.

Haack, S. (1974). *Deviant Logic: Some Philosophical Issues*, Cambridge University Press, London.

Hayes, I. (ed.) (1993). *Specification Case Studies*, Prentice Hall International Series in Computer Science, edited by C. A. R. Hoare, second edn, Prentice Hall, Hemel Hempstead.

Hindley, J. R. and Seldin, J. P. (1986). *Introduction to Combinators and λ-calculus*, Cambridge University Press, Cambridge. London Mathematical Society Student Texts, vol. 1.

Hoare, C. A. R. (1969). An axiomatic basis for computer programming, *Communications of the ACM* **12**: 576–580 and 583. Reprinted in (Hoare 1989), pp. 45–58.

Hoare, C. A. R. (1989). *Essays in Computing Science*, Prentice Hall International Series in Computer Science, edited by C. A. R. Hoare, Prentice Hall, Hemel Hempstead.

Hoare, C. A. R. and Wirth, N. (1973). An axiomatic definition of the programming language pascal, *Acta Informatica* **2**: 335–355. Reprinted in (Hoare 1989), pp. 154–169.

Holyer, I. (1991). *Functional Programming with Miranda*, Pitman, London.

Hunter, G. (1971). *Metalogic: An Introduction to the Metatheory of Standard First-order Logic*, Macmillan, London.

James, G. and James, R. C. (eds) (1976). *Mathematics Dictionary*, fourth edn, Van Nostrand Reinhold, New York.

Jones, C. B. (1980). *Software Development: A Rigorous Approach*, Prentice Hall International Series in Computer Science, edited by C. A. R. Hoare, Prentice Hall, Hemel Hempstead.

Jones, C. B. (1986). *Systematic Software Development Using VDM*, Prentice Hall International Series in Computer Science, edited by C. A. R. Hoare, Prentice Hall, Hemel Hempstead.

Kaldewaij, A. (1990). *Programming: The Derivation of Algorithms*, Prentice Hall International Series in Computer Science, edited by C. A. R. Hoare, Prentice Hall, Hemel Hempstead.

King, S. (1990). Z and the refinement calculus, *Technical Monograph PRG–79*, Programming Research Group, Oxford University Computing Laboratory.

Lakatos, I. (1976). *Proofs and Refutations: The Logic of Mathematical Discovery*, Cambridge University Press, Cambridge. Edited by John Worrall and Elie Zahar.

Lakatos, I. (1978). *Mathematics, Science and Epistemology: Philosophical Papers*, Vol. 2, Cambridge University Press, Cambridge. Edited by John Worrall and Gregory Currie.

Lemmon, E. J. (1965). *Beginning Logic*, Nelson, London.

Lewis, H. A. (ed.) (1991). *Peter Geach: Philosophical Encounters*, Vol. 213 of *Synthese Library: Studies in Epistemology, Logic, Methodology, and Philosophy of Science*, edited by Jaakko Hintikka, Kluwer, Dordrecht (Holland).

Macdonald, R. (1991). Z usage and abusage, *Report 91003*, Royal Signals and Radar Establishment, Malvern (Worcestershire).

MacLennan, B. J. (1987). *Principles of Programming Languages: Design, Evaluation, and Interpretation*, second edn, Holt, Rinehart and Winston, New York.

Martin-Löf, P. (1984). *Intuitionistic Type Theory*, Studies in Proof Theory Lecture Notes, Bibliopolis, Napoli.

Mason, I. A. (1987). Hoare's logic in the LF, *Technical Monograph ECS–LFCS–87–32*, Laboratory for Foundations of Computer Science, Department of Computer Science, University of Edinburgh.

Mates, B. (1972). *Elementary Logic*, second edn, Oxford University Press, Oxford.

McMorran, M. and Powell, S. (1993). *Z Guide for Beginners*, Computer Science Texts, edited by A. M. Gibbons, M. C. Henson and V. J. Rayward-Smith, Blackwell, Oxford.

Mendelson, E. (1964). *Introduction to Mathematical Logic*, The University Series in Undergraduate Mathematics, edited by John L. Kelley and Paul R. Halmos, Van Nostrand Reinhold, New York.

Morash, R. P. (1987). *Bridge to Abstract Mathematics: Mathematical Proof and Structures*, Random House, New York.

Morgan, C. (1990). *Programming from Specifications*, Prentice Hall International Series in Computer Science, edited by C. A. R. Hoare, Prentice Hall, Hemel Hempstead.

Neilson, D. S. (1990). From Z to C: Illustration of a rigorous development method, *Technical Monograph PRG-101*, Programming Research Group, Oxford University Computing Laboratory.

Newton-Smith, W. H. (1985). *Logic: An Introductory Course*, Routledge & Kegan Paul, London.

Nielson, H. R. and Nielson, F. (1992). *Semantics with Applications: A Formal Introduction*, Wiley Professional Computing, Wiley, Chichester.

O'Donnell, M. J. (1982). A critique of the foundations of Hoare style programming logics, *Communications of the ACM* **25**: 927–935.

Paulson, L. C. (1987). *Logic and Computation: Interactive Proof with Cambridge LCF*, Cambridge University Press, Cambridge.

Popper, K. R. (1975). *Objective Knowledge: An Evolutionary Approach*, Oxford University Press, London. Originally published in 1972.

Popper, K. R. (1992). *Unended Quest: An Intellectual Autobiography*, Routledge, London. Originally published in this form in 1976.

Rohl, J. S. (1983). *Writing Pascal Programs*, Cambridge University Press, Cambridge.

Sanford, D. H. (1989). *If P, then Q: Conditionals and the Foundations of Reasoning*, The Problems of Philosophy: Their Past and Present, edited by Ted Honderich, Routledge, London.

Schumm, G. F. (1979). *A Teaching Companion to Lemmon's* Beginning Logic, Hackett, Indianapolis (Indiana).

Shoesmith, D. J. and Smiley, T. J. (1978). *Multiple-conclusion Logic*, Cambridge University Press, Cambridge.

Sperschneider, V. and Antoniou, G. (1991). *Logic: A Foundation for Computer Science*, Addison-Wesley, Wokingham.

Spivey, J. M. (1988). *Understanding Z: A Specification Language and its Formal Semantics*, Cambridge University Press, Cambridge.

Spivey, J. M. (1989). *The Z Notation: A Reference Manual*, Prentice Hall International Series in Computer Science, edited by C. A. R. Hoare, first edn, Prentice Hall, Hemel Hempstead.

Spivey, J. M. (1992). *The Z Notation: A Reference Manual*, Prentice Hall International Series in Computer Science, edited by C. A. R. Hoare, second edn, Prentice Hall, Hemel Hempstead.

Sufrin, B. A. (1981). Formal specification of a display editor, *Technical Monograph PRG-21*, Programming Research Group, Oxford University Computing Laboratory.

Sufrin, B. A. (1982). Formal specification of a display-oriented text editor, *Science of Computer Programming* **1**: 157–202.

Suppes, P. (1957). *Introduction to Logic*, Van Nostrand, London.

Turner, D. A. (1986). An overview of Miranda, *ACM SIGPLAN Notices* **21**: 158–166.

Welsh, J. and Elder, J. (1988). *Introduction to Pascal*, Prentice Hall International Series in Computer Science, edited by C. A. R. Hoare, third edn, Prentice Hall, Hemel Hempstead.

Wing, J. M. (1988). A study of 12 specifications of the library problem, *IEEE Software* pp. 66–76.

Woodcock, J. C. P. and Loomes, M. (1988). *Software Engineering Mathematics: Formal Methods Demystified*, Pitman, London.

Wordsworth, J. B. (1992). *Software Development with Z: A Practical Approach to Formal Methods in Software Engineering*, Addison-Wesley, Wokingham.

Index

abbreviation definition, 14, 282
abstraction, 25
    lambda, 292
    procedural, 4, 120
    representational, 4
Accept, 109
Account, 204
AddAnotherCopy, 245
AddEntry, 48, 53, 166
addition ($+$), 7
AddMember, 60
AddNewBook, 244
AddSales, 211
AddSalesOkay, 211
adequacy, 140
after, 99, 293
after state, 46
allroutes, 231
AlreadyAcceptable, 109
AlreadyMember, 60
AlreadyPresent1, 168
AlreadyStocked, 110
animation of a specification using Miranda, 271–278
antecedent, 12
anti-restriction
    domain ($\triangleleft$), 61, 288
    range ($\triangleright$), 74, 288
apodosis, 12
append, 174
application
    function, 91, 93
    generalized ($\_(\!|\_|\!)$), 55, 289
argument
    natural language, 125
    of a function, 91

    represented as a sequent, 125
assignment
    in a programming language ($:=$), 192, 198
    in model-theory, 86
AuthorizedRequestor, 240
axiom, 131
    schema, 118
    set
        comprehension, 152, 303
        empty, 152, 303
        enumeration, 152, 303
        equality, 151, 303
        power, 152, 303
    tuple
        equality, 156, 304
        membership, 156, 304
axiomatic description, 73, 281

bag, 103, 295
    difference ($\uplus$), 296
    generalized ($bag_\pm$), 335
    sum ($\uplus$), 296
    union ($\uplus$), 104, 296
bank account specification, 204–205
base
    case, 157
    name, 79
before state, 46
bi-implication ($\Longleftrightarrow$), 13
    distributive laws, 22
    elimination rule, 129, 300
    introduction rule, 129, 300
    truth-table, 13
biconditional ($\Longleftrightarrow$), 13
bijection ($\rightarrowtail\!\!\!\rightarrow$), 94, 291
bill of materials specification, 223–227

Bonus, 213
BonusOkay, 213
BookInfo, 235
BookNewToLibrary, 246
BooksBorrowedBy, 251
Buy, 111
ByAuthor, 249
BySubject, 250

calculating preconditions, 165
Capacity, 106
CapacityExceeded, 111
cardinality, of a set ($\#$), 38, 286
casino, 32
ChangeEntry, 84
Char, 255
CheckOutCopy, 239
ChoosyRoutes, 232
Class1, 162, 171, 182
Class1Class2, 181
Class2, 182
classroom specification, 161–163
closure
    reflexive-transitive ($\_^*$), 73, 290
    transitive ($\_^+$), 73, 290
CODoAddEntry, 63
CODoAddMemberCommand, 63
CODoAddSales, 214
CODoBonus, 214
CODoCommission, 214
CODoFindCAB, 214
CODoFindNamesCommand, 63
CODoFindPhonesCommand, 63
CODoRemoveEntryCommand, 63
CODoRemoveMemberCommand, 63
COInitSalesDB, 214
Commission, 212
CommissionOkay, 212
commuting diagram, 174, 187
completeness, 140
composition
    relational
        backward ($\circ$), 72, 289
        forward ($;$), 71–72, 289
    schema ($;$), 79–84

comprehension, set, 31, 32
    axiom, 152, 303
concatenation
    distributed ($^\frown/$), 100, 293
    sequence ($^\frown$), 98, 292
conclusion, 128
    of a sequent, 16
conditional, 12
conjunct, 11
conjunction ($\wedge$), 11
    distributive laws, 21
    elimination rule, 128, 300
    introduction rule, 129, 300
    truth-table, 11
conjunctive formula, 11
connective, truth-functional, 10
consequence
    semantic ($\models$), 16
    syntactic ($\vdash$), 131
consequent, 12
constituent, 10
    immediate, 10
contradiction, 17
CopyAvailable, 243
CopyCheckedOut, 241
CopyNotOwned, 241
CopyNotPreviouslyBorrowed, 252
CopyOwned, 245
corestriction
    domain ($\lhd$), 61, 288
    range ($\rhd$), 74, 288
correctness
    of a thema, 131
    of design, 181
    of operation modelling, 174
count, 103, 295
criticism
    immanent, 161n
    transcendent, 161n
Curry, Haskell, 96n
currying, 96
cyclefree, 224

data
    decomposition, 4, 172

refinement, 172

reification, 4, 172

type

baroque, 4

mathematical, 4

de Morgan's laws, 22

declaration, 32

declaration-part, of a schema, 6

decomposition, data, 4, 172

decoration, schema, 46

definite description operator (μ), 27, 287

definition

abbreviation, 282

generic, 98, 282

schema, 283–284

DeleteLeftDoc1, 256

DeleteRightDoc1, 260

description, axiomatic, 73, 281

deviant logic, 3n

diagram, commuting, 174, 187

difference

bag ($\uplus$), 296

number ($\neq$), 7

object ($\neq$), 285

set ($\setminus$), 36, 286

symmetric ($\triangle$), 36, 286

disjoint , 100, 294

disjointness, 100

disjunct, 11

typical, 144

disjunction ($\vee$), 11

distributive laws, 21

elimination rule, 129, 300

introduction rule, 129, 300

truth-table, 11

disjunctive formula, 11

display-oriented text-editor specification, 255–268

distributed concatenation ($\frown/$), 100, 293

distributive laws

bi-implication, 22

conjunction, 21

disjunction, 21

implication, 21

division (**div**), 7

DoAccept, 109

DoAddAnotherCopy, 246

DoAddEntry, 55

DoAddEntryCommand, 63

DoAddMember, 60

DoAddMemberCommand, 63

DoAddNewBook, 245

DoAddSales, 211

DoAddSalesCommand, 214

DoBonus, 213

DoBonusCommand, 214

DoBooksBorrowedBy, 252

DoBuy, 113

DoByAuthor, 250

DoBySubject, 251

Doc1, 256

Doc2, 264

Doc3, 268

DoCheckOutCopy, 242

Docherty, Rosemary, 233n

DoCommission, 212

DoCommissionCommand, 214

DoDeleteLeftDoc1, 257

DoDeleteLeftDoc2, 265, 266

DoDeleteRightDoc1, 260

DoDeleteRightDoc2, 265

DoEnter1, 169

DoFindCAB, 213

DoFindCABCommand, 214

DoFindNames, 59

DoFindNamesCommand, 63

DoFindPhones, 57

DoFindPhonesCommand, 63

DoInsertLeftDoc1, 259

DoInsertLeftDoc2, 265

DoInsertRightDoc1, 261

DoInsertRightDoc2, 265

DoInsertRightDoc3, 268

dom, 44

domain

anti-restriction ($\lhd$), 61, 288

corestriction ($\lhd$), 61, 288

of a relation (dom), 44, 288

restriction (◁), 60, 288
subtraction (◂), 61, 288
DoMoveLeftDoc1, 258
DoMoveLeftDoc2, 265
DoMoveRightDoc1, 261
DoMoveRightDoc2, 265
DoPreviousBorrower, 253
DoPrice, 108
DoRemoveEntry, 59
DoRemoveEntryCommand, 63
DoRemoveLast, 249
DoRemoveMember, 62
DoRemoveMemberCommand, 63
DoRemoveMoney, 114
DoRemoveOther, 247
DoReStock, 111
DoReturn, 243
double negation, elimination rule, 130,
        301
DoWithdraw, 207
drop, 99, 293

ElectNewLeader, 88
elimination rule, 128, 300
    bi-implication, 129, 300
    conjunction, 128, 300
    disjunction, 129, 300
    double negation, 130, 301
    existential quantifier, 142
        restricted, 302
        unrestricted, 302
    false, 130, 301
    identity, 142, 302
    implication, 129, 300
    negation, 129, 301
    set
        comprehension, 152, 303
        enumeration, 152, 303
        equality, 152, 303
        power, 152, 303
    true, 130, 301
    tuple
        equality, 156, 304
        membership, 156, 304
    universal quantifier, 141

restricted, 301
    unrestricted, 301
empty
    bag (⟦ ⟧), 103
    sequence (⟨ ⟩), 97
    set (∅), 34
entailment
    semantic (⊨), 16
    syntactic (⊢), 131
Enter1, 162, 182
Enter2, 182
EntryAlreadyExists, 54
enumeration, set, 31
equality (=), 7
equivalence
    semantic (⫤⊨), 18
    syntactic (⊣⊢), 131
ErrorAtBottom, 260
ErrorAtTop, 257
Europe, 24
ExactChangeUnavailable, 113
excluded middle, law of, 17n, 23
existential quantifier (∃)
    restricted, 25
        elimination rule, 302
        introduction rule, 302
    unrestricted, 26
        elimination rule, 142, 302
        introduction rule, 142, 302
expl1, 225
expl2, 226
extraction (↑), 99

F, 286
F₁, 286
f, 9, 13
false, 13, 130
    elimination rule, 130, 301
false-elim, 130, 301
falsehood, logical, 17
falsity, retransmission of, 337
family, 103
figs1, 225
figs2, 226
filtering (↾), 99

FindCAB, 213
FindCABOkay, 213
FindNames, 58
FindPhones, 57
finite
    injective function ($\rightarrowtail\!\!\!\!\rightarrow$), 94, 292
    partial function ($\rightarrow\!\!\!\!\rightarrow$), 94, 292
    sequences (seq), 292
    sets (**F**), 286
flatten, 263
for, 100, 293
ForeignCoin, 113
formal
    semantics, 9, 125
    syntax, 125
formula
    always false, 13, 130
    always true, 13
    biconditional, 13
    conditional, 12
    conjunctive, 11
    disjunctive, 11
    hypothetical, 12
    implicative, 12
    primitive, 140
free type, 115
front, 99, 293
Full1, 168
function
    argument of, 91
    injective, 291
        finite ($\rightarrowtail\!\!\!\!\rightarrow$), 94, 292
        partial ($\rightarrowtail$), 94, 291
        total ($\rightarrowtail$), 94, 291
    partial, 91, 290
        finite ($\rightarrow\!\!\!\!\rightarrow$), 94, 292
    retrieve, 172, 173
    successor (*succ*), 7
    surjective, 291
        partial ($\rightarrow\!\!\!\!\!\twoheadrightarrow$), 94, 291
        total ($\twoheadrightarrow$), 94, 291
    total ($\longrightarrow$), 291
    value of, 91

Geach, Peter, 126n

generalized
    application ($_-(\!|_-|\!)$), 55, 289
    bag ($bag_\pm$), 335
    intersection ($\bigcap$), 38, 286
    union ($\bigcup$), 38, 286
generic definition, 98, 282
Good, 106
GoodsNotPriced, 110
greater than
    or equal to ($\geq$), 7
    strictly ($>$), 7
Groves, Lindsay, 233n, 235n

head, 99, 293
heterogeneous relation, 72
hiding, schema ($\backslash$), 79
Hoare triple, 190
    getting from a schema, 203–204
homogeneous relation, 72
horizontal form, of a schema, 283
hypothetical, 12

id, 72
identity
    elimination rule, 142, 302
    relation (id), 72
    start sequent, 142, 302
iff (abbreviation), 11
image, of a relation ($_-(\!|_-|\!)$), 55, 289
immanent criticism, 161n
implication ($\Rightarrow$), 12
    distributive laws, 21
    elimination rule, 129, 300
    introduction rule, 129, 300
    truth-table, 12
induction
    mathematical, 157, 305
    sequence, 158, 174, 306
inductive step, 157
inequality, object ($\neq$), 285
InitBookInfo', 238
initial state, 66
initialization, proof obligation, 163
InitLibraryDB', 238
InitLibraryState', 238

InitMaterials', 227
InitPhoneDB, 66, 78
InitPhoneDB', 66
InitSalesDB', 210
InitSalesDBCommand, 214
InitVendingMachine', 108
injection, 291
    partial ($\rightarrowtail$), 291
    partial surjective ($\rightarrowtail\!\!\!\rightarrow$), 291
injective
    partial surjection ($p\rightarrowtail\!\!\!\rightarrow$), 291
    sequence (iseq), 292
injective function, 291
    finite ($\rightarrowtail\!\!\!\rightarrow$), 94, 292
    partial ($\rightarrowtail$), 94, 291
    total ($\rightarrowtail$), 94, 291
input variable, 5
inputs, 48
InsertLeftDoc1, 259
InsertRightDoc1, 261
inter, 176
interactive process, specification of, 62
internal telephone directory specification,
    41–65, 271–278
interpretation, in model-theory, 86
intersection
    generalized ($\bigcap$), 38, 286
    set ($\cap$), 35, 285
introduction rule, 128, 300
    bi-implication, 129, 300
    conjunction, 129, 300
    disjunction, 129, 300
    existential quantifier
      restricted, 302
      unrestricted, 142, 302
    implication, 129, 300
    negation, 130, 301
    set
      comprehension, 152, 303
      enumeration, 152, 303
      equality, 152, 303
      power, 152, 303
    true, 130, 301
    tuple

equality, 156, 304
    membership, 156, 304
    universal quantifier
      restricted, 301
      unrestricted, 141, 301
intuitionistic logic, 130n
invalidity, retransmission of, 337
inverse, of a relation, 58, 288
isconstit, 224
iseq, 98, 292
ItalianElection, 88
items, 105, 296

Lakatos, Imre, 151n, 336
λ, 95, 292
λ-calculus, 95
λ-notation, 95
lambda abstraction, 292
language, typed, 24
last, 99, 293
laws
    de Morgan's, 22
    distributive, 21
    useful, 22
leap, 76
Leave1, 162, 171, 182
Leave2, 182
less than
    or equal to ($\leq$), 7
    strictly ($<$), 7
library database specification, 233–253
LibraryDB, 236
LibraryState, 237
Line, 262
Lisp, 118
list, 115
logic, 125
    classical, 9
    deviant, 3n
    Hilbert-style, 115
    intuitionistic, 17n, 130n
    many-valued, 9n
logical
    falsehood, 17
    truth, 17

LookUp, 93

Map, 230
maplet, 287
Materials, 227
mathematical induction, 157, 305
membership
    bag ($\in$), 104
    set ($\in$), 33
meta-language, 16
Miranda, 271–278
model, 172
model-theory, 9, 125
modelling, correctness criterion for, 174
modulo (**mod**), 7
modus ponendo ponens, 118
    as a sequent, 132
modus ponendo tollens
    as a sequent, 132
    as a thema, 133
modus tollendo ponens
    as a sequent, 132
    as a thema, 133
modus tollendo tollens
    as a sequent, 132
    as a thema, 133, 139
Monarchy, 86
Month, 74, 76
MoveLeftDoc1, 258
MoveRightDoc1, 261
multi-set, 103

N, 32
N$_1$, 36
name, base, 79
negation ($\neg$), 11
    double, elimination rule, 301
    elimination rule, 129, 301
    introduction rule, 130, 301
    truth-table for, 11
Neilson, David, 255, 259, 268
neither _ nor _, truth-table, 29
non-contradiction, law of, 23
nondecreasing, 106
NonPositiveWithdrawal, 207

NotAuthorizedRequestor, 252
NotConfirmed, 211
NotEnoughMoney, 207
NotInStock, 112
NotMember, 54
NotNewBook, 244
NotOnlyCopy, 248
number range (..), 31, 287

occurrence (of a variable)
    binding, 25
    bound, 25
    free, 25
one-to-one correspondence, 291
OnlyCopy, 247
operation refinement, 169
ordered pair, 287
output variable, 5
overriding, relational ($\oplus$), 76, 290

P, 35
P$_1$, 35
pair, ordered, 42
parameter, formal generic, 282
parameterization, partial, 96
partial
    function, 290
        finite ($\nrightarrow$), 94, 292
    injection, 291
    injective
        function ($\rightarrowtail$), 94, 291
        surjection, 291
    parameterization, 96
    surjective
        function ($\twoheadrightarrow$), 94, 291
        injection, 291
partition, 56, 100
partition, 100, 294
pattern, 282
Peirce's law, 23
Person, 43, 271
Phone, 43, 271
PhoneDatabase, 64
PhoneDB, 46, 77
PhoneDB', 47

piping, schema ($\gg$), 84–85
post-weak, 191
postcondition
    of a Hoare triple, 190
    weakening, rule of, 191
Power, 5, 6
power set (**P**), 35
pre, 165
pre-strength, 191
PreAddEntry, 167, 168
PreAddSalesOkay, 215
PreBonusOkay, 215
PreCommissionOkay, 215
precondition, 48
    calculation of, 165
    of a Hoare triple, 190
    schema, 165
    strengthening, rule of, 191
predicate-part, of a schema, 6
PreDoEnter1, 169
PreEnter1, 165
premise, 128
premises, set of
    of a sequent, 16
PreNotConfirmed, 215
PreUnknownSalesperson, 215
PreviousBorrower, 252
PreWithdraw, 205
Price, 108
procedural abstraction, 4, 120
product
    Cartesian, 42
    cross, 42
Profiteering, 114
promoting operations, 265, 268
promotion, 265, 268
proof
    obligation
        applicability, 184, 187
        correctness, 181, 184, 186, 187
        correspondence of initial states, 181, 186
        initialization, 163
    rigorous, 151

sequence, 116
tree, 130
proof-checker specification, 119
proof-generator specification, 120
proof-theory, 9, 125
ProofChecker, 119
ProofGenerator, 120
proper subset ($\subset$), 34
protasis, 12

quantifier
    existential ($\exists$)
        elimination rule, 142, 302
        introduction rule, 142, 302
        restricted, 25
        unrestricted, 26
    unique ($\exists_1$), 27
    universal ($\forall$), 25
        elimination rule, 141, 301
        introduction rule, 141, 301
        restricted, 25
        unrestricted, 26
quantity, 108

ran, 45
range
    anti-restriction ($\rhd$), 74, 288
    corestriction ($\rhd$), 74, 288
    number (..), 31, 287
    of a relation (ran), 45, 288
    restriction ($\rhd$), 74, 288
    subtraction ($\rhd$), 74, 288
reasoning
    immanent, 161n
    transcendent, 161n
recursive structure, 115
refinement
    data, 172
    operation, 169
reflexive-transitive closure ($\_^*$), 73, 290
Region, 91
reification, data, 4, 172
relation, 42
    domain of (dom), 44
    heterogeneous, 72

homogeneous, 72
  identity (id), 72
  range of (ran), 45
relational
  composition
    backward ($\circ$), 72, 289
    forward ($;$), 71–72, 289
  image ($\_(\!(\_)\!)$), 55, 289
  inverse, 58, 288
  overriding ($\oplus$), 290
RemoveEntry, 59
RemoveLast, 248
RemoveMember, 62
RemoveMoney, 114
RemoveOther, 247
renaming, schema, 78
Report, 65, 234, 255, 271
representational abstraction, 4
Republic, 86
ReStock, 110
restriction
  domain ($\lhd$), 60, 288
  range ($\rhd$), 74, 288
retransmission
  of falsity, 337
  of invalidity, 337
retrieve
  function, 172, 173
  schema, 180
Return, 242
rev, 100, 294
reversal, sequence, 100
rigorous proof, 151
roulette, 32, 38
route planner specification, 228–232
Routes, 232
rule
  elimination, 128, 300
  introduction, 128, 300

sales database specification, 208–214
SalesDatabase, 214
SalesDB, 210
schema, 5, 46, 283
  as formula, 162

composition ($;$), 79–84
  utility of, 81
  declaration-part of, 6
  decoration, 46
  deriving a Hoare triple from, 203–204
  hiding ($\backslash$), 79
  horizontal form, 283
  inclusion, 51
  piping ($\gg$), 84–85
  predicate-part of, 6
  renaming, 78
  retrieve, 180
  vertical form, 283
scope, 141
SelfRequestor, 251
semantic
  consequence ($\models$), 16
  entailment ($\models$), 16
  equivalence ($\models\!\mid$), 18
  turnstile ($\models$), 16
semantics, formal, 9, 125
seq, 97, 292
seq_1, 98, 292
sequence
  concatenation ($\frown$), 98, 292
  empty ($\langle\,\rangle$), 97
  induction, 158, 174
  proof, 116
  reversal, 100
sequences
  finite (seq), 292
  injective (iseq), 292
sequent, 128
  conclusion of, 15
  constructor ($\mapsto$), 15
  input, 128, 299
  output, 128, 299
  set of premises of, 15
  start, 142, 195, 299, 302, 304, 305
set
  comprehension, 31
  difference, 36, 286
    symmetric ($\triangle$), 36, 286

empty ($\emptyset$), 34
enumeration, 31
  axiom, 152
intersection, 35, 285
  generalized ($\bigcap$), 38, 286
membership ($\in$), 33
power (**P**), 35
union, 35, 285
  generalized ($\bigcup$), 38, 286
Sheffer's stroke, 14
  truth-table for, 14
shortestroutes, 231
Sørensen, Ib, 161n
Sort, 106
sorting, specification of, 105–106
soundness, 140
spec-conj, 192
specification
  animation, 271–278
  case study
    bank account, 204–205
    bill of materials, 223–227
    classroom, 161–163
    display-oriented text-editor, 255–268
    internal telephone directory, 41–65, 271–278
    power, 5–7
    proof-checker, 119
    proof-generator, 120
    route planner, 228–232
    sales database, 208–214
    sorting, 105–106
    theorem-prover, 119
    vending machine, 106–114
    weather map, 91–93
    Wing's library database, 233–253
  conjunction, rule of, 192
  format of, 64
  of an interactive process, 62
  structure of, 64
standard Z, 4
start sequent, 142, 195, 299, 302, 304, 305

state
  after, 46
  before, 46
  initial, 66
  invariant, 48
structure, in model-theory, 86
SubComponents, 227
subset, 33, 285
  proper, 34, 285
substitution, 141, 192, 301
subtract, 178
subtraction, 7
  domain ($\lhd$), 61, 288
  range ($\rhd$), 74, 288
succ, 7, 101
Success, 54, 109, 169, 206, 211, 242, 257
successor function (*succ*), 7
Sufrin, Bernard, 255, 259
sum, bag ($\uplus$), 296
sumbag, 112
sumseq, 231
SuperComponents, 227
surjection, 291
  partial injective ($\rightarrowtail\!\!\!\rightarrow$), 291
surjective
  function, 291
    partial ($\twoheadrightarrow$), 94, 291
    total ($\twoheadrightarrow$), 94, 291
  injection, partial ($\rightarrowtail\!\!\!\rightarrow$), 291
symmetric set difference ($\triangle$), 36, 286
syntactic
  consequence ($\vdash$), 131
  entailment ($\vdash$), 131
  equivalence ($\dashv\vdash$), 131
  turnstile ($\vdash$), 131
syntax, formal, 125

t, 9, 13
tail, 99, 293
take, 100, 293
tautology, 17
tertium non datur, 23
thema, 126, 128
theorem-prover specification, 119
TheoremProver, 119

TooLittleMoney, 113
TooManyCopies, 241
total
    function ($\longrightarrow$), 291
    injective function ($\rightarrowtail$), 94, 291
    specification, 54
    surjective function ($\twoheadrightarrow$), 94, 291
totality, of a specification, 168
transcendent criticism, 161n
transitive closure ($\_^+$), 73, 290
transmission
    of truth, 337
    of validity, 336
tree, 115
    proof, 130
triple, Hoare, 190
    getting from a schema, 203–204
true, 13
truncate, 266
truth
    logical, 17
    transmission of, 337
truth-table
    bi-implication, 13
    conjunction, 11
    disjunction, 11
    implication, 12
    negation, 11
    neither $\_$ nor $\_$, 29
    Sheffer's stroke, 14
truth-value, 9
Turner, David, 271
turnstile
    semantic ($\models$), 16
    syntactic ($\vdash$), 131
type, 24
    free, 31, 115

UnauthorizedRequestor, 240
UnboundedDisplay, 263
union
    bag ($\uplus$), 104, 296
    generalized ($\bigcup$), 38, 286
    relation, 46
    set, 35, 285

universal quantifier ($\forall$)
    restricted, 25
        introduction rule, 150, 301
    unrestricted, 26
        elimination rule, 141, 301
        introduction rule, 141, 301
UnknownAuthor, 250
UnknownBorrower, 251
UnknownCommand, 214
UnknownEntry, 59
UnknownName, 57
UnknownNumber, 59
UnknownSalesperson, 211
UnknownSubject, 251
Unregistered, 241
Update, 92

validity
    semantic, 16
    transmission of, 336
value, of a function, 91
variable
    input, 5
    occurrence of
        binding, 141
        bound, 141
        free, 140
    output, 5
    primed, 46
    unprimed, 46
VDM, 3, 224n
vending machine, specification of, 106–114
VendingMachine, 107
verification conditions for
    assignment, 198
    conditional, 198
    for-loop, 199
    sequencing, 199
    while-loop, 199
vertical form, of a schema, 283
Vienna Development Method, 224n

weather map specification, 91–93
WeatherMap, 92

well-formed formula, 118
wff (abbreviation), 118
Wing's library database specification, 233–
    253

Withdraw, 205
WithdrawOkay, 206

Z, standard, 4